PENGUIN BOOKS

THE PENGUIN ECONOMIC HISTORY OF BRITAIN
GENERAL EDITOR: DAVID CANNADINE

MAKING A LIVING IN THE MIDDLE AGES

Christopher Dyer was Professor of medieval social history at the
University of Birmingham and is now Professor of regional and local
history at the University of Leicester.

D1337388

THE PENGUIN ECONOMIC HISTORY OF BRITAIN

Making a Living in the Middle Ages

THE PEOPLE OF BRITAIN 850–1520

CHRISTOPHER DYER

PENGUIN BOOKS

PENGUIN BOOKS

Published by the Penguin Group
Penguin Books Ltd, 80 Strand, London WC2R ORL, England
Penguin Putnam Inc., 375 Hudson Street, New York, New York 10014, USA
Penguin Books Australia Ltd, 250 Camberwell Road, Camberwell, Victoria 3124, Australia
Penguin Books Canada Ltd, 10 Alcorn Avenue, Toronto, Ontario, Canada M4V 3B2
Penguin Books India (P) Ltd, 11 Community Centre, Panchsheel Park, New Delhi – 110 017, India
Penguin Books (NZ) Ltd, Cnr Rosedale and Airborne Roads, Albany, Auckland, New Zealand
Penguin Books (South Africa) (Pty) Ltd, 24 Sturdee Avenue, Rosebank 2196, South Africa

Penguin Books Ltd, Registered Offices: 80 Strand, London WC2R ORL, England

www.penguin.com

First published in Great Britain by Yale University Press 2002
Published in Penguin Books 2003

1

Printed in England by Clays Ltd, St Ives plc

Contents

Illustrations

Plates

Maps

Figures

Preface

This book surveys the society and economy of medieval Britain. It covers the seven centuries from the Vikings to the Reformation, and it aims to deal with Britain, that is England, Scotland and Wales. I have approached the subject by seeking to understand the perspective of those who lived at the time. Changes in the society and economy came about because men and women, as individuals or in groups, made decisions and acted accordingly. We can therefore appreciate why they behaved and acted as they did if we can reconstruct their thinking in the light of their circumstances. Such an exercise requires some imagination, as one of the purposes of this book is to explore the economic contribution of the working population, who are not very fully documented. This is difficult, but is intended to add to the interest of the book, and in the same spirit while scholarly debates and controversies are reflected in these pages, they will be presented without lengthy accounts of the views of contending schools of historians. The writing consciously avoids jargon and technicalities and the more specialized terms will be explained when they are first mentioned.

A book dealing with a long period and many themes is inevitably the product of many years of research, reading, listening and conversation. I could not possibly name the dozens of people who have helped me in various ways, and I hope that they will understand and forgive the omission. The only exception must be Rodney Hilton, whose early tuition and later advice has been an influence and inspiration. To focus on those who helped specifically with the production of this book, David Cannadine suggested that I write it, and commented helpfully on a first draft. I was advised and encouraged by the editors for Penguin and Yale, Simon Winder and Robert Baldock. Chapters were read and improved by Dawn Hadley, Keith Stringer, Phillipp Schofield and two anonymous readers.

The final version of the typescript was prepared by Sue Bowen and Nancy Moore. Jenny Dyer read drafts and helped in other ways. John and Geraldine Brown gave me hospitality when I worked in Edinburgh. Help with preparing illustrations came from Duncan Brown, Bob Croft, Geoff Egan and Andy Isham. Candida Brazil of Yale University Press gave care and encouragement. The University of Birmingham and the Arts and Humanities Research Board allowed me a generous period of study leave.

Christopher Dyer
Birmingham, April 2001

Note on the text. Places are identified here with reference to the counties before the reorganization of local government in the 1970s. Money, length, distance, area, volume and weight are given in measures prevailing before metrication. There were 240d (pence) in a pound (£1), and 12d (pence) made a shilling (1s). To gain a sense of the value of money, a cow could be bought for about 24d (2s) or 36d (3s) before 1200, and between 6s and 11s after that date. A foot is equivalent to 0.3 metre, a yard to 0.9 metre, and a mile to 1.6 kilometres. An acre is 0.4 hectare. Grain was measured in bushels (36 litres) and wine in gallons (4.5 litres). Wool and tin were weighed in pounds (0.45 kilogramme).

Introduction

Approaching the economic history of medieval Britain

We should explore the economic history of medieval Britain for many reasons. It is the only branch of history which gives pride of place to the whole population, and through the study of the economy we can understand the everyday lives of working people. The economy was important. All other human endeavours depended on the production of food and other goods, which means that any investigation of non-material things must take into account the material base. Economic history is a unifying subject, not taking us into an obscure byway of the past, but acting as a crossroads from which we gain access to the history of the environment, culture, politics and thought.

Economic historians are concerned with two types of change. One focuses on the ups and downs of economic life, both the short-term fluctuations in prices and trade, and the long-run movements of growth and decline. The other is concerned with the structural changes, such as the emergence of towns, or the shifts in the distribution of land and the control of farming between social groups. Both are necessary for understanding the course of history.

Why go back to such a remote period? The past has always attracted our curiosity, and there is no reason to think that the period before 1520 offers us any less interest than the twentieth century or any other period in between. Medieval people were as lively, active and complicated as at any other time, and they are as worthy of our attention as those of later centuries. They pose at least as many dilemmas and puzzles of interpretation. Indeed there is a particular fascination in revealing the thoughts and actions of people living in an age unlike our own, when most people worked on the land, and were dominated by an aristocracy and an all-embracing church. The past fascinates us because it was different, and the middle ages were very different. Lastly, but not least, later periods cannot be fully understood if we do not appreciate their predecessors. We owe the majority of our villages and towns, boundaries, roads and institutions to the middle ages. The words that we use to describe economic life, such as farmer, wages, fees, capital and interest were all used (often with distinct meanings) in the middle ages. Our world is based on foundations laid before 1520, and we consequently need to know about that phase of our development.

Choosing the dates for the beginning and the end of a historical period always presents dilemmas. The economic history of the middle ages could be said to have begun with the large-scale clearances of land in the third millennium BC. Much land under the plough in 850 had been cultivated since prehistoric times. It might be tempting to start with Roman Britain, when cities and lines of communication of lasting importance were established. The barbarian invasions of the fifth and sixth centuries offer another convenient point to begin, when English-speaking settlers arrived, and embryonic states and the Christian church developed. The ninth century has been chosen because it marks the beginning of a great formative period, when essential elements in the political, social and productive structure were put in place. The pattern of villages and towns which provided the place of residence and work for many medieval (and modern) people was established in the period 850–1100. The basic principles of the social hierarchy, with a dominant aristocracy living on the rents and services of a subordinate peasantry, and a network of exchange based on towns, all owe their origins to this period. The Norman Conquest of 1066 had economic repercussions, but it cannot be regarded as an important turning point in economic history. Choosing an ending point creates less difficulty. The two centuries after 1100 can be summed up as a time of expansion, followed by a profound crisis in the fourteenth century, marked by the Great Famine (1315–17) and the Black Death (1348–50), but we could not end the story at that point because a combination of contraction and new developments flows from the crisis, and these must be followed through until the early sixteenth century. A new era began with the end of a long period of low population in about 1540, the price inflation which is visible just before 1520, and the redistribution of property associated with the Reformation from the 1530s.

This book deals with Britain, that is the whole island including England, Scotland and Wales. Some common factors united all three countries, such as the influx of northern French or 'Anglo-Norman' elites in the eleventh and twelfth centuries. However, for most of the middle ages the three countries were separate political entities, which makes generalization difficult or impossible. But this is not political history, and the varied regional economies prevent us from generalizing about the experiences of any single kingdom or principality. In many ways this is the history of a collection of regions. East Anglia had its own patterns of settlement, agricultural methods and hierarchy of towns, which were totally different from those of the west midlands or the Lake District. Indeed, the Lake District had much more in common with parts of southern Scotland than with southern and eastern England. A broad distinction can be made between those parts of Britain which by the thirteenth century were characterized by extensive cornfields, a disciplined dependent peasantry and strong urban influence, and the highland regions such as northern and western Scotland and part of central and north Wales, where lords collected tribute from an independent, pastoral and scattered peasantry, and exchange based on money was slow to develop. Regional differences were also important on the small scale, and we can identify a close patchwork of different types of countryside, including the champion or felden districts where large villages and great open arable fields dominated, the woodlands with dispersed hamlets, enclosed fields and a good deal of pasture as well as woods, the wolds and chalk downs which combined extensive hill pasture with cultivation, and the wilder moorlands and marshlands. A traveller through the midlands in 1300, in the 60 miles from Oxford to Lichfield, would have been acutely aware of a succession of varied landscapes: woodlands in west Oxfordshire, the low hills of the Cotswolds, the flat open fields of the Vale of Evesham, and the woodlands again in the Forest of Arden in north Warwickshire. In each case the size and layout of the fields, the balance between cultivated land and grassland, the local road system, the size and distribution of settlements would have offered sharp contrasts. These environments had at least as profound an influence on the productive activities, social organization and mentality of the inhabitants as their location in one kingdom or another.

National differences still had an impact on the economy, especially in such matters as the coinage and international relations. For two centuries the silver coins of England and Scotland were essentially the same, but they diverged in the late fourteenth century when the Scottish money was debased. Scottish and English merchants exported their wool to different continental ports as the result of political decisions about the location of staples. Often the differences cannot be easily explained, such as the absence of records of peasant revolts in Scotland, or Scotland's apparent growth in settlement and farming in the late fifteenth century, when in much of England there was no great expansion. Unfortunately these questions are difficult to answer because the evidence, both written and material, is relatively scarce for Scotland and much of Wales.

We might say that 'Britain' is too big to be easily understood because of regional differences. But in a significant dimension it is too small, because the economic history of the offshore island of Britain cannot be separated from that of continental Europe. This is not just because of the importance of overseas trade, which made the economies of Britain and Flanders in particular interdependent. Nor is it because of continental invasions and migrations which brought new ideas and institutions to Britain between the ninth and eleventh centuries. Continental European culture was a vital influence on mentality and administration, from the ideas of chivalry and crusade among the secular aristocracy, to the religious orders and methods of church government which spread through the international church. Much more significant for economic history were the characteristics that were common across Europe, which meant that people solved problems in similar ways, such as adopting open fields with intermixed strips. All parts of Europe experienced the same trends and setbacks, notably the expansion of the thirteenth century and the crisis in the fourteenth. These parallel developments affected regions in different ways, which helps to identify the special character of each.

Any book on 700 years of complex and varied developments must be built on the work of generations of scholars, and this work reflects the body of knowledge and thinking which has accumulated since the birth of economic history in the 1880s. The early writers on the subject were primarily interested in law and government, so they tended to focus on institutions, such as the manor, serfdom, boroughs and guilds. They often shared the prevailing view that mankind had progressed, and so they looked for evidence in the middle ages for the origins of the modern economy. They thought that the towns were early islands of freedom and capitalism within a more backward agrarian society, and believed that the use of money, trade and the middle class grew in importance, and from that growth emerged the industrial revolution and the modern capitalist economy. A similar strand in the thinking of historians from the United States drew them to study peasants and villages because they traced the origins of American democracy in the communities of the English countryside.

In the middle decades of the twentieth century, the progressive 'Whiggish' view of economic change was challenged by M. M. Postan, who questioned many of the assumptions of his predecessors. He showed that there was no 'rise of a money economy' because the use of money both expanded and receded, and he emphasized the cyclical nature of economic change. There had been growth up to about 1300, and then contraction, and he believed that the roots of change lay in the countryside. The key determinants of economic growth and decline were the level of population and the productivity of the land. The great expansion in numbers of people in the thirteenth century put excessive pressure on land, which created the conditions for the catastrophes of 1315–17 and 1348–50. He argued that much production was for direct consumption in the peasant household, and therefore the market, towns and trade were peripheral to the rural economy.

Postan's interpretation of the changes in the later middle ages was influenced by the ideas of the classical economists, such as Malthus and Ricardo, both of whom predicted contraction as the inevitable consequence of growth. Postan was in no sense a Marxist, and yet his ideas bore some resemblance to the Marxist theory that a feudal mode of production reached its peak of development in about 1300, after which internal contradictions led to a general crisis of the social order. The most eloquent advocate of this view, R. H. Hilton, sees the struggle between lords and peasants for rent as a key factor in precipitating the late medieval crisis. R. Brenner has pursued the Marxist view that demography was not the determinant of economic change, and that class relations explain the circumstances which enabled the gentry around 1500 to impose capitalist agriculture by expelling peasants to create large farms.

The generation of historians that grew up in Postan's later years, and since his death in 1981, have developed alternative ideas which have eroded his great thesis without replacing it with some new grand narrative. The Cambridge demographers have argued for essential similarities between early modern and medieval population structure, which implies that adjustments in marriage rates and fertility caused population growth and decline, replacing the rather cataclysmic view of excess populations and crises of mortality. Postan thought that medieval cultivators could not escape from a cycle of falling yields and fields damaged by repeated cultivation because of an inability to improve their technology. Now we appreciate that the period was one of constant innovation, in the use of mills, in the rotation and mix of crops, in methods of drainage and water management, and in the use of draught animals. Instead of the gloomy views of nineteenth-century classical economists, who argued that excessive numbers of people would be an unsupportable burden, economists like Boserup have shown, using observations of the modern third world, that labour can be used to increase production, and indeed we can see this in the most densely populated English regions. Finally, towns and trade have been rediscovered as an important dimension of the medieval economy. The towns were early to develop, became large by around 1300, acted as a stimulus to production, and promoted specialization. The influence of the commercial world penetrated deeply into the countryside, affecting every region and all levels of the social hierarchy.

The flourishing of archaeology in the last thirty years has made an especially valuable contribution to the period before 1100. Excavation and fieldwork have shown that villages formed between about 850 and 1200, not in the fifth and sixth centuries as was once thought. Work on towns of the tenth and eleventh centuries reveals their large size and concentration of crafts and commerce – in other words, they were real towns. In the later middle ages material remains tell us about housing, trading patterns and the shrinkage of settlements. Archaeological interpretation makes us aware of the social meaning of material things, such as conspicuous consumption or the emulation of social elites, and archaeology demonstrates continuities and technical achievements. Archaeology has altered thinking about economic history in the last few years, but economic historians have always been influenced by other disciplines, especially the social sciences, which include anthropology and sociology as well as economics, and by literature and cultural studies.

The approach to the economic and social history of the middle ages which is represented in this book is based on the assumption that the period mattered. The modern economy owes something to its medieval predecessor, and we should note the emergence within the period of, for example, shareholding or industrial mechanization. But the middle ages should not be studied merely to seek the origins of more recent developments. Those who lived a thousand years ago are worthy of investigation in their own right, and we can learn from their differentness, as well as from the similarities with our experience. For example, medieval lords devoted a large amount of resources to building and maintaining ponds for freshwater fish. Their ponds now lie abandoned, and the rearing of freshwater fish has played a negligible role in modern Britain. Yet the ponds and their management are worth our attention because they meant a great deal to those who built and used them. Once we have appreciated that species such as bream and pike were regarded as a luxury food, the ponds tell us much about dietary preferences and medieval status seeking.

There is always a tendency to belittle the achievements of the past and to assume in a patronizing way that medieval people were primitive and ignorant. For example, the yield of corn in the fifteenth century was low by modern standards, and indeed had fallen since the thirteenth century. Does this mean that the people who grew the crops were stupid and lazy? In fact, if we look at the price of grain and the consumption of bread we find that food was cheap and plentiful. Corn production was adequate for society's needs, and as it was unnecessary for cultivators to strain themselves to increase their output, we should not criticize them for their imagined failings. Recent experience of technological failures, such as the BSE epidemic and the threat of climate change, has perhaps made us rather less confident of our superiority, and a little more appreciative of common sense and skilful management in the middle ages. Scottish economic history has suffered in particular from assumptions about that country's backwardness before modern 'improvement'. Scottish agriculture was not very productive, but the country was thinly populated and not especially prone to famine. In the thirteenth century the abundant Scottish currency and urban growth suggest that the country participated in the general European expansion.

As we adopt a more sympathetic approach to medieval economic management, we appreciate that people had to make a series of difficult decisions about which crops to grow or which type of cloth to weave. As the economy became more complex, the decisions included the raising of credit, marketing strategies and investment plans. Historians once tended to determinism, which means they believed that circumstances forced society along particular channels, and that events unfolded with a certain inevitability. Now we recognize an element of choice. For example, we do not know why some rural communities in the early middle ages lived in scattered hamlets with fields irregularly disposed around them, while others moved into large villages with well-organized open fields. They were influenced by the soils which they worked and the social pressures around them, but we must doubt if the decision was predestined.

It is sometimes believed that the crucial decisions were taken by powerful elites of rulers, aristocrats and merchants. We often find, however, that when kings or great lords initiated some change, the results were unplanned and unforeseen. At the beginning of our period King Alfred ordered the building of a system of forts to keep the Danes out of his kingdom of Wessex. Many of those forts would become towns, but it is not certain that the king intended that result. More often change emerged from the combination of thousands of uncoordinated actions, involving people at all levels. Formal descriptions of medieval society imply the subordination of the masses. Yet even serfs had some use of property, and had some choice in the management of their holding of land, though they were of course restrained in many ways. One of the dynamic forces in medieval society, and the motive force behind many economic changes, was not dictatorial decisions, but the opposite – the competition and frictions between different groups, not just between lords and peasants or merchants and artisans, but also between laymen and clergy, higher aristocrats and gentry, and subjects and the state, and between individuals within those various groups. A society that appears to be governed by rigid laws and customs, in reality allowed people to take initiatives.

Change was based on combinations of interconnected movements, such as the simultaneous emergence of lordship, villages, towns and the state in the period between 850 and 1050. Selecting which came first, or which dominated over the others is often a fruitless exercise. Those who advocate a single explanatory mechanism, such as changes in population, or innovations in technology, or climate change, are usually oversimplifying. We know the difficulties in tracing the origins of the industrial revolution, or the slump of the 1920s, and the argument that single causes can be applied to an earlier period again suggests a patronizing attitude which underestimates the varied and interlocking nature of the medieval economy.

Finally, because we are dealing with a culture and economy very different from our own, various terms and concepts are used which cause problems for modern readers. These are terms in use in the middle ages, and also those coined by modern historians, which as much as possible will be defined when they are first mentioned. Some modern words are so fundamental, and yet have been subject to so much controversy, that they need brief discussion here.

It has become commonplace to describe medieval society and economy as 'feudal'. Some historians regard this as a misleading modern invention to describe an ideal type of society which never existed. The word will be employed here as useful shorthand for a social organization in which lords had powers over others, through private jurisdiction and other non-economic means, which enabled them to extract rents, services and other dues. Feudalism in a more specialized sense refers to the ties between lords and their aristocratic vassals, based on the granting of land (fiefs) in exchange for military and administrative services. Here the word 'aristocracy' will be used to describe the whole landed elite, from the gentry to earls and dukes, but also including the higher clergy. 'Nobility' is used on the continent but is not easily applied in Britain, and the aristocracy can be recognized as a coherent group from its landed incomes and style of life. 'Peasant' refers to small-scale cultivators, who possess land, and are subordinated to lords and the state. There has been a move to deny the existence of an English peasantry, on the grounds that they were not as closely bound to family groups as in other cultures, but peasantries differ, and the economic position of those dependent on small holdings of land (usually below 60 acres) is a defining characteristic. This excludes farmers (who had large holdings) and those entirely dependent on wages. 'Serfs' were peasants who were legally unfree, that is they were judged in their lord's court and could not usually appeal for justice to the king's court. The term 'serf' derives from legal status, and tells us little about wealth. 'Towns' and 'urban' refer to places with a dense and permanent concentration of people who pursued a variety of non-agricultural occupations. The population need not have been very large – a town could have had 300 inhabitants – and many towns were unwalled, and had not been granted a borough charter or other privileges.

PART ONE

Origins of the medieval economy, c.850–c.1100

The late ninth century saw the first stage of a great formative episode in history, when key elements in society and economy such as villages, manors and towns were created and states were forged. Of course people had been organizing production and consumption for a very long time before the ninth century. The whole of mainland Britain up to central Scotland had been brought into a sophisticated urbanized and commercial economy as a Roman province in the first and second centuries AD. The villa estates, cities, industries and tax system had largely collapsed in the fifth and sixth centuries when the Roman army withdrew and the province was taken over by its native British population, some Anglo-Saxons from across the North Sea and migrants from Ireland. The legacy of the Roman empire can be seen in the survival and later re-occupation of many of the towns, and the continued cultivation of much of the land. Changes in England in 650–850 had long-term importance: towns and coinage were revived, and major churches were given property rights over extensive lands. But the main features of the economy at that time – great estates, rural settlements and towns such as the predecessors of London and Southampton – did not survive in their original form or on the same sites.

Understanding the economy in the period 850–1100 is surrounded by difficulties, not least being the shortage of written sources. Two thousand charters, some law codes, narrative sources such as chronicles and the lives of saints, and religious literature such as sermons provide some fragmentary information. Fortunately, at the end of our period we have the unique and comprehensive survey of England (except its most northern counties) made in 1086 and recorded in Domesday Book. Domesday and later documents mention thousands of place names, most of which were formed before 1000, and can tell us about settlements, people and the use of land. Archaeological evidence, accumulated mainly since the 1950s, has provided information about the plan and size of settlements, houses, churches and other structures, graves, artefacts such as pottery and metalwork, and the remains of animals and plants which allow the past environment and its use by man to be reconstructed.

The evidence is difficult to interpret. The most satisfying results are often obtained by bringing together information from different sources. Each type of evidence has to be understood and approached critically. The documents were produced by the elites of church and state, and so reflect a partisan 'official' view. The material evidence which at first sight appears 'objective' has in fact been selected, by the accident of survival, and by the choice of particular sites for excavation.

There is much room for disagreement in making historical sense of this period. Some scholars doubt whether much economic activity existed at all, suggesting that apparent sales of goods and land were really exchanges determined by social and political relationships. Even when we assume that there was an economy as we understand the term, the time scale of change is open to many interpretations, with some putting more emphasis than is shown here on the period before 850, and others regarding the Norman Conquest as having important economic consequences. Archaeologists point to continuity: the same agricultural land, defined by similar boundaries, remained in use for many centuries, even millennia. The processes that underlie economic change are just as controversial, with some favouring the formation of the state as the key to understanding change, while others give more attention to shifts in climate, or the growth and decline of population. Here emphasis is placed on decision-making in all sections of society.

CHAPTER ONE

Living on the land, c.850–c.1050

Most medieval people made their living from agriculture, and had to arrive at decisions about the best methods of production. Their choices were not made freely, because they worked within the limits imposed by their social circumstances and technical knowledge, and by the soil, terrain and climate. Their resources were more restricted than those of later cultivators, but that did not leave them at the mercy of nature. They moulded and exploited the landscape, and indeed were the inheritors of a countryside already changed by centuries of human intervention. It was once believed that great tracts of primeval woodland survived into this period, which made the clearance of trees so that the land could be used more productively one of the main tasks of early medieval cultivators. We know now that in much of England the area under trees was not much greater than at the present day. Patches of 'wild wood' had survived since early prehistory, but some woodland was quite new, the result of the regeneration of bushes and trees on former cultivated land since the end of the Roman period. Woodland was not left as wilderness, but was managed to produce timber or fuel, and feed for livestock. Bears had been hunted to extinction throughout Britain by the eleventh century, and in the following century beavers were to be seen only on a few rivers in Wales and Scotland. Wolves still survived, but only in the more remote parts of England and other parts of Britain. Wild animals which were valued as food and for sport, such as deer and boar, were protected and nurtured. Nature had been tamed.

i. Farming

In managing the earth, vegetation and animals, the first priority of medieval men and women was to produce food, but they also expected to receive the benefits of their work in the foreseeable future, so they prac- tised (to use the modern term) 'sustainable' agriculture. They planned for the same land to yield crops regularly, and they appreciated that well-managed resources renewed themselves. They anticipated the changeability of the seasons and the harvests, and hoped that their farming methods would allow them to survive in a year of unusual weather, for example by planting a variety of crops. At no time or place within our period can they be described as 'subsistence farmers', in the sense that they ate only food that they had grown, or that they produced solely for their own consumption needs. They always expected that their land would yield a surplus, whether for the benefit of the state, the church or their lords, or for exchange for goods and services which they could not obtain from their own land.

These aims were most easily achieved in the favourable environments created by the wide river valleys, such as the Wye, upper Thames, War- wickshire Avon, Nene, Great Ouse and upper Trent, and in low-lying districts such as eastern Norfolk, as well as on coastal lowlands in Kent, Sussex, south Wales, and eastern Scotland. Here were light soils that could easily be turned by the plough, which gave a good seedbed for cereal crops. The level ground gave easy access, and implements could be used at all times, as the free-draining soil did not become waterlogged. The topsoil on flat land or gentle slopes was not easily washed away by the rain. The fields were sheltered from extreme weather and in the south there was a long growing season, so that crops would ripen even in a wet summer. In the most favoured locations water was near to hand, and the land adjoining rivers and streams yielded long grass for haymaking. Cultivation extended over much larger areas, which offered many, if not all, of the advantages of the river valleys. The limestone hills like the Yorkshire wolds and the Cotswolds gave good opportunities for growing corn, as did the heavier clay and marl lowlands which prevailed in much of the country from central Scotland, through eastern and midland England, to Somerset.

In these regions which offered fertile land for cultivation the inhab- itants devoted their main productive effort to growing large acreages of grain – wheat, rye, barley and oats, together with legumes, mostly peas and beans. This was the most efficient way of producing basic foods. Wheat gave the most nutritious and palatable bread; barley and oats could be made into an inferior bread, or could be malted and brewed into ale, or, like the peas and beans, be boiled for pottage; oats and beans could also be fed to animals. The cultivators had to be careful to combine their arable with grassland and wood. The best way of maintaining the quality of the soil – or even of creating a decent seedbed in the case of the heavier clay soils – was to keep a good proportion of land as grass or hay meadow, so that animals could be fed and their manure used to spread on the fields. Sheep were especially efficient sources of fertilizer, because they could be fed on pasture land in the day, and penned at night on the land on which crops were to be sown. Not only would they deposit their manure, but their small sharp hoofs would tread the droppings into the surface. Animals were themselves an important source of food – medieval people lived not by bread and pottage alone – and their muscle power was essential for ploughing and hauling. Woodland was also a vital asset for fuel, timber for building and making implements, and acorns and beech mast for fattening pigs. So those who lived in the regions with the best potential for grain-growing kept a balance between different types of land. If they extended the arable, they rested it regularly with fallow, on which animals found stubble, grass and weeds to eat, as well as keeping some land as permanent pasture. The descriptions of boundaries attached to the charters of the tenth and eleventh centuries of the Vale of the White Horse in Berkshire reveal the local concentration on arable. The writers of the charters defined the edges of estates not by the usual trees, stones and ponds, but instead by reference to parcels of cultivated land – acres (meaning strips that had been ploughed), furrows and headlands (the strip at the end of a field where the plough turned). If the outermost fringes of these territories were fully occupied by arable, the centre was also likely to be cultivated.

Not everyone was so heavily involved in growing corn. Across the southern counties, from Essex and Kent to the Chiltern Hills and north Wiltshire, and in much of western England, the arable land was interspersed with patches of pasture and woods, some of them commons to be shared among a number of settlements (Map 1). In north Worcestershire, for example, the local informants quoted by the clergy who wrote boundary clauses for charters often mentioned hedges and crofts (meaning hedged fields) as landmarks. In East Anglia much land was given over to arable, but important features of the landscape were the large greens, consisting of uncultivated land used as common pasture. Around the Wash, and along both sides of the Severn estuary, in the Somerset Levels, on the south coast at Romney Marsh and the Pevensey Levels, south of the Humber estuary, and in the south-west of Scotland were fens and marshlands around which communities combined cultivation with summer grazing, peat-digging and fishing. The people of the uplands of western and northern England, Wales and Scotland aimed at a very different balance in their management of the landscape, cultivating arable as much as possible, but inevitably depending on pastures for their main livelihood. An extreme example is provided by the people who

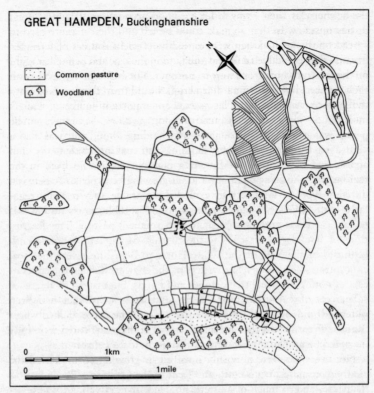

Map 1. A woodland village and its fields: Great Hampden, Buckinghamshire. In the
Chiltern Hills, as in much of Britain outside the 'village belt', people lived in dispersed
settlements (in this case stretched along a green and scattered among the fields). They
cultivated land in limited areas of open field, and also in enclosed fields. Grazing land
and wooded areas were plentiful. This map of 1741 reflects a much earlier landscape.

Source: A. H. R. Baker and R. A. Butlin (eds), *Studies of Field Systems in the British Isles*
(Cambridge, 1973).

lived in the ninth century on Gauber High Pasture above Ribblehead in
the Pennines, in a house at 1,100 feet above sea level, who in spite of the
adverse climate were able to grow a few acres of oats, as well as grazing
sheep and cattle. In environments lacking easily cultivated land, as in the
Scottish islands, soils suitable for growing corn were created by concentrating all of the manure, and other sources of compost such as turf and
seaweed, on to small fields. Barley and oats could be grown, but people

made much of their living from keeping sheep and cattle, fishing and catching sea birds.

One means of making use of varied types of land was to lay out territories which included hill and valley, wood and arable, so that natural resources would complement one another. The boundaries of an estate or a village would run in parallel across the contours from the crest of a hill to a river bank some miles away, encompassing hill pasture, wooded hill slopes, lowland arable and riverside meadow. Sometimes arable and woodland could be associated only by abandoning the ideal that an estate would consist of a single block of land, and attaching to the main arable-based estate a piece of woodland, even if the two properties were ten miles or more apart. A balance could also be achieved among the possessions of a monastery, for example, which might include among the land scattered over a region some specialist woods and pastures as well as manors devoted to corn-growing.

ii. *Expansion*

The landscapes and territories of the tenth and eleventh centuries were often very old. Much of the arable had been cultivated continuously since Roman times, and some field and estate boundaries dated from that period or even earlier. Building on these foundations, the peasants and estate managers were imposing some major changes on the landscape. Two tendencies can be identified – one to change the use of land in woodland and pastoral regions, and the other to restructure the regions which already contained much arable. The first tendency led them to fell some woodlands and turn them into either arable or pasture, or to bring them under more intensive management. The weald of Kent, one of the largest wooded areas in the country, was divided among the inhabitants of the north of the shire, who gained their main living by cultivating the fertile lowlands. In the autumn, herds of pigs had traditionally been driven to the south-west along well-marked tracks from the Isle of Thanet or the settlements around Faversham to feed on beech mast and acorns, and at the appropriate seasons firewood and timber were cut and carried back considerable distances – often between 8 and 20 miles. The wealden denns, which consisted of pastures and small settlements, some of them occupied seasonally by swineherds and woodcutters, by the late eleventh century had expanded into quite large and permanent communities. The denn attached to Thanet, for example, became the permanent settlement of Tenterden. The use of the land shifted towards arable, though this did not necessarily involve wholesale removal of woods. In a similar way the wolds of the midlands, relatively high ground with limestone or clay soils, which had gained their name from their wooded appearance in the sixth or seventh century, were being brought into more extensive cultivation. On the uplands of Cornwall and the Lake District, shielings occupied in the summer by herdsmen accompanying cattle and sheep on to the high pastures were being converted to permanent farmsteads. The ploughed area was being extended in parts of northern England, south-west Scotland and the isle of Arran at the expense of woodland and pasture, the change in vegetation having its effects on the proportions of pollen of different plants preserved in peat deposits. In the fenland and Somerset Levels, land was being drained and brought into agricultural use. A number of these local changes were not necessarily designed just to expand the bounds of cultivation – often they also increased the amount of pasture, as in East Anglia where intensive grazing turned woodlands into large open greens. The hay meadows of the upper Thames valley were being enlarged by ditch-digging at this time.

Not everyone welcomed this growth in the productive capacity of the countryside. Kings and aristocrats were devoted to hunting, which they valued above all other pastimes. The game, especially deer, would flourish only in a well-wooded environment, and those in authority were anxious to conserve the habitats that still survived. A rigorous forest law of continental type was not applied – that is, the king could not restrict landowners hunting on their own land, but areas of woodland seem to have been put under special protection by kings and major landowners, and they enclosed areas of wood and grazing land into parks. The charters mention 'hays', which in some cases were enclosed woods and in others 'deer hedges' designed to assist in the hunt. Near Oxford, at Shotover, in opposition to the normal trends, the area under trees was actually increasing around the tenth century, presumably in response to royal orders to improve the hunting, and after the Norman Conquest the area became a royal forest. Concern for maintaining areas of wood and pasture was probably a reaction to the prevailing tendency towards its reduction. Outside the aristocracy few people ate venison (deer bones are relatively scarce in excavated rubbish deposits), perhaps because it was reserved for the elite social groups, but also reflecting the domination of the landscape by agriculture.

The main changes in the rural landscape were not on the fringes of woods, moors and marshes, but in the well-developed arable lands, where the tenth and eleventh centuries were an important phase in the creation of villages and their associated fields. Before the tenth century almost everyone lived in small and scattered settlements. These are known from archaeologists' finds of groups of pottery fragments on modern ploughed fields – sites located in this way in the east midlands are usually dated before *c*.850. Excavation reveals ditched enclosures round fields and paddocks, pits for rubbish, and the remains of rectangular buildings with walls consisting of rows of vertical posts set into the ground, which were used for dwelling houses and barns. The houses occasionally seem to have stood alone, and are assumed to have been isolated farms, or sometimes are found in groups. One site with more than sixty structures, at Catholme in the Trent valley in Staffordshire, at first looks like a large village, but the buildings were arranged in farmsteads, each containing a dwelling and agricultural buildings such as barns and cowsheds, and not all of these were occupied throughout the life of the site from the sixth to the ninth century. At its height the settlement consisted of five households, which means that it rates as a hamlet rather than a village.

Dozens of pre-tenth-century settlements have been discovered in eastern and midland England, the majority of them in the fields of the medieval and modern periods, not under modern villages. So people have not lived on the same sites throughout history: a sharp break came when peasants abandoned farmsteads and hamlets, and moved into larger villages. The new settlements which emerged in the tenth, eleventh and twelfth centuries had populations of between twelve and sixty households. They were stable, as the majority are still inhabited; they were compact, consisting either of rows of houses along a street or green, or of a cluster of dwellings; and their inhabitants usually cultivated land in adjoining open fields.

Why was there this remarkable change in the size, site, layout and durability of rural settlements? No contemporary wrote about the transformation that was going on, perhaps because it was so commonplace that no one thought it remarkable, and in any case the literate members of society had their minds on higher things, such as religion and government. Rather we have to reconstruct thought processes from the material evidence of the hamlets and villages. Any explanation of the move into nucleated villages must take into account their localized distribution. The villages were confined mainly to a belt of Britain from eastern Scotland through Northumberland and Durham, broadening to include most of the midlands and central southern England, and ending in Dorset and Hampshire (Map 2). To the east and west of the 'village belt', in south-east England and East Anglia, and in the whole of the west of Britain from Devon and Cornwall up to the Highlands and Islands of Scotland, people lived in various types of hamlet, or in single farms. In these regions of dispersed settlement the farms may have persisted for centuries on the same site, as in the western and northern isles of Scotland; by contrast, hamlets and farms in East Anglia migrated even more than in the midlands, and many of the late medieval and modern hamlets of western England do not seem to sit on sites going back earlier than

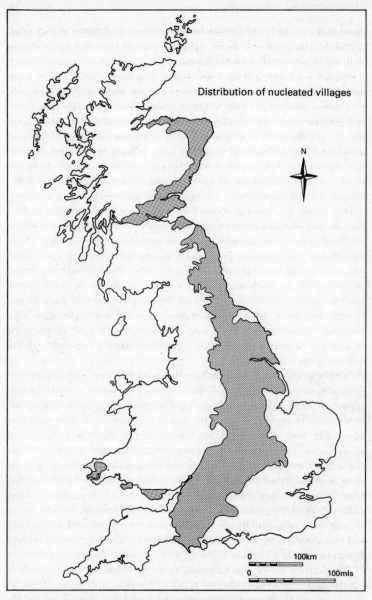

Map 2. Distribution of nucleated villages. The shading shows the regions where nucleated villages, rather than hamlets or single farms, were the main form of settlement in recent times. This distribution reflects, approximately, the settlement pattern of the middle ages.

Sources: B. K. Roberts and S. Wrathmell, *An Atlas of Rural Settlement in England* (2000); B. K. Roberts, *Rural Settlement in Britain* (Folkestone, 1977).

the eleventh century. So the settlement pattern underwent widespread upheaval, but it was only in the central belt that the inhabitants ended by living in large nucleated villages.

Perhaps the term 'village revolution' exaggerates the speed of this change. While hamlets of Northamptonshire were abandoned soon after 850, signalling the beginnings of village formation, the first phase of occupation in many villages came no earlier than the eleventh century, and the whole process may not have been complete – in north-east England, for example – until about 1200. Precise dates often cannot be assigned to the origin of many villages, and much of the evidence consists of plans recorded in recent times. Perhaps we should see the formation of each village in evolutionary terms. As the density of farms and hamlets increased, the amount of land under cultivation grew, and fields fragmented as a result of inheritance, marriage and other transfers. A crowded and complicated countryside was inconvenient to cultivate, and generated disputes. Meanwhile, the house of the lord, his church and the cottages of slaves and servants provided the nucleus for a large settlement. More and more peasants found it efficient to move their dwellings to the centre, and gradually they organized their landholdings in more systematic ways, ending with all of the houses in one central grouping, and the fields laid out and regulated by the community. This reconstruction of events is supported by some villages which seem to have stuck at intermediate phases of development, notably the 'polyfocal' villages where there may be three groupings of houses in close proximity – as if people had never brought their movement towards a single centre to its final and logical conclusion. Occasional single farms or small hamlets lay interspersed among the large villages, as if a few individuals managed to avoid the general trend towards living in groups. The evolution continued with the replanning of some villages, or their enlargement with new groups of houses. And villages might split into two: as a settlement became large, its inhabitants might decide to form a new nucleus nearby, which helps to explain why we find so many twin villages, called Upper and Lower, or Great and Little, or East and West.

Another explanation of village formation is based on the formal and disciplined nature of many of the settlements, which appear to be the product of a deliberate act of those in authority. Villages were planned, with each house occupying a plot identical in size and shape to its neighbours: the houses were regimented in rows along a street or beside a green, and each was attached to a standard holding of 15 or 30 acres also set out in dozens of strips in strict order in the surrounding fields. Such a planned settlement, it is said, could only have been accomplished by orders from above, most likely from the lord, whose motive was to

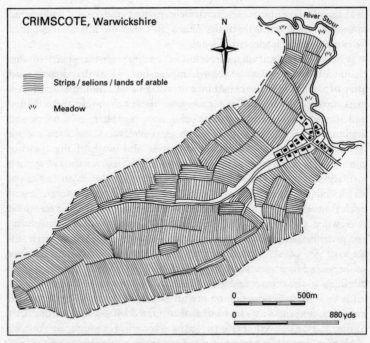

Map 3. A champion village and its fields: Crimscote, Warwickshire. The main features of this village, though not recorded on a map until the nineteenth century, developed in the early middle ages. Its characteristic features were the houses closely packed into the settlement, its high proportion of land under the plough, and limited area of pasture and meadow. There were *c.*1,500 strips, gathered into 46 furlongs, and divided (along the road into the village) between two fields.

Source: A. H. R. Baker and R. A. Butlin (eds), *Studies of Field Systems in the British Isles* (Cambridge, 1973).

impose his control on the peasants. This must have taken place in a short time, perhaps a single year. In fact the two reconstructions of events could both have occurred – a gradual nucleation in the tenth century, followed by a reorganization into a more regular plan in the twelfth. The measuring and allocation of land necessary for all of these changes is most likely to have been the work of the villagers themselves, as they alone would have had detailed local knowledge. Indeed the whole process could have been initiated by them.

Though views vary about the formation of the village, everyone agrees that behind these new large settlements lay an economic logic (Map 3). They are located in regions with a strong commitment to arable farming, and there was a close connection between the villages and their fields. The fields had a rational purpose. Each peasant household ploughed and harvested its own holding of land, which was regarded as its property. The holding was scattered evenly over the whole territory of the village, in the form of strips, called 'acres' at the time. The working and cropping of the land was regulated by common rules. Everyone had to fallow part (often half) of the land each year, while cultivating the rest. The fallow ideally formed one block of land, a single field consisting of hundreds of acres belonging to each of the villagers' holdings, so that animals could wander over it after harvest and until the next sowing, finding grazing in the stubble. The fallowed land after its rest and manuring should have been more productive when it was its turn to be cultivated and cropped in the following year, and the former arable turned over to fallow. If these rules were not observed, animals would not have been able to graze over the whole fallow field, and crops were in danger of being eaten by wandering animals. In the same spirit, the areas of permanent grassland were available to everyone, and restrictions had to be put on the number of animals lest the community suffer from the effects of overgrazing. Similarly, meadows were carefully allocated to each holding in proportion to the holders' other assets. The details of these arrangements are not recorded until the twelfth and thirteenth centuries, and it may well be that the whole package of rules was not in place until then, but the references to land in intermixed strips (it was said to lie 'acre under acre'), to common land, and to land being divided into two blocks implies that some of the main elements of the open-field system were functioning in the tenth century.

This package of regulations had advantages and restrictions for the individuals. The routine of cultivation and fallowing was designed to maintain a balance which ensured that the grain gave reasonable yields from one year to the next. No one participating in such a system was likely to become very rich, but neither were they liable to starve. All the shareholders in the village felt that they were fairly treated, as everyone lived in the same place, equally near to their strips and the other facilities such as streams and woods. The scattering of the strips ensured that everyone worked some of the best and worst land, and if there was a poor harvest everyone would have the same chances. Each peasant was committed to the common fields – there was no way in which they could withdraw. The village was by no means unchanging, as its size could be increased, by ploughing up pastures for example, or by adding to the number of cottagers by subdividing holdings, or by lords granting out parcels from their land. But in some senses the formation of a village signalled that expansion was coming to an end. Villages developed within fixed limits – many of the boundaries detailed in tenth-century descriptions coincide exactly with those of modern parishes. And by the tenth century, as we have seen, the ploughed land reached up to the edge of the territory. The village provided a means of rationalizing an already full countryside. The standard peasant holdings served the interests of lords because rents and services were levied from them, but they also protected the families who occupied them from impoverishment. Land and people were working together in equilibrium within the village, and any future transformations would be more likely to occur outside the village regions.

The field systems which grew alongside the villages represent one of the principal technological changes in the early middle ages. We do not have precise information about agricultural methods at this early date, but the two-course rotation, by which half of the arable was fallowed every other year, was used. This could well mark a stage in the intensification of farming, because we might expect that in earlier periods when arable was not fully extended the land would have been cropped only intermittently or occasionally, or that 'infield–outfield' husbandry would be practised, whereby a small area (a much-manured infield) was cropped every year, and the remainder of the territory intermittently. Ploughing techniques varied from region to region. The light plough, the ard, which stirred the soil with an iron-pointed share attached to a beam, was being used in some parts of the country, while illustrations in manuscripts show heavy ploughs with both shares and coulters, and sometimes wheels, which were capable of turning furrows and creating the ridged fields which have been recognized by archaeologists, for example near Montgomery on the Welsh border. Ploughs were cumbersome implements, drawn by teams of eight oxen in some cases, and in order to turn them round as infrequently as possible the parcels (acres) in the fields were long and narrow. One early type of strip field was so extended that it might stretch for hundreds of yards from the edge of the settlement to the boundary of its territory. In villages in Northamptonshire smaller parcels, each containing between a quarter- and half-acre, but retaining an elongated shape, were formed by subdivision and reorganization of the original long strips.

Place names, charters and preserved vegetation found in excavations reveal the main crops that were planted in this period. Rye increased in importance in East Anglia, probably reflecting an extension of cultivation on the light, sandy soils of the region. Old wheat varieties, spelt and emmer, were being replaced with bread wheats which were more easily threshed. While such field crops represent one of the main priorities of cultivation, much effort went into growing vegetables and fruit, probably by women, and their husbandry was probably also responsible for crops used in textile manufacture, notably flax, hemp and dyestuffs, which were grown everywhere, but with special intensity on the edge of the growing towns.

The methods of livestock farming are reflected in the bones found discarded on settlement sites, most plentifully in towns, and these varied from region to region: for example, cattle were especially important in the vicinity of York, but a higher proportion of sheep grazed in Norfolk and Lincolnshire. Sheep were kept for the sake of their wool rather than meat, so that most of them were slaughtered as mature adults. Some cattle were killed young, for meat, and others kept for many years for dairying and haulage. Animals were not very large. At York, the sheep resembled in size the rather small breed now kept on the Welsh mountains, and the cattle were by modern standards stunted – they probably weighed live about 440 pounds, half the weight of even a small modern breed. This lack of stature may be partly a comment on the cattle owners' failure to breed animals selectively, and partly on the feed and shelter available. One indication of careful management is the lack of many signs of disease on the bones.

Managing woods, in order to ensure a steady supply of both large building timbers and the smaller underwood for fuel and fencing, was not a new technique at this time. But growing demand, especially from towns, must have led to a closer and more systematic control of a limited resource. Many woods were coppiced, that is cut on a rotation in order to crop each new growth of underwood every few years. This must lie behind the deliveries of hundreds of cartloads of wood fuel to the salt works at Droitwich in Worcestershire, recorded as a well-established practice in 1086. Larger trees, which grew either among the coppiced wood or in 'wood pastures' where stock grazed, would be conserved for eventual use as timber. Another woodland product exploited at this time was honey, which is mentioned so often in documents that it must be rated a major product of the countryside. Its plenty reflects the abundant flora, and the skilful management of many hives. In regions where woods were less plentiful, notably eastern Norfolk, turbaries (peat diggings) provided towns like Norwich with fuel as well as supplying the needs of a dense rural population. The pits were on such a scale as to create eventually the pattern of inland lakes now known as the Norfolk Broads. In other parts of East Anglia, and in Somerset, the wetlands were being reclaimed by means of dyke systems, suggesting that drainage methods, knowledge of which had lapsed since Roman times, were being learned again.

Technical advances depended on small-scale cumulative improvements, rather than dramatic new inventions. The story of water mills suggests that we should not always assume that 'improvements' moved in one direction. The 6,000 English water mills that we know existed in

1086 need not have been installed in the previous two centuries – a considerable number were built before 900. Nor should we assume that the more efficient vertical-wheeled mill (in which the power was connected through cogs to the millstones on the floor of the mill building) expanded at the expense of the horizontal mill (where the wheel was fixed in the channel of water, and turned the millstones directly). At Old Windsor in Berkshire, a horizontal mill was built in about 900 on the site of a mill with vertical wheels which had been recently destroyed. Mills were growing in number and efficiency, freeing labour from the time-consuming drudgery of milling by hand for more productive purposes, but a great number of hand mills were still in use.

The tendencies that we have reviewed so far – the growth in towns, the filling up of the countryside implied by village formation, the extension of cultivation and the more efficient exploitation of resources – could be seen as stimulated by a growth in population. Were people living longer, marrying younger, rearing more children to adulthood? Our sources are capable neither of telling us the intimate details of family life, nor of giving exact global population figures. Roman Britain could have had a population of 5 million, and by 1086 a figure for England in the region of 2.2 to 2.5 million seems likely (see pp. 94–5). The main decline of the early middle ages probably occurred in the three centuries after 400, when the collapse of the Roman economy, social disruption and recurrent epidemics were likely to have been linked with low fertility and high mortality. Population numbers may have fallen well below 2 million, so the tenth and eleventh centuries would have been a period of recovery, a preliminary episode in the great population increase which quickened in pace in the two centuries after 1086 (see Figure 2 below, p. 235). If population levels were not rising very rapidly, we should not think of those who moved into towns or restructured the countryside as impelled by some urgent crisis caused by high levels of population. Perhaps they were able to make radical changes precisely because they did not feel the pressure of rapid growth in numbers, but were free to innovate and experiment. They were having to adapt to increased demands from their rulers and lords, and they were encouraged to adopt more intensive methods of production as they became enmeshed in the market.

iii. *Estates and lords*

How did the various sections of society gain a living from the land in the two centuries after 850? At the beginning of the period the magnates and major institutions depended on very large holdings of land, to which various terms are applied: in the north the word 'shires' appears in 'Richmondshire' or 'Aucklandshire'. In Scotland, at a later time they were known as 'thanages' as well as shires. 'Multiple estate' and 'land unit' are terms currently used, but here they will be called 'great estates'.

As with so many aspects of society and economy before 1050, we are dependent on later evidence. Most of our knowledge of the boundaries and subdivisions of the great estates comes from the survival of a few of them in the centuries after 1050, or of traces of their former existence. Occasionally a charter gives a description of a great estate. In 959, for example, King Edgar, quite soon after the northern counties had been taken from Scandinavian rule into the English kingdom, granted to a woman who was evidently a great landed magnate the estates of Howden and Drax, adjacent places in Yorkshire. The land thus conveyed was characteristically extensive – from north-east to south-west it measured more than 10 miles. Also typical of the 'multiple estate', it had a federal character: the charter lists the dependencies of Howden – Knedlington, Barn Hill, Caville, Thorpe, Hive, Eastrington, Belby and Kilpin, most of them settlements still flourishing today in the neighbourhood of Howden. Finally the charter describes the boundaries of the estate, which was easily done because they consisted mainly of rivers – the Ouse, Derwent, Foulness and Aire. It therefore had a geographical coherence with 'natural' boundaries, which has led to the speculation that great estates had very early origins. Great federated estates like that based on Howden have been found throughout Britain. In Scotland, many thanages had a dozen or so constituent 'touns', and the thanes (lesser aristocrats with service functions), who had their own holdings on the estate, made sure that the estate worked. The estate centre in Wales, the *llys*, stood at the head of a group of hamlets or *trefi*. The *maenor* of Meddyfnych (now Llandybie in Carmarthenshire) is recorded in sixth- and ninth-century documents, and in the later middle ages contained seven *trefi* (see Map 4 below, p. 28). The estate measured 7 miles across, and its boundaries included both upland and valley land, which gave the lord access to cornfields, meadow and hill pasture.

The kings, bishops, monasteries and nobles who controlled the great estates expected from them regular supplies of food and rent. Lay lords and bishops would travel from estate centre to estate centre, lodge with their servants in the residence that was maintained there, and order delivery of enough food to keep the household for a specific amount of time: the king with his huge following would demand one night's food only, whereas lesser lords who had fewer estates to visit would stay longer. A typical food rent for an itinerant household in England consisted of

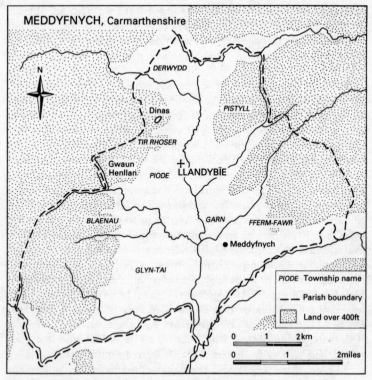

Map 4. A great estate: Meddyfnych, Carmarthenshire. This *maenor* is described briefly in *c*.800. Its boundary coincided roughly with that of the modern parish of Llandybie, which contains about 12 square miles. In the later middle ages it included seven townships (*trefi*) and its varied resources (arable land and meadow in the stream valleys, and upland grazing) would have been exploited from a number of settlements in the early middle ages also. The church is now at Llandybie, but an earlier church is recalled by the place name *Gwaun Henllan* ('meadow of the old church').

Sources: G. Jones, 'Post-Roman Wales', in *AgHEW*, vol. 1, part 2; W. Davies, *Wales in the Early Middle Ages* (Leicester, 1982).

hundreds of loaves of bread, many barrels of ale, cattle, sheep, bacon and dozens of cheeses. Monasteries demanded specified quantities of food from their estates, rather like a bishop or lay magnate, but as their residence was fixed, made arrangements for the food to be sent to them. A food rent attached to Hickling and Kinoulton in Nottinghamshire when the estate passed to Ramsey Abbey in about the year 1000 consisted of 80 bushels of malt (for brewing), 40 bushels of oatmeal, 80 bushels of flour (for bread), eight sides of bacon, sixteen cheeses, two fat cows and eight salmon in Lent. This was enough to feed the monks and servants of a large monastery for a week or two. In Wales food rents consisted of loaves of bread, oats, cattle, sheep, pigs, butter, ale and honey.

The estate was not geared to squeezing the land and its people with any great intensity. The food rents represented a tiny fraction of the produce of the areas of land in the estate – the grain element in the rent from Hickling detailed above, for example, represents the produce of about 30 acres of land. Howden or Meddyfnych could have produced many thousands of bushels of grain and dozens of surplus animals for meat, but its lord would have received only a fraction of these. The estates themselves played a limited role in actual production, because much of the food that was sent to the lord had been gathered as tribute or rent. Descriptions of ancient tenant obligations often include services such as feeding dogs or helping in the hunting field which, though troublesome to perform, cannot be compared with the burden of continuous heavy labour services found in later centuries. There was probably a piece of land, a home farm of some kind, attached to the residence, and the local peasants would have been expected to labour on this land as part of their obligations, with work also provided by slaves. Certainly bond hamlets supplying labour services to cultivate land under the lord's direct control formed part of the idealized Welsh scheme – though as descriptions of estates were written down in the thirteenth century, they may not reflect accurately earlier conditions.

An estate was organized for production in the sense that it contained complementary resources, and different parts of the federation had functions assigned to them, which are commemorated in place names recording their specialisms, like Shipton (which means 'sheep settlement') or Wootton ('wood settlement'). At the estate centre various craft activities were concentrated, such as iron-working. Co-ordinating the estate's activities depended on officials who were granted holdings of land: thanes in Scotland, riding men in western England, and drengs in the north. In Wales the settlement called the *maerdref*, where agricultural work was concentrated, was appropriately the home of the reeve, who supervised agricultural work. However, the emphasis on tribute means that the great estate resembles not a farm, but a unit of government, an agency for collecting rents.

In the period after 850 the great estates were often broken up. For example, Bampton, which had dominated the south-west corner of Oxfordshire, had its outliers granted away one by one, including Chimney, Ducklington and Brighthampton, in 955–84. The formation of smaller units of landholding was not entirely new. The great estates had never covered the whole countryside; relatively small estates lay in the interstices of their larger neighbours. In any case the estates had always been 'multiple' or 'federal', consisting of a number of smaller blocks of land. Some of these had been held on tenancies in the eighth and ninth centuries, and so were already becoming detached from the estate centre. But after about 850 the tendency to fragmentation accelerated. Some of the small estates were entirely new. In regions with extensive arable the new unit of landholding was defined by means of a zigzag boundary turning a series of right angles as it was drawn through the strips and furrows of a well-established field system. In others it was impossible to detach a single piece of land, and the new lord received dozens of strips scattered through the common fields (he might be awarded 'every third acre'), with a separate parcel of meadow or pasture to complete the holding.

The great estates were split up by inheritance, or parcels were granted by will, or they were given away as part of a marriage settlement, or pieces were acquired by the church. Most important of all, the followers and retainers who had previously lived in the household of a magnate or bishop expected to be rewarded with a holding of land, which they could call their own and pass on to their descendants. The English thegns were taking part in a Europe-wide process by which the lesser nobility were receiving landed endowments, and were to become a numerous and influential group of smaller landowners – later known as the country gentry or the squirearchy in England. The lords of the great estates did not make these grants for nothing – they expected that the thegns would give loyal service, in administration and war, for example. The more fortunate received their portion of an estate as bookland, which gave them complete security, but many of the thegns gained *loenland* (leasehold), usually in the form of a grant for three lives, supposedly then to return to the lord, though in practice the lease was renewed. Some of the land was simply sold. In eastern England a great upheaval in landholding was caused by the growth of the estates of the newly reformed or founded monasteries at Ely, Crowland, Ramsey and Thorney in the late tenth century, when the monks bought land, some of it in relatively small units. The transactions recorded by the monks were just part of a busy land market already operating among the laity. Finally, some land was stolen, when powerful individuals, especially in troubled times, put pressure on churches to make leases, or converted a temporary tenancy into permanent possession.

Over much of England, then, the great estates were being fragmented. The wider consequences were firstly the change in the whole scale of landholding. The old estates were often rated at 20, 30 or 40 hides, while the new thegns' landholdings, and many of the grants to the new monasteries, had an assessment of between one and six hides. The hide had originally meant 'land for a family', but it came to be an assessment, a means of apportioning liability to tax and service. In terms of more modern measurements, the great estates like Bampton and Howden might stretch over 50 or 100 square miles, while the new units of landholding covered no more than 2 or 3 square miles. Secondly, the exploitation of the land was transformed: instead of delivering produce for the occasional visits of a household, we have an estate fulfilling the daily needs of a lord. The great estate was one among many of a magnate's possessions, while a thegn would often depend on a few pieces of land, or even a single property. The new lord would expect to be a resident, and indeed we find aristocratic houses being built in the ninth and tenth centuries on previously unoccupied sites. These dwellings became castles or manor houses in later centuries.

There could be no question of living on tribute – the thegn would develop an area of land beside his house as a home farm which under his direct supervision became the main source of produce for his household. He would hope to squeeze labour from his peasant tenants, but later evidence suggests that the land under the thegn's direct control, then called the demesne, was worked mainly by slaves or servants. Land detached by the early eleventh century from the great estate of Stratford-upon-Avon in Warwickshire, at Luddington, consisting of only about 200 acres of arable, was provided with twelve slaves. The great estate had balanced its resources, but when the constituent parts were broken away the combination of contrasting types of land could no longer be guaranteed. Some of the parts consisted almost entirely of arable, others mainly of wood and pasture, so the new lord either had to change the use of land to make it more self-sufficient, or continue with the specialism and sell surplus produce. In either case the new small scale of landholding led to more intensive use of the land. New lords would add to their profits by investing in a water mill, which would pay for the effort and cost of construction from the tolls paid by the local peasants to grind their corn. Attitudes to property and management changed. The thegns in particular now regarded the land as their own, as the ideas about property rights originally designed by the church to protect its endowments became more widely diffused through society. Laymen saw their lands as long-term investments, which would pass to their children and grandchildren. Many new place names were coined at this time which identified the place by its owner: Ardwick in Lancashire, for example, means the farm of Aethelred. In contrast with the rather relaxed regime of the great estates, production and rent-gathering were watched hawk-like by the resident lords, anxious to protect their interests and gain the maximum returns.

We can see how the new regime may have worked in the case of a thegn called Haehstan, who was granted a three-life lease of Pendock and Didcot in Worcestershire in 967. Haehstan was something of a carpet-bagger, as he came from eastern England, where his family had been founded by a Danish immigrant in the late ninth century. One of the Dane's descendants, Oswald, became bishop of Worcester, and he looked after his relatives, including Haehstan, by granting them pieces of land from the church's estates. Pendock and Didcot may have been Haehstan's only possessions. They were both quite small, rated in total at three hides, and they were quite awkwardly placed 13 miles apart. Didcot, located in the valley of the Carrant Brook on the edge of the Avon valley, consisted entirely of arable land. Indeed, when Didcot was detached from the parent estate of Overbury, a single block of land could not be defined, so it was formed of scattered strips in the open fields. Pendock, on the other hand, was easily carved out of a relatively underdeveloped wood-land landscape. It included a small amount of arable, with a good deal of marsh, open pasture, enclosed fields, a hedged pasture for pigs, and woodland. Haehstan could have supplied his household with corn, mostly from Didcot, and meat, dairy produce and fuel mainly from Pendock. The properties complemented one another in production as well as consumption, because pigs bred in the valley would have been brought to the woods to be fattened on acorns, young cattle reared at Pendock may well have have been sent to Didcot to work as plough oxen, and if a barn was to be built at Didcot, Pendock would have been the source of timber.

Didcot offered limited opportunities for expansion, as the land there was fixed in a routine of cultivation as part of an established field system. At Pendock, however, there was more scope for development, as its pastures could have been ploughed to extend the arable under Haehstan's direct management. New tenants could have been found land there. People were already established in Pendock, whose names – Osric, Eadred and so on – were used to identify points round the boundary in 967. But a mainly pastoral landscape would be bound to be thinly peopled, and the lord could only increase his revenue from rents and gain labour for his own cultivation if more tenants were recruited from Didcot and its neighbourhood. Another strategy for developing Pendock would have been to take advantage of its special resources, to stock it with more animals, or manage its woods with the intention of producing a saleable surplus of bacon, cheese or honey which could be taken by road to Gloucester, the nearest town. The purchaser of a Kentish swine pasture similar to Pendock was willing to pay £2 40d for it, suggesting its potential to earn money from the sale of produce. Thegns like Haehstan would expect to have cash to spend on aristocratic luxuries like a fine horse, armour, weapons and cloth. A thegn's heriot (death duty paid to his lord) was set at £2 soon after Haehstan's time. So he needed to earn cash from his land.

The lords of the great estates were also forced into new attitudes and policies by fragmentation. As places like Bampton and Overbury lost their former dependencies, their lords had to compensate themselves for the loss of revenues by focusing their efforts in a more concentrated way on the lands remaining under their direct control. The lords had the advantage that they were often located on the best land, and had plenty of peasant tenants capable of doing agricultural service. They emphasized the efficient cultivation of the land, while putting pressure on the peasant tenants to contribute more labour.

The greater landlords seem not to have been driven by the same energy as the lords of small estates. Their assets were so great, and their power over tenants so well established, that they may have felt no need for radical innovations. The wealthier churchmen worried about encroachment on their estates by acquisitive laymen, and the charters that they kept and the boundary clauses that were recorded in so much detail were clearly intended to protect their properties. On the other hand, unlike their contemporaries on the continent, they did not write surveys of their estates, containing the names of peasants and lists of their obligations. The omission may reflect their lack of administrative flair, or a rather complacent attitude towards management. But the existing customs and practices delivered the right results, and would not be helped by a time-consuming bureaucracy. The lay magnates seem not to have put any effort into keeping records. Their estates were so extensive that they may not have been greatly concerned with the details of agricultural profits. Their chief means of expanding their wealth was to add more land to their holdings through their political skills, and they expected to grant away many of their assets in pursuit of patronage. They wished to protect their estates from unnecessary losses, and many of the new acquisitions made by the new monastic estates of the late tenth century had to be fought through the courts as relatives of the donors disputed the legality of the church's possession of their family property.

Magnates of all kinds – kings, earls, bishops, monasteries – faced a dilemma about who would be responsible for the details of cultivation, enforcing service and selling produce. Were these difficult tasks to be supervised by an official appointed for the purpose, a reeve? Or should each estate be leased out for a fixed farm of food, or cash, or a combination of the two? Both direct management and leasing ('farming') are recorded. Farming out their manors would have suited the major lay landlords best, as their estates were often widely scattered, and management would be greatly simplified if it consisted essentially of making a bargain with a lessee, and then ensuring that the farm was paid promptly and in full.

Lords of all types had coped for centuries with the problem of finding the best way to translate their control of land into the revenues of food, fuel and money. As tribute played an important part in the running of the great estates, in theory the practice could have continued and intensified with lords demanding higher proportions of the crops of their tenants. The church received the ancient tax of churchscot, usually levied as grain, and in addition imposed the much more onerous tithe, by which a tenth of all produce – grain, wool, young animals, fruit and so on – was paid to the local clergy. Lords also continued to demand payments in kind, which on the estate of the Winchester monks at Hurstbourne in *c.*900 involved the peasants (the word *ceorl* was used to describe them) paying wheat, barley, ale, firewood and sheep to their lords. As a principal method of taking revenue from an estate, however, payments in kind were rather inflexible and clumsy.

The most effective way for lords to gain income was to develop a demesne, land set aside for their exclusive use, with a core of workers directly employed either as slaves or as hired hands, but which could also draw on the labour of the local peasantry. The whole organization consisted therefore of tenant land, on which peasants were settled on condition that they paid rents and worked for the lord, linked to the demesne on which the labour services could be used. At the centre stood the buildings of the manor, where the lord could live and his officials were based. Both the produce of the demesne and any rents in kind could be collected and processed at this centre of management. Manor (or hall in English) meant a dwelling, but by extension came to refer to the administrative unit which gathered revenues from demesne and tenants.

The concern for the effective management of the demesne was expressed in a treatise written in the early eleventh century known as 'The Reeve' (*Gerefa*), which advised an estate official to know the best seasons for ploughing and mowing, to look after all of the manor's assets, remembering to mend hedges and ditches and clean out sheds. The reeve should be acquainted with a long list of equipment, from an axe to a mousetrap. The section on labour relations advised that the lord's authority should be kept, but that the servants (hired men) should be treated fairly. The treatise resembles a literary exercise rather than a practical handbook, the list of implements being designed to show off the author's encyclopaedic knowledge and wide vocabulary. The subject matter is, however, a guide to the preoccupations of its author, a churchman. Like many of his contemporary landlords, he needed to take an interest in practical agricultural matters. The main message of 'The Reeve', though dressed in rather bookish language, was that anyone in charge of a demesne should protect his lord's interests by paying attention to detail.

The growth of towns, especially in the south and east, influenced the management of estates, as even the 800 inhabitants of a town of modest size would eat and drink the produce of 1,000 acres of arable land, and over a large area would generate demand for livestock and wool. The penetration of cash into the rural economy by the end of the tenth century stimulated a land market which enabled the monasteries of eastern England to build up their estates. The monks of Ely kept a book that recorded for posterity their acquisitions. They proudly entered payments of £15 for a two-hide manor here, £60 for ten hides there, and a purchase of two hides and 37 acres for £11 (see p. 75).

The close connection between the growth of exchange, more intensive production, and the fragmentation of the estates is underlined by the lack of these developments in Wales and Scotland. Here, in countrysides which persisted in traditions of self-sufficiency and tribute payments, the great estates continued to function in the eleventh century, though they soon changed as towns and new political and social formations exercised their influence after 1100.

iv. *Peasants*

The peasant tenants provided much of the labour on many manors, a typical burden according to one early eleventh-century treatise being two or three days each week for a peasant with a yardland, a substantial 30-acre holding, and one day per week for a cottager, but with another day each week during the harvest season. Lords were anxious to gain as much labour as possible, but they were also interested in the payments of rents in cash and kind. They were able to create a dependent peasantry by two routes, one by reducing the independence of tenants, and the other by settling slaves on the land. Lords cajoled lightly burdened peasants to do more work on the demesne. In troubled times, such as a famine year, peasants would have been willing to make concessions for material help, while in times of political troubles the lord could offer his protection in exchange for a promise to labour on the demesne. Perhaps he imposed his protection, and bullied the tenants into doing more work for him. But we should not necessarily envisage such dramatic circumstances, but rather see the lord putting a slow and relentless pressure on his tenants, sometimes threatening them with some loss of privilege, such as access to pasture, sometimes acting as their benefactor, but expecting material returns from that friendship. A lord would, for example, provide food if the whole peasant community turned out to help with the harvest or haymaking.

The freeing of slaves provided another route to a dependent labouring peasantry. Slaves seem to have been very numerous in the ninth, tenth and eleventh centuries. Modestly sized estates were provided with as many as twelve or thirty 'men'. A will written in 992 mentions no fewer than seventy-two of them. In some ways they resemble chattel slaves, like those in the American south in the nineteenth century, as they were listed along with the animal livestock of an estate, and could be bought and sold, the price of a man in the tenth century being £1, eight times that of an ox. They were expected to work in jobs requiring continuous labour, especially as ploughmen, each plough requiring two workers, one to drive the oxen and the other to hold the plough. Many were employed on herding sheep, cattle and pigs, and women worked as dairymaids. Their owners fed the slaves on bread, mutton, beef (for males only) and beans. Slaves, however, seem to have had rather more independence than this picture of subjection and constant work might suggest, as we find them occupying plots of land, marrying and rearing families, attending markets, and accumulating goods and money.

Slaves were being freed in the tenth and eleventh centuries in such numbers that the institution had virtually died out soon after 1100. Various explanations have been offered for this development. Slavery was undoubtedly regarded as morally tarnished, and freeing a slave counted as an act of charity, but this had been the case in earlier centuries. Churchmen disapproved of aspects of the slave trade, and at the same time kept slaves on their estates like other lords. Perhaps difficulties were encountered in recruiting new slaves, with a shortage of war captives. There were other ways of gaining new slaves, among those who sold themselves in times of famine, for example, and in any case married slaves would help to maintain numbers, as the children of slaves were themselves slaves. The conventional view that slaves were lazy and in-efficient and that granting them holdings of their own would motivate them does not accord with recent research on the productivity of slave labour. They were, however, difficult to discipline, and tended to run away, or disobey orders. Those who did manage to sell goods and save money would buy their manumission, and so escape legally. Perhaps the estates found the administrative burden of managing the slaves unsupportable, and decided that it was much simpler to settle them on holdings, while still retaining a claim on their labour.

Thousands of slaves were granted tenant holdings, and so they joined the ranks of the peasantry. The descendants of the freed slaves of the tenth and eleventh centuries can be identified after 1100 because they held small tenements in return for heavy services, such as carrying out full-time tasks as ploughmen or shepherds. The manorial tenants owing labour services therefore consisted partly of people who had come 'up from slavery', and partly of an older stratum of dependent tenants pressurized into doing more work for the lord, and perhaps peasants previously free of major obligations who had been caught in the manorial net. We will never know for certain which route into dependence on the manor was more important, and indeed this must have varied with the region or type of estate. Our view is partly obscured by the versions which lords liked to believe. Just as they presented an image of themselves as the friends and protectors of their tenants, they also justified their dominance by claiming that peasants had been granted parcels of the lords' land, together with livestock and equipment, in exchange for heavy services, making the whole arrangement seem like a reciprocal exchange. But very rarely were lords filling up an empty piece of countryside. A more common situation was that they took over an inhabited territory, and then had to subject it, and above all its population, to their control. In these circumstances they had not given their peasants their holdings, but took away lands they already held, and granted them back on more oppressive terms.

Some lords were much more successful than others in forcing the peasantry into manorial discipline. The regions which have produced the best early evidence for a regime of heavy labour service tend to lie in the west, in Worcestershire, Gloucestershire, Hampshire and Somerset, and the documents come from the archives of the major church landlords. To the north and east social organization seems much looser, with large manors provided with relatively small demesnes, associated with outlying dependent parcels of land, known as berewicks when they were under manorial control, and sokes when the peasants enjoyed a great deal of independence. These groups of free peasants may have come under the jurisdiction of lords as late as the tenth century, when kings granted rights over them to English aristocrats moving back into territory formerly held by the Danes. In Kent we find some peasants under close lordly control, and others who were much more independent, who were able to practise partible inheritance into later centuries. In Wales and Scotland, although details survive only from a later period, bond tenants owed services to estate centres, but there were also numerous lightly burdened peasants. The latter were expected to pay rents in cash and kind, or contribute occasional labour dues, but were exempt from the more oppressive routine of manorial labour. These differences to some extent reflected varied types of agricultural production, as pastoral husbandry did not need so much labour, and peasants travelling with their herds were much more difficult to tie down. The different types of landlord had a strong influence, as large church estates were better established in western England than in the north and east.

Peasants' reactions to all these changes are not recorded, but we can attempt to reconstruct their views from the comments of their superiors and their overall behaviour. To begin with the slaves, they clearly felt the disadvantage of their status, and sought to escape from it. In the words put into the mouth of a slave ploughman by a monastic writer, Aelfric, in *c*.1000, 'Yes, the work is hard, because I am not free'. We have seen that slaves contributed to their own liberation in a small way by buying their freedom, or by flight. They welcomed the grants of land which gave them at least a measure of economic independence, and an inheritance for their families. Slave specialist workers such as swineherds and beekeepers were contracted in the eleventh century to deliver to the lord a fixed quota of produce – fifteen pigs or five sesters (a sester weighed nine pounds) of honey – after which they could keep or sell any surplus. They were gaining some control over their working lives.

The smallholder, sometimes called the *cotsetla*, was recorded in the *Rectitudines* (rules), a description of peasant conditions in western England written near to 1000. He contributed relatively small amounts of labour service to the manor – a quarter of his working time was spent on the demesne. As their holdings were probably too small to feed their families, we can deduce that these people formed part of the force of hired workers who were employed on the demesnes, or in towns if they lived nearby, or most often by the wealthier peasants.

The peasant with a yardland (30-acre) holding known as a *ceorl* or *gebur* formed the key figure in the manorial structure, providing the bulk of the labour service and rents in cash and kind. The obligation to work on the lord's demesne for two or three days per week was undoubtedly a burden, and a drag on his ability to produce from his own holding. One imagines in particular the problems he experienced when the sun shone in the haymaking or harvest seasons, but the days had to be spent working for the lord while the crops on his own holding were damaged by neglect. Although technically free, in the sense that he attended the public courts of the hundred, he was subject to manorial discipline, which prevented him from moving without the permission of his lord. We can also glimpse behind the descriptions of peasant obligations the *gebur* and his household as substantial producers in their own right, with a holding of arable, and access to grazing and woodland. The house, judging from peasant buildings that have been excavated, measured 15 feet by 30 feet and was built of substantial timbers, as were the barn and other outbuildings. At least 15 acres of crops were planted each year, and peasants kept oxen as draught animals, and cows, sheep and pigs, from which in normal years the family could feed itself, pay the rent and have a surplus to exchange. The holding was associated with others in a hamlet or village, which was essential for agricultural production, as each *gebur* usually owned two oxen; it would only be through joining with neighbours that the full team of eight could have been assembled. It was also from his neighbours that he gained the labour for harvesting and other seasonal work, employing the cottagers who needed earnings to supplement the produce of their smallholdings. The *gebur* or *ceorl* emerges then not as a mere appendage of a manor, but as a producer, trader, member of a community, and as an employer.

More obviously independent was the *geneat*, a peasant without a heavy commitment to labour services, whose obligations to his lord often involved riding, carrying messages, escorting his lord, helping with the hunt and general carriage work. A *geneat* had a larger holding than a *gebur*, and therefore enjoyed better opportunities to sell produce. He was less burdened with time-consuming labour services, and gained in status from his light and honourable duties.

The manor played a significant part in the economy, but rural society was not entirely dominated by lords and their officials. The village had responsibilities to the hundred court, and the peasant community managed its fields and pastures. Where the village was divided between two or more manors – a common situation at the time of Domesday Book, but going back to much earlier times – the villagers protected the unity of the community, and ensured in the absence of any other single authority that the rules of husbandry were obeyed.

The peasants' ability to conduct their own lives emerges from an examination of their involvement in buying and selling. They paid cash rents to their lords, for which the usual figure given in the tenth and early eleventh centuries was 10d or 12d per yardland, though at the estate of Tidenham in Gloucestershire each *gebur* paid another 6d. In addition, the geld payments to the king were paid in cash, and though not demanded every year, they could amount to 6d or more per yardland. This money could only have been obtained by selling produce. Certain crops, notably wool, bacon, cheese and other animal products, may have been available in quantities beyond the subsistence needs of the family, and were suitable for the market. We find peasants employed in non-agricultural occupations aimed at yielding a cash income, such as the large-scale fishing at Tidenham, presumably reproduced all round the coast and along major rivers, and wood-cutting and transport. They worked in rural industries such as pottery manufacture at Michelmersh in Hampshire and quarrying at Taynton (Oxfordshire) and Barnack (Lincolnshire). Near towns, peasants worked the hemp and flax gardens which kept an important urban craft supplied with raw materials. It could be said that peasants were forced to produce for the market to pay rents and taxes. They paid some of the money that they earned to lord and state, but they also had to buy essential goods for their farming and domestic lives, and wished to indulge in expenditure for pleasure, status-seeking and other familiar motives. In eastern England they bought pottery manufactured mainly in towns, and all over the country they acquired functional iron implements and hand mills, ornamental bronze belt attachments and brooches.

Contact with the market meant that peasants travelled into towns or the less formal gatherings outside churches or estate centres. These visits sometimes turned into longer stays and permanent migrations, hence the growth of the urban population. The manorial authorities attempted to control the movements of the *geburs*, but they could not be prevented from taking opportunities outside their native village. A list of *gebur* emigrants from Hatfield in Hertfordshire was compiled by officials working for the monks of Ely around 1000. Among others they found that three of the peasants had sons – their names were Duding, Ceolmund and Aethelheah – who had moved to Walden (now King's Walden), which would have involved a journey of about 10 miles, perhaps in a concerted move by a peer group of ambitious young men. Marriage provided the motive for a number of Hatfield migrations. Peasant society of the tenth and eleventh centuries was clearly not rooted in one spot or unaware of the wider world.

There are hints in documents written by their superiors about peasants, and in the traces of peasant culture that still survive, in the naming of minor features in the countryside, that tell us a little of peasant mentality. They were aware of local myths and legends, but to some extent they were practically minded, knowing the crops for which a piece of land was best suited (for example 'beanfield'), and had a detailed appreciation of the subtleties of the landscape, so that they had numerous words for 'valley' and 'hill'. They had strong family attachments, and could remember their ancestors; they had a memory for custom, which estate managers were warned to ignore at their peril. This was not just a matter of mindless loyalties to familiar people and old ideas, but a necessary means of protection against dangerous forces in a world that was not always changing for the better. For the same reason they valued the collective organizations like the village community which regulated cultivation, but also offered companionship and support among those of similar status and common economic interests.

A development in the countryside which brings together all of these varied but connected trends was the building of local churches. In the days of the great estate, a few widely scattered rich minster churches provided the main centres of religious life. When the great estates fragmented, hundreds of local lords founded churches on their manors, which became the parish churches that still exist as institutions, even if their fabric has been renewed in later centuries. By 1086, and mainly in the previous century or two, 416 churches had been established in Suffolk, three-quarters of the total that ever existed in the middle ages. These new churches reflect the change in the pattern of lordship, and the ambition of the lesser lords to gain the status symbol that a church represented: it was often built on land adjacent to the manor house. The lords profited from church dues, and like a mill, the church generated valuable revenue for the manor: spending on its construction was an investment. The new pattern of churches also reflects the expansion of the rural landscape, as many were sited on the edges of the old estates, on land that had been brought into intensive use in the previous century or two, as in the weald of Kent. The churches were built for congregations in rural communities, and often stood near one of the relatively new nucleated villages. We do not always know whether the church or the village came first, and perhaps they were built simultaneously. The actual construction, furnishing and decoration of the church shows the growing division of labour and craft specialization. The mason's craft as a major occupation for hundreds of workers was born in the wave of church-building in this period, as these were the main stone structures. Other crafts found employment too. Quarrying new stone seems to have developed around 1000, earlier churches having often been built from reused masonry. Carpenters made the roofs of the stone churches, and the whole of the structure in the numerous churches which were built entirely of timber. Painters, stone carvers, bell founders, goldsmiths, embroiderers of vestments and other specialists equipped and ornamented the interiors of the buildings. Not just the furnishings and fittings were traded over a distance – the building materials could have been brought from far off, like the stones used for the tower of Sompting church in Sussex, which came from Quarr in the Isle of Wight and Caen in Normandy. Here was a society co-ordinating itself at every level, which at the same time was generating disposable wealth. (Plate 1)

The rural economy in the period 850–1050 was growing in the sense that overall production expanded, and was stimulated by changes in

institutions and the market. The aristocracy undoubtedly benefited from
these developments, emerging at the end of the period more numerous
and wealthy. The peasantry had more mixed experiences, with the freeing
of slaves balanced by the extension of the power of the manors, and the
opportunity of gains in the market being offset by the increasing burden
of rents, services and taxes. One guide to the overall health of agriculture
may be the incidence of hunger. The *Anglo-Saxon Chronicle* reported
famines in 975–6, 1005, 1039 and 1044. These reflect the problems of
variable weather, or even the desire of a partisan cleric to emphasize the
depth of crisis in times of political troubles. It is surely significant,
however lacking in objectivity the reports may be, that the chronicler
chose to indicate the severity of the food shortage in 1039 and 1044 by
quoting the very high prices paid for grain – 55d and 60d for a sester
(quarter) of wheat. The unconscious assumption that this was the best
way to measure shortage reveals the strength of the market's influence,
not just on agriculture, but also on people's minds.

CHAPTER TWO

Crisis and new directions, c.850–c.1050

Economic history often deals with slow and even imperceptible changes in population or trade, and dramatic events are the concern of political history. Sudden upheavals were sometimes so profound that they had an impact on economic and social life. The Viking invasions were a cataclysmic episode of this kind, when people from Scandinavia surged into the rest of Europe. We need to consider whether an influx of settlers, who certainly regarded themselves as brave, innovative and resourceful, changed the economy, or whether their main impact was to energize the existing population.

i. *The Viking invasions*

The Viking attacks shocked the people of Britain. The first recorded violent contacts came in the years 789–95, when monasteries were sacked at Lindisfarne off the north-east coast of England, and at Iona in western Scotland. In Dorset a group of intruders killed the king's local official who rode to meet them. They moved swiftly and purposefully by sea and along the major rivers, in well-designed ships propelled by both sails and oars, which could carry between thirty and sixty men. In the ninth and tenth centuries people from Norway took over the northern and western isles (Orkney, Shetland, the Hebrides and the Isle of Man) and parts of the mainland of Scotland such as Caithness. The raids against England, mainly by Danes, built up in scale and intensity through a phase of attacks in the 830s. In 850–1 an army stayed over the winter, and from 865 until 896 (with some lulls) armies ranged over the whole country. At the end of that period of warfare the south of England, thanks to the efforts of the inhabitants of Wessex, co-ordinated by its king Alfred

(871–99), retained its independence, but in the north and to a lesser extent in East Anglia, the land was ruled by Scandinavians. The former English kingdoms of Northumbria, Mercia and East Anglia ceased to exist. York became for a time the capital of a Viking kingdom.

In the tenth century successive kings of Wessex conquered the areas under Scandinavian rule, finally capturing York in 954. Northern and eastern England, the Danelaw, retained distinct customs and culture. In a new phase of attacks beginning in earnest in 991, well-organized forces from Denmark extorted tribute from the English (Danegeld) and ultimately in 1016 the king of Denmark, Cnut, became king of England, to be succeeded by two of his sons. At about this time, between about 975 and 1025, the earls of Orkney were leading raids in the north and collecting booty and tribute. Wales was subjected to sporadic raids in the ninth century, and the south of the country was invaded in 914. In the late tenth century north Wales, especially Anglesey, was vulnerable to incursions from the Scandinavians then dominating the Irish Sea.

This brief recounting of events does not convey the full impact of the Vikings on Britain. They had their effects throughout Europe, and played some part in precipitating the breakdown of the Carolingian empire which had brought together much of western Europe, including the territories now called Germany, the Netherlands, Belgium, France and Italy. In addition, they had a role in the formation of the embryonic Russian state based on Kiev, and they explored the north Atlantic, colonizing the Faeroes, Iceland, Greenland and, briefly, Newfoundland. But nowhere felt the force of Viking activity as intensely as did the British Isles. In the north and west, virtually independent Norse colonies were created, including a state based on Dublin, and the isles around Scotland and the Isle of Man were settled intensively. For a time in the late ninth century England faced the full force of Danish aggression, and around 1000 the attacks and invasion were organized by the Danish state.

We often presume that medieval warfare concerned only the political elites, who fought battles and made peace with little direct influence on the rest of society. But the Viking attacks left no one untouched. Their raids were directed against wealthy establishments, such as churches, but their tendency to descend on a monastery when people were gathered to celebrate a special saint's day, which attracted worshippers and would have been a suitable occasion for a market, shows that they intended to plunder the goods and money of the assembled laity as well as the chalices and ornaments of the monks. Captives were carried off into slavery, so poverty gave no protection. Those who lived in the areas of Scandinavian colonization, whether the Picts of Orkney and Caithness or the northern English, were liable to violent expulsion from their homes, or (more commonly) subjection to new lords. Hoards of coins were hidden through fear of the invaders: eighteen of them have been found in England alone from the period 868–75, and no doubt many more still lie undisturbed in the ground. The fact that they remained to be discovered in modern times demonstrates the real social disruption which prevented the recovery of the money by the person who deposited the hoard. The many English who never encountered a Dane face to face were drawn into the conflict because of the demands that were made by the kings of Wessex for labour and cash to sustain the war effort. Under Alfred, conditions near to 'total war' prevailed in southern England, especially in the programme to build a chain of burh fortifications: these were strong points to provide a protective chain along the south and west coasts, and in the Thames valley. Peasants were drafted in to dig defensive ditches and heap earth, to haul timber to make the ramparts, and to take part in related construction projects such as road- and bridge-building. Once a burh was complete, the local population contributed to its maintenance, and to the manning of the walls. A fifth of the adult male population of Wessex was required to garrison the burh system by *c*.900. A century later, under Aethelred (978–1016), new burh works were under way, this time sometimes with stone walls, but above all a heavy burden of taxation was needed to pay Danegeld. The Danes expected to receive even more cash once they had become the masters in 1016, and heregeld (silver to pay troops) was levied until 1051.

This effort was sustained partly by compulsion, but also by the conviction among the population, fostered by rulers and churchmen, that the Vikings were pagan barbarians who were especially cruel, destructive and ruthless in their pursuit of plunder and captives. This demonization of the enemy went further than in other wars, and was established so effectively that it is still widely believed, hence the familiar modern image of early medieval Scandinavians as helmeted warriors leaping from their ships to spread havoc. Here I have followed common custom in referring to all the migrants as 'Vikings', though the word was used in Scandinavia to identify those who went on expeditions, not the whole people. The hostile perception of the Vikings was a real factor in the political and economic life of the period, and it helped to mobilize resources against them.

Did the Scandinavian invaders themselves make a contribution to the economy? Their activities are commonly divided into piracy, trade, settlement and organized invasion to collect tribute and conquer territory. In practice these different sources of profit were closely connected. In the ninth century the Vikings operated as raiding parties, acquiring goods such as precious metals, ornaments and slaves, either by direct seizure or by demands for tribute. These goods could be exchanged, so the raiders became traders. Scales and weights are found as part of the equipment for the afterlife buried with the dead in Scandinavian graves. These could have been used in the course of trade, to weigh gold and silver or precious commodities, or to share out booty after a raid. They are also found in women's graves, so these transactions were not confined to the warriors. Raiding could lead to settlement, as the attackers observed attractive opportunities for farming. The settlements could serve as bases for further plundering expeditions.

In the rural economy, they played a role as colonists. The *Anglo-Saxon Chronicle* says that the Danish 'great army' shared out the land in northern and eastern England in 876–80. 'Great' armies were not very large in the early middle ages, but this suggests that at least a few thousand men took land, and these numbers were swelled later by wives and children and other colonists, who came to account for a substantial proportion of the population of counties such as Yorkshire and Lincolnshire. The place names of the northern and eastern counties of England, the northern and western isles, and parts of north-east Scotland and Galloway, reflect the presence of many people speaking Scandinavian languages. Names like Grimsby (Lincolnshire) combine a Danish personal name with the Danish word *by* that means a village; and in north-west England names ending in -thwaite indicate a Norwegian presence. Norwegian speakers also named many places in Orkney, such as Grimbist, which derives from the word *bolstadr*, meaning a farm.

Linguistic contact with the native population produced hybrid names like Grimston, which combine a Scandinavian personal name with the Old English word for an estate or village. In all, more than a third of the place names listed in Domesday Book in the East and North Ridings of Yorkshire contain Scandinavian elements. These were applied to places of all kinds, both key administrative centres and minor hamlets on poor land. The Grimsby type of name is especially important, because it implies a Scandinavian presence not just in the place itself, but also in the surrounding district, because it would only be a local population of speakers of Danish who would need to distinguish one 'by' from another. The numerous field names in north Lincolnshire based on Scandinavian words points also to the presence of Danish-speaking villagers. In the eleventh century and later we find that the northern English counties have distinctive institutions, such as subdivisions of the shires which are called wapentakes: this derives from a Scandinavian word for an assembly where those attending indicated their will by brandishing their weapons. The most intense colonization occurred in the northern and western isles, where the language was transformed, and a dialect of Norwegian persisted for centuries. Settlements were established there which modern excavations have shown to consist of long houses of Scandinavian type with benches built along the side walls and a hearth in the centre.

While all of this provides compelling evidence that much land was taken over by Scandinavian immigrants, we need to be cautious about assuming a wholesale transfer of population from Denmark and Norway. The process by which a new language was imposed is difficult to understand, but it would certainly be wrong to assume that everyone who spoke a dialect of Danish in Lincolnshire or Yorkshire in the tenth century had come from Denmark or was descended from a Danish settler. Danish words spread eventually throughout England, into regions where virtually no Danes ever set foot, like the word 'toft' meaning a plot of land on which a house was built. Personal names, for example, do not necessarily prove the ethnic origin of their bearers, as a fashion developed among the native English of giving their children Scandinavian names. Place names like Grimsby do not prove that everyone in that part of north Lincolnshire was of Danish origin, and the Grimston type of name shows that English speech persisted: place names indicating a Scandinavian influence are often mingled with those deriving from the native languages of England and Scotland.

The Scandinavians are unlikely to have played a major role as pioneering developers of new land. They found a countryside already cultivated, and took over existing settlements, or infiltrated local communities. The more powerful took over the centres of the great estates, while their followers acquired the attached hamlets, and hastened the break-up of the estate by making these outer parts independent. This is most likely to have led to a renaming of the more remote sections of an estate in the language of the invaders, hence the tendency of Scandinavian place names to be attached to the less desirable land. Many of the settlers took over not as groups of peasant cultivators but as a conquering elite: a contemporary chronicle says that they put East Anglia 'under the yoke'. They seem not to have imposed new agricultural methods or new ways for extracting money and goods from the peasant population. Types of estate organization in northern England are recorded in the eleventh and twelfth centuries in which sokes – outlying parcels of land – were attached to estate centres. The inhabitants of the outlying places, sokemen, were lightly burdened and were once thought to be the descendants of free Danish soldiers. But these free peasants and the distinctive ways of exploiting the resources of the countryside had been established before the Danes arrived, and were also changed by the process of reconquest by the English in the tenth century. So the Danes may not have introduced their own methods of land management. In general the newcomers, far from stamping their customs on the land that they occupied, accepted the culture of their new country, converting to Christianity within a generation or two. The characteristic styles of decoration developed in Scandinavia are most commonly encountered in England on stone crosses and church monuments, so even when they were bringing their own ideas they worked within a framework of existing institutions.

Even in the northern isles, where the Scandinavian presence seems so dominant, not many new settlements were being founded. Jarlshof in Shetland shows that a ninth-century settler built a farmhouse of distinctively Norwegian type, with stone foundations, benches and a long hearth in the main room, and this then expanded into a hamlet of houses either through subdivision of the land among the succeeding generations or the arrival of more colonists. Birsay and Buckquoy are more typical of Viking colonization in that houses of a Scandinavian type were constructed on top of Pictish buildings. The immigrants seem to have been attracted to existing settlements, from which they continued to farm land already under cultivation. The animal bones found in the deposits of the pre-Viking and Viking periods show that there was no abrupt change in the methods of agriculture. Fish formed part of the diet in both periods, but after the Scandinavian migrations more deep-sea species, notably cod, were consumed, suggesting that the newcomers brought with them techniques for fishing expeditions beyond the shore. The inhabitants' use of ornamental metalwork of 'Celtic' type suggests a period of coexistence and cultural contacts between the natives and immigrants, and they may have intermarried.

If the Vikings' innovations in the countryside were on a limited scale, perhaps they brought new life and vigour into the towns? Their raids were linked closely to exchange, as we have seen. Church plate and ornaments which had previously been hoarded were now put into circulation, and stimulated trade. The Vikings have a reputation for technological innovation, especially in the design of ships. They built not just fast, light ships for warfare and raiding, but also heavier trading vessels able to carry bulky cargo. Helped by colonizing ventures, sea routes were developed around northern Europe, linking Scandinavia with Iceland, the British Isles, the Low Countries, the Rhineland and northern France. Scandinavian products, such as soapstone and amber, were imported into York. Towns grew in areas under Scandinavian rule, at Dublin, York and Rouen, as well as in the homelands at such places as Haithabu, Birka and Kaupang. Eastern routes connected the Baltic through the Russian river systems with Byzantium and the Arab states of the middle east. The

Vikings' network of trade brought distant economies into contact, so that 'kufic' coins, minted in the east with Arabic inscriptions, were owned by residents of northern England and Scotland. A hoard buried at Golds-borough in Yorkshire in the 920s contained coins minted at Samarkand in modern Uzbekistan. The Viking rulers of York minted high-quality silver pennies, and thereby brought northern England into the monetary system prevailing throughout western Europe.

By such activities Scandinavians were contributing to economic growth, but this statement needs some qualifications. Expansion in towns and trade was not confined to the Scandinavian sphere of influ-ence; rather they were participating in a general tendency of the period. For example, a community of Scandinavians lived in eleventh-century London, where churches were dedicated to saints such as St Olaf of Norway and St Clement Danes, and the chief legal assembly was known by a Scandinavian word, the Husting court. But they were just one element among a number of groups of continental merchants who traded in the city. The successful town foundations tended to lie in territories already showing signs of growth in exchange before 850, like York, and in some of the areas of most intensive Scandinavian settlement, in the Northern Isles or the Isle of Man, they may have founded trading centres but no real towns. The Vikings looted and damaged towns; the trading settlements at Southampton (Hamwic) and London (Lundenwic) were abandoned in the ninth century, and were re-established, eventually, on more secure sites. The stimulus to exchange which is said to have flowed from Viking activities may not always have worked very rapidly. In the 'five boroughs' of the Danelaw, at Derby, Leicester, Lincoln, Nottingham and Stamford, much of the urban growth may have come in the late tenth century, after they had come under English rule. The number of objects of 'Viking' character found at York, or goods which were imported from Scandinavia, are limited in quantity. The construction of the buildings was not based entirely on Scandinavian types. No doubt the Viking rulers of the city gave the impetus for the growth of new towns, but most of the people who moved in to work as artisans and traders were likely to have been of local origin.

The Scandinavian invaders cannot be dismissed as barbarians but their background ensured that they could influence, but not transform, the economy. Scandinavia had no experience of Roman rule, and had escaped inclusion in the Carolingian empire. Centralized monarchies were devel-oping during the Viking age, and were assisted by the conversion to Christianity in the tenth and eleventh centuries. But the Scandinavians lacked the state institutions, social hierarchy and literacy which had evolved in the English kingdoms between *c*.600 and 850. They were receptive to influence from the cultures and economies which they encountered. In Yorkshire, they joined in the processes of urbanization and developing the use of money. When they operated in less complex economies, they adopted different attitudes towards acquiring and exchanging wealth. This is apparent from the silver hoards deposited in Scotland between about 940 and 1065, which contain 'hack silver' (pieces of metal resulting from cutting up jewellery and other objects), ingots, coins and arm rings or ring money which were made in standard weights. Clearly these objects had been used in exchange because they had often been pricked or nicked with a knife point to ensure that they were made of pure silver. Coins are found with these marks also, showing that they were accepted for their silver content, not at face value. The population had apparently not become accustomed to the use of money, but weights of precious metals were being bartered. People acquired quantities of bullion and stored it as proof of their status, or used it in the exchange of gifts rather than in commercial transactions, or even handed it over in payments to compensate the relatives of someone killed in a feud. Similarly in the countryside the Vikings adopted the farming methods and settlement patterns which already existed. Economic activity was unlikely to be determined by ethnic make-up or national character. Enterprise and invention arose, as at other times and places, from a combination of circumstances, pressures and incentives. (Plate 2)

ii. *The growth of the state*

Important economic changes followed the Viking incursions. The economy before the Viking age was not very productive or sophisticated. The great estates were designed to gather foodstuffs for consumption by the itinerant households of kings, nobles and bishops, or to send to monasteries. The lords were not exploiting their rural resources very intensively, judging from the fixed quotas of produce, in rather modest quantities, which they expected to receive from each estate. Peasants did not enjoy any great plenty, and their tendency to move their dwellings suggests an unsettled and shifting agricultural system. Slaves did much of the agricultural work, and may not have achieved high levels of productivity. Trade was conducted from a few towns, which were very unevenly distributed. The imported goods were aimed at a luxury market, the small scale of which can be judged from the normal method of unloading ships by hauling them on to beaches. Manufactures were produced by itinerant craftsmen, or by non-specialists. The only potters who made high-quality ware on a large scale seem to have been those working in Ipswich, and their products had a restricted distribution, mainly in East Anglia.

The Vikings shook society, and one indirect contribution that they made to economic growth was to unify and animate the machinery of the state. The Vikings destroyed weaker states, and galvanized others into effective action. They contributed to the unification of the Scottish kingdom by weakening Pictish rule in the east of the country, and by putting pressure on the Scots in the west, which led to the king of the Scots, Kenneth Macalpine, taking over the territory ruled by the Picts in 843. Scandinavian incursions did not pose such a major threat to the rulers of Wales, but nonetheless a prince who vigorously opposed the invaders, Hywel Dda (922–50), enjoyed greater authority than any of his predecessors.

In England, the kings of Mercia in the eighth century, and especially Offa (757–96), had increased state power to build a system of fortifications on the Welsh border (Offa's Dyke), and to defend centres such as Hereford, Tamworth and Winchcombe. They mobilized manpower by insisting that landowners should contribute to military service, and to the building of fortifications and bridges. Similar demands were made on a much larger scale by Alfred and his tenth-century successors as rulers of Wessex and then England. A chain of forts was built around Wessex, and then extended into the midlands, at such places as Bedford, Buckingham, Warwick and Worcester. With the conquest of Danish territory the system was pushed further north, and Leicester, Lincoln and York were taken under English royal control. Forts were also built along the Welsh border, as far west as Rhuddlan.

Before this surge of burh-building, government was based on the king's *tuns*, which were estate centres, usually provided with a residence, where food rents and dues could be collected. A burh was often sited at or near a king's tun, but was larger and more strongly fortified, enclosing an area of between 40 and 300 acres, enough space for an army to be based and to provide shelter for the population of the district. A burh was originally conceived as a military strong point, to block off a river or road route, such as the fort which occupied an island in the Thames at Sashes near Cookham in Berkshire. A number of these strategic defences, including Sashes, fell into disuse once the Viking emergency had passed. But many of the forts in the tenth century became formidable centres of royal authority, and behind the security of their ramparts, sited on main roads and river crossings, officials (the king's reeves) could hold courts, enforce law and order, levy troops, supervise the minting of coins and collect taxes. The burh became the basis of a new system of local government, most readily apparent in the twenty shires north of the Thames, each of which took its name from a burh at its centre – Nottinghamshire from Nottingham, Herefordshire from Hereford, and so on. The shires were not entirely new, because they were often formed from putting together many old administrative districts. Henceforth the kingdom of England would be a centralized state, because the burh network gave the king authority in every part of his kingdom. Through the officials in the shires – the ealdormen and shire reeves – the king had a direct line of communication with the provinces. The shire courts, run by the king's representative, dealt with a wide range of business: administrative, military and financial. With the gradual development of written documents in government, the king could send a brief letter of instruction authenticated with his seal, a writ, to the shire authorities to ensure that his will was done. A further tier of government below the shires, hundreds in the south, wapentakes in the former Danish territories, ensured that royal government functioned in every locality. The hundred courts met regularly, settled disputes and enforced law and order, being charged with catching thieves and recovering stolen goods. Each household and community was responsible for the good behaviour of its members, and the smallest unit of government of all, the village, was represented by its reeve and leading men at the hundred court.

The state planned for resources to be assessed and obligations apportioned in a systematic fashion. Every piece of land had for centuries been assigned a hidage – the typical village would be rated at five hides. Hides had ceased to mean 'family land' but had come to be a unit of assessment which bore some relationship to the resources available. Assessments were built up into wonderfully elaborate statistical edifices, so that a model shire like Worcestershire (recorded in the eleventh century) consisted of twelve hundreds each of 100 hides, making a round total of 1,200. If troops were levied at one man for a hide to defend the burh of Worcester, 1,200 would be assembled. If taxes (geld) were levied at 2s to the hide, the king could expect to receive 2,400s. The larger and richer shires in the south owed much more – Hampshire, Wiltshire, Berkshire and Surrey together had originally consisted of 120 hundreds, and perhaps therefore 12,000 hides. The hides went back to very early times, but the system of assessment could be adapted to new needs. When a navy was needed to repel the Danish attacks at the end of the tenth century, hundreds were grouped in threes, and each of the resulting 'shipsokes' of 300 hides was expected to find a crew of sixty men at a rate of one man for each five hides.

The hierarchy of administrative units at the king's command, allowing rational deployment of money and manpower through universal fiscal assessments, resembled in many ways – and indeed was modelled on – the arrangements within the continental Carolingian empire that reached its high point a century before the reign of Alfred. Like the Carolingians, kings of Wessex and England, notably Alfred and Edgar (957–75), as well as developing their practical powers, allied themselves with churchmen. Alfred had a programme for education, to improve the quality of the clergy and to spread literacy among the lay aristocracy. Edgar encouraged the foundation of new monasteries and the reform of existing communities of clergy. Clerics aided government through their literacy, but more importantly for the rulers they gave secular government a moral basis, and held out an ideal of a harmonious society that could develop under Christian royal rule. Bishops, as in the Carolingian system, supported the state as advisers at court and provincial governors. The Carolingian institutions, for all of the official propaganda, had many flaws, and perhaps the same is true of the apparently logical and efficient English royal government.

One gap in the administrative symmetry is apparent in the north, where the large and clumsy shires of Lincoln and York were clearly not formed according to the midland model, and in the far north shires were not created until after the Norman Conquest. The state was no bureaucracy. The king's household probably contained a professional writing office, a chancery, on the lines of continental practice. However, its main task was to produce charters and writs, and there is little evidence that the state kept any quantity of written administrative documents. Geld rolls, recording tax liability, were evidently held in the eleventh century in an archive at Winchester. Law codes and special documents, like the 'burghal hidage' detailing the arrangements for defence in *c*.900, were compiled occasionally. But the main operations of the state depended on oral instructions, custom and memory. The absence of detailed evidence for the day-to-day running of government means that we do not know if it worked as intended. A group of 'agents of the state' have been identified – minor aristocrats and small landowners who delivered messages, collected money and carried out other government tasks. But even this group would have been hard pressed to conduct all of the work required. In the end, the whole machine depended on the co-operation of subjects, and no doubt the rulers were able to call on their loyalty, persuading them that their self-interest coincided with that of the central government. Everyone with property wished to maintain order, and those who helped the state would find that some of its authority rubbed off on them. Still, we cannot avoid some scepticism about the efficiency of government. Why, for example, was the legislation of the period so concerned with theft and dishonesty, unless it was a major problem that the hundred courts were unable to control?

Finally, the main problem that had faced the Carolingian empire was the necessity for the rulers to delegate power to the local nobility, who at a later stage could become independent rulers. While the centralized monarchy was developing in England, political power on the continent was coming under the control of counts, dukes and castellans whose predecessors had been the 'faithful men' of the Carolingian dynasty. This has become known to historians as the 'feudal revolution'. Such an extreme devolution was prevented in England by the king's continued grip on the shires. The landholdings of the great magnates were usually widely scattered, so unlike their continental contemporaries they lacked a local power base. There was still a degree of delegation of authority, which meant that royal rule could be challenged and undermined by members of the nobility. At the end of Edgar's reign a group reacted against the growing influence of monks, so that monasteries lost land and new foundations ceased for a time. In 1007–17 a great magnate, Eadric Streona, was said to rule like a 'sub-king' in the midlands, and from 1016 to 1066 the earls, bearing a newly created title, were prone to plots and rebellions. The great landowners were able to count on the support of numerous followers among the lesser aristocracy, who formed part of their households, or who held land from them on leasehold or some other dependent tenure, or who were 'commended' to them in a bond which obliged them to provide service. The English magnates did not enjoy the privileges of private jurisdiction which allowed counts and dukes across the Channel to wield a great range of royal rights, from capital punishment to the minting of coins. The English were granted minor legal powers, known as 'sake and soke', though we do not know what this meant precisely in terms of their treatment of the tenants on their estates. An apparent disadvantage of the English aristocracy was their lack of private castles, as the major fortifications, the burh system, were retained firmly in the hands of the king. The aristocracy, however, built some defences around their houses so the idea of a private fortress was not entirely absent from England (see pp. 75–6 and 80). Nor was the strong English state immune to persuasion and lobbying in the interests of individual landowners. The universal hidage assessments for judging taxable wealth could be manipulated through patronage, resulting in reductions in hidage for favoured subjects. No doubt the courts of hundred and shire were also strongly influenced by the local lords.

The English and continental aristocracies inhabited the same world of extensive privileges and private power. We can conclude that the English state that had been formed out of the turmoil of the Danish invasions was a very incomplete organization, in which kings and aristocrats had to work together. But the kings could do more than any of their European contemporaries, and in particular commanded more effective machinery for tax collection than any polity in Europe since the decline of the Roman empire.

The growth of the English state contributed to economic change by providing a plentiful and reliable coinage. Kings kept close control over the currency, much of which was minted in burhs. In the late eighth century the penny had been produced for the first time, and this was to be the main type of coin minted and circulated in England throughout the middle ages. Silver of a high degree of purity (that is with 8 per cent or less of base metal alloyed with the silver) was beaten into flat sheets and out of these were stamped discs of the right size, 18–20 millimetres in diameter. Each disc was placed on an iron die, on which the design of one face of the coin had been cut in reverse. The moneyer held a punch bearing the design of the other face of the coin on top of the disc of silver. A sharp blow with a hammer would impress the relatively soft metal of the disc with the design on both faces simultaneously, and a coin would result. The process was repeated thousands of times, depending on the supply of silver.

Minting practice indicates the kings' aims in managing the currency, which are especially clear after Edgar's reforms of 973. Anxious that the coins should be widely distributed, the kings set up mints all over the kingdom. By the end of the tenth century seventy mints had been established, not just in the obvious centres of population and trade such as London and Canterbury, but also in small places such as Bruton in Somerset and Horncastle in Lincolnshire. No one could claim that they could not pay their taxes because coins were unobtainable, as almost everyone lived within 15 miles of a mint. Kings ensured that only their coins were available by insisting that any foreign currency that entered the country was handed in for minting. Indeed, only new money was in circulation, because every few years (not more than six) the pennies were called in and recoined, which was mainly for the king's profit, as he gained revenue from each recoinage. This involved the trouble of making large numbers of new dies at frequent intervals, but had the advantage of reassuring the users because all of the coins had a standard appearance. Coins were maintained at a good weight (around 1.4 grams on average) and were made from pure metal. Moneyers who cheated were threatened with severe punishments. The reverse face of the coins recorded the name of the moneyer and the place where the coin was minted, so the producer of a bad coin could be immediately identified. The weight and purity of pennies was reduced in the stress of political upheaval and Danegeld payments at the end of the tenth and in the early eleventh centuries, but even this relaxation of high standards was co-ordinated from the centre. The coins carried messages – the king's head and name made clear whose authority lay behind the issues, and the representation of the head often mirrored Roman coins, in a delib-erate bid to associate the monarchy with imperial grandeur. Religious images on coins such as the 'hand of providence' symbolized the divine origin of royal power.

The kings' efforts in controlling the issue of coins seem to have worked. Good-quality coins had beneficial economic effects: buying and selling could be conducted in confidence if both parties to the transac-tion knew that the money could be trusted. This went with a number of other measures, such as the regulation of markets, insistence on the pres-ence of witnesses when a sale was agreed, and the punishment of thieves and frauds. Concerned to maintain law and order, kings recognized that markets were potentially dangerous sources of quarrels, and special measures had to be taken to prevent disputes. Kings also appreciated the contribution of merchants, who brought luxury goods for royal con-sumption, but also performed a vital task in spreading the cash in which taxes would be paid. Realizing their vulnerability when travelling with valuable goods, the kings made a special point of taking them under their protection. Each burh, though built mainly for military purposes, pro-vided shelter for a market. Bridges were often associated with them, partly because the burh often stood at a river crossing, and partly because bridges had a military function in blocking passage up and down nav-igable rivers. The bridge-building and rebuilding of the decades around 900 helped the flow of peacetime traffic once the Viking threat had receded. We might wonder also if the various naval initiatives from Alfred onwards had some impact on sea transport, perhaps increasing the number of vessels available in peacetime, or spreading shipbuilding and sailing skills. In short, then, royal policies which were mainly directed to military, political and fiscal ends smoothed the path for commercial growth. A modern economist looking at the period sees two forces at work. The first was 'emergency conversion' in the periods of threat from the invaders, which brought hoarded precious metals into circulation. The levying of taxes and mobilization of resources by rulers increased economic activity and stimulated exchange in general. The other development was the longer-term reduction in 'transaction costs', as improvements in the network of markets, availability of money and reduction of risks taken by purchasers all encouraged people to trade.

Calculations of the volume and circulation of currency confirm that this was a period of expansion in the economy. The most striking figures for the amounts of money in circulation are the *Anglo-Saxon Chronicle*'s statements that £137,000 was paid in Danegeld between 991 and 1012, and a further £82,500 after the Danish victory in 1018. These seem incredible sums when we remember that £5 was the annual income of a lesser aristocrat, and that cattle cost 24–30d each. Chronicles are notorious for overestimating figures. Perhaps there was not enough money in England to send so much out of the country? Some of the payments, however, may have been spent by Danes in England, and so came back into the economy. Undoubtedly a great number of silver pennies were paid in Danegeld and were taken overseas, as reflected in the 30,000 English coins of the late tenth and early eleventh centuries discovered mostly in hoards in modern times in Sweden. Estimating from the number of dies used by moneyers, and the quantity of coins produced by each die, 20 million pennies could have been minted in six years, 979–85, worth £83,000. The modern discovery of coins as single finds provides evidence for their actual circulation. More than 150 have been found in England dating from the reigns of Aethelred (978–1016) and Cnut (1016–35), an impressive figure when compared with earlier periods. These were lost in towns and villages, showing that they were really used. Many have signs of wear caused by being 'passed from hand to hand on a daily basis' (D. M. Metcalf) and they reflect the real economy of buying and selling. Although the rulers of Scotland and Wales did not mint their own coins, pennies minted in England circulated in limited numbers in those countries, and made some contribution to the growth of exchange.

Concentrating on a sequence of political events with economic consequences may give the false impression that politics determined the history of the economy, or even that economic expansion was part of a master plan. It has been said by R. Hodges that this period shows that 'great men . . . alter their cultural circumstances to their own ends'. But a more plausible interpretation is that rulers like Charlemagne and Alfred pursued military, political, religious and fiscal objectives, and usually in the short term; any economic effects resulted from the backwash of the main flow of policy. The writings of the kings and their advisers make little reference to economic matters. At least as important as the policies of rulers were the quiet actions by millions of their subjects, which in combination, reacting to a range of circumstances, changed patterns of production and exchange. The significance of broad social and economic movements can be seen by comparing developments in Britain and on the continent. As we have seen, the fragmentation of the Carolingian empire coincides with the centralization of the English state, yet both sides of the Channel experienced some similar economic tendencies, such as the growth in towns and trade.

iii. *The origins of towns*

An examination of urban origins and growth should help to define the respective roles in promoting economic change of the state (or even great men) and the underlying shifts in the economy. The term 'town' needs definition. In the early middle ages there were many settlements which had some administrative or religious function, such as king's tuns, burhs, cathedrals or minster churches (which housed a group of clergy to serve a district). These centres must be carefully distinguished from towns. The usual definition of a town or urban settlement is that it should have a permanent concentration of population, some hundreds at least, who made their living from a variety of non-agricultural occupations. These people might include officials and clergy, but usually in order for a large population to find employment the inhabitants would be occupied in trades and crafts. A town would also have a range of institutions, a complex social structure, and would be closely involved in the economic and cultural life of a rural hinterland. But occupational diversity was its most distinctive hallmark. Very often the town grew in or around a fortress or church (the 'pre-urban nucleus') and our task, made difficult by the small quantity of evidence, is to determine when, how and why the place acquired a commercial and manufacturing community.

Some features of early English towns suggest that they were conceived as part of the royal policy of fortress-building. The ideal site for a burh was on a route that was used for the movement of armies, but trade goods were also carried on main roads. Some of these towns were provided with a street plan as well as walls. The best examples are found in Wessex, such as Wallingford and Wareham. At Winchester the Roman walls were refurbished by Alfred to create a burh, and soon after, by about 900, a rectilinear pattern of cobbled streets was laid out. A series of side streets at regular intervals joined the long High Street to a road that ran inside the circuit of the walls. The arrangement suited the defence of the burh, allowing troops rapid access to any part of the walls that was under attack. The layout of streets defined a series of rectangular blocks of land that could be allocated to various Wessex landowners, and the blocks in turn were subdivided into small plots suitable for the houses, outhouses and workshops of traders and artisans. During the tenth century the fortified space filled up and became a thriving city (Map 5a).

The transition from fortress to town in dozens of places was fostered by the siting of mints, and by legislation that required the sale of valuable goods to be conducted in a burh or 'port' (trading centre, often also a burh) before witnesses. Some of the town's inhabitants were recruited by kings and aristocrats: the royal officials and moneyers, the clergy serving new or reformed monasteries, and craftsmen who were settled in the town to serve their lords' needs, and who eventually made goods for general sale. The kings defined a rural territory for each burh, from which defenders of the walls were levied, or which were administered from the burh, and when trade developed, this piece of countryside would form the commercial hinterland of the town. Sometimes a burh had no hope of becoming a town because it was sited in an inaccessible place. Pilton was founded on a hilltop to defend the north Devon coast, but a town developed on lower ground nearby, at Barnstaple. The creation of a fortress was not always a single act: at Worcester there were two phases of burh foundation, one in the 890s and another about a century later, so the authorities seem to have been responding to the growth of the settlement by giving it additional secure space. On the basis of such evidence it is argued that Alfred and his successors intended that the forts they founded would become towns, and ensured that this happened by their initial planning and subsequent encouragement.

The complexity of the history of different towns does not support the idea that kings alone founded them. A few were 'greenfield sites' where the story began with the building of the fortifications, so it is fairly easy to show the connection between the burh and the town. In many cases the town had begun to grow around the 'pre-urban nucleus' that had existed before the late ninth century, and continued within the burh fortifications, which served only as a secondary focus for urban development. In Oxford, crafts like linen-weaving and shoemaking that would be expected in a town were being practised in a settlement near the monastery of St Frideswide (a pre-urban nucleus) in *c.*750–850, well before the burh was fortified. If the burh marks only an intermediate stage in urban development, the royal founders of these fortifications seem less important as initiators of towns.

Most towns do not conform to the Winchester model, in that they lack a single, regular street plan. Instead they were subject to piecemeal development. In the towns of the east and north of England the lines of some streets wandered like country lanes, and did not form a grid, but

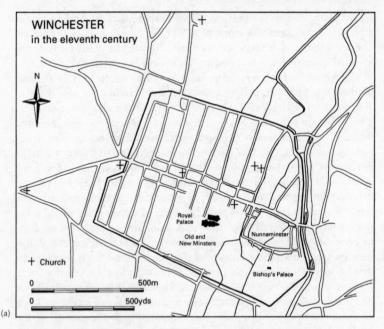

Maps 5a and b. Town plans of Winchester and Northampton. The modern streets of these towns developed in the period 870–1000. Winchester's regular layout contrasts with Northampton's more piecemeal and less coordinated plan.

Sources: D. M. Wilson (ed.), *The Archaeology of Anglo-Saxon England* (Cambridge, 1981); E. Jones, J. Laughton and P. Clark, *Northampton in the Late Middle Ages* (Leicester, 2000).

converged on points within the town. Northampton, Lincoln and York each have this type of 'organic' plan (Map 5b). In both Lincoln and Norwich the town seems not to have been conceived as a single entity, as at Winchester or Wallingford, but was created from the growing together of a number of once separate centres of settlement. These towns were not necessarily unplanned, but were formed out of a series of small-scale planning ventures. When there was a plan, it did not always work: Cricklade, a burh site with considerable potential, failed to attract settlers, and the extensive walled area never filled up with townspeople.

Where the town was a success, the process of urbanization seems to have been a slow one. In London, taken over by Alfred and fortified in the 880s, many of the subsequent developments within the walls, and the building of wharfs along the Thames waterfront, were delayed until the late tenth and eleventh centuries. The stimulus provided by those in authority apparently met with a delayed reaction.

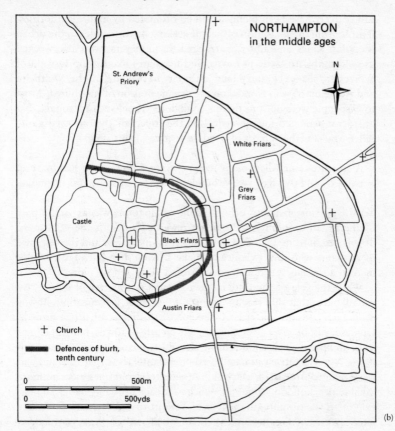

NORTHAMPTON
in the middle ages

N

St. Andrew's
Priory

White Friars

Grey
Friars

Castle

Black Friars

Austin Friars

+ Church

▬▬▬ Defences of burh,
tenth century

0   500m

0   500yds

(b)

The inhabitants of towns who are recorded in documents tend to be the elite of officials, aristocrats and clergy. The way in which they contributed to the filling up of the urban space can be reconstructed at Worcester, where initially the burh was laid out in large blocks of land, called *hagae* (literally, enclosures) on which houses were built. Pieces of property in the town were attached to estates of land in the surrounding countryside and granted to thegns, clergy and other landowners. They no doubt sold produce and bought goods from their houses, but the initial blocks of land were larger than was necessary for this purpose, and they split them up and rented them to incomers who intended to trade and practise crafts. The entry of such obscure people into the town can scarcely have been planned and co-ordinated by higher authorities: it arose from the migration of people seeking opportunities in the urban economy. Kings undoubtedly arranged for moneyers (who also worked as goldsmiths) to settle in towns, and magnates like Bishop Oswald of Worcester (962–92) granted land in the city to two goldsmiths, Wulfhelm and Aethelmaer, who worked on the ornamentation of his church. Most townspeople were not prestigious enough to attract such patronage. No aristocrat arranged for the arrival on the streets of the one-eyed garlic seller who was the subject of a riddle written at this time:

A creature came where many men . . . were sitting . . . ; it had one eye, two ears and two feet, twelve hundred heads . . . Say what is my name.

Yet the pursuit of many such mundane occupations was as vital a part of the urban economy as the better-rewarded work of the goldsmith. Towns began from a combination of official initiatives and the response of migrants who saw a chance to make a living. If a burh lacked commercial advantages, it remained a fortified place and no more.

While the role of the state in town origins is a matter of debate, we can all agree that this was an important period of urbanization. Towns achieved a considerable size. At the end of this phase of urban growth, Domesday Book gives a very incomplete picture of towns, but still allows us to glimpse their distribution and size either in 1066 or 1086 or at both dates. A conservative estimate based on its statistics is that England had more than 100 towns, of which at least seventeen contained 2,000 or more inhabitants. London, York and Winchester each probably had a population of 10,000 or more (in the case of York in 1066, but not twenty years later) (see Map 6 below, p. 63). If all of the urban figures are added together, and compared with the national total for peasants, slaves and other country dwellers, we arrive at the conclusion that near to 10 per cent of the English population lived in towns in 1066–86. The towns that existed before 850 could be quite large, notably the predecessors of London and Southampton, but much of the country lacked such centres, and a reasonable guess would be that less than 2 per cent of the population lived in towns.

The main period of town growth, with perhaps a fourfold increase in the proportion of town dwellers, lay in the years 850–1066. In towns that were flourishing in the tenth and eleventh centuries where there have been extensive excavations, and systematic records have been made of casual finds of pottery, coins and other evidence of occupation, the area settled at this time was large – 200 acres in Norwich, and at Cambridge, York and Winchester the built-up area seems similar to that

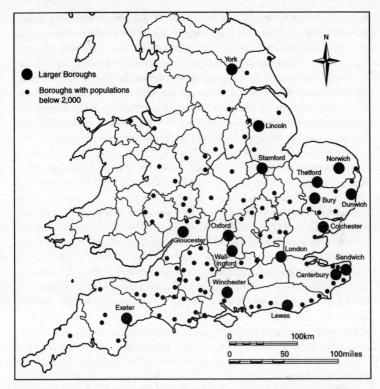

Map 6. Boroughs in Domesday Book (1086). Those boroughs with populations likely to have exceeded 2,000 are named. The larger towns were concentrated in southern and especially eastern regions.

Sources: R. A. Dodgshon and R. A. Butlin (eds), *An Historical Geography of England and Wales* (1990); D. Palliser (ed.), *The Cambridge Urban History of Britain*, vol. 1 (Cambridge, 2000).

of the thirteenth century. Towns like Worcester were spilling outside their walls into suburbs, and by the eleventh century communities of cottagers had formed outside some towns, who were making their living from working in the town or selling garden produce in the market.

Not only were the towns large, but space within them was arranged in distinctive patterns. Land was divided into long narrow plots, with houses towards the street. Such was the demand for building room in the centre of York, along Coppergate, that the width of the plots was only 18 feet. A more open plan prevailed in Thetford, but in general the density of housing was increasing in the larger towns. One clue comes from the destruction of buildings when castles were built in towns soon after the Norman Conquest. At Shrewsbury, for example, fifty-one houses or plots for houses were lost to the castle, implying perhaps ten houses to the acre. The concentration of people into a limited space caused a number of familiar environmental problems. Rubbish disposal on the plot led to the accumulation of middens and the digging of pits for cess and other household waste. At Durham some attempt was made to contain the smell by shovelling layers of sand periodically over a midden. But the inhabitants of York had a remarkable tolerance of rotting organic material, which sometimes lay scattered over the floors of houses, together with the scavenging insects that the rubbish attracted. Mice, rats, jackdaws and ravens moved in to take advantage of urban waste. Fish bones recovered at York show the disappearance of shad and grayling during the tenth and eleventh centuries. These freshwater species were especially sensitive to the pollution of rivers, so it seems that they were driven from the Ouse by the effluent of York. The close-packed wooden houses were vulnerable to fires, which are recorded both in chronicles and in excavation. No fewer than six phases of occupation on the early medieval site at Flaxengate in Lincoln ended in fires.

The large size and high density of urban populations could only be sustained by a lively economy. The full variety of non-agricultural occupations has only become apparent from the archaeological research, especially where waterlogged soil has preserved organic materials. Excavation at such towns as Lincoln, London, Stamford and York has produced plentiful evidence for crafts, not just the finished objects themselves, but tools and pottery kilns, raw materials and the residue from the process of manufacture, such as pieces of leather and bone discarded by the artisans, or broken crucibles containing traces of metal. The range of activities includes food-processing and sale, for example by butchers who have left bones bearing the marks of their work. Woodworking involved the carpenters who built houses and applied their skills to furnishings and boats, and the turners who made wooden cups and bowls on lathes. Smiths forged a variety of tools, locks and weapons, and workers in copper alloys and precious metals cast or hammered ornaments, jewellery and coins. Beads were made from glass, jet and amber, and stone was carved for gravestones. Leather was processed by tanners, and cut and stitched, probably by different craftsmen, into shoes, scabbards and belts. Furs were cured for use as clothing. Wool, flax and hemp were spun, woven into cloth and dyed, and then made into garments. Fine embroidery work satisfied a specialized luxury demand. Potters made cooking pots, pitchers and oil lamps, while bone-carving resulted in the manufacture of elaborate combs, as well as simpler pins and toggles, and ice-skates.

The remarkable feature of these craft activities is not just their number, but the evidence they provide for the relocation of industry in towns, and the economic consequences of that shift. Pottery before *c.*850 was manufactured largely in the countryside, on a small scale, the clay being shaped by hand and the resulting vessels fired rather unevenly. In the late ninth and tenth centuries we find pottery being produced on a large scale in Stamford, Thetford and Norwich, and in significant quantities at Lincoln, Northampton, Torksey and York. In the west, where pottery-making had scarcely existed previously, it began at such centres as Chester and Stafford. Stamford ware catches our attention among these new urban products: one type involved the striking innovation of applying a yellow or pale green glaze to a hard cream or pink fabric. The technique may have been invented in the Lincolnshire town, but is more likely to have been introduced by a migrant from Huy, now in Belgium. The wares produced in other towns, and indeed the ordinary cooking pots from Stamford, were unglazed, but they were turned on a potter's wheel and fired in efficient kilns. Towns were not the obvious place to make pots – the fuel had to be carried in from the country, and the kilns posed a fire hazard. On the other hand, there was plenty of labour, and the pots were easily marketed and distributed in the town's hinterland and further afield. Clothmakers also seem to have moved into towns. Archaeological finds of clay weights from vertical looms dating from before the tenth century show that much weaving went on in rural settlements, at Goltho in Lincolnshire in a large shed beside the lord's house. By the eleventh and twelfth centuries weavers appear in numbers in towns, and the vertical loom gave way to the horizontal treadle loom. Similar concentration of crafts in towns probably occurred in the case of metalworkers, and the larger urban communities gave employment to specialists serving the food market, such as bakers and fishmongers.

The move from country to town had implications for the organization and productivity of the industries. The concentration of artisans practising different crafts in close proximity gave them the opportunity to work together. Knife blades could be forged, fitted with bone or wooden handles, and provided with scabbards by specialists working side by side. Although all larger towns supported a variety of crafts, a degree of specialization, like large-scale iron-working in Northampton and Stamford, may have increased the efficiency of production. The whole process of migration into new towns and the adoption of new styles of working was clearly conducive to technical innovation. Artisans sometimes adopted methods from abroad, as in the case of glazed pottery, or ideas spread from one town to another, leading to the manufacture of pottery in Norwich and Ipswich that imitated wares originally made at Thetford. If workers turned out a standardized product, which was especially the case for pottery, their productivity would be raised. Located near markets, they could be sure that the wares were available to the largest possible number of customers, both within the town itself and in its hinterland, and they were well placed to respond to changes in demand. In short the newly urbanized industries could make new and better products, in greater quantities, more efficiently and more cheaply; and these were more readily saleable.

Long-distance trade, especially international commerce in high-value goods, was the most prestigious and profitable part of the urban economy. It was alleged by an early eleventh-century writer that a merchant who travelled three times overseas at his own expense was eligible for the status of thegn (see p. 73). English merchants went to northern Italy, presumably in pursuit of spices and silks, and paid tolls at Pavia. Merchants from Germany, Flanders and northern France are recorded in the port of London in the early eleventh century, bringing cloth, wine, fish and timber. Chester traded with Wales and Ireland, and handled such goods as furs. Imports in eastern towns included millstones and pottery (the high-quality Pingsdorf ware) from the Rhineland, soapstone, amber and walrus ivory from Scandinavia, silk from the Mediterranean, and figs, also from the south. Exports included cloth, the prestigious embroidered garments for which England was famous, tin, lead and agricultural produce, notably cheese and wool.

Trade, particularly in luxury goods, had been going on for centuries, but urbanization was associated with changes in the size and character of cargoes. Although no statistics for the volume of trade are known, it is worth mentioning the development of ships able to carry bulky goods, which included wider, slower, heavier versions of the famous Viking ships, and another type of merchant vessel, the hulk. At London, new techniques of handling cargoes are evident in *c.*1000, when a jetty was built at the place later called New Fresh Wharf, which would have allowed ships to be unloaded. A shift in the character of trade may also have occurred at this time, because if the imports and exports included herrings, planks, wool and other high-volume and relatively cheap goods, this must point to international trade aimed at a wide market.

Most urban trade, and the basis of the growth of towns at this time, involved carrying quite mundane goods over short distances. Organic deposits from urban excavations show how much was brought into the towns from the surrounding countryside – not just grain and animals to keep the townspeople fed, but also fruits and nuts, together with hay for animal feed, and straw and bracken for their litter. Wood and turf were needed for fuel, and flax, hemp, wool, dye-plants, timber, antler and skins as raw materials. The townspeople depended on the flow of trade from the country, and in turn they had their impact on the rural economy. Land near the town would be turned into garden plots and hemp fields, and over a much larger area husbandry would be influenced by urban demand. Sheep, for example, would be sent to the towns' butchers not as lambs, but when they had yielded an annual fleece for three or four years to help to satisfy the demand from the cloth industry. The trade in urban manufactures is best traced from the distribution of pottery such as Stamford and Thetford ware. Stamford ware is found on numerous rural sites in the town's region, concentrated within a radius of 15 miles. It is also found at York and Northampton, reflecting the traffic between towns at greater distance. Much of this trade was carried by the roads which radiated from every town, some of them of Roman or prehistoric origin, but also new routes: Stamford was served by major north–south roads diverted from the course of the Roman road, Ermine Street. Cheap and easy communications were provided by navigable rivers such as the Thames, along which Londoners were supplied with pottery (shelly ware) made in Oxfordshire. The pottery was probably carried in boats, with grain and fuel as the main cargo. The river was judged so important that at one point south of Oxford a new channel was dug in 1052–66 to aid navigation. The sea brought both vessels from the continent and coastal traffic. Small ports and landing places developed, for example along the coasts of Sussex and Kent, and Hastings from small beginnings grew into a town.

Urbanization transformed the lives of thousands of migrants who worked in trade and crafts. The countryside exchanged agricultural produce for traded and manufactured goods from the urban markets. Did town growth have some more profound effect on the workings and outlook of society? Continental historians used to believe that the merchants and artisans of the towns were separated by a great gulf from the land-based, aristocracy-dominated feudal world. The townspeople were thought to have originated in the marginal elements of society and to have acquired their capital for trade by accumulating small profits. Town dwellers were said to be hostile to the traditional aristocracy. But in fact many leading townspeople were descended from officials and lesser nobility, and they launched their trading careers on the basis of landed wealth. In English towns the aristocracy had a key role, owning houses attached to rural estates, and on occasions they lived in the town. At

Thetford, a large hall appropriate to a thegn was built in the town not far from potters' workshops. A number of guilds for thegns and cnihts provided occasions in towns for convivial assemblies of the local landowners. Great lords encouraged towns, like the monastery of Bury St Edmunds, around which 310 households (c.1,500 people) had gathered by 1066. The upper classes in general were not distrustful of towns, but valued them for practical reasons as sources of rent and traded goods. No doubt they appreciated that they had cities which resembled in some ways those on the continent.

The lower classes in the towns were recruited from peasants who had migrated, or whose villages had been absorbed into the town's economy as it expanded, like Stepney in London or Holywell on the edge of Oxford. Many towns were provided with some agricultural land – Colchester in the late eleventh century had an average of 8 acres per household, and ploughs worked extensive fields outside Cambridge, Derby and many others. Few towns had enough land to feed the population, and the inhabitants still had to gain much of their living from trade and crafts: even at Colchester less than half of the households had any land. The towns' agricultural interests, like the investment in urban land by the aristocracy, show that they were not cut off from rural society.

Townspeople developed a distinctive culture and style of life. They built houses appropriate to their restricted living space. In York they lay end-on to the street, and were inevitably quite small – those at Coppergate measured 14 feet wide and c.25 feet long. In other towns a type of urban house was built with a sunken floor, perhaps serving as a cool store for ale or cheese. A number of institutions gathered within town walls, like the fifty parish churches at Norwich, or ten each at Cambridge and Gloucester, founded in many cases by wealthy individuals or groups. In terms of privileges and rights of self-government, English towns seem less developed than those on the continent. Holders of urban property had the advantage of paying rents in cash rather than labour services, but towns had no political independence – the king and lords remained firmly in charge. Laws and customs made concessions to the needs of urban living, and leading townsmen would play a central role in running the courts. The firmness and stability of town government is suggested by the fixed nature of property boundaries: once established in the tenth century, these remained on the same line until modern times.

At the end of the eleventh century, English towns had grown impressively, and had a key part in the economy. The foundations that had been laid were remarkably durable, so that the leading towns in 1086 remained important in later times. Urbanization had certainly begun, but still had some way to go, because town dwellers accounted for a minority, and the urban system was still immature. This latter judgement is based on the hierarchy of towns, which in a fully formed urban system consists of a series of ranks, with regional capitals and provincial towns at the top, and numerous market towns below. In England the upper range of a hierarchy can be readily identified, with London at the apex; York, Winchester, Norwich and Lincoln occupied the next tier, followed by about twenty-nine towns below them with more than 1,000 inhabitants. When we turn to the bottom rank, we can see a fair scatter of small towns in Somerset and Wiltshire, but none at all in some midland shires, so that places like Derby and Leicester stand apparently in lonely isolation (see Map 6 above, p. 63). The people of these regions cannot have regularly trekked long distances into their shire town to buy and sell. More likely there were occasional local markets, for example when groups of traders and artisans had gathered at centres of administration or minster churches (see p. 59), such as Chesterfield in Derbyshire or Breedon in Leicestershire. Still, these trading occasions were no substitute for a network of permanent towns in view of their transient and unstable character.

In Scotland and Wales centres of exchange are known. The monastery at Whithorn in Galloway, on a peninsula jutting into the Irish Sea, had become a 'monastic town' in the seventh century, with evidence of crafts and overseas trade. This role continued in the period 850–1100, when a settlement of small buildings clustered around the monastery, and trade contacts were maintained with Ireland and northern England. One speciality among the craftsmen was the manufacture of elaborate bone combs. Whithorn was too small and restricted in its range of occup- ations to be called a town, and a conventional town did not develop on the edge of the church precinct until the thirteenth century. Scottish towns which gained formal status as burghs (the equivalent of boroughs north of the border) in the mid-twelfth century, such as Dunfermline and Aberdeen, may well have begun to show signs of development as towns around 1100. A site with trade contacts across the Irish Sea in the ninth and tenth centuries has been excavated at Llanbedryoch in Anglesey. In south-east Wales, Monmouth may have been a centre of trade before 1000, judging from the number of charters granting land in its vicinity, and a find of tenth-century pottery brought from Chester. A later saint's life recalls a tradition that at around 1050 a trading place existed at the mouth of the River Usk, probably at or near Newport. By the 1080s rents and tribute in that region were being paid in cash, and a mint had been founded at Cardiff.

England in the eleventh century has been described as a wealthy country, by which is meant that it was able to pay vast sums in Danegeld and heregeld, and that an abundant coinage circulated. The silver cannot have come from mines within the country, as these were few and small, so it is said that much silver flowed in from the continent, specifically in return for exports of wool. The evidence for this is entirely circumstantial, notably the large sheep flocks recorded in Domesday Book, and no document tells us that their fleeces were carried in bulk overseas. We cannot be sure that the cloth industry of Flanders was really working on large enough scale to need so much wool. In addition, England was importing luxury goods, like wine, which must have absorbed a high proportion of the money paid for goods sent abroad.

The real wealth of a country should be measured not by the amount of silver issued by its mints, but by its ability to produce sufficient goods to give its people an adequate living. It was in the countryside that most people lived and most income was generated.

CHAPTER THREE

Conquest c.1050–c.1100

The English suffered a shocking defeat in 1066, when an army from northern France under William, duke of Normandy, won a decisive battle near Hastings and conquered the whole kingdom. The invaders were soon to penetrate into Wales and Scotland. The humiliation reverberated through the centuries. From the seventeenth century onwards the myth of the 'Norman yoke' fostered the misconception that social inequality and political oppression began with the imposition of Norman rule. These ideas influenced modern historians, and in the twentieth century it was possible to attribute the origins of towns, serfdom, the manor and feudal services to the Norman invaders. We have already seen that urban growth and the imposition of heavy burdens of service on peasants can be traced back to the ninth and tenth centuries, and indeed earlier, and so we cannot regard the Norman Conquest as having a transforming effect on the grass roots of the economy. Our assessment of the impact of the Conquest must therefore be focused on the aristocracy. Here we will analyse the elite in the two centuries before 1066, before examining the subsequent upheaval, and then make some overall judgement of the economic importance of the Conquest.

i. Old aristocracy

'Aristocracy' is used here to mean the whole social elite, both the laity and the leading churchmen. In English writing of the tenth and eleventh centuries the use of the catchy phrase *'eorl and ceorl'*, meaning 'lord and peasant' or 'noble and commoner', indicates clearly enough the fundamental division in society. A slightly more refined approach to describing social structure comes from the pens of two writers at the

beginning of the eleventh century, Aelfric and Wulfstan, one the abbot
of the monastery at Eynsham in Oxfordshire, the other archbishop of
York. Both refer to an idea first mentioned in English by King Alfred,
that society can be divided into those who fight, those who pray and those
who work. All of these groups supported the monarchy, and their separate and reciprocal functions provided the basis for a harmonious society.
In the real world disharmony prevailed, as churchmen often complained,
but their suggested ideal of mutual support and co-operation was based
on a very unequal distribution of obligations and rewards. Half a million
or more peasant households worked to support a few thousand of the
fighting elite, yet the aristocracy signally failed to carry out their protective function in 991–1016. The peasants were exposed to Viking
attack, and were expected to contribute large sums to the Danegeld.
Churchmen could deliver their obligation to pray for the rest of society
with more consistency. Although they emphasized the differences
between the functions of those who fought and those who prayed, we
cannot avoid noting that the top churchmen and secular nobles enjoyed
similar landed wealth, and that the upper clergy were often recruited
from high-ranking families.

The 'three orders' idea took a very masculine view of society, yet
women played a more prominent part than the theory suggests. Among
the aristocracy women could hold landed property independently of
men. They were granted land, managed it, and from their surviving wills,
bequeathed it, even to other women. Sometimes they were carrying out
the wishes of their fathers or husbands, but they could also follow their
own judgement. They were not just the transmitters of property to the
next male generation. Wulfwaru, who made her will in *c.*1000, held a
considerable landed estate in Somerset. She left goods and lands to the
monastery at Bath, but also made bequests of land and moveable wealth
to her two sons, and to her daughters Aelfwaru and Gode. She reveals a
lower stratum of women of some standing, as she remembered in her
will four male high-grade servants, and her household women who were
probably of similar status. At any one time a sizeable proportion of
landed estates lay in the hands of women, and this is reflected in a
number of place names which still bear the name of a female owner of
this period.

An aristocracy can be defined by reference to its special characteristics – birth, legal status, functions, wealth and style of life.
Contemporary members of the group liked to believe that birth was all
important: they prided themselves on belonging to a race apart, and
could justify their position by reference to their illustrious ancestors. It
was said that marriage into a noble family was restricted to nobles. In

practice the aristocracy could not be so exclusive, but had to admit new recruits to replace the families which died out. Much clearer was the definition of the upper rank, called ealdormen in the tenth century, and earls in the eleventh, because these titles were granted to individuals by the king. The ealdorman was assigned a shire, the earl a larger province (Wessex, Mercia, East Anglia, Northumbria), in which they carried out government functions, such as leading the shire's contingent in the army. They were entitled to a third share of some revenues, and could profit from estates belonging to their office. Bishops and abbots, like the ealdormen, were appointed to specific positions in the church hierarchy, and were expected, in addition to their duties in governing the church, to lend their support to the state by attending local courts and advising the king. Permanent and substantial landed endowments were attached to their church offices. Members of the second lay aristocratic rank, the thegns, also performed various tasks in local government, such as running the hundred courts and collecting taxes. The superior group of king's thegns had a special status and greater wealth, and can be found at the king's court and acting as his advisers. 'Thegn' originally meant 'servant', and they were often called on to perform administrative tasks for kings and greater lords, but men in this rank did not have specific offices assigned to them. Consequently the status of thegn was not granted by any superior authority, but was gained by reputation and the judgement of society.

The ealdormen, earls and thegns had a military function, as the theory of 'three orders' noted. This role is celebrated in heroic poetry, most notably the *Battle of Maldon* which recorded the last stand of Byrhtnoth, ealdorman of Essex, with his band of household retainers, against a Viking attack in 991. A more practical indication of the universal involvement of the aristocracy in war comes from the rules about the heriot, the death duty, by which the earl was expected to render to the king when he died the equipment of eight soldiers (horses, spears, shields and so on), the king's thegn four sets of military gear, and the thegn one. Bishops paid heriots too, because they were responsible for the military service owed from their estates, and the death of a bishop of Hereford in battle against the Welsh in 1056 shows that in emergency the division between those who prayed and those who fought was not strictly observed. Unlike the situation of their contemporaries on the continent, aristocrats' privileges did not include exemption from the justice of the local courts, but when geld (tax) was levied, the 'inland', that is the demesne or land under the direct control of a lord, did not pay.

The landed wealth of the aristocracy provides the clearest way of characterizing the whole group and subdivisions within it. The minimum qualification for a thegn was five hides of land. This was the assessment of an average village, so if it was organized along conventional lines the thegn with five hides would have had a demesne of at least 200 acres of arable land, and perhaps twenty peasant tenants paying rents and doing services. According to Domesday, in 1066 (and values had not changed radically during the previous century) a five-hide manor generated an annual revenue of £5, or the selling price of forty cattle. A monk writing in the early eleventh century at Ely believed that to be a 'noble' (*procer*) you needed to hold forty hides, and on the eve of the Norman Conquest there were at least eighty-eight people with that much land (and presumably an income of £40 per annum or more). But these were modest landholdings compared with the huge accumulations of the ealdormen and earls. An ealdorman of Hampshire, Aelfheah, who made his will in about 970, had land stretching over six shires, including some very large estates, and totalling at least 700 hides. The earls of the eleventh century acquired even greater tracts of property, and Godwin, earl of Wessex and his family gathered lands worth more than £5,000. The lands of both ealdormen and earls, while often including a good deal of property in their shire or province, were widely scattered, over a half-dozen shires or even more. The more modest landed fortunes tended to be more localized. Eadric of Laxfield, for example, in 1066 had assets in thirty-three villages, most of which lay in Suffolk and the adjoining shires. Some of these more concentrated groups of land were the result of a deliberate policy of consolidation, by which a thegn would dispose of outlying properties, and acquire (by purchase or marriage) parcels nearer to the family's base. Bishops, whose landed fortunes can be compared with those of ealdormen and wealthier king's thegns, often held most of their estates within their dioceses, and like their lay counterparts travelled from one property to another to consume the produce. Monasteries developed estates in which a number of food-growing manors lay within convenient carting distance, because the community could not move. Lesser thegns might hold a single piece of land, on which they lived.

With the growth in towns and a market for agricultural produce, lords' demesnes could yield revenues in money from the sale of surplus foodstuffs and cash crops such as wool. Lords could expect their peasants, who also had access to the market, to pay some rent in money. The aristocrats of the tenth and eleventh centuries disposed of large sums in cash, and we can add monetary to landed wealth as one of their distinguishing characteristics. The heriot payments, already quoted as evidence of their military role, included a cash payment, of 200 mancuses of gold in the case of earls, and 50 mancuses for a king's thegn, which, converted into silver pennies at 30d to a mancus, means that an earl paid £25 and a king's thegn £6. Lesser thegns contributed £2. These payments to the king at death did not by any means exhaust the cash reserves of many magnates, who made large bequests of money in their wills. Ealdorman Aethelmaer, for example, when he made his will at some time between 971 and 983, bequeathed 500 mancuses of gold (£62), four gold armlets worth another 300 mancuses, and £56 in silver coin. A further guide to the monetary reserves of the great landowners comes from the purchase of land, which often required expenditure in excess of £10, and for major monasteries like that at Ely, which were building up their estates at the end of the tenth century, these totalled hundreds of pounds.

The magnates also mentioned in their wills goods which reflect their wealth and provide insights into their lifestyle. The value of the weapons lay in the specialist skills and great amount of time that went into making a sword blade or a mail shirt (birnie), and also in the decoration of military equipment with precious metals. Military display figured prominently in the culture of aristocrats who did not always distinguish themselves in war itself. Cups and dishes of silver, often mentioned in the wills, showed off the riches of the host at the lavish meals for numerous guests which played a central role in the lives of the great families. They built residences which accommodated their following and provided the setting for social gatherings.

Houses have been excavated at Goltho in Lincolnshire and Netherton in Hampshire, which belonged to families below the level of the magnates. In the tenth century each contained complexes of buildings, a hall for public meals and drinking, together with 'chambers' or 'bowers' – rooms, separate from the hall, where the lord and the household slept – and service buildings such as a kitchen and a latrine. The buildings, like those found in towns and peasant settlements, were of wooden construction, but they were quite large: the hall built at Goltho just before 1000 measured 42 feet by 29 feet. They sometimes used lavish quantities of timber, and the chamber at Netherton had stone walls lined with plaster on the inside. Fortifications were expensive ways of securing protection and obtaining prestige. Those at Goltho, enlarged early in the eleventh century, enclosed a space 325 feet by 270 feet with a ditch and earthen bank 6 feet high, pierced by two gates. At about the same time the lord at Netherton was building a church on a site adjoining the house: at this time local churches were seen as useful estate assets, and another means of asserting the superior status of their owners. A sign of luxurious consumption comes from the presence at Netherton in the tenth century of a craftsman working in bronze and gold, probably an itinerant worker attracted to the house by the promise of patronage;

here he made ornaments and jewellery commissioned by the lord and his family. We have seen that much of the countryside was set aside for hunting, and this is reflected in the consumption of quantities of venison by the households who stayed at the two residences. Of the bones left over from their meals which have been excavated and analysed, 6 per cent of those from Goltho and 10 per cent of those from Netherton came from the various species of deer, which contrasts with the much smaller quantity known from non-aristocratic sites. (Plate 3)

The aristocracy went through important changes in the pre-Conquest centuries. Their growing numbers are immediately apparent. This is not so true of the highest rank of the laity, as the twenty or more ealdormen of the tenth century were replaced by only four earls in the eleventh, but as the earls' landed wealth was shared out among brothers, wives and other family members the size of the top rank did not diminish so much. The thegns increased in number: not so much the hundred or so king's thegns, but the lesser thegns who must have risen to 4,000 or more by the mid-eleventh century. New landed endowments were found for them from the fragmented great estates, as inheritances were divided or those who had previously lived in the households of the magnates were provided with their own lands. Others could make their way upwards in a society in which the land market and patronage offered increasing opportunities. There were also the invaders to be accommodated – the new wave of Danes who arrived with Cnut, a significant element among whom were the huscarls, the troops who had originally formed the king's retinue.

The church aristocracy was growing at the same time. The bishoprics did not change much, apart from some rearrangements in the south-west and the trend for two sees to be held simultaneously, such as the bishopric of Worcester and the archbishopric of York: this was thought necessary because the latter, despite its grand title, had low revenues. The dramatic change came in the reform or foundation of Benedictine monasteries, which numbered sixty-one by 1066. There had been no shortage of monasteries before the reform movement: hundreds of 'minsters' were well-endowed local churches, served by a group of clergy, some of whom who were married and who might each hold separate pieces of land. These arrangements did not accord with the strict rule of St Benedict, now reinterpreted by continental monks. The new reformed monasteries, like Glastonbury, Winchester, Abingdon, Peterborough, Ely and Bury St Edmunds, were based on large landed estates, often exceeding 300 hides, which were held by strictly celibate monks committed to a collective life in both economic and spiritual matters.

It could be said that these communities were scarcely aristocratic, because the monks possessed very little as individuals and their ethos was based on a rejection of worldly materialism. Monasteries are, however, best regarded as a dimension of the aristocracy, as collectively they received vast revenues and lived in grand buildings, and were provided with sumptuous vestments and precious church ornaments. They were closely bound in to the secular elites, who patronized a monastery as a matter of family prestige, to ensure that they would be remembered in the monks' prayers and buried in an honoured place in the church. Byrhtnoth, for example, the ealdorman who died in a celebrated battle against the Vikings in 991, had close associations with Ely, and his headless bones are still buried in the cathedral there, in his day a monastery church. Needless to say, the monks tended to be recruited from aristocratic families. The clergy who were attached to the new dense network of local churches were often poor and badly educated, the sons of peasants, but those who served the survivors of the old minster churches might still be rich enough to be equated in wealth and style of life with the lesser thegns. To some extent monastic reform involved no more than the reordering of existing church property, and changes in the conduct of the monks within the religious house, but in eastern England significant quantities of lay property were transferred to the new monasteries in the Fens.

Contemporaries who observed the increasing numbers of thegns felt unease at the threat that they posed to the old social order. Conservatives like Archbishop Wulfstan and a number of anonymous writers of law codes and statements about social rank, mainly in the early eleventh century, were concerned at the rise of parvenus. One said that it was not enough for a *ceorl* (peasant) to acquire flashily ornamented arms to become a thegn – he had to have land as well. Another celebrated statement of the qualifications for thegnly status was written in the past tense, so it was referring back to the customs of the 'good old days'. It said that a *ceorl* needed to acquire a bell (or in another version, a church), a fortified house, a seat in the king's hall (an official position) and five hides of land – of his own. The implication is that *ceorls* were in reality achieving social promotion without all of these attributes, above all by acquiring money. At the same time, disloyalty and irreligion were being criticized, and the whole of society, but particularly its highest rank, was seen as declining into a corrupt morass. The word *ceorl* is used to describe these unworthy candidates for higher status, which perhaps, if we translate it as 'peasant', gives an exaggerated impression of the speed of social mobility. We are aware of a group below the thegns with sizeable holdings – a hide or two – who might be called cniht, *radman* or sokeman, who were in a much better position than an average peasant to aspire to thegnly status.

The background to these complaints of excessive dilution of the aristocratic ranks lay in the Danish attacks that began in 991. The whole episode amounts to a profound political and economic trauma for the English aristocracy. They failed to prevent the invasion, some families died out in the struggle, and Danes acquired land even in regions like the west midlands which had not seen any earlier Danish settlement. The heavy taxation, initially to pay the Danegeld and then owed to the conquerors, strained the resources of lords, who may not have contributed very much themselves but were still damaged by the demands made on their peasants. Churches complained that they had to sell their ornaments. Further signs of social tension were the attempts by lay families to prevent transfers of land to the church. The upheaval in 1066 repeated for the English (who strictly speaking should be called 'Anglo-Danish' because of the various Scandinavian migrations, but will be called English here for convenience) the crises which their parents and grandparents had faced. In the early eleventh century there had been not just a drastic change in the personnel of the aristocracy, but also a shift in the structure of landholding with the rise of the enormous fortunes of the earls.

Continental society, particularly in France, was also apparently going through a great transformation around the year 1000, but that was associated with the fragmentation of state power and the rise of territorial lordships, in which the former servants of the Carolingian state, the counts, dukes and castellans, seized control of their localities. They wielded judicial powers that had formerly belonged to the state, and dominated the local population from castles with the aid of mounted knights. This was the 'feudal revolution' or 'feudal mutation' of modern historical writing. In England, we can recognize some similarities in the energy and aggression shown by the elite, for example in the factional struggles of the reign of Edward the Confessor (1042–66), and the proliferation of the thegns who bear some resemblance to the knights. But the cohesiveness of the kingdom, though sorely tested by both the Danish conquest and the independent spirit of the new earls, was not destroyed. The centre held, and at the end of the reign of Edward the Confessor we find a relatively stable hierarchy of earls, including the successors of Godwin of Wessex, and below them in the scale of wealth and status the hundred or so middling lay aristocrats with forty hides or more, and then some thousands of thegns of various ranks. The church elite, though troubled by individual scandals, had settled down at the end of the main period of the reform and foundation of monasteries. The king's own new Westminster Abbey, which was acquiring lands partly at the expense of other religious houses, stands out as a notable exception.

The aristocracy was held together by ties of kinship, well illustrated by the numerous members of earls' families recorded as former land-owners by the compilers of Domesday Book. Their common acceptance of the superior power of the monarchy, and their participation in the running of the state, also helped to maintain the aristocracy's cohesion. They could not contemplate directing their political energy towards the creation of independent lordships, because their lands were dispersed and they lacked a concentrated territory over which they could rule. This did not prevent the ealdormen, earls and superior thegns pursuing their own interests, and forming a clientage among the lesser aristocrats. Thegns were expected to perform political, administrative, military and legal services for the king, but they were often committed also to serve greater lords. This could take the form of commendation of a thegn to a lord, by which the lesser man accepted a personal obligation of loyal service. This did not necessarily mean that the client held land from the lord, or if he did he was sometimes able to sell it as he wished. On the other hand, a thegn or cniht might hold property on a three-life lease, often from a bishop or monastery, under the restriction that the land still belonged ultimately to the church and should be returned at the end of the third life. Occasionally we have direct evidence that the subordinates held their land from a lord and were under a personal obligation to serve him, like the thegns in Gloucestershire who had 'submitted themselves and their lands under the power of Beorhtric (son of Alfgar)'. Everyone contributed to the king's army, and if a magnate owed military service from his estates, he would organize those who held land from him, or who were commended to him, into a contingent of soldiers, as when bishops were required to assemble ships' crews on the basis of sixty men from every 300 hides. The lord could offer to his followers, as well as grants of land, protection if they were involved in disputes or lawsuits, and influence in high places.

All of these bonds within the ranks of the aristocracy bear a strong resemblance to the feudal structure of service and authority found on the continent, though the flourishing of a strong state made English society distinctive. It is sometimes said by those who emphasize the contrasts between England and the continent that the absence of the castle in England shows that royal authority was all important, exercising control through public fortifications (the burhs) while on the continent the nobility could build private strongholds, from which they could compel the local peasantry to obey their commands. But on closer examination the differences do not seem so great. A specific type of castle, in which a tower was built on an earth mound both as a vantage point for observing the surrounding countryside and as a defensive citadel in the event of a siege, is not found in England before 1066, but lords like those at Goltho or Sulgrave in Northamptonshire threw up banks, ditches and palisades around their houses, and may have used timber gates with their superstructures as strong points. English lords may not have had the legal and political power of continental castle owners, but their defended houses bolstered their status and authority. (Plate 3)

Aristocrats, both in England and the continent, are often represented as being mainly concerned with the relationships between superiors and inferiors – magnates had clients among the lesser aristocracy, and all of them depended for their living on their domination of the peasants. But they also developed associations among equals, most readily identified in the guilds of thegns and cnihts which met in towns such as Cambridge and Canterbury, but no doubt also based on more informal contacts when thegns attended hundred courts, or gathered to carry out official duties in the shire towns, or at some religious ceremony, or in the household of a magnate. They had interests and a culture in common, shared similar duties and privileges, and intermarried. While they might sometimes be in competition, they could also eat, drink, worship and deliberate as a group.

ii. *New aristocracy*

The Norman Conquest brought disaster to the old English aristocracy. The government of the country continued to function in the former style, as the well-run state could deliver to William, duke of Normandy and his followers the financial benefits of an efficient tax system. But the years between 1066 and 1086 also saw the largest transfer of property ever seen in English history. Virtually a whole upper class was displaced, as in the revolutions of 1789 in France and 1917 in Russia, but we cannot properly call the events after 1066 a revolution because the property was not seized by the lower orders: the new rulers were aristocrats themselves. How was this done? Was this just a change of personnel, or was there a shift in the structures of landholding? Were any economic changes involved? What was the state of England at the end of the upheaval?

In the autumn of 1066, having defeated King Harold and his army near Hastings, and taken over London, William and his men expected to enrich themselves. One of their first objectives was to secure military control, notably by building castles at strategic points, and then to take over the land. This was inevitably a slow process, but the task was made easier by the decisiveness of the victory. Many English thegns died in battle, either at Stamford Bridge (fighting the Norwegians just before the Norman invasion), or at Hastings. The widows and heirs of the dead, and those who fought and lived, were deprived of their property by application of the argument that William had been the rightful king, so that those who had supported the usurper Harold were traitors. Those who resisted the new regime by joining the many rebellions in the first five years after Hastings shared the same fate. Those who were left could be forced out by financial exactions. They were compelled to pay cash to redeem their lands, so that a thegn might have to find £5 to £12, a year's income, in addition to the heavy tax that was immediately demanded by the Conqueror. The English landowners had to borrow money, and then became so burdened by debt that they needed to sell or abandon their lands, and many went into exile abroad. Others were submerged because they sought the protection of the powerful newcomers, but found that their lords treated them harshly. Whether through debt or other pressures, former thegns or lesser aristocrats were pushed so far down the social scale that within two decades after the Conquest they joined the ranks of the freemen or sokemen as rich peasants. English churchmen were squeezed out under the new archbishop of Canterbury, Lanfranc. A few survived, and even prospered, like Colswein of Lincoln, who was promoted as a major landowner after the Conquest, and a scatter of thegns and their widows, like Ketel, Osward, Edith and others in Gloucestershire. But in general the lesser lords named in 1086 reveal their origins across the Channel by their names: Geoffrey, Henry, Hugh, Ralph, Roger, William and the rest.

As the English were removed or gave up the struggle, newcomers from northern France acquired their lands (the conquerors came from Picardy, Brittany, Flanders and other provinces, as well as Normandy, but for the sake of convenience here they will be called Normans). In the most straightforward method of transfer, the king granted all of the lands of some pre-Conquest lord to a newcomer. This is apparent from Domesday Book, which records in 1086 that, in a typical case, the lands of Asgar the Staller, who had a strong base in Essex, had been made over to Geoffrey de Mandeville. An estate with a western focus, held in 1086 by Queen Matilda, had previously belonged to Beorhtric, son of Alfgar. Such a transfer could have been achieved in some cases by forcing an heiress to marry a Norman, but most commonly lands were confiscated and then granted by the king. If a Norman succeeded an English lord in this way, he was more likely to continue the management of the estate in the former style. This simple transition would not help the Norman who deserved a particularly large quantity of land to establish his status or to reward his contribution to the Conquest, which must explain why some incomers received the lands of two, three or more English predecessors. Sometimes we find that in 1086 a Norman was holding land previously belonging to a dozen Englishmen, scattered over the length and breadth of a shire. One explanation could be that after the king had granted more coherent groups of land to followers, he granted to a latecomer all of the leftover pieces. A rather special example of the creation of a new landed fortune from the properties of a number of English predecessors is provided by the royal estates, as William held lands worth double those of Edward the Confessor, valued at £11,000, or a sixth of the landed revenues of the whole kingdom. This was not just a question of increasing the income of the crown, but involved a strategy of extending the king's direct influence throughout the country. Sections of rural England which did not belong to the royal estate were placed under forest law. This continental concept was designed to protect game animals and the woods in which they lived, and restricted hunting by the forest's inhabitants. The forests included settled and cultivated land as well as wilder country, and in the long run were to yield the kings valuable, but much resented, revenues.

Another dimension of royal policy gave Norman lords the lands of many pre-Conquest owners because the Conqueror decided that in contrast with the normal pattern of scattered possessions, consolidated lordships should be created in strategic positions on the Welsh border and along the south coast. Trusted lords like Roger of Montgomery, who was given much of Shropshire, or William of Warenne, who acquired a large section of Sussex based on Lewes, were set in place in the first case to keep the western boundaries of the kingdom free of Welsh attack, and in the second to secure vital lines of communication with Normandy. On a smaller scale, local castleries appeared, in which the lords of strongholds like Tutbury in Staffordshire or Tickhill in Yorkshire were granted groups of adjacent lands.

Sometimes landholding before and after the Conquest shows a complete transformation, with the properties of English lords being broken up and distributed to many Normans. This absence of central planning or policy in the transfer of land points to the activities of Norman lords which have been called 'private enterprise'. Individual incomers did not wait for grants from the king, but took advantage of the troubles of the English owners to grab their land. They may have forced a widow or daughter to enter into marriage, or they took on a supposedly temporary lease and extended it indefinitely, or used their control of the courts to force out those with debts or disputable legal claims. Such activities would be aided by the connivance of the new Norman officials, especially the sheriffs, who in some localities earned a reputation for ruthlessness and partiality, and indeed for enriching themselves with the lands of the conquered. When disputes were reported to the Domesday commissioners in 1086, the parties would refer to the use of the king's seal to legalize the questionable transfer, and to the role of a 'liberator' (deliverer), that is someone using the king's authority to convey land to a new owner. This freebooting pursuit of landed wealth after 1066 resulting in completely new estate structures was especially characteristic of parts of eastern England.

A further extension of 'private enterprise' took the Normans of the Welsh border into Wales itself. Herefordshire, initially under the lordship of William fitz Osbern, threatened south Wales, and fitz Osbern's subordinates, who included such formidable families as the Lacys, penetrated a considerable distance to build castles at Caerleon and Brecon. Along the north coast, where the threat to the Welsh came from Cheshire under Hugh of Avranches, the kingdom of Gwynneth lost a great deal of territory, though by 1100 the Normans had been pushed back to the River Conwy. In the north of England the Normans began to put in order the shires north of Yorkshire, with the development of Carlisle both as a stronghold and as a bishopric, but the movement into southern Scotland was delayed until the early twelfth century.

Historians debate which change in landholding predominated: the transfer of whole estates from a single English predecessor (antecessor), or the more complicated assembling of new estates from many previous lords. If the latter was normal, then the Conquest seems more 'revolutionary' than if estates were handed over intact. The evidence is incomplete, because our main source for the process, Domesday Book, does not give complete information on the various layers of lordship before the Conquest, so it will tell us that the pre-Conquest holder of a manor was 'Wulfwine', and not mention Wulfwine's overlord. The overlord's dozen manors may have been granted to a Norman successor in a single, coherent transaction, but the record suggests that the new lord had scrambled together a new combination of manors from Wulfwine and eleven other minor English thegns, as they, the subtenants, are named as the holders in 1066. The eastern counties seem to have experienced more complicated and 'revolutionary' transfers of property than those in the west. The conservation of old estates in some regions resulted partly from the continuity of the holdings of the major churches, which held a high proportion of the countryside in the south and west, from

Kent to Worcestershire. They survived the Conquest, and helped to preserve an important dimension of the old economic order into the new
post-Conquest world.

In the reconstruction of the policies and behaviour that lay behind the
upheaval of property-holding after 1066, Domesday Book has been used
as our main source. The enquiry which assembled the information for
the book demonstrates conclusively that the old state machinery was
functioning efficiently, but at the command of new masters. No other
comparable documents exist in Europe, not because they once existed
but have been lost, but because no other government was capable of
such an ambitious project. The basis of the survey came from the tax-
gathering rolls containing the names of places and landholders. This
skeletal information was then greatly expanded by enquiries in local
courts, and by the seven groups of commissioners who went off to the
shires (each group was assigned four, five or six shires each) to gather
from lords and from local juries details of manors, the numbers of
ploughs, peasants and mills, and the size of woods. Animals were
counted too, though these statistics were discarded for most shires during
the process of abbreviation and collation when the data from the shires
were assembled into the main record, 'Great Domesday'.

The survey had three main aims. First, it was designed to provide a
comprehensive picture of the landed assets of the aristocracy, with a calculation of annual value for each manor, so that if they came into the
king's hands on the death or disgrace of their lord the potential revenues
would be known. A short-term objective arose from problems when
troops were assembled to counter a threat of Norwegian invasion in
1085. Information about the resources of landowners would enable the
billeting of soldiers to be shared out efficiently. Secondly, the pleadings
that accompanied the survey were intended to settle some of the disputes
that had arisen from thousands of grants and seizures of property – the
twenty years after 1066 had seen an upheaval in landholding, not just
through the replacement of the English, but also because some of the
new Norman lords had died or rebelled, which meant that the holders
of land in 1086 were often the third in succession in a relatively short
period.

Thirdly, the king wanted an overview of resources which could in the
long term be used to reassess the tax system. The well-established
method of collecting geld levied the tax at a rate, for example, of 2s on
the hide, so that a five-hide manor paid 10s. The Domesday survey
included for some shires a calculation of 'ploughlands' – 'there is land
for eight ploughs' a typical entry reads – and the figure often bears little
resemblance to the number of ploughs said to be working on the demesne

and in the hands of the peasants. One possible explanation was that the ploughlands, which like the hides were designed to reflect the overall taxable capacity of the land, would replace the hidage to form the basis of a new tax, but if this was the case it was not implemented. Another objective that was never realized may have been a plan to extend the tax system to lords' demesnes, which explains why the Domesday enquiry paid such close attention to demesne assets, even to the point of counting pigs, which the English monk who wrote the *Anglo-Saxon Chronicle* regarded as 'shameful'.

As well as changing the people at the top, the Conqueror was distributing landed wealth in quantities which would forge a new social hierarchy. At first William apparently contemplated rebuilding the very large and rich earldoms that he found in 1066. But the political dangers were soon appreciated, and earldoms that developed in the 1070s were conceived on a smaller scale. The new earls resemble the tenth-century ealdormen in their attachment to a shire, which we now call a 'county' after the continental 'count', the equivalent of an earl. In fact the English and continental institutions cannot be equated exactly. The county in the old Carolingian empire had once been a unit of royal government, but by the eleventh century it had become a virtually independent small state, of which the county (later duchy) of Normandy is an outstanding example. The shire/county in England remained under the control of the monarch, with a sheriff appointed by the king. The landed fortunes of most earls were not confined to their shire/county. Some of the great landowners were adding English possessions to large estates in Normandy, but other newcomers made their fortune through their English lands – Bigot, Mandeville and Warenne had only modest properties across the Channel.

In place of the pre-Conquest hierarchy of wealth consisting of a few super-magnates towering over many modestly well-off thegns, the new social order established about 200 substantial tenants-in-chief, earls and barons holding directly of the crown, who together owned about half of the land. Below them were another 1,000 landholders with land worth at least £5, and 6,000–7,000 lesser men, some resembling pre-Conquest thegns, many with only a hide. The overall effect of the Conquest had sometimes been to increase the landed wealth of the higher ranks. In Cambridgeshire, for example, of the seventy-four landholders in 1066, only three were worth £100 per annum or more, while in 1086 the forty-three tenants-in-chief included five with £100. This impression of a changed distribution of land must be qualified by the problem of Domesday's incomplete record of landholding before the Conquest. Its tendency not to refer to overlords may lead to an underestimate of the number of rich lords in 1066. One of the major lords in Cambridgeshire throughout was the monastery of Ely, and stability in the church's share of property is typical of the whole country. Various pressures were applied on the church to grant land to Norman lords, resulting in some losses, but on the other hand the Normans made pious gifts, both to monasteries across the Channel and to a handful of new foundations, such as the priory of Lewes in Sussex.

Conquest, and the continuation of Norman rule, depended on armed power. The numerous new castles had to be garrisoned, and both the aristocrats and the king needed the ability to summon armies to suppress rebellions and counter threats from overseas. The key figures were the knights, who included both well-off aristocrats with lands assessed at between five and twenty hides and people who were called 'country knights' on the continent, with only a hide or two of land. In addition, many knights still lived in the households of the greater lords. The king gradually assigned quotas on the tenants-in-chief by which they were required to provide a set number of knights, later known as the 'due service'. This figure was only loosely based on the landed resources of the lord, and indeed sometimes seemed to reflect political loyalty. So the rich monastery at Evesham was expected to provide only five knights, while Peterborough Abbey was burdened with sixty. Wealthier lay lords were usually assigned a quota of forty or above, giving a total potential over the whole country of an army of 6,000 knights.

These arrangements, by which a social hierarchy of king, tenants-in-chief and knights were bound together by obligations to provide military service in exchange for landholdings, have been seen as a major change, introducing continental feudal notions of social and political dependency. Indeed, the social vocabulary was new and largely French. We have seen already that the top rank of aristocrats were called counts and the second rank barons; the sheriffs were known as viscounts. Knight (cniht) is an English word, but the terms *miles* (Latin) and *chevalier* (French) were commonly used. The lands and rights of a magnate, an honour, included among its tenants knights who held fiefs in the continental style, though in English this later became a 'fee'. Tenants symbolized their subordinate (yet still honourable) relationship to their lord by swearing an oath of fealty (faithfulness) and performing an act of homage. They owed him, as well as service, 'aid and council', meaning that they might be expected to pay money in emergencies, and attend his private court to make judgments and offer advice. On death and inheritance the English paid a heriot, but under the new arrangements the heir paid a relief. In important respects the new language was describing old practices, and before the Conquest thegns held tenancies, commended themselves to lords, and served in the army in their lord's contingent.

All of this has significance for economic history because the definition of rights and obligations established a relationship between crown and magnates peculiar to England, in which the central state maintained control over the localities, while still delegating a great deal of power to the aristocracy. Everyone in England could regard the king as an ultimate authority, in spite of the import from the continent of a strong tradition of private justice. Much was made of tenancy, which defined the conditions on which land was held, and the rights of lords. Even the greatest earl was a tenant-in-chief, and his land could be confiscated if he was disloyal; in the event of any tenant's death without a male heir, or if the heir was under age, the lord could take over, and either marry off the daughter, or act as ward of the young heir and exploit the lands. But the recognition of hereditary rights ultimately made the tenant, even the lowliest knight, the effective owner of his land. As the pre-Conquest custom of divided inheritance was replaced by the succession of a single heir, it was possible for property to be accumulated and passed on to future generations. Tenants could also expand their landholdings by acquiring properties from the tenants of other lords, which obliged them to serve two or more lords. The tenants could use the land in the way that they thought most effective, and had lordship over the peasants living there, and they made the decisions about extracting revenues from their manor.

All of these changes in the upper levels of society had a limited impact on the economy. The new lords were anxious to make a regular income from their newly acquired estates, and their best course at first was not to disrupt the existing customs and practices, but to let the routines of production and rent collection continue. The officials who ran the manors or groups of manors, the reeves, remained in office. The main impact of the conquerors can be seen in the destruction of selected parts of the country, and in the reordering of manors in order to expand their profits. There were also some new developments in the towns.

Destruction refers both to the incidental consequences of military operations, and to the deliberate wasting of rebellious districts. The first type of damage affected the area around Dover, where the conquering army moved after the victory at Hastings, and then along the line of march from the south coast to London. Presumably the troops took animals and grain to feed themselves and their horses, and like armies at all times intimidated the inhabitants by burning houses. Manors on this route dropped in value after 1066, but usually had recovered again after twenty years. Deliberate devastation was concentrated in the north after the rebellion of 1069–70, apparently reflected in Domesday in more than a thousand villages described as 'waste', notably in the West and North

Ridings of Yorkshire, with 267 and 367 reports of 'waste' respectively. We cannot take the statements in Domesday at face value, however. A puzzling feature is the concentration of 'waste' in the uplands, on the slopes of the Pennine hills. Perhaps the rebels lived in the wilder country? Or the destruction had originally covered the lowlands, but the more attractive villages on the most fertile soils could be repopulated more quickly, even at the expense of the uplands? Another explanation is that while destruction undoubtedly occurred, it was followed by reconstruction which also involved the reorganization of estates, and that when places were absorbed into some new unit of lordship, they were described as 'waste', which therefore had an administrative rather than a physical meaning. Parts of towns were destroyed to make space for royal castles, the number of houses affected varying from four at Warwick to 166 at Lincoln. The reality of the demolition is proved by modern excavations beneath castle earthworks which have revealed the remains of the houses.

These acts of destruction were compatible with the conquerors' aims of profiting eventually from their newly acquired territory. The short-term loss of revenues in a few parts of the countryside could be justified if the shock convinced the English as a whole of the futility of rebellion. The castles in the towns kept the inhabitants, and the surrounding country, under observation, and the prominent towers made everyone fully aware of the potential violent power of the new regime. The remarkable continuity in the flow of revenues proved the value of the display of ruthlessness and military might. A limited amount of pain inflicted at the beginning of the process of Conquest ensured long-term gain for the invaders.

The Conquest must have been regarded by the peasants with mixed feelings. They may have felt a strong loyalty to the lords it displaced. More likely they had found the restrictions imposed by their English lords irksome, judging from the pre-Conquest lists of peasants who had left the manor, and the hints in the treatises on estate management on the need to avoid trouble by observing custom and ruling with a firm hand. Before 1066 they would have had limited opportunities to form any bond with the many lords who were infrequent visitors to their manors or even total absentees. The replacement of their former superiors may not have been regarded as a disaster. They had often changed lords before, especially after 1016, and although they would have had some sense of nationality, they may not have reacted with hostility to 'foreign' Normans. Again, they were used to being ruled by strangers – Danes, or aristocrats from remote provinces. But whatever their initial reactions, they would soon have good economic reasons for regretting and resent-ing the Conquest. For a start they faced heavy tax demands, like the geld demanded in 1067, and contributions to the redemption payments that their English lords were expected to pay. The new Norman lords kept up the pressure for rents and services to maintain a high level of profit from the manor.

When we know the changes in the values of manors between 1066 and 1086 they often show an increase. This must have been achieved by lessees or farmers to whom the running of manors was delegated for a fixed annual rent or farm. These middlemen were squeezed by lords, and in turn would have passed on the demands to the peasants below them. As the lords' demesnes do not seem to have expanded, the extra revenue must have come from the peasants. The jurors who reported to the Domesday commissioners sometimes expressed an opinion on the high 'renders' or values that they recorded, and made comments such as 'it cannot bear it'. The manor of Coggeshall in Essex was reported as having been worth £10 per annum in 1066, but in twenty years the sum had increased to £20. Its actual value was judged at £14. These statistics tell us much more than the mechanics of estate administration: the high sums that had to be found each year must have entailed stress for the farmer and anguish among the peasants. Specific methods by which lords or their farmers could increase revenues included, in the east and north, pressing the sokemen to pay more. One group of sokemen in Norfolk found their annual payments rising from £2 to £20 in the ten years after 1066. In Yorkshire a 'sokeland', where the inhabitants enjoyed considerable independence, might become a 'berewick', an appendage of a lord's demesne manor, with consequent increases in the services owed by the peasant population. Numerous former sokemen and freemen had by 1086 been reclassified as villeins and bordars: presumably this was not just a change of name, but committed them to more rents and labour. In 1066 there had been eight free men at Frostenden in Suffolk. Twenty years later, under the lordship of Ralph Baynard, only three were counted, but the number of bordars – smallholders closely subjected to the manor – had increased from fourteen to twenty. In the north, such developments may have been associated with more radical changes whereby new manors with demesnes were formed out of sokelands, and the peasants were required to provide labour services. This was not just part of reconstruction after the devastation of the north, but can be linked with a longer-term reorganization of the countryside, as the great estates were breaking down in Yorkshire at a later stage than in the south and the midlands.

Many of the tendencies after the Conquest disadvantaged the peasants, as lords' control was extended and everyone had to pay more to the manor. The decline in slavery might suggest that there was some compensatory improvement. At Frostenden the two slaves of 1066 had disappeared twenty years later: perhaps one of them had joined the bordars. In general the ex-slaves reappear as oxmen or bordars, having gained a tenancy of land, but were still required to work on the lord's demesne, so the lord had not lost a great deal. The lords of eastern England in particular were pursuing a policy of reducing all the different categories of peasant to a common state of subjection, which involved loss of independence for some, and a token liberation for others. All of this had been a long-term tendency, and the phase of social change after 1066 may not have been a consequence of the invasion. The Normans took over existing manors, working demesnes and dependent peasants, and made the most profitable use of them, observing local customs and no doubt taking advice from the English reeves and farmers who dealt with the detailed running of the manors. Occasionally changes were made on the initiative of a Norman lord, notably in the case of Ernulf de Hesdin, who held land in ten shires. He enjoyed a reputation in the twelfth century as an agricultural improver, and in 1086 his manors had unusually large demesnes, some of them, such as Chipping Norton in Oxfordshire and Kempsford in Gloucestershire, exceeding 500 acres in area, and were well provided with slaves to man the ploughs. He was rewarded for his apparent vigour in management with increases in values, which in view of the size of the demesnes must have partly derived from the sale of produce.

The invaders recognized the importance of the towns that they found in England, and made sure that they acquired urban property. For example, the list of owners of houses in Leicester – Hugh de Grentemaisnil, the earl of Chester, the bishop of Lincoln, and so on – echoes the distribution of rural manors among the tenants-in-chief in the county. The town dwellers remained mainly English, though an influx of migrants from across the Channel established separate 'French' boroughs, notably at Norwich, Southampton and Wallingford. These newcomers were presumably attracted by commercial opportunities, and their presence made a contribution to the expansion of towns. The towns along the south coast – at Chichester, Pevensey and Sandwich – prospered from the increase in cross-Channel traffic and trade, but reports of poverty and vacant holdings are found in East Anglia, at Norwich, Thetford and Ipswich, and towns such as Huntingdon and York suffered from destruction after rebellions. Elsewhere the reports of waste and destroyed houses – at Shaftesbury and Dorchester in Dorset, or at Oxford – might suggest that the urban economy was going through a difficult patch when Domesday was being made, perhaps unrelated to political events. On the other hand, small towns seem to have been growing to fill the gaps between larger centres, sometimes encouraged by the patronage of monasteries, such as Battle in Sussex (the religious house founded on the field of victory by William I). Some developed at the gates of new castles, and therefore presumably under the stimulation of the new lords, like the forty-two men gathered at a market 'around the castle' of Tutbury in Staffordshire, or the forty-three burgesses who had been established at Clare in Suffolk, the stronghold of Richard fitz Gilbert.

The setbacks suffered by the towns, as well as the examples of growth after 1066, provide one set of guides to assessing the overall effects of the Conquest. We might expect that by putting pressure on their manors to generate more revenue, by squeezing free tenants to produce more rent, and by granting to slaves land on which they could produce their own food, the newcomers would have been giving some stimulus to the economy in terms of both productivity and the increase in exchange. More money was spent than ever before on building work: perhaps the local inhabitants were compelled to dig earth and haul timber for the new castles in the initial assertion of power, but the continued work on aristocratic construction, such as the great stone White Tower that dominated the east of the city of London, must have given employment to masons and the carters and boatmen who brought materials to the site. More widespread was the rebuilding programme on the major churches, both cathedrals and monasteries, which were now to reflect more closely continental Romanesque styles (which we now call 'Norman' architecture) and were conceived on a larger scale than their predecessors. Many small local churches were also rebuilt. (Plate 4)

The undoubtedly negative effects of the invasion on the economy included not just physical destruction, but the disruption of trade and estate management by violence. High rents and taxes may in some circumstances have pressurized peasants to grow and sell more actively, but when we are told that a manor that had doubled in value 'cannot suffer it without ruin', the peasants were apparently being impoverished by excessive demands. Some of the money that the Normans gained in this way was carried out of the country and not spent to the benefit of English merchants or artisans.

iii. *England in 1086*

We can sum up both the aftermath of the Conquest, and the longer-term developments in country and town discussed in the last three chapters, by examining the state of England in 1086, an analysis made possible by the Domesday survey.

Before looking at the wider picture, the nature of the evidence and its meaning can be examined through a single manor, Pinbury in Gloucestershire, which lay on high ground to the north of Cirencester. It had been given to the nuns of Caen in Normandy in a pious act by King William. We are told that in 1086:

> There are 3 hides. In demesne are 3 ploughs. 8 villeins and a smith with 3 ploughs. There are 9 slaves. A mill at 40d. It was and is worth £4.

The information is so compressed, and the terms so unfamiliar, that it seems to be written in code. Fortunately we can use other, less enigmatic evidence to help to decode the message, in the form of a survey made by the Caen nunnery for its own purposes as landlord thirty years later, in about 1120. This later survey contains similar information, confirming the essential accuracy of the Domesday entry, but it supplies more details. The three hides need not detain us, as this was an assessment, used by the state in determining tax liability, which shows that Pinbury, falling towards the lower end of a range which mostly lay between two and ten hides, was rated as a small but not insignificant manor. Such assessments were inevitably artificial and archaic, but other information is based more closely on agricultural realities. The three ploughs of the demesne were real implements of wood and iron, pulled by teams of eight oxen each, which was almost the case in c.1120, when Pinbury was provided with twenty-two oxen and two cows, the latter perhaps substituting for the missing pair of oxen. The number of ploughs gives a clue as to the amount of land in the Pinbury demesne, as a plough could, according to later records, cultivate about 100 acres in a year. In fact at Pinbury in c.1120 205 acres were recorded as under crops (wheat, wheat mixed with rye, and oats) which means that the demesne totalled 400 acres, of which half was planted each year while the other half lay fallow. Extra ploughing was provided by the villeins, who had three ploughs between them, suggesting that each peasant owned two or three oxen, and they joined together to make complete teams, mainly to work their own holdings, but with spare capacity for the demesne. The contribution of the villeins to demesne cultivation has to be presumed from Domesday, but it is confirmed by the later survey which tells us that they each owed the lord five days' work each week. The smith presumably had a holding of land, but his main task was to make and mend the lord's ploughshares, iron bindings on carts, sickles and other implements. The nine slaves worked full time for the lord, six of them as ploughmen, as each plough needed a crew of two. The other three would have looked after the animals on the demesne, which are not recorded in 1086, but in *c.*1120 there were seventeen cattle, a horse, 122 sheep and ten pigs. The mill made a profit from tolls on grinding the corn of the peasants (toll corn), and perhaps those from neighbouring manors as well.

Both surveys suggest a self-sufficient system of production, in which the lord could obtain all the labour for the demesne from the villeins and slaves, and did not even have to go elsewhere for the specialized skills of a smith. In fact the long distance between Pinbury and Caen meant that the produce cannot have been used by the lord, except perhaps for cheese and wool. The value of £4, that is the annual payment from the manor to the lord, could only have been achieved if the main product of the demesne, grain, was being sold in the locality, perhaps at the market in Cirencester, in the same way that the miller could obtain money for the toll corn. Judging from the small numbers of sheep in *c.*1120, which at other times formed the main Cotswold cash crop, there was a limited demand for wool.

While surveys give the lord's view of the manor, they must be used cautiously to reconstruct the lives of the peasants. Pinbury had a single manorial lord, so the numbers of peasants and slaves suggests a village with eighteen households, if we think of the slaves as married and having their own dwelling. The figure would be nineteen if we include the priest, who is mentioned in *c.*1120 but not in 1086, which might mean that the church had been founded in the intervening years, or more likely was omitted from the Domesday survey. The village consisted therefore of 80–90 people, if the average family contained between 4.5 and 5 individuals. The villeins each cultivated 30–40 acres, so their fields totalled about 300 acres, less than the demesne. If their farming resembled that of the lord, they concentrated on corn, with wheat as the main crop, and kept a few cattle, sheep and pigs as well as their plough oxen. We can begin to visualize the village surrounded by about 700 acres of cornfields, but with some pasture and meadow for feeding the animals, and perhaps a small wood, which would not be mentioned in Domesday if it did not provide revenue for the lord, but was a source of fuel and pasture for the peasants. The villeins grew their own food, but sold the surplus if they grew more corn than they needed to eat, and part of the lord's £4 annual income would have come from rent. The smith would not have been fully employed making and mending the lord's implements, and no doubt sold his services to his neighbours and in the surrounding villages. In the thirty years after 1086, the main change seems to have been the 'freeing' of six of the slaves who were called oxmen, who still manned the three demesne ploughs, and the appearance of four cottars, who may have been provided with land from the subdivision of one of the larger peasant holdings, as the number of villeins had fallen from eight to seven.

By decoding the information for a single manor, we can apply it cautiously to the thousands of manors recorded in 1086 to give a more general picture. Having calculated the population of one place, can we now estimate the population of the whole country? Domesday records a total of 269,000 individuals (villeins, cottars and so on) in its descriptions of manors, and a little more than 20,000 people, houses, plots and other indications of urban households. If we multiply these combined figures by 4.5 or 5 to allow for whole families, the result is between 1.3 and 1.5 million. However, many people were omitted from the survey, such as the households of the lords, which each contained officials, servants and soldiers, the garrisons of the new castles, monks and nuns and their servants, and the population of the four northern shires, together with a considerable proportion of those living in Lancashire. Large towns – London, Winchester and Bristol – were not described in detail; nor were smaller ones like Coventry and Tonbridge. Other towns were clearly not as systematically surveyed as the rural manors, and we sometimes have near-contemporary surveys which show that hundreds of households were omitted. At Gloucester, for example, more than 600 properties are implied in a survey in c.1100, but fewer than 150 houses and burgesses are mentioned in Domesday. The actual number of townspeople throughout the country may have been near to double the recorded figure.

In the countryside the record was also incomplete, as can be suspected from the small numbers of slaves listed in some northern counties, which might suggest that the officials there did not collect information about that social group. A more widespread problem arose from the concentration on the peasant tenants who made the main contribution to the demesne economy, the villeins and bordars, so that those who paid money rents were not counted. Judging from those known to have been living shortly after 1086 on one Staffordshire estate, that of Burton Abbey, and not mentioned in Domesday, their numbers could run into many thousands over the whole country. Priests were recorded inconsistently, as were officials and craftsmen. There were at least 6,000 mills, but apparently only eight millers or mill-keepers; demesne sheep must have numbered well over a million, but only ten shepherds are mentioned; similarly, the hundreds of square miles of woodland must have been supervised by more than four foresters and one huntsman. An important category of people, who would not appear in Domesday because they held no land, were the servants who worked on demesnes when slaves

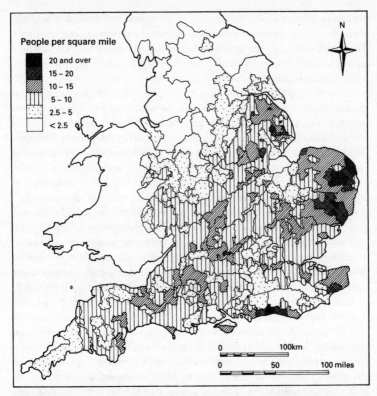

Map 7. Distribution of population according to Domesday Book (1086). The high density of population in the east persisted throughout the middle ages. There was a band of districts with relatively high population densities running from the Humber south-west to southern Somerset and Dorset.

Source: H. C. Darby, *Domesday England* (Cambridge, 1977).

were in short supply, and indeed were employed by the better-off peasants. Their presence must explain how the numerous small manors were operated which had a plough and a single tenant or slave, or even a plough and no recorded population at all. Making conservative allowance for these gaps in the Domesday survey would give a population figure of 2 million in 1086, but a more likely estimate would lie somewhere between 2.2 and 2.5 million (Map 7).

The example of Pinbury shows how the acreage of arable and patterns of land use can be calculated. For the country as a whole, the cultivated area probably lay in the region of 7 or 8 million acres, while woodland took up perhaps 4 million acres, or 15 per cent of the total available land. The arable was concentrated in a belt across the middle of the country, from Herefordshire to Norfolk. The woods were most extensive in the west and the south-east.

Comparing these statistics with those from other periods, we arrive at the conclusion that the population in 1086 was about half of that in 1300 or 1700, but the numbers were comparable with those of the period 1377–1540, that is after the Black Death and other epidemics. William I ruled almost as many English subjects as did Henry VIII. The cultivated area in the mid-twentieth century, when the population was twenty times greater, was 8.3 million acres, and 1.8 million acres were used for forests and woods – figures which are remarkably similar to those of the eleventh century. Domesday mentions 13,000 places, and the great majority exist now as hamlets, villages and towns with similar names. The general impression we gain is of a country with few very large empty spaces, in which agriculture, though not intensive, had attained a high level of development. The regional distribution of arable and pasture bears some resemblance to the patterns of land use in modern times. Another way of looking at the statistics is in terms of the experiences of those living in 1086. The cultivated area amounts to three acres or more per head. If half of the land was actually producing crops each year and yields were comparable with those recorded 150 years later, the land could have provided everyone in normal years with about 2 pounds of grain per day, more than sufficient to sustain healthy life if combined with other foods. Each person needed an acre of woodland for fuel for heating and cooking. This would have come from managed coppice woods, of which there were many among the 4 million acres of woodland, and together with the peat in East Anglia and the north, the supplies were ample for the population.

The survey of 1086 was mainly concerned with describing manors, and these provide a huge amount of evidence for the management of human resources. At Pinbury the demesne and tenant lands were fairly evenly balanced, which is characteristic of small manors in general. Minor lords, both monastic, as in our example, and the much more numerous laymen and women, kept quite a high proportion of their land in demesne, in some cases to feed their households, in others to produce a saleable surplus. As they did not have numerous tenants, and many of them were not burdened with very heavy labour services as was the case at Pinbury, they depended on slaves, or in eastern England, where slavery was dying out, they employed a good deal of hired labour. On the larger manors a higher proportion of the land was held by the peasant tenants, so that on many of the well-established church manors only a fifth of the land was held in demesne: in terms of Domesday statistics, peasant ploughs exceeded demesne ploughs in a ratio of 4 to 1. Such manors were therefore amply supplied with labour services from the peasants, especially the villeins. On very large manors, and particularly those in the king's direct control, the demesnes were relatively small, and as the numerous tenants were superfluous to the labour needs of the demesne, they were evidently paying rents in kind and cash.

The varied distribution of the different types of landowner gave each region its own social and economic character. Church estates were especially numerous in parts of the east midlands, notably in Huntingdonshire, and also in the west midland counties of Gloucestershire and Worcestershire. They also formed a large part of the southern shires of Hampshire and Kent. But other factors influenced the manorial regime, such as the large manors with their many dependencies and high proportions of sokemen and freemen in the old Danelaw, which gave rent payment a prominent role. Slaves were especially numerous in the west.

Domesday tells us much about villages and peasants as well as manors and tenants. The village had a part to play in law enforcement, and sometimes the peasants were sufficiently well organized to take on collectively the farm of the manor. The cohesiveness of the peasant community was not always reflected in compact nucleated villages, which were still being formed at this time, and in many parts of the country the settlement pattern remained dispersed. The Domesday survey of Devon records numerous tiny named manors which clearly represent a scattered spread of farmsteads.

The most numerous category of peasant tenants was that of the villeins, who account for about 40 per cent of the recorded rural population. On average they owned about three oxen each, and held yardlands or half-yardlands of 30 or 15 acres. They were important producers from their own holdings, had a surplus for exchange, and contributed much labour to the demesnes. The bordars and cottars, with holdings of 3 to 5 acres, accounted for 30 per cent of the rural population. They did not have enough land to feed themselves, and acted as hired workers for the demesnes and their better-off neighbours. They were most numerous in woodland and pastoral counties, where they could keep animals and find employment in such work as wood-cutting and turf-digging. In East Anglia they may have found paid work easier to obtain because of the commercial influences on the region, and more intensive farming systems. This was also an area with little slave labour, and bordars probably did the full-time work on the demesnes. Although villeins, bordars and cottars were tenants on manors, and in many cases had heavy obligations to their lords, they were carefully distinguished by the Domesday survey from the slaves. The words used to describe them by the Domesday clerks were derived from a continental vocabulary, in which 'villein' meant villager, and 'bordar' a tenant of a small house or smallholding. These names did not imply that they were servile, and indeed, like the pre-Conquest *gebur*, *ceorl* and *cotsetla*, these peasants were still legally free. The balance of public and private jurisdiction was beginning to change, as in continental style some of the hundreds were taken under private jurisdiction.

Domesday depicts an economy in which money and commerce played a central role. Its pages are littered with references to small payments of cash in rent, whether the valuations of mills or the obligations of groups of tenants, like the twenty-two sokemen of South Leverton in Nottinghamshire who together paid 20s. Above all, every manor could be assigned a render or value related to the annual income from that property to the lord. The whole country was thus valued cumulatively at £72,000, which cannot all have been paid at once, as the evidence of coins suggests that the total of pennies in circulation came to no more than £37,500. In the real world many lords obtained little or no cash from a manor, but took delivery of foodstuffs for consumption by the household. The values show that estate managers and the compilers of the survey envisaged that every manor was capable of producing an annual revenue in cash. Lords had to pay out in order to obtain these profits: for example they invested in 6,000 mills, which contained machinery built by specialists, and materials such as steel and the stones for grinding the corn which had to be purchased. Some of the demesne crops were put on the market, but much grain, together with cheese and meat from the animals kept, was consumed directly. Not so the wool from the sheep which, judging from the 13,000 to 50,000 listed in each of the south-western and eastern counties in the Domesday survey, would have numbered more than a million for the whole country – and that accounts for demesne flocks only. Some fleeces may have been processed and woven on the estates, but much of this production was sold to the increasingly specialized urban cloth industry both in England and overseas.

Town dwellers accounted for almost a tenth of the English population. Such a figure implies that the countryside was producing a substantial surplus for consumption by townspeople with limited access to land of their own, and that the towns were producing or trading goods and services that the country could buy. Towns were not just centres of population, but also generators of wealth, which the state recognized and exploited when it could extract annual sums of £50, £60 and more from individual towns. The interaction of town and country encouraged the development of property relations which bound urban centres to rural manors – boroughs belonging to a single lord were intended to serve as markets for the produce of the nearby estates, and for the larger and more complex royal towns, urban houses were attached to the rural manors of various landholders within the hinterland. Towns, as well as providing points of sale and processing facilities for agricultural produce, also specialized in expensive goods for the wealthy, like the furs traded at Chester. Country dwellers, as well as producing agricultural surpluses, extracted raw materials by quarrying, and by mining iron and lead, and also processed goods for sale, such as salt on the coast and pottery inland. Fishing was sometimes concentrated in towns, such as Sandwich with its large herring catches, but was also widely distributed along the coast and on the major rivers. In addition to the fully urban communities, markets were held in administrative centres, such as Luton (Bedfordshire) and King's Sutton (Northamptonshire).

This account of Domesday has focused on its picture of a rationally organized, well-populated and productive country. There were many weaknesses, including uneven development, with thin populations, low values and pastoral economies in the north and west. The lack of basic security on the Welsh border, to take an obvious example, and political instability everywhere discouraged investment. The activities of a predatory aristocracy who were still disputing the ownership of land and seeking short-term profit at the expense of the long-term interests of their tenants damaged confidence. The incomplete hierarchy of towns, in which the smaller towns were absent, and the limited marketing network, meant that much production was either for direct consumption, or surpluses might be wasted. Weaknesses in technology condemned many to such drudgery as milling by hand, and gave low agricultural returns. To some extent the problems of the eleventh-century economy were general difficulties felt before the industrial revolution, and we should still be impressed by the changes in the two centuries before the Conquest which had created many of the structures that would endure in subsequent centuries – villages, field systems, manors and towns.

PART TWO

Expansion and crisis, c.1100–c.1350

Many of those who lived between the time of Domesday and 1300 experienced varied types of economic growth. If they lived in the countryside they saw the number and size of settlements increase, and they were aware that land was being brought into more productive use through clearance of woodland, scrub, moors and heaths, or the drainage of fens and marshes, or the enclosure of open land and woodland. Town dwellers realized that new houses and streets were being built around them, and many new towns were being founded, sometimes in rivalry with existing places. By 1300 the numbers of towns can be estimated at around 700 in England, 80 in Wales, and over 50 in Scotland, compared with little more than 100 in Britain in 1100. Urban and rural workshops were making more goods, and demanding increased supplies of raw materials. By 1212, for example, a million pounds of tin were being smelted each year in Devon and Cornwall, and the extraction of ore was scarring the landscape. Carts and pack-horses were moving along the road system in ever greater numbers, and by 1300 hundreds of ships were passing in and out of the ports annually, with the fleeces of 12 million English sheep among their cargoes. Observers in the thirteenth century were conscious of the growing numbers of people, without feeling the need to calculate how many, but we can make some estimate for 1300 of about 6 million in England, a million in Scotland, and 300,000 in Wales, about three times the totals in 1100. These people carried in their purses the silver pennies minted in especially large numbers by Edward I of England and Alexander III of Scotland, and indeed the amount of money in circulation had grown more rapidly than the rise in population. In England more than £1 million in coin was circulating in 1320 compared with £37,500 at the end of the eleventh century. In Scotland from about £20,000 in the middle of the twelfth century the total had grown to between £130,000 and £180,000 in 1280. From the point of view of individual adults that meant 4–5 shillings each at any one time.

The strengthening of the state in part provided a secure environment for an expanding economy, and in part was made possible by growth. In England Henry II (1154–89) made legal reforms which extended the jurisdiction of the royal courts, and the extension of powers to judge and tax the king's subjects reached its high point under Edward I (1272–1307). Frictions with the aristocracy in 1212–16 (during which time Magna Carta was issued by King John) and 1258–65 (when Simon de Montfort sought to reform the rule of Henry III) were part of a process by which the magnates lost some independence, but were brought into close association with royal government, to form a 'community of the realm'. King and barons conquered that part of Wales which remained independent, and unsuccessfully attempted to subdue the Scots. The Scottish kingdom entered a new era under David I (1124–53), who introduced the main features of a west European state: a local government structure based on sheriffs and sheriffdoms; royal castles; burghs; and a penny coinage. He reorganized the church with a system of dioceses, and founded monasteries belonging to the main European orders. He encouraged outsiders, especially Anglo-Norman aristocrats, to settle, granting them lands in exchange for service. His successors continued the same policies, extending royal rule of the new type into the north and west of the country. Although troubled by rebellions and problems of succession to the throne, the country enjoyed relative peace under Alexander III (1249–86).

The reign of Stephen (1135–54) was a political episode which probably disrupted the English economy. As two rival claimants competed for the allegiance of the aristocracy, the normal processes of government were interrupted. Lands were confiscated from enemies, and used to reward supporters. Monasteries were granted lands to which the donor had dubious title. Coins of inferior quality were issued, some from unofficial mints. In the civil war, armies ravaged sections of the countryside and towns were damaged, especially during sieges of castles. The prevalent insecurity and lack of stable property rights were reported by chroniclers at the time, and were remembered long after order had been restored in the 1150s. The extent of the destruction is apparently reflected by the amount of geld (tax) collected by the officials of Henry II in 1156. The sum had fallen by 24 per cent since 1130, and the local officials blamed 'waste', especially in the midland counties. This word could refer to administrative disruption rather than physical devastation, but Henry II's officials did have to pay very large sums to restock royal manors, apparently because cattle had been stolen and other damage done. Some of the places complaining of waste are known from chronicle accounts to have been the scene of fighting. This period of insecurity and sporadic damage to property may have contributed to the rather slow growth in landed incomes in the twelfth century (see below, p. 121). Kings had a direct influence on the economy of substantial parts of the kingdom through their administration of the royal forests. These reached their maximum extent in the early thirteenth century.

The increase in written documents represents for historians an especially important aspect of growth in administration. Economic activity and record-keeping were directly connected. First, an economy with a large surplus was better able to pay for an educational system, and to reward specialist writers such as administrators, clerks and poets. Secondly, such documents as accounts were desirable as transactions became more numerous and complicated. In an age of rapid change, property owners needed the assurance of written proof of their title, and customs previously entrusted to the memory of old people were now preserved in more durable form. Finally, and most importantly, those in power found that, when different groups were competing for wealth and privilege, documents increased their authority and efficiency. Before Domesday a relatively small number of charters, law codes and chronicles give us a very patchy and imprecise glimpse of economic life, and we are not sure about the main long-term trends. From Domesday onwards the records accumulate in ever greater quantity. The first surviving financial account for the English kingdom relates to the year 1129–30, and records of the royal court begin in 1193; detailed tax lists survive from 1225. The earliest estate surveys were drawn up in the teens of the twelfth century; the first manorial accounts relate to the year 1208; and lords' court records have survived from the 1230s. The earliest urban court proceedings begin at the end of the twelfth century. From the 1270s onwards we can gather information from thousands of charters and deeds, and hundreds of surveys, tax lists, court rolls and bishops' registers. Most adult males alive in 1300 in England, even lesser peasants and ordinary artisans, must have had their names written in documents a number of times, often when they paid a rent or tax or because they came before a court on some routine matter. In spite of the destruction and loss of documents, enough have survived for a good proportion of those names to be known to us.

Now, these documents were produced by and for governments, and they can only give us a very incomplete and even misleading picture of economic activity. They tell us much more about the thirteenth century than the twelfth, which retains rather an air of mystery. About southern, eastern and midland England we have much more information than about the north and west. Wales was partly incorporated into the English state and eaten up by English lords, so it is quite well represented in the archives, especially after its conquest in 1282. Many Scottish charters survive, but there are few detailed local surveys, accounts or court records. Even when the documents are abundant, the poor and under-privileged are under-represented. The peasant economy has to be reconstructed from indirect evidence, and those who lacked land are almost hidden from view. Women and children are much less prominent than adult males.

The records tell us often about how things should have been, viewed from the perspective of those in authority. A charter issued by the king may grant to a lord the right to hold a weekly market on his land, but it does not tell us that trading has been taking place on that spot unofficially for many years, and that the charter is merely confirming an existing event. To take an opposite possibility, the charter will not explain that the grant was a speculative venture which failed dismally – no one wished to trade there, and the market existed only as a theoretical privilege. The purpose of the charter was to record the grant from king to subject, not to describe the local economy. Fortunately we are not entirely dependent on written evidence, and the mass of material remains from the period provides welcome confirmation that settlements were being founded, towns were growing in size, goods were being manufactured and traded in bulk, and large quantities of rubbish were accumulating. The archaeological evidence is also selective, because more substantial remains survive of the public works of the crown (such as Edward I's great Welsh castles), or cathedrals, than of the houses of the peasants and townspeople. But the material remains have been selected in different ways, and so we gain greatly from putting the written and unwritten evidence together.

The documents, and to some extent the buildings and artefacts, have a value beyond giving us routine information such as the figures for industrial production and levels of population that have just been quoted. If we are to glimpse the outlook of those who lived and worked in the medieval economy, to have some notion of their motives, intentions and ideas, then the 'bias' of the evidence is valuable to us. Medieval people have left us few explicit explanations for their behaviour, and when they did we should be suspicious because they were often seeking to justify their actions for some political or moral purpose. We must reconstruct their intentions from their actions, and attempt to understand the thinking behind the documents or the artefacts. The market charter mentioned above, which reveals so little about the realities of trade, speaks volumes about the pretensions of kings and lords, in their desire to regulate and profit from the activities of their inferiors.

The main theme of the first three chapters of this section is growth. The fourth deals with the early fourteenth century, when expansion faltered and ceased. This crisis deserves our attention as a significant episode in itself, but also compels us to re-examine the period as a whole.

CHAPTER FOUR

Lords, c.1100–c.1315

The lords had established themselves in a strong economic position after the upheavals of the eleventh century, and here we need to consider their involvement in the age of expansion. Did they develop their control over property and expand their landed assets? How successful were they in managing their estates and incomes in a time of rapid change? And did they make their own contribution to growth?

i. *Aristocracy and property*

To begin with property, the word is linked in our minds with ownership, but such modern concepts cannot be applied to the world of the twelfth and thirteenth centuries without reservations. The English magnates, that is the earls and barons among the lay aristocracy, and the bishops and larger monasteries in the case of the churchmen, thought of their collection of lands and rights as an 'honour'. By this they meant a great lordship, at the core of which lay demesne manors yielding great quantities of food and cash. Dozens of tenants of substance held their lands from the magnate in 'fee', and therefore owed military and administrative services. Some were themselves known as barons, with perhaps five or more demesne manors, but most of them were knights and lesser landholders with a single manor. At the centre of an honour in secular hands lay a castle, as much a centre of government as a military stronghold. Visitors would be impressed by the nucleus of buildings and people around the castle, as at Tutbury in Staffordshire or Pontefract in Yorkshire, because next to his stronghold the great lord would have founded a monastery, where his family would be buried and their memory perpetuated in the prayers of the monks, and a planned town was laid out at the castle gates. Nearby, to confirm the high status of the lord, there would often be a park full of deer and great ponds for fish. The appearance of wealth and power was not just show, because the honour was run like a small state, with officials like the steward (originally in charge of the household), the butler (who supplied the wine), the marshal (who looked after the stable, and had military duties) and chamberlain (who managed the finances), just as in any kingdom. The more advanced honours had their own exchequers, where the revenues from land, towns, profits of justice and feudal dues were collected and any debts noted. The lord's judicial authority was exercised through the honour court, in which the tenants in fee assembled to deal with any disobedience in their ranks, such as failure to do services, and to settle internal disputes. The tenants could be summoned to advise the lord: the foundation of a monastery, for example, might be approved at such a gathering. Revenues came to the lord from his rights over the tenants, whose lands, if they died leaving a young heir, would be managed in wardship by the lord for his own profit while he acted as guardian. If the lands came to a female, her marriage was arranged by the lord, often for a considerable sum of money. When an heir succeeded, he paid a relief in cash to be accepted as tenant, and on certain occasions lords could demand financial help from the tenants, the aid.

The honour appears to stand as a denial of the property rights of the tenants, who formed the great majority of the aristocracy. This powerful organization, especially in the twelfth century, enabled a few magnates to exercise a very real control over their subordinates. The honour might seem to have provided the basis of the social and political lives of the tenants in fee. It was said that they could not grant away their land, or let land to subtenants (subinfeudate it), without the lord's permission. The lord was able to take their money, in reliefs for example, and through his rights of wardship and marriage he was making crucial decisions about the future of his tenants' families and lands. In short, everyone was a tenant – even the magnates held their honours of the king. Can words like property and ownership be applied in a feudal world where society functioned on the principle that land was held in exchange for service?

If we adopt this view of twelfth-century society we are in danger of accepting the image that the magnates projected. They claimed great powers and dramatized their social position, but their authority was limited from many directions. Crucially, they were never independent of the king. In the later twelfth century the royal courts extended their jurisdiction and offered to all free tenants, that is to the tenants of the honours, protection from eviction through the assize of novel disseisin, by which aggrieved tenants could bring a complaint against anyone who deprived them of possession (seisin); in addition, the assize of mort d'ancestor enabled a tenant who was deprived of his inheritance to reclaim the land. This was not an unprecedented attack on the honours, as the royal courts had always been there, and had dealt with cases involving the tenants of honours for decades. Even in the late twelfth century the kings and their lawyers thought that they were seeking to force the magnates to remedy abuses and judge their tenants fairly, not to undermine the honour courts. Whatever the intention, the opportunity to use the royal courts was welcomed by the tenants, and private justice was weakened. The growth of the common law exercised in the king's courts marks an important stage in the development of a state in which citizens depend for their security and property rights on a single authority.

The upper ranks of tenants, even before 1100, had not been entirely under the thumb of the honours. Many of them lived on substantial estates, had built castles and held their own courts, and so rivalled the jurisdiction of the honour from within. The Tourville family, for example, held lands from the honour of Leicester, and were close to the Beaumont family who were earls of Leicester in the early twelfth century. Geoffrey de Tourville based his considerable wealth and power on his castle at Weston Turville in Buckinghamshire, and in c.1150 was owed service of castle guard by the knights who held land from him. The tenants like the Tourvilles formed a group who met regularly, could co-operate in their own interests, and exercised influence in the honour court. Judgments often took the form of compromise settlements and arbitrations rather than the lord handing down orders. In the ladder of tenures which made up a feudal society, magnates could not behave as dictators, because they were the king's tenants, and if they expected their lord to behave reasonably and listen to their advice, they could scarcely adopt a different standard in their own lordship. When King John assented to Magna Carta in 1215 he was accepting limitations on his feudal powers, on such matters as marriage, wardship and reliefs, but at the same time the barons who imposed the charter had to concede that they could not treat their tenants in an arbitrary way. For example, the standard relief of £5 for a knight's holding became normal throughout the feudal hierarchy.

The main obstacle to the power of the honour came not from direct challenges from above or below, but from the independent attitudes of the tenants, which eroded the authority of the magnates. They, like the magnates, thought that they had earned their lands as rewards for past service. They expected to enjoy hereditary succession by right. There had always been an element of fiction in the notion that they performed

military service in person for their lands, because at any one time a proportion of them would have been too old, too young, too ill or disabled
to ride and fight, and so they paid for a substitute. More often than not
in the twelfth century the tenants paid money (scutage) and the lord or
king engaged professional soldiers for wages. In the thirteenth century
the principle of military service was kept going, but each magnate was
expected to provide a much smaller quota of knights, and soon after 1300
armies were paid entirely from tax revenues. Similarly the ideal that lords
and tenants enjoyed a close personal bond had probably never been true,
and was certainly receding, in view of the scattered nature of the great
estates.

In practical terms, by the early twelfth century lords had limited
powers over the tenants in fee, who could do much as they wished with
their holdings. The exploitation of resources was left entirely to the
tenant. Land could be sold or given to the church on the tenant's initiative, and no one questioned that when a tenant died the successor in possession of the land would be the heir, ideally the eldest son. The custom
developed by the middle of the twelfth century that if there were no male
heirs, and the tenant had more than one daughter, the inheritance would
be divided between them. Only in exceptional circumstances, such as
total disloyalty, would a lord step in and take the land away. If the tenant
wished to sell the land, he would 'subinfeudate' the property, that is make
the buyer his subtenant, which added to fragmentation of holdings and
the complexity of the honour's tenures. Alternatively the tenant could
convey land by substitution, that is by asking the lord to accept the buyer
as a tenant instead of the seller. These alienations of land were allowed
on condition that the tenant looked after the interests of those who might
be damaged by the transaction – members of the family who might be
deprived of their inheritance would give permission, and the lord would
be guaranteed that any change to the tenancy would not result in a loss
of service.

Tenants acquired land from a number of lords, by purchase or marriage. This was not a deliberate policy to create divided loyalties, but
the inevitable consequence of expanding landholding in localities where
there were normally a number of overlapping magnate lordships. Lords
in search of political or military support, who may at one time have
depended on their tenants, instead sought the services of those with skills
(as lawyers for example), or influence among their neighbours, and rewarded them with money payments or promises of protection. In other
words they built up a retinue of supporters, and this rather than the
honour became the basis of lordly power and influence. This process
extended over a long period. Lords were recruiting supporters among

people who were not their tenants before 1200, but they still expected their tenants to attend their private courts and to form an important element in their circle of allies and helpers as late as the 1260s.

The English aristocracy did not have the full control over their land that we associate with modern concepts of ownership, but nor can we regard the majority of the aristocracy as living under the overwhelming restrictions of an overlord's honorial authority. In the long run the magnates' political power was completely overshadowed by the state. Edward I asserted royal power when he enquired into the franchises of his subjects, and objected if they were claiming (for example) hunting rights (free warren) or supervision of the sale of bread and ale, but could show no written evidence for those privileges. He was still willing to sympathize with their complaints that their tenants were depriving them of feudal rights of wardship and marriage by subinfeudating their lands, or by granting land to the church without permission. The Statutes of Quia Emptores (1290) and Mortmain (1279) forbade these practices. In future if land was sold a new tenant should be substituted who would recognize the rights of the overlord, and gifts to the church required a royal licence which was granted after an enquiry to establish that other interests would not be damaged. The crown's self-interest was served by these measures, but they show that at least some dimensions of lords' interests in their tenants' property still survived at the end of the thirteenth century. But the aristocracy regarded themselves as the owners of their land, and we can confirm that they were the effective masters of their own estates.

The secular aristocracy took a lofty view of their obligations. They justified their position by the services that they owed to overlords and ultimately the king, but also claimed a more general role as the protectors and defenders of the whole community. They believed that this function on earth was sanctioned by God. Their collective sense of duty was given a more specific focus in the twelfth and thirteenth centuries by the growth of ideas of chivalry, which in some versions emphasized the close link between knights and the church – knights were portrayed as soldiers of Christ, protecting the weak and defending Christendom against the heathen. More often, knights regarded themselves as uniquely skilled practitioners of the arts of war, and in peacetime found a place in the households of the lords and kings, winning the praise of women with their civilized accomplishments. In the same period the higher clergy also gained in self-confidence, as the church reform movement separated more clearly the clergy and the laity.

The aristocracy had more selfish aims. The laity were attached to their lineage, so they were conscious of their debt to previous generations of their family, and of their responsibility for the well-being of their offspring. They competed for land that could be added to the main inheritance, ultimately for the benefit of the eldest son, and also for land which could be handed on to younger sons and daughters. In a comparable fashion, monks focused on the landed assets of their monastic house, and they took a long-term view. Many monasteries kept a chronicle, which perpetuated a collective memory of any 'bad' abbots whose mismanagement caused debt or the loss of land, and recorded the virtues of those who had been successful in running the estate and adding to its resources. Monastic houses competed with rivals. Benedictines, who were well established, not to say complacent, by the twelfth century, resented the austerity of the Cistercian order (which seemed to smack of hypocrisy) when they were attracting patronage, and were affronted in the thirteenth century by the enthusiastic and fashionable orders of friars. Their hostility to the latter was sharpened by the friars' preaching of a doctrine of poverty, which included criticisms of the wealth of the traditional religious orders.

There were acquisitive individuals who advanced themselves by using their talents and good fortune, like William the Marshall, a younger son of a minor baronial family who embarked on a career under royal patronage fighting in wars and tournaments from 1168, until eventually he received the reward of loyal service in marriage to the heiress of a rich marcher lordship in 1189. His counterpart among the clergy was one of the great pluralists, like Walter de Merton, who served successive kings as chancellor in 1261–3 and 1272–4, and ended his days as bishop of Rochester. In the course of his career, which began in 1233, he drew income as a cathedral canon at Wells, Exeter, Lincoln, London and Salisbury, and was either vicar or rector (in name) of ten churches. In 1270 his income from these offices alone must have been near to £400 per annum.

These two extreme examples show that aristocrats became richer most rapidly by gaining political favour, as the patronage of magnates and kings could be translated into acquisitions of land, or offices which would yield the profits in cash with which land could be bought. The aspiring careerist had to show appropriate talents and find the right patron. Backing the losing side, as those who supported Simon de Montfort's cause in 1258–65 found, could lead to confiscation of land, and to ruin. The important chances for an up-and-coming courtier or soldier came when old families died out in the male line, leaving the lands to a marriageable heiress. In the late twelfth and early thirteenth century, risk-takers could 'proffer' money to the crown – often hundreds of pounds – for a wardship or marriage, calculating that the income they gained would cover the investment.

One route to success lay in moving into frontier territories, where lands of conquered enemies could be acquired, but also where underdevelopment in the economic and administrative sense gave the opportunity for carving out new lordships. Norman lords can be seen taking risks by moving into Yorkshire and the other northern counties after the pacification of the region in 1071: here they could build castles like that at Richmond and develop the surrounding countryside. The Welsh marches provided such opportunities, and lords established themselves there by seizing land and building castles as the basis of their lordships at such places as Wigmore (Herefordshire) and Grosmont (Monmouthshire). Anglo-Norman lords were welcomed by David I and his successors in Scotland, where they were granted feus (fiefs). Intervention in Ireland extended the colonial territories from the late twelfth century, and many English and marcher lords acquired lands there. Often the occupation of new territory was followed by a colonizing movement by monasteries belonging to the new orders of the twelfth century, especially the Cistercians and Augustinians.

Once established, the land accumulated by aristocratic families had to be protected against erosion. There were constant pressures to detach pieces of land as rewards for deserving followers, or to endow the local monastery. Children who had no formal claim on the main inheritance expected to receive some land – daughters to take it with them into marriage, or younger sons who could be made subtenants or under the prevailing custom could be given land that had been acquired during their father's lifetime, as distinct from the property that he had himself inherited. The most successful operators looked after the whole family, made good marriages which would bring useful alliances for the future, and endowed monasteries, without ruining their estates. As old families faltered, or most likely when the careful calculations of successive generations were frustrated by biology and the main inheritance went to a female, there were plenty of new men anxious to acquire land and establish their families. Lesser barons like William Marshall sought promotion into the ranks of the magnates, and replacements for losses among the lesser aristocracy came from officials, soldiers, merchants or rich peasants. The aristocracy was always an 'open elite', proclaiming that only high birth and long ancestry qualified them for their privileges but accepting that in the real world landed wealth was the main qualification.

Individual aristocratic families rose and fell, and some died out and were replaced by new recruits, but we might expect to see an overall pattern. There are so many examples of magnates prospering – such as the constant accumulation of land, mainly through a successful marriage policy, of the Clares, earls of Gloucester, throughout the twelfth and thirteenth centuries, or the purchase of land from indebted lay families by monasteries in the thirteenth century – that contemporaries commented on the growth of larger estates, which they sometimes deplored. Soon after 1300 a chronicler complained that 'the earls and other magnates who could live according to their status on their inheritance . . . pester their poor neighbours to sell what they have inherited'. Because the surviving documents come from the successful landowners, the land market may appear to have worked in favour of the large estates.

The routine records of enfeoffment, however, and the emergence of new small manors, can leave no doubt that land became more fragmented and the lesser aristocracy multiplied. Magnates rewarded their supporters and officials, and indeed renewed old obligations of service by granting land to families already endowed with fiefs in an earlier generation. The new estates were not always the result of splitting existing units, but were also created by the clearance or drainage of new land. In the same way lesser aristocrats multiplied especially rapidly in the frontier areas, such as the north of England or the Welsh marches in the twelfth century, when there was not so much room for new manors in the older countries of the midlands and the south. In Scotland at this time, magnates who had benefited from the initial grants of feus were using part of their estates to reward lesser aristocrats. In the monastic world, as well as the growth in the size of the large estates, we should not ignore the hundreds of new small foundations – priories and nunneries in the twelfth century, friaries, colleges and hospitals in the thirteenth, many of which were provided with annual revenues of less than £100. The proliferation of small units of landholding was not always controlled by superior lords, but often resulted from initiatives among the knights and gentry, who were carving out new manors for themselves by buying parcels of land or making clearances. They were using as capital money acquired from their office-holding or profits gained from farming and trading. Throughout our period most land was in the hands of the lesser aristocracy, and their share increased through time.

An example of the multiplication of small manors is Hanbury in the wooded country of north Worcestershire. In 1086 it was described in Domesday Book as being divided between two large manors, one belonging to the bishops of Worcester and the other part of the royal demesne. A minor lay lord held one very small sub-manor. By 1300 the territory was divided into ten or eleven units of exploitation. The king kept a fragment of his original estate, a 1,000-acre park, and his park keeper held a small manor in keeping with his gentry status. The bulk of the former royal land had been granted to Cistercian monks from Bordesley Abbey, who farmed it in two separate granges, one of which was formed by clearing new land from wood and rough grazing. The bishop retained a much-truncated manor, having ceded a large section of underdeveloped land to a lay family who then granted it to the Knights Templar. Four other gentry families had created small manors by a combination of grants from the bishops, purchase and clearance, which joined the small manor surviving from the time of Domesday. The bishops were not left out of the move to expand, as they had developed a detached area of former woodland into a virtually separate manor, and they also bought up an area of newly cleared land from one of their tenants, but the general tendency clearly favoured the multiplication of small manors in the hands of gentry and the new religious orders.

The balance of landholding between the laity and the church moved in two directions immediately after 1066. Bishops and monasteries were required to provide landed endowments for knights perfoming military service. The opposite tendency of lay families endowing the church was probably on a larger scale. It began slowly with a few new Benedictine houses such as Lewes in Sussex and Much Wenlock in Shropshire, both initiated by Norman magnates, and the royal foundations at Battle in Sussex and Reading in Berkshire. A significant wave of monastic expansion came with the arrival of the new monastic orders in the twelfth century, of which the most important were the Cistercians (with various allied orders such as the Premonstratensians), the Augustinian canons (including the Arrouasians and Victorines), the native English order, the Gilbertines, and the military orders of the Templars and the Hospitallers. They attracted enthusiastic aristocratic support. A prominent family would wish to be associated with a particular monastery, and would gain spiritual benefits and social status from the size of the endowment and the quality of its monks and buildings. A typical example would be the new earl of Leicester, Robert de Beaumont, founding on a lavish scale Leicester Abbey, an Augustinian house, in 1138 or 1139, which would ever after be regarded as an asset to his earldom.

The greatest number of new monasteries were founded in the north and the marches, where older Benedictine monasteries were relatively few, and where new lay families were anxious to make their mark. The numbers are impressive – there were more than sixty Cistercian houses by 1200 in England and Wales and at least 150 Augustinian foundations. In Scotland, where new monasteries were founded later, twenty Cistercian, seventeen Augustinian, seven Tironian and six Premonstratensian houses had been established by 1300. They were not given many great manors occupying prime agricultural land in the fashion of the earlier Benedictine establishments. Cistercians and some branches of the Augustinians attracted lay benefactors by their preference for occupying wild places (deserts, as the monks called them), in order to contemplate spiritual matters away from the corrupting influence of secular society. They could be established in remote valleys like Rievaulx in Yorkshire or Llanthony on the Welsh border, and their colonizing effort would contribute to the development of the whole region, without great cost to the founder. (Plate 5) The Augustinians sometimes occupied former minster churches, so they had some landed basis for the new monasteries, and they were often given parish churches with their glebe lands and tithes, which laymen were being discouraged from owning in the new climate of the church reform movement. Monasteries added to their estates by purchase, especially in the thirteenth century. The new centres of religious life of this time, such as the orders of friars and the foundation of colleges of priests to pray for the souls of the founder, added yet more property to the church's considerable possessions, but were not as well provided with land as the monasteries had been. We can estimate that the church's share of landed wealth in England had grown from about a quarter of the total in 1086 to almost a third in 1300.

Finally the king lost land. The 'royal demesne' had been inflated by the Conquest, but was then granted to loyal subjects as part of the crown's patronage, and was used to endow religious houses. The land said by Domesday in 1086 to have been held by the king, at £11,000, amounts to about a sixth of the total value of land in the kingdom. Around 1300 the royal demesnes yielded £13,000–£14,000 annually, a small increase in money terms, but after a major inflation and much general economic growth, the king's share of landed income had fallen to about 2 per cent. A king such as Edward I suffered no great hardship from this loss – his predecessors had gained valuable political support from the grants of land, and the monarch disposed of many other sources of income such as taxation.

The landowners of the twelfth and thirteenth centuries had made great efforts to increase and keep the amount of land under their control, and as a result estates rose and fell in size, and parcels of land large and small were constantly moving through inheritance, marriage, purchase and gift. In the long term the church acquired land from the laity in general, small church institutions multiplied, and among the laity the knights and gentry gained at the expense of the magnates and the crown.

Scottish landholding deserves some separate consideration. The language of continental feudalism arrived in the reign of David I, when the crown began to grant feus to immigrant aristocrats from England and Normandy, who grew in numbers and influence during the late twelfth century. One of these 'infeftments' gave Robert de Brus, from a family which originated near Cherbourg, a great tract of country in Annandale from the Solway to the source of the Clyde in 1124 for the service of ten knights. The charters issued at this time, and those that they in turn used to grant lands to their supporters, give the impression of a pyramid of landholding for service, which has been seen to mark the 'feudalization' of the kingdom. The Scottish common law came under the strong influence of English law, with its concern to regulate property relations within a framework of lordship and tenancy. The grants of feus (many of them much smaller than Annandale, and for the service of a single knight) to the Anglo-Norman elite was concentrated in the south and east of the country, where royal power was most securely established and which contained the most developed agricultural land and urban centres. Gradually the new form of tenures was extended into the west and north, where more traditional forms of lordship tended to persist and royal rule remained a more remote influence.

During the twelfth and early thirteenth centuries, magnates built up great accumulations of land which ignored the frontiers of kingdoms, and in some cases combined estates in Scotland and England, and Ireland. So David, earl of Huntingdon (1152–1219) held Garioch, a great compact lordship north-west of Aberdeen, with smaller holdings in the east and in Midlothian, near Edinburgh. He was also a considerable lord in the east midlands of England (Map 8). He did not see these lands as separate but ran them as an integrated enterprise. He recruited in England some of the lesser aristocrats whom he established with grants of land in Scotland, and one of his Scottish estate stewards came from his midland properties. A handful of great magnates can be compared with the earl of Huntingdon, including the Stewarts, hereditary stewards to the Scottish kings and major lords in the west, with a base at Renfrew

▶

Map 8. Examples of estates in the twelfth and thirteenth centuries. The map is designed to show the characteristic estate patterns of different types of lord: a bishop's manors tended to be concentrated in his diocese, though in the case of the very rich bishopric of Winchester there were important outliers, from Taunton in the west to Southwark in the east. An earl's estates were much more scattered, for the earl of Huntingdon in his English honour, the manors were stretched across the east midlands and, in addition, he had a string of lands, some of them very extensive, up the east coast of Scotland. Monastic lands tended to lie within carting distance of the monastery, but the granges of Margam Abbey (a Cistercian house) were more tightly concentrated than those of the older and richer Norwich Cathedral Priory. The rich knightly family the Longvillers had scattered manors in one region, mostly in Yorkshire, but stretching into Nottinghamshire and Lincolnshire.

Sources: J. Z. Titow, *Winchester Yields* (Cambridge, 1972); K. Stringer, *Earl David of Hunting-don 1152–1219* (Edinburgh, 1985); D. H. Williams, *Atlas of Cistercian Lands in Wales* (Cardiff, 1990); I. Atherton et al. (eds), *Norwich Cathedral* (1996); C. Clay, 'The Family of Longvillers', *Yorkshire Archaeological Journal*, 42 (1971).

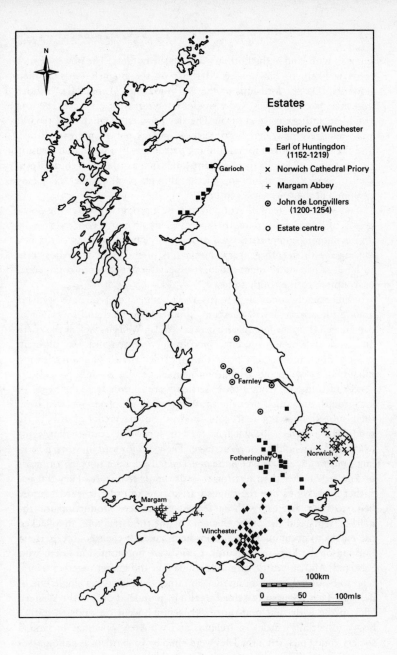

Estates

♦ Bishopric of Winchester
■ Earl of Huntingdon
  (1152-1219)
× Norwich Cathedral Priory
+ Margam Abbey
⊙ John de Longvillers
  (1200-1254)
○ Estate centre

Garioch

Farnley

Fotheringhay

Norwich

Margam

Winchester

0   100km

0   50   100mls

but also with land in the Lothians and on the borders. The power of such lords is likely to have exceeded those of the English lords in their honours. Like the lordships of the Welsh marches, Annandale, Garioch and their like stretched over a single, large territory, and gave the lord complete and exclusive control. The ties between magnate and tenants were relatively new, hereditary succession was not always established, and the tenants looked for continuing patronage. In a very large lordship the tenants were less likely to acquire land from a number of lords. Royal control was a less inhibiting factor, though royal justice was being extended in the thirteenth century.

This view of a 'feudal' Scotland may be a product of surviving documents, and charters apparently recording simple grants concealed social and economic complexity, such as sales of land and loans of money. During the thirteenth century the tenants of the great magnates seem to have gained more independence, especially in the more commercial envronment of the south and east.

While broadly common patterns of economic and social developments among the aristocracy of England, southern Scotland and south Wales can be seen from the late twelfth century, Welsh Wales as well as the north and west of Scotland present a poorly documented and very different picture. English observers at the time regarded these as alien territories, inhabited by wild and barbarous people. Feudal tenures provided a veneer of influence from a more settled world. Lords were the heads of kin groups, and ruled over men rather than lands. They received from their subordinates not rents and services, but payments of tribute, in kind, which were acknowledgements of superiority rather than rents calculated on a holding or an acreage. The word for lord in western Scotland, *mormaer*, and in Welsh the *pencenedl*, both refer to chiefs or heads of kindreds rather than territorial lords in a feudal state. They did not gather possessions like the English aristocrats in order to enrich future heirs to their estates. Without towns, commerce, production for the market, rents and the other elements of the infrastructure, they lacked the means to accumulate wealth in the manner of their counterparts in Lothian or the English midlands. Coins were not minted in north-west Scotland. And any cattle or goods which they did gather together would tend to be distributed among the kin rather than kept in a single line of descent. They sometimes gained wealth by plunder. Lords in the Western Isles in the early and mid-thirteenth century went on raids to gather booty (especially cattle) in Ireland, and with few openings in landed society young men from the Isles were hired by Irish rulers as galloglasses (mercenaries). The prince Owain Gwynedd in 1162 took a plundering expedition to Arwystli (Montgomeryshire). These freebooting societies were introduced gradually to the feudal world through migration, inter-marriage and the cultural influence of such western European concepts as knighthood, but also in the case of Wales through conquest.

ii. *Managing the estate*

In addition to the decisions that had to be made over acquiring and losing property, landlords had to consider various options is relation to the exploitation of their estates. For the greater lords – the earls, barons, bishops and larger monasteries – these decisions became more urgent as time went on. In the eleventh century, both before and after the Conquest, the landholdings of the greatest magnates seem so enormous that we cannot imagine that they had to worry about their incomes. But we know from our own times that even the greatest millionaires seek new ways to expand their fortunes, and they justify themselves, as would the medieval earls, by pointing out their expensive responsibilities. A handful of families belonged to the super-rich category, and among the leading 200 in 1086 were many lords with perhaps a dozen manors in demesne worth in total about £50 per annum who understandably felt a need for more income.

Estates consisted partly of land held directly by the lord, the manors in demesne, and of lands held as fiefs by tenants. Even in the midlands and the south, where the bulk of grants in fee had been made before 1100, parcels of land were still being given out to tenants during the twelfth century. They were lost to the lord as sources of substantial income, so lords hung on to their largest and richest manors, and tended to grant to subordinates or to the church smaller, outlying and less valuable prop-erties. The Lacy family, based at Weobley in Herefordshire, illustrate the point. They kept in demesne large manors located on fertile soils, like Stanton Lacy in Shropshire, and Weobley itself. Here they had their main residences, and so their household could be fed directly from their own produce. They also kept large and valuable demesne manors further east, such as Painswick in Gloucestershire, which were safe from devastation if war broke out on the Welsh border. Land out on the border itself, further west than Weobley, which was not very productive and which was vulnerable to attack, was either granted to knights who could give valuable service defending the border, or was used to endow the remote Augustinian monastery of Llanthony.

Lords' resources of land were constantly diminishing, and there were limits on their other sources of income. They were prevented from demanding large sums in feudal dues, as custom developed to protect the tenants in fee – for example, the £5 maximum relief on a knight's fee, which was becoming customary in the late twelfth century, was fixed by Magna Carta. Profits of justice were limited as the royal courts became more active at this time. The franchises which allowed lords to take fines and charge tolls on their subordinates – in markets, for example, or from the regulation of ale-selling, or by seizing the goods of those convicted of felonies in the royal courts – were defended by lords against royal enquiries in the thirteenth century, but even when their rights were upheld under the Quo Warranto investigations of Edward I's reign, they were not very lucrative. In the lordship of Holderness in east Yorkshire, for example, which was especially powerful, the franchises were valued at £14 annually, a small fraction of the income from land.

The magnates felt beleaguered in the 1190s and in the reign of John (1199–1216) because the royal courts were attracting business, to the long-term damage of their own honorial courts, while at the same time the crown was subjecting them to demands for very large sums of money. In 1213–14 William fitz Alan, a Shropshire baron, was an extreme example of a general trend when he was expected to pay a relief of 7,000 marks (£4,666), a sum well in excess of the annual income from his estates. The sums demanded for a wardship or marriage rose to near impossible levels. To make such payments, the magnates had to borrow money on the strength of their future income. On top of these problems came severe inflation. A load (later known as a quarter) of wheat had cost on average 2s for most of the twelfth century, but soon after 1193 it had increased rapidly, soaring as high as 8s, and settling to an average of between 3s 8d and 4s 10d in 1210–50, nearly double its old price (see Figure 1 below, p. 230). Oxen, the main source of pulling power in twelfth-century agriculture, increased in price by a similar amount, fetching 3–4s before 1200, and an average of 6s 8d in subsequent years. Foot soldiers in the king's army had been paid a penny a day in the reign of Henry II but by 1200 their wages had doubled. The rate of pay of agricultural workers probably also doubled at the same time, from a halfpenny to a penny per day.

Unlike the soldiers and labourers, the incomes of the landed aristocracy did not rise in the general inflation. Those lords who supplied their households directly from their estates were at least protected from the increase in the price of basic foodstuffs, but the cost of any grain and meat bought on the market, and of other goods and services, was rising, while many of their demesnes were leased out for fixed rents. Demesne leases were recorded by some church landlords, but were apparently generally employed throughout upper landed society. The canons of St Paul's Cathedral in London in 1152 leased their manor of Kensworth in

Bedfordshire to a farmer, Henry Bucvinte, a member of a local lesser aristocratic family, for an annual rent of £10 for the rest of his life (they helped him to become established with lower rents in his first four years). For this he received farm buildings including a manor house, barn and housing for animals, 220 acres of arable land, and enough pasture for at least 24 cattle and 120 sheep, together with the labour services of the peasant tenants – sufficient assets to enable him to pay £10 to the canons and to make some profit for himself. Such an arrangement was based on the assumption that prices and profits remained relatively stable. In 1181 the rent of Kensworth had risen to £13 annually, but such an increase would not have protected the canons against the effects of inflation if Bucvinte's successor had lived through the 1190s while prices were doubling. Many farmers found themselves in the happy position of holding a lease of a demesne for quite a long term – for the remainder of their lives, or for twenty years – paying a fixed cash rent, while their profits increased.

The landlords had grown up with stable prices, which meant that they thought of land values as fixities – a farm, in Latin *firma*, a leasehold rent, was described by a twelfth-century official as so-called because it was firm and unchanging. Many manors between the late eleventh and late twelfth century increased their annual revenue but not by a very large margin: Charing in Kent, for example, was worth £34 in 1066, and £40 at the end of the twelfth century. Lords on the eve of the inflation received much the same income as their predecessors at the time of the Domesday survey. The archbishop of Canterbury, one of the great church magnates, had estates valued at £1,246 in 1086 and £1,375 in 1172. The landlords' world fell apart when these apparent fixities in their lives shifted. Between 1184 and 1214 the greater lords converted their system of management from leasing of demesnes by taking over each manor as the farmer's term ended, and putting it under the control of officials directly responsible for the profits. Apart from the shock of inflation, the lords may have had other motives for the change; they may have solved the problem of the price rise by leasing out the demesnes for very short terms of a few years, negotiating a higher rent at each renewal. More likely they were concerned about the improvement in tenants' security which had resulted from the legal reforms of the late twelfth century, and became worried that leasehold tenants, like tenants in fee, would be protected by the royal courts. Bringing demesnes into direct management would certainly prevent such a disaster.

Lords were taking a far-reaching step when they brought demesnes under their direct control. It involved other developments which were still having repercussions two or three generations after the initial decisions were made around 1200. One of the advantages of the old system of leasing lay in its administrative simplicity. Once a suitable farmer had been found, and the bargain struck with him, the central estate officials had no more complicated task than collecting the money or agricultural produce when it was due (often at four dates through the year), checking that payment was made in full, and ensuring that the buildings were not being neglected.

Under the new system, the lords' officials were working full time on the detailed supervision of agricultural tasks. Each manor was put under a local official, a reeve, sergeant or bailiff, who either served as a condition of holding land or was in receipt of rewards in cash and kind. These officials took charge of a large agricultural enterprise, as each demesne on a large estate usually consisted of between 200 and 500 acres of arable land, with meadow, pasture and wood. The official had to assemble a labour force of full-time servants, hired workers and tenants, supervise their work, and pay and feed them. On a mixed farm the tasks on the arable of ploughing, harrowing, sowing, weeding, harvesting, threshing and grain-processing had to be conducted alongside mowing and making hay, milking cows and shearing sheep, as well as the daily routines of feeding and caring for animals. Decisions had to be made about marketing – when and where and what quantity of grain or animals should be sold. The local official was often expected to collect rents and other dues. The reeves who carried out these tasks in the thirteenth century were servile peasants with experience of cultivating a holding of perhaps 10, 20 or 30 acres. They brought to the management of the demesne a wealth of detailed local knowledge about the soil, the crops which grew best, the most suitable animal breeds, the nearby markets, and the tenants and workers on the manor. It was this expertise which made the reeve such a useful asset for the lord, but he had no experience of large-scale agriculture, and he took a great risk in venturing into an operation of such size and complexity.

The lord took an even greater risk, as he was entrusting his valuable assets to a peasant who might prove incompetent or dishonest. Accordingly the lords created a new central management to supervise the reeves and bailiffs. There would be regular visits to the manors by the lord or members of the household. On a monastic estate monks would call in, and some of them established a system of monk wardens who looked after a group of manors. The steward would arrive regularly as he went round the manors to hold the lord's courts, and the receiver or treasurer, or a representative, came to collect money. These higher officials would not expect the reeve to make major decisions; such matters as wool sales or large items of expenditure would be arranged centrally. Their primary concern was to check on the reeve's conduct, which could be done through informal observation, but more officially through the manor court. One accusation made to the court was that the reeve used the lord's servants, ploughs and seed to cultivate his own holding.

The main check on the reeves' honesty and efficiency was made by the lords' auditors. They sometimes held an interim 'view' of the account, but their main meeting with the reeve came after the end of the farming year, at Michaelmas (29 September), when they examined the account that he had compiled with the help of a clerk. The audit involved a search for inconsistencies which would expose the reeve's tendency to exaggerate expenditure and minimize income. In the first part of the account the reeve would list the rents that had been received and the money gained from the sale of grain, cheese and other produce, and in the second part show how much of this income had been spent on wages, repair of buildings and implements, and purchase of animals or goods such as a new bucket for the well. Most of the surplus money would already have been sent to the treasurer or receiver. The auditors would check the reeve's figures by referring to a survey of the manor, which, for example, listed the rents, and they consulted the accounts for previous years. They would keep themselves informed about local conditions such as the performance of crops and the price of corn. The reeve could answer some of their sceptical enquiries because he kept evidence of transactions: written records or at least tallies on which the sum paid would be recorded with notches on wooden sticks. If the reeve could not provide a satisfactory answer the item on the account would be crossed out, the auditors would substitute their version, and the reeve would be expected to pay the difference. A clever reeve would make a profit from his term of office, but skilled auditing prevented him from lining his own pocket too lavishly.

The auditors, and the other estate officials, were helped in their work by a number of treatises, textbooks as we would call them, on the philosophy and practice of estate management, which carry such titles as the *Husbandry* or *Stewardship*, though the most famous, written around the 1280s, is always known by the name of its reputed author, *Walter of Henley*. These were mainly in French, and clearly aimed at an educated readership of clergy and aristocrats. *Walter* addresses itself to the lord himself, and gives rather moralistic advice about the need to calculate the resources of an estate, and to match expenditure to those assets. Such books dispense some useful agricultural knowledge, but they are mainly concerned with management, including the choice and control of employees, and above all calculations about yields of grain and animals, which would help auditors to make informed judgements about the performance of the reeves and their manors. *Walter*, for example, informs its readers that every two cows on salt marsh pasture will produce every week enough milk to make a stone of cheese and a half-gallon of butter, while three animals grazing ordinary pasture – in woodland or on meadows after haymaking – yield the same amount of dairy produce. The authors take a rather pessimistic view of the staff of lesser officials and farm servants, who are assumed to be potentially dishonest, lazy and malicious. Another type of textbook from the thirteenth century contains formularies which demonstrated to clerks the correct form of accounts, surveys and other records. These books were used in schools, at Oxford for example, where clerks who had received a conventional education were given a more practical training in producing the documents needed for running an estate. The change from leasing to direct management created thousands of new administrative jobs for clergy and gentry.

In addition to employing staff to run their estates from year to year, lords needed advice on more strategic matters, such as the purchase of property, or the clearance of new land, or major new building works. This was provided by a council of officials and lawyers. Monasteries recognized the need for expert management, and some of them took manors away from the individual departments of the monastery (the office of the almoner, precentor, sacrist and so on) and put the bulk of the land under a single powerful official, often the cellarer or the treasurer.

Did the lords and their advisers make the right decisions? They clearly believed that direct management was the right way to increase their revenues, because this method was employed by all types of lord over a large section of the south, east and midlands of England for the best part of two centuries. The combination of local responsibility and checks from the central officials overcame the problem of running a large scattered estate. Indeed, scattered estates had their advantages, because manors on different soils were less likely all to suffer crop failure in the same year. Also they could be linked to complement each other's resources: sheep and cattle from lowland manors could spend the summer on hill pastures, or pigs might be driven to woodland to be fattened on acorns and beech mast. Dispersed manors could also be convenient for providing food for the household, if they lay in districts which an itinerant lord (such as an earl or a bishop) might wish to visit. Lords and their households would stop for a few days or weeks at each residence, conduct local business, entertain their supporters, and consume the food from the demesne. Provincial lords who held a manor in the vicinity of London often made regular use of it when travelling to the capital, and it would serve as a retreat if the city became too uncomfortable (see Map 8 above, p. 117). Many estates inherited their geography from the remote past, but they modified their structure in the interests of efficiency and profit. An inconveniently remote manor would be sold or leased out. Large productive demesnes would be divided into two to create more easily manageable units of production. A small demesne could be increased in size by purchase.

In view of the relative uniformity of the accounting system, and the widespread knowledge of the textbooks such as *Walter of Henley*, we might expect to find that different demesnes were exploited along similar lines. It is true that mixed farming was usually practised, and most demesnes planted four different types of corn, and kept the main types of livestock – horses, cattle, sheep and pigs, with some poultry. A degree of centralization was practised in the management of sheep. Large estates would place all of the scattered flocks under a stockmaster or master shepherd, who orchestrated their movements from one manor to another according to a central estate strategy. One of the richest heiresses of the late thirteenth century, Isabella de Fortibus, had a stock-keeper for the lordship of Holderness in eastern Yorkshire, a lowland district with a tradition of mixed arable and pastoral farming. From a base at the manor of Keyingham he supervised shepherds at eleven places on the estate, who looked after more than 7,000 sheep. He would arrange for the flocks to move to the best pastures at the right time – for example on to rich grazing on the Humber estuary in the summer. The stock-keeper could assemble all of the wool together in order to sell it in bulk to a major merchant. The Holderness clip was bought between 1260 and 1280 for as much as £200 in a single year by the great international trading company, the Riccardi of Lucca. They provided a banking service for the lady, so they would not give the money to the estate officials in Yorkshire, but would credit it to Isabella's account.

Further west in northern England, on the Scottish border and in Scotland itself, hilly country was ill suited to much arable farming, and on the slopes lords set up specialist stock grazing centres, vaccaries (for cattle) and bercaries (for sheep). On the estates of the Lacy family based on Pontefract in 1295 a stockman called Gilbert de la Legh was in charge of twenty-seven scattered vaccaries in Lancashire, in such places as Accrington, Pendle and Rossendale, each with local keepers with more than eighty animals in their charge, making a total of almost 2,500. The estate invested in buildings to shelter the stock, which were moved frequently as a precaution against disease. They bred oxen for sale as draught animals and for beef in the markets of northern England.

Stock-rearing, whether managed separately within a mixed farming estate or practised as the main agricultural activity on remote hillsides, shows that estates were capable of specialization. On the lowland manors that made up the bulk of the great estates the managers left the choice of crops and agricultural methods largely to the reeves and bailiffs who knew the local conditions. In some districts wheat was chosen as the main winter-sown corn, but in others rye or a mixture of rye and wheat, maslin, was preferred. In some districts, notably in parts of Norfolk and Suffolk, barley occupied a very large acreage and not much wheat was grown. Oats and pulses (peas and beans) varied a great deal in their importance as a crop. Oats in some districts (parts of Essex, for example) were sown on more acres than barley, and in the south-west, the north-west and parts of Scotland the crop was grown almost as a monoculture.

The combinations of crops were chosen by the managers in the light of a number of complicated calculations. They were influenced by the local environment, so oats, which tolerate acid soils and have a short growing season, were grown in upland regions, while rye, which is well suited to light soils, was cultivated in gravelly river valleys and the sandy districts of East Anglia. The managers also had an eye on market opportunities, and would grow wheat for the urban market, though they also devoted land to oats and rye near to large towns, because traders used horses a great deal, for which they needed oats for fodder, and the poor ate rye bread, though these relatively cheap grains could only be carried relatively short distances. Manors sited away from towns, and from waterways which could be used for relatively cheap transport, had more limited opportunities to sell crops. A high proportion of the crops were consumed on the manor, which encouraged the cultivation of at least a small acreage of oats for the horses, even when the crop did not yield very highly. Similarly, if the demesne was to supply the lord's household, wheat for baking and barley for brewing would be produced. The demesne managers grew peas, beans and vetches partly for their value as animal feed, but also because of their beneficial effect on the following crop, as these legumes helped to add nitrogen to the soil.

The same mixture of motives governed the choice of animals, and while certain environments suited the various species – sheep were kept on hilly country, cattle in river valleys and pigs in woodlands – livestock also complemented arable cultivation, so many lowland manors practised sheep and corn husbandry, in which the flocks spent much of the time in the stubble and fallow fields, finding grazing in the vegetation that grew with the corn, and contributing their manure to the next year's arable land. Some demesnes found ways of feeding animals without relying on the natural resources of the locality. Manors which had limited access to woodland could still keep pigs, allowing them to feed on grain or peas and beans. The managers were aware of the ecological importance of selecting the right balance of arable and livestock, and of different crops and animals. They also insured themselves from complete failure in the event of bad harvests or diseases among the animals. At least part of the demesne's range of products would be likely to succeed even in a disastrous year.

The frequency of cropping varied from region to region. Through much of north-eastern, central and southern England, demesnes sowed crops on half of the arable land each year (following a two-course rotation) in step with the field systems operated by the peasants; while many other demesnes were organized on the basis of a three-course rotation, by which a third of the land was fallowed each year. In parts of the south-east and in Norfolk the land was cropped more frequently and nine-tenths or an even higher proportion of the land was cultivated. The managers of some manors, such as South Walsham on the earl of Norfolk's estate, had by the 1260s given up fallowing entirely, and cultivated all of their arable every year. Such intensive methods were adopted in north-east Norfolk not just because the soil was naturally fertile, but also because the high population density allowed labour to be concentrated on the land, with repeated ploughing, weeding, and spreading of manure and marl. Peas were cultivated in quantity, which added nitrogen directly to the soil, and provided fodder for animals fed in stalls, which was a good source of manure. Seed for grain and legumes was applied thickly; oats on one demesne were sown at 6–8 bushels to the acre rather than the 4 bushels which was normal in most of lowland England: the purpose was to smother the weeds. The ploughs were pulled by horses, which worked more quickly and efficiently than oxen. These methods were designed to raise the productivity of the land as much as possible in a region where towns such as Norwich and Yarmouth generated a high demand for foodstuffs, and there were many rural consumers. The demesne managers achieved the highest level of production of grain per acre recorded in medieval England, in good years climbing above 20 bushels per acre.

Most lords away from the agricultural hothouse of north-east Norfolk were content to leave a half or a third of the land to lie fallow, to plough the land with slow ox teams only once or twice before sowing, to sow only 2 to 4 bushels per acre, and to harvest between 8 and 16 bushels from each acre. Therefore their crops achieved only a three or fourfold increase over the seed sown. They were not betraying conservative attitudes in following this agricultural system – it was well suited to the conditions, and gave them acceptable returns.

It has been said that the level of investment in buildings, equipment and other assets on the large estates was often low, with only 5 per cent or less of income being spent in this way. The productivity of the demesnes' arable seems generally unimpressive. Even the profitable sheep was so small and ill-fed that its fleece often weighed little more than a pound and a half. For comparison, modern grain cultivation achieves a yield ratio of twenty-five times the seed, and a modern sheep's fleece weighs 4–6 pounds. The great lords could be seen as rather complacent because of the scale of their resources, like the successive bishops of Winchester whose estate contained more than forty manors with demesnes with a total of 10,000 to 14,000 acres sown each year (see Map 8 above, p. 117). Such lords did not need to be so concerned about the productivity of the land per acre, and were slow to learn from better practices in other regions or on other estates. Also, they gained much of their revenues from rent, and indeed a proportion of the labour supply was obtained as labour services of peasants.

We ought not to be censorious and over-critical in making judgements about medieval demesnes. It is not appropriate to compare their yields with those of the twenty-first century, because modern farmers have the benefit of chemical fertilizers, machinery and veterinary science. The manorial managers had limited opportunities to invest, given the level of technology, and in their society great benefits flowed from the status and patronage associated with high expenditure on entertainment and high living. Rather than judging them by modern standards, we should appreciate the way in which they managed their affairs in difficult circumstances. It was, for example, an impressive achievement for the demesnes of Norfolk to produce yields around 1300 which are comparable with the performance of farmers in the same county in the eighteenth century.

Demesne managers were capable of innovations in their farming. Monastic lords who were active around 1300, such as Henry of Eastry of the cathedral priory of Christ Church Canterbury, or John of Laund of Bolton Priory in Yorkshire, have enjoyed a reputation as improvers akin to that of Coke of Norfolk in the agricultural revolution of the eighteenth century. Modern historians have applied the term 'high farming' to the great estates of the late thirteenth century, again borrowing an idea from recent agricultural history. The estates under their energetic lords were administered in more effective ways, and they reacted to the stimulus of the market, as demand for produce of all kinds increased and pushed up prices.

England had the most agriculturally minded aristocracy in Europe, who were prepared to innovate. Among their triumphs of administrative ingenuity was the second phase of manorial accounts which appears from the 1270s. Earlier accounts tend to be very formal records compiled centrally for all of the manors of an estate, but the 1270s saw some decentralization, in which the reeve gained more responsibilities but also more freedom of action than before. The accounting officials in the late thirteenth century were calculating profit (*proficuum*), which included not just the gains that the lord made in cash, but also valued the goods that were sent to the household. They understood the concept of productive investment, as they regarded the cost of building a barn or spreading marl on the fields as expenditure contributing to the profitability of the manor. There were different methods of calculating profit, but at this time the officials were anxious to know if agricultural activity was making adequate returns. Any manager examining long-term profitability found his task complicated by the fluctuations from year to year as yields and prices rose and fell with changes in the weather. The fellows of Merton College, Oxford, for example, found that their manor of Ibstone in Buckinghamshire returned no profit in 1299–1300, but in the following accounting year made about £8. It was difficult in these circumstances to make long-term plans, or even to decide that direct management was the most profitable method of running the estate, but we must appreciate their efforts to make rational calculations.

The managers knew of good practices, and these methods spread from estate to estate. Often they were adopted in particular regions, where they were appropriate to specific social and economic circumstances, like the package of intensive methods that developed in northeast Norfolk. These practices were not confined to Norfolk. Increased acreages of legumes, mainly for fodder, were grown in many regions. Horses were used for ploughing in Kent, the Chiltern Hills and south Hampshire, while mixed teams with both horses and oxen were adopted by some manors in south-east England and the east midlands. The trend toward the use of horse power had begun in the twelfth century and gathered pace in the thirteenth; it had a universal impact on transport, as carts pulled by horses replaced ox wains. Horses and carts carried goods by road more quickly, and therefore could cover greater distances, which was especially useful for travelling to market. As plough animals the horses also gave more speed, so that while an ox team could plough only a half-acre in a day, a mixed team could plough a full acre. While a plough team of oxen often contained eight animals, a horse team consisted of six at most, and often four or even two, which compensated for the higher cost of feeding the horses with oats: oxen usually managed on grass. Particular types of plough were appropriate for the different draught animals, so horse teams tended to haul wheeled ploughs, while ox teams or mixed teams pulled swing ploughs or ploughs with a 'foot' and no wheels.

Demesnes participated in the expansion of cultivation by ploughing up pasture and clearing woods, and by draining areas of marsh and fen.

The work often involved adding a few acres to an existing demesne, but estates could carry out reclamation on a large scale. The bishop of Winchester, for example, spent £44 in two years in 1251–3 on an assart near Downton in Wiltshire. More than two miles of ditches were dug around the new enclosure, and at least 500 man days were devoted to spreading marl to improve the newly cleared land. Such additions to the arable could contribute to the productivity of land in the short term, as new ploughing of pasture released nutrients for the benefit of grain crops, as has been observed on another Winchester manor, at Rimpton in Somerset. In the long term, of course, reducing the amount of grazing might not be good for productivity, as there would be less manure for the arable. A reclamation project was carried out in the early thirteenth century by the monks of Glastonbury Abbey in the Somerset Levels around the villages of Chedzoy and Westonzoyland. The scheme to build dykes called the Aller Wall and the Lake Wall, and to divert the courses of the Rivers Parrett and Cary, reveals remarkable surveying and constructional skills and an audacious ability to conceive of transforming the landscape over many thousands of acres. One of the main results of the drainage scheme was not to extend cultivation, but to raise the quality of grassland, allowing meadows with abundant hay crops to replace rather soggy marshland that was only available for grazing in the summer. (Plate 9) Any means of increasing the supply of fodder aided the whole farming system. We also find lords cropping their woods more efficiently, by extending the coppices from which fuel could be cut on a rotation, for the benefit of their own household supplies, and for sale to local peasants and to industry and towns. Woods do not represent land kept in its natural and unproductive state: on the contrary, they provided valuable grazing, timber, fuel and raw materials for crafts.

The demesnes' main contribution to technology lay in the management of resources rather than in new inventions or mechanical devices. They realized that they could maintain and improve yields by finding ways to combine arable and pasture to the advantage of both, through changes in rotation or combinations of crops. *Walter of Henley* advised them to carry out experiments – to show that seed brought in from outside gave better yields, he said, plant a strip with your own seed alongside another strip sown with purchased grain, and observe the results. That spirit of trial and error was practised. An Oxfordshire manor of Merton College, Cuxham, appears to have followed the tedious routine of a three-course rotation, in which winter-sown corn was followed by spring-sown corn and then fallow in repetitive sequence, but in the 1280s quite radical changes were made in the crops on the spring-sown field, with a reduction in the quantity of oats sown; instead more peas and dredge (a mixture of barley and oats) were cultivated.

Agricultural buildings achieved a higher standard in the thirteenth century, with more use of stone foundations and advances in carpentry. The greatest care was taken in building barns which, by providing secure and dry storage, prevented losses to crops after the harvest. The building costs appear on the manorial accounts, and monks sometimes boasted of new barns in their chronicles, but the robust nature of construction is signalled most emphatically to us by the survival of barns, some of them still employed for their original purpose: for example, two barns at the manor of the Knights Templar at Cressing Temple in Essex, which had an exceptionally large demesne of 1,000 acres. The barley barn was built in the 1230s, and the wheat barn in about 1290; the differences in the timber framing and the joints used in the construction show that the techniques of building these large structures was developing during the intervening half-century.

Mills were built at considerable cost for the sake of the revenue that came to the lords either in tolls collected by a miller employed by the lord, or as rents paid by a tenant miller. The number of water mills was already high in 1086, when Domesday records more than 6,000, but many were valued at such modest sums that they must have been small, weakly powered 'horizontal' mills (see pp. 25–6). In the next two centuries these were upgraded as vertical mills, which needed much more investment, both in machinery and in the building of ponds, weirs and leats to provide a sufficient flow of water. As well as improving the performance of existing mills, lords built them on new sites, and in the west midland counties of Gloucester, Warwick and Worcester the number increased from about 500 in 1086 to 800–900 in 1300. If lords in the rest of the country behaved in a similar way, the total of English mills by 1300 probably exceeded 10,000. Some of this increase came from new corn mills constructed on streams which had not previously been harnessed for this purpose. Corn mills driven by wind, and water-powered fulling mills were introduced in the late twelfth century. The fulling mills enabled lords to take some profit from the growing cloth industry, much of it in the countryside, which had developed outside the control of the manor. Windmills proliferated in districts where streams were few and small, or where the flat landscape, notably in eastern England, made the water flow so sluggishly that it gave insufficient power for water mills. These new machines, invented either in the east of England or on the shores of the North Sea, were the product of the daring imagination of craftsmen who raised the machinery on to a post above the ground, and designed sails which would turn the mill but not make the whole structure topple. Lords spent about £10 on building a new windmill, and would have to make regular outlays on repairs, but could expect to gain an annual return of a pound or two. (Plate 7)

Mills contributed to peasant production as they freed for more useful tasks labour which had previously been spent on milling by hand. The peasants resented attempts made to force them to use the lord's mill, and objected to the rate of toll that the miller charged, but nonetheless took their grain to be ground. Lords seem on occasion to have behaved like entrepreneurs in their management of mills: when complaints were voiced that their tenants were not using the manorial mill, the peasants were often not grinding the corn at home, but taking it to the mill of a neighbouring lord which offered lower tolls, less queueing, or a less dishonest miller.

Lords also aided the commercial economy by building bridges. Bolton Priory, for example, spent £90 mostly in the years 1304–8 on Kildwick Bridge across the Aire in Yorkshire, naturally for the convenience of their own carts, but indirectly the whole neighbourhood benefited. All of these changes show that lords were not conservative and hostile to technological innovation, but they cannot be seen as leaders. Such developments as the introduction of horses were taken much further by peasants. And the brilliant carpenters or millwrights who invented the windmill in about 1180 had to wait a long time for the new machine to be taken up on a large scale by lords. The bishop of Ely, whose East Anglian estates were ideal sites for windmills, did not begin to build them in any numbers until the 1230s and 1240s.

The lords were part of a society undergoing economic growth. They participated in that expansion, gaining from such trends as the specialization in crafts, and interacting with others involved in production and marketing. Their great contribution lay in the resources that they could mobilize, and their ability to pay for major projects, though they were often reluctant to commit themselves too heavily. The aristocracy were not the directors and controllers of change, but sometimes joined with enthusiasm, and sometimes held back with caution.

Landlords were faced with dilemmas in the deployment of labour on their demesnes. The manor had grown up by combining the productive capacity of the demesne land with the labour of the tenants. We have already seen that at the time of Domesday manorial structures with a high proportion of land in the hands of peasant tenants gave some lords much more abundant peasant labour services than others. In the east midland counties covered by the Hundred Rolls of 1279, the only general survey of lords' resources in this period that can be compared with Domesday, 13 per cent of manors can be described as large, and were served by numerous customary (servile) tenants owing heavy labour services. These manors must not be ignored, because by virtue of their size they accounted for a high proportion of the English countryside, and they are most likely to have kept records. But most lords held land on a limited scale, and two-thirds of manors were small (with 500 acres or less). These manors tended to have a small proportion of tenant land, and in particular lacked servile tenants and labour services. Even on the larger manors, the labour services would not have supplied all of the needs of the demesne even if they had been demanded in full, and often much of the lord's income from tenants came in the form of cash, not labour service. Around 1300, many lords decided to collect rents, commuting a proportion of the service for cash, and used the money to pay labourers to do the work. Throughout the twelfth and thirteenth centuries lords relied on a group of farm servants (*famuli*) as the core of their labour force. Some of them were tenants, usually of small holdings, who were obliged to work full time in a vestige of slavery, but most were contracted to serve for a year in exchange for a cash wage and an allowance of grain.

The monks of Crowland, for example, in the 1290s employed on their Northamptonshire manor of Wellingborough eight ploughmen (enough to man four ploughs throughout the year), two carters, three shepherds, a dairymaid and cowherd. With the addition of various part-time servants such as a swineherd and tithe collectors for the harvest season, these workers accounted for about a half of the labour needed to cultivate the 300-acre demesne of the manor. Extra occasional wage earners were hired for specialized and skilled work. At Wellingborough in 1292–3, smiths and woodworkers mended the ploughs and carts, and for 6d the piglets were castrated. But in addition workers were hired to carry out routine tasks that might have been performed by tenant labour services – a modest 2s 2d was spent on weeding the corn, and 24s 3d on threshing. On other manors at this time, wages were being paid for mowing hay and harvesting corn. The best estimate is that around 1300 only 8 per cent of tasks on demesnes came from tenant labour.

The demesne managers should have welcomed labour services. The labour owed was directly related to the peaks of demand in the agricultural year. A peasant who owed two days per week through the winter, spring and summer might be expected to do three days per week in August and September when the corn was cut and carried, and additional 'boons' when the whole community was expected to turn out in the harvest field, including older children and servants. Lords were able to harness not just the labour resources of the peasant household, but also its equipment, as some services expected the peasants with middling and larger holdings to plough and cart with their own implements and draught animals.

Labour services, however, were not without their problems for the managers. They were fixed by custom, which made them inflexible. Smallholders often were obliged to work on Mondays, but if bad weather prevented work on that day, the lord lost the work. Sometimes a 'work' was defined as labour for a full day, and sometimes only until noon. There was much ground for dispute about working hours, and other conditions such as the quantity and quality of the food to which workers were entitled when they attended a 'boon'. The feasts provided on these occasions had been established by custom at quite a generous level, and at a 'meat' boon the workers would consume large loaves, meat and ale. The accountants would sometimes find that the food and drink cost more than the wages of hired workers, and questioned the benefit of enforcing the service. The main problem lay with the compulsion by which the work was obtained.

The workers approached their task without enthusiasm, especially when by the mid-thirteenth century they were well aware of the alternative of commutation of service. Working on urgent seasonal tasks, such as haymaking or harvest, would be especially resented because these interrupted the completion of the same job on the peasants' own land. There would be problems of absenteeism, even of co-ordinated boycotts, and when the workers attended, as they normally did, they did not work as carefully and efficiently as the lord would have wished. At the haymaking at Wisbech in Cambridgeshire in the mid-fourteenth century, the productivity of tenants doing their services can be compared directly with that of hired workers. An average day's labour service produced one-third of a cartload of hay, while a wage earner doing the same task yielded a half-cartload. More precisely, hired labour was 36 per cent more efficient. Presumably this discrepancy, though its extent may have varied in time and place, was found throughout the country, and the demesne managers must have been aware of the problem. This helped them to decide that in some circumstances it was more profitable to let the tenants pay their commutation money – to 'sell' their works, to use the language of the accounts – and to use wage earners instead. This decision was made in the light of the knowledge that the commutation money, fixed before the thirteenth-century inflation, did not cover the full cost of the hired workers.

Demesnes were run on rational lines, and were not trapped in a mindless routine. Managers made investments and adopted new methods in the interest of greater profits. But we must beware of exaggerating the achievements of agriculture under the control of lords. The Cistercian order of monks seems to represent a special case. They appear as a radical force sweeping with a new broom through the orthodox world of estates and manors. The monasteries were founded mostly in the early to mid-twelfth century, inspired by an austere conception of religious contemplation set apart from the distractions of the world. They sought out sites remote from existing settlements, and rejected endowment with parish churches which provided other orders with an income from glebe land and tithes. Their desire for a self-contained religious life led them not just to choose isolated and remote sites for their monasteries, but also to found on their estates granges which consisted of blocks of land under the monks' exclusive ownership, and which were separated from the common fields of villages. They selected sites for their granges on moors, marshes and woods, which often involved them in enclosing, clearing and draining land and earned them an enduring reputation as agricultural improvers. If they acquired land on the edge of a village's territory, they would set about extending it, consolidating scattered parcels by buying up land or by making exchanges, and even arranging for any peasants who lived on the land to move elsewhere. These processes took some time, and it was not until the middle of the thirteenth century that the Cistercians (together with orders with similar ideals, such as the Gilbertines and Premonstratensians, together with some Augustinian houses) had developed their grange system fully (see Map 8 above, p. 117). By 1300, confining the calculation to the Cistercians, there were almost a hundred houses in Britain, many of which had provided themselves with between ten and twenty granges.

The granges resembled modern farms, and have been represented as agricultural enterprises ahead of their time. With their compact group of buildings on a new site, surrounded by land free from the restraints and complications of communal farming, the 'grangers' who managed them could use their compact group of fields as they and the central monastic adminstration wished, ignoring conventional crop rotation, and specializing if appropriate. The size of the granges, often about 300–400 acres, was chosen for reasons of efficiency. In the early days the labour force consisted of lay brothers (*conversi*) – laymen who had chosen to live a religious life, but without becoming fully-fledged monks – and later hired workers, full-time farm servants and day labourers. No labour services were available, because the grange often had no peasant tenants attached to it. Setting up the grange involved much investment in buildings, enclosures and land clearance. Sometimes industries such as tanning were sited on the granges. The whole unit of production was integrated into the market, as the land was often purchased, the labour hired, and the produce, such as the famous Cistercian wool, was sold. The Cistercians rarely founded towns on their lands, as this would not accord with their ideal of isolation, but they acquired houses in urban centres such as York where wool could be stored and sales negotiated. They acted as middlemen in the wool trade, buying up fleeces from their neighbours and putting them up for sale with their own produce.

The granges' reputation for modernity is supported by the belief that Cistercians stood apart from feudal society, because their ideas about the religious life and the world prevented them from receiving services, or even tithes, and they were exempted from the usual obligations to do military service for their lands, or to pay tithes. But on closer inspection the order does not seem so distant from the rest of medieval society. Their estate management was intimately bound up with lordship. They held much land outside their granges, from which they collected rents, and where they held courts for their tenants in much the same style as other lords. The lay brothers bear a close resemblance to types of servile workers, and the institution developed in the early twelfth century as a replacement for slavery, like the tenants who acted as full-time farm servants on conventional demesnes. Indeed, the *conversi* recognized the anomaly of their position, resented the inadequacy of their quasi-religious status as a reward for their hard work, and rebelled. Their ambiguous situation was so difficult to sustain that the *conversi* were phased out in the thirteenth and fourteenth centuries.

The Cistercians represented themselves as heroic settlers in 'deserts', where they transformed unproductive land. But when their houses were founded in really bleak places, they persuaded their patrons to move them to more hospitable sites. A group of monks established at Barnoldswick in the Pennines in 1147 survived five years of hunger and cold before migrating to a fertile valley at Kirkstall near Leeds. Similarly most granges were not carved out of windswept moors, but were assembled out of parcels of already cultivated land near existing settlements. The exploitation of a compact block of land was by no means confined to the Cistercians, as many demesnes consisted of fields separated from the common fields of the village. On the hills Cistercian vaccaries and bercaries resembled those belonging to other lords, both churchmen and laity. Demesnes of conventional manors, as we have seen, could specialize in husbandry systems, such as sheep and corn, or they might concentrate on particular crops, such as barley in East Anglia. Demesnes and granges of all kinds produced partly for consumption in the household, and partly for sale. The Cistercians were not uniquely wedded to the market, except that their location in northern and western hills naturally encouraged their involvement in the wool trade. They certainly developed a commercial relationship with overseas merchants, judging from the lists of those selling wool to Italians in 1294, which included two-thirds of the Cistercian houses in England. This was not always a very advantageous arrangement for the monasteries, as the merchants from the great financial centres of Lucca and Florence were lending them money and contracting to take the wool in the future for fixed prices which no doubt benefited the buyers in a rising market. The granges do not seem to have been technically more sophisticated than other demesnes. In short, the Cistercians' 'progressive' farming and their supposed separation from feudal society seems to have developed as a modern myth, as indeed has the belief that monks in general were unusually inventive and efficient.

We can appreciate the quality of aristocratic management of agriculture without accepting the excessive adulation sometimes accorded to those involved in 'high farming' or to the Cistercian order. The achievement of aristocratic direct management has to be kept in perspective. Demesnes in general occupied a great deal of land in the midlands, south and east, but still only a third of the land in some regions, and a fifth in others. In the south-west and the north-west of England, and throughout Scotland, demesnes could be very small, or even non-existent. Many English lords leased out their demesnes, and either failed to adopt direct management, or abandoned it before the end of the thirteenth century. Neither should we exaggerate the commitment of estates to the sale of produce. We can find large scattered estates, like those of the bishopric of Winchester or the earldom of Cornwall, where the most convenient policy was to sell valuable crops like wheat, and indeed between half and three-quarters of wheat went on the market. On others, even in *c.*1300, where the manors were grouped around a monastery, such as Norwich or Durham Priories, most of the wheat went for consumption by the monks, their servants and their guests (see Map 8 above, p. 117).

iii. *Lords and peasants*

Direct production on demesnes after *c.*1200 attracts attention because it was new, because it shows lords responding to wider economic changes, and because it distinguishes the English aristocrats from those of continental Europe. But lords continued to gain most of their income from rents. Even at the peak of 'high farming' at the end of the thirteenth century, English estates striving to maintain and increase their demesne profits were deriving 50 or 60 per cent of their income from rents of various kinds. In Scotland, where there is little evidence for direct management of demesnes, rents were even more prominent. In the south and east of Scotland, tenants' rents in cash yielded a high proportion of lords' revenues, and in the north and west where the great 'multiple' estates dominated the countryside, peasants paid traditional rents in kind, which were sometimes commuted for cash, known as cain and conveth. At Strathearn in *c.*1200, tenants contributed payments in grain, malt, cheese, fowls and game.

Landlords could raise more revenue by increasing the number of tenants, or by taking more from them in cash rather than in kind or labour, or they could squeeze more from each peasant household. None of these routes to gaining higher rent was straightforward, and every policy decision encountered obstacles, but lords were helped by the growth in population and the expansion of the market which made land a valuable asset. An obvious means of creating new holdings was to clear woodland or waste. Land-hungry peasants would be eager to occupy new land. Lords did not, however, control large areas of such underdeveloped land if their estates lay in districts where the arable area was already extensive. Loss of woodland and pasture endangered the livelihood of the existing population, even in areas with large areas of uncultivated land, so a lord who encouraged colonization of the wastes might find himself facing vociferous opposition, and even if he succeeded would risk impoverishing, and therefore reducing the rent-paying potential of, tenants already established. The tenants of new land were not always major sources of income, as the normal custom was to grant assarts on free tenure for modest cash rents. Another way of expanding tenant numbers, subdividing holdings, could result in a numerous but poor body of tenants who could not pay as much as those with large holdings, and would not be able to bring ploughs and carts to their labour services as they could not afford to buy and maintain implements, or own oxen and horses. Land could be taken from the demesne for peasant holdings, but surely the land gave a higher return under direct management? The calculation of advantage was not always easy, especially in the long term. Changing the form in which rent was paid, or raising its level, would again risk peasant resistance. Free tenants might take the lord to the king's court, and those governed by the customary law of the manor could cause trouble in the lord's court, or in some circumstances appeal for protection to royal justice.

The lords steered round these restrictions and made substantial increases in rents. In the twelfth century the bulk of lords' income came from rent because the demesnes were often leased to farmers. In addition, some lords shifted the balance between demesne land and tenant land by granting out parcels of demesne land to tenants for cash rents on hereditary tenures. At the same time, partly because of the reduction in the demesne area, but mainly in view of the growing opportunities to sell produce, holdings that owed labour services were converted to paying money rents. Lists of tenants sometimes divide tenants into those owing works (*ad opus*) and those paying rents (*ad censum*). Both developments are recorded in a survey of Blockley in Gloucestershire in about 1166, when a tenant called Girard held 12 acres formerly in the demesne for 2s and six labour services, and a cotland (a smallholding attached to a cottage) which had previously done labour services was rented for 18d.

In both the twelfth and thirteenth centuries lords took advantage of the expansion in cultivation by taking rents from the newly cleared or drained land. In some cases the lord may well have caught up with settlers after they had taken over the new land, but some clearance ventures were planned and encouraged by lords. A typical group of such tenants was listed by the canons of St Paul's Cathedral at their manor of Navestock in Essex in 1222 under the heading of 'New assarts'. Over the previous forty years the holdings of twenty-five tenants had been established, most of them smallholdings – an acre, a half-acre, a curtilage and so on. The tenants paid the usual moderate cash rents – in this case at an annual rate of 6d per acre, but these gave a total of 12s 10d per annum, a useful addition to the value of the manor which yielded £7 7s 1d for its lord in 1181.

Most manors added to the number of free tenants paying cash rents in the twelfth and thirteenth centuries, not all of them holding newly cleared land. One group consisted of servants and clients of the lords who were granted the land as rewards, but their rents brought in modest sums of money. The main benefit for lords came from additions to the numbers of customary tenants who owed heavy burdens of labour service and cash payments. The well-established standard units of land holding, were called virgates or yardlands in southern England, bovates or oxgangs in the north, and in parts of Scotland. Lords often agreed to their subdivision, so that by the late thirteenth century many customary tenants held half- or quarter-yardlands, or half-oxgangs, which usually produced for the lord more than half or a quarter of the rents owed by a full unit. Lords were reluctant to allow excessive subdivision lest the rents and services attached to the original holdings be forgotten, and the tenants be impoverished. No such inhibitions seem to have applied in parts of East Anglia, where the original 'tenements' were highly fragmented as a result of partible inheritance, a lively land market and weaker control by lords. Landlords in that region may even have favoured the splitting of holdings into very small acreages: at Gressenhall in Norfolk, a manor of the Stuteville family, it was believed in 1287 that a steward called Crowe some time before 1259 had changed the custom from inheritance by the eldest son to division among all sons 'because he wished to have more tenants'.

Lords faced a serious problem in their relations with tenants around 1200. Their most privileged tenants, the tenants in fee, had become virtually independent, helped by the protection of the royal courts. The king's common law was being extended to all free tenants, preventing lords gaining any more income from them. But where could the line be drawn between the free and unfree? Before about 1180 the distinction had been imprecise, and a tenant could be described as 'more free' than another. A clear distinction was now essential, so that the royal courts could decide who fell within their jurisdiction, and so that lords could be reassured that there were to be limits on the king's encroachment on their powers. The lawyers in the royal courts developed means of testing the legal status of individuals. If a tenant owed the heavy labour services known as week-work, or paid marriage fines (merchet), or was liable to serve as reeve, then the individuals and their families were judged to be of villein or servile status. Words changed their meaning, so that 'villein', which had once described a villager with a middling or larger holding of land, came to mean an unfree tenant, holding by a servile tenure – in villeinage. A customary tenant, that is someone holding land under the custom of the manor, which was enforced through the lord's court, was excluded from the common law of the royal courts, and therefore categorized as servile in status. The term 'neif', in Latin *nativus*, had meant someone born into servility, and this stigma was now being attached to many of those who held by customary or villein tenure. It was still possible for a personally free individual to hold land in villeinage, but increasingly legal status was being equated with the tenure of land.

Take for example the case of William, son of Henry of Pilton in Rutland, who complained to the king's court in 1224 that he had been deprived of his free holding by Bartholomew, son of Eustace. He was bringing an action under the assize of novel disseisin, as free tenants had been doing for more than forty years. Bartholomew responded with a claim that William was a villein, and he had no right to appear before the royal court. The case had been heard before, in the reign of King John (1199–1216); reference back to the earlier hearing showed that William owed heavy labour services and that neither his daughter nor son could marry without his lord's permission. This proved that William was unfree, and that he would have to take his case before the court of his lord, Bartholomew, son of Eustace, where he may not have been heard with much sympathy.

There were distinct advantages in establishing the villein status of tenants. Certainly it confirmed the labour services which were becoming so valuable to lords when they were introducing direct management of demesnes. But they were always conscious of the financial benefits from villein tenants. The many restrictions on the unfree, such as those controlling their marriage and movement from the manor, became opportunities to levy fines in money. The lord would happily give permission, or lift a restriction, in exchange for a few shillings. The tenants in villeinage, because they were not 'free men', were not subject to the provision in Magna Carta of 1215 that new tenants should pay only a 'reasonable' relief. Free tenants would therefore pay one year's rent, usually no more than a few shillings, but when a villein wished to take over a holding, including when he inherited after the death of his father or mother, the lord demanded an entry fine or *gersuma*. On some manors this became fixed by custom – perhaps at a mark or half-mark (13s 4d or 6s 8d) – but most lords resisted any move towards such a restriction, and levied fines that varied with the demand for land, the size and quality of the holding, and the capacity of the new tenant to raise the money. Entry fines around 1300 commonly rose to three times the annual rent of the holding. A yardland of about 30 acres of arable could command a fine of £3.

The acute shortage of land made it possible for lords to make these demands, and the profits that could be made from the sale of agricultural produce enabled the peasant to pay, or at least to borrow the money and eventually pay it back. Servile tenants were also expected to contribute to collective payments, notably tallage or aid, which often amounted to £5 or £10 on a large manor, to which the more substantial tenants in villeinage contributed 2 or 3s each. The recognition fine, again a collective sum of a few pounds, was demanded from servile tenants when a new lord took over an estate. Heriots, or death duties, were often owed by free tenants, but in the north-west midlands, where rents and services were not usually very onerous, lords compensated themselves by demanding from customary tenants not the usual heriot of the 'best beast' but a number of animals, pots and pans, beehives and other goods.

Powers of private justice were given a new lease of life in the thirteenth century. The manorial courts administered the customs under which serfs lived, and many of the dues such as marriage fines and entry fines were collected through the court. In addition, the courts dealt with matters of tenancy and services, such as failure to do labour services or to maintain the buildings on the holding. Trespass on the demesne land, whereby tenants pastured their animals on the lord's pasture, or even on his crops, was punished. The courts also gave the tenants an opportunity to settle disputes by hearing small claims for debts, trespasses and detention of chattels: if one peasant bought a cow from another and failed to pay the agreed price, or a straying animal trampled the plants in another's garden, or if an axe was borrowed but not returned, the court would help the injured party to recover the money, goods or compensation for damages. The courts provided a forum for community matters to be discussed – by-laws might be issued relating to the protection of grain in the harvest period, or to regulate the grazing of animals on the commons. The contribution that the court made to good order in the community came at a price, as each stage in the inter-peasant lawsuits or each breach of the by-laws resulted in the lord collecting a few pence in amercements (a money payment in order to gain the lord's mercy). In a single court, dozens of amercements, each of 2d, 3d, 4d or 6d, accumulated to a few shillings, and as the courts were held regularly through the year, sometimes every three weeks, and rarely with an interval of more than three months, the profits of justice amounted to a few pounds over the whole year. In lowland England the 'perquisites of the courts' could amount to a tenth of the income of an estate, but in the Welsh marches, where lords enjoyed much wider powers of justice and could use the courts to levy substantial collective fines, lords were gaining as much as a third of their revenues from this source.

From a lord's point of view the dues arising from servile tenants or from profits of justice had a special value because they were variable and not supervised by any other authority. Lords could imagine themselves as independent rulers, boasting that they could tallage their tenants 'high and low, at will', that is they could demand as much payment, and as often, as they wished. In practice they received the same sum annually, so the rhetoric was not applied. The state exercised some restraint on lords, for example in reviewing their franchises and in providing channels for tenants to appeal against injustice. Some payments, like entry fines, reflected the growth in land values and the scarcity of land.

A typical tenant of a yardland on a large church estate in the early thirteenth century, Jordan de Legh of Street in Somerset, a manor of Glastonbury Abbey, had his obligations recorded in 1241. Jordan was expected to pay a cash rent of 2s 6d, together with 'lardersilver' of 14d, on 11 November, when the lord could claim that he needed help with stocking his larder with salt meat for the winter. He also paid 1d for 'hurtpenny' (called Peter's pence elsewhere – a contribution supposedly for a tax to the pope, though in practice part went to the lord) and 2 bushels of wheat for churchscot (payment originally to the local church). But his main obligation was to work for three days each week through the year, with extra days in the harvest, making an annual total of 170 days, that is two-thirds of the working days in the year. These customary obligations were written into a formal document kept by the abbey, and etched on the memories of the peasants, and any move by the lord to increase them would breach custom and provoke a storm of protest that even the monks would have found uncomfortable. However, the lord could decide to take part of the labour service in cash, and by the end of the thirteenth century many tenants of Jordan's type would be paying 10s rent, and working on the demesne for 100 days or less. In general, tenants seem to have preferred to pay cash rather than do labour services.

Some lords would arrange for some of the holdings that owed labour services to pay cash only. For example, at King's Ripton in Huntingdonshire the lord of the manor, Ramsey Abbey, increased the number of holdings carrying a rent entirely in cash from three to nine between 1250 and 1275, while still requiring labour services from fourteen others. Rents in kind were also converted into cash payments. These figured especially prominently in the dues owed by peasants in north Wales. In the commote of Ardudwy in Merioneth, for example, 200 bond tenants were expected to do only one day's labour service each per annum, but were obliged to pay cattle, pigs, milk and flour, and to entertain the prince's men when they visited the district. But in the decades before the English conquest in 1282, many of these dues were rendered in money – the rent in animals, for example, was valued at £10 18s and paid in cash.

Ways were found to increase tenants' obligations, not just to move from one mode of payment to another. Occasionally lords could establish new villein holdings. The manor of Cuxham in Oxfordshire was undersupplied with villein half-yardlands, which were the main source of rents and labour services. The number was more than doubled from six to thirteen between 1276 and 1293, by converting cottage holdings with additional acres from the demesne. Lords could find ways of taxing activities not covered by the customary rules. In the thirteenth century peasants were anxious to sublet land, which enabled lessors to raise money or reduce the size of a holding that was becoming burdensome, and allowed lessees to add to their acreage. Lords were ambiguous in their attitudes to subletting, as it threatened the unity of the holding and contributed to the remoteness of the lord from those actually working the land. On the other hand they saw in this a source of profit, and so some lords insisted that sublettings, especially those for more than a year or two, be reported to the court and be subject to fines.

Another route to extra profit for lords came from the conversion of both free and customary holdings into leasehold, a form of tenure in which a contract was made between lord and tenant which fixed the rent in relation to the market for land. This could be used when lords bought up freeholdings, which produced low rents, and then let them to new tenants on short terms. This was a policy pursued on the estates of the Berkeley family on the rich valley land between Bristol and Gloucester. The land that the lords recovered was rented out for 9d per acre, even 20d per acre, reflecting local demand for fertile land, but acquiring the holding was expensive for the lord. On the nearby estate of Gloucester Abbey villein tenants would offer substantial lump sums – £6, £8, even £16 13s 4d for their tenures to be converted from customary tenure to leasehold. William the reeve of Coln Roger, for example, with Agnes his wife, was able by an agreement of 1289 to hold his half-yardland for 8s per annum, and be exempt from all labour services. Leasehold made its greatest advances in Cornwall, where 'conventionary' tenure gave tenants a seven-year term. The cash rents were not very burdensome, but each renewal was agreed with a large fine, payment of which was spread over the first six years of the term, and therefore became an extra rent. On the largest estate in the county, that of the earls (later dukes) of Cornwall, conventionary tenure was introduced in the 1280s and became widespread by the 1330s. Parcels of demesne were also leased out in growing quantities around 1300 as lords became more doubtful about the profits they were gaining from direct management.

There were obvious advantages for lords in extending leasehold, so why did they not lease land on a larger scale? The answer must be that leasing was often seen as a short-term measure, and serfdom represented a fundamental institution, at the very centre of their way of life.

Lords may have had a strong regard for custom and their ancient rights over their peasants, but their outlook was not entirely conservative and inflexible. They introduced ways of maintaining control through written records. Admittedly the surveys that church landlords in particular compiled seem very formal: each tenant was named, the holding described, and the tenant's services and rents listed in considerable detail. These were useful for auditors checking accounts, and could be consulted in the event of tenants querying their duties. They carried such authority that the title of 'Domesday' was sometimes given to them. But gathering the information was troublesome, and the circumstances that they described quickly changed. The matters that might be disputed with tenants, such as the customs governing the transfer of holdings, were not usually recorded in surveys.

Much more effective were the court rolls, which estates of all kinds, including those of knights and gentry, were writing and preserving in the last quarter of the thirteenth century. Instead of making a formal list of tenants at one point in time, the court roll recorded each change of tenant. Settlements of disputes, declarations of customs and statements of inheritances and transfers of land provided precedents, and lords and peasants alike respected the rolls as evidence. Peasants had some regard for the court and its deliberations, because they participated as jurors and pledges, and their interests were in some ways served by its judgments. They would give money to have items written into the court rolls – for example, John and Alice Tonestal of Weedon Bec in Northamptonshire in 1296 paid 5s to occupy 2 acres jointly, and for the new tenancy to be 'enrolled' as a permanent record of the arrangement. The procedures of the courts were going through continuous development partly under the influence of the common law in the royal courts, but also because lords and their officials were anxious to make their courts efficient. Around 1300, greater use was being made of juries for settling disputes, which was a more decisive and speedy way of arriving at judgments than depending on the deliberations of the whole court. The courts compelled tenants to attend, but new procedures were also designed to attract business. The joint tenancy of husbands and wives, as in the Weedon case mentioned above, was wanted by peasants. It made no difference to the lord – he would gain his rents and services whether or not the land was held jointly – but agreeing to the change yielded an extra 5s.

iv. *Lords and towns*

Lords took a number of initiatives in order to profit from the growth in trade: they promoted new towns, founded markets and fairs, and invested in urban property. A few new towns founded by lords are recorded in Domesday Book, but their numbers increased dramatically in the succeeding two centuries. A common procedure was to create a borough by conferring on the tenants the privileges of burgesses, which gave them the right to hold a plot of land (usually less than a half-acre) for a fixed money rent without any labour services or servile dues. They were able to sell, sublet or mortgage their land, and could trade in the borough market without paying tolls. Some boroughs were formed by attaching new privileges to an old settlement, some were entirely new towns, laid out on greenfield sites and depending on migrants to inhabit the plots. In England the hundred or so boroughs recorded in 1086 had increased to 218 by 1200, and to more than 500 by 1300. The king had founded the majority of boroughs before 1086, and another seventy in the next two centuries. Between 1086 and 1300, church landlords accounted for ninety-five, a little more than their fair share in view of the proportion of land that they held, while lay lords (mostly the higher ranks) founded about 170. Boroughs appeared for the first time in Wales in the late eleventh century, but they then proliferated quite quickly, with twenty-eight recorded between 1070 and 1200, and another fifty-five in the thirteenth century. In Scotland royal burgh foundations dominated, with thirty in the twelfth century, and eleven created by church and lay lords. In the thirteenth century ten of the nineteen new burghs were non-royal (see Map 9 below, p. 189).

The obvious advantage to an estate from a borough or burgh foundation lay in the rents paid by the burgesses, which would often yield £4 even from a small place with eighty burgage plots paying a shilling each. But with the market tolls, profits of the borough court, and tolls from a mill the profit could easily rise to £10. The area of land on which the borough stood would have been worth no more than £1 if it was still in agricultural use. Lords could always hope for a booming success and the growth of a large town like King's Lynn, originally Bishop's Lynn from its founders, the bishops of Norwich. After shadowy beginnings around 1100, Lynn had at least 800 inhabitants by 1167, and by 1300 it ranked twelfth among all English towns, and its judicial profits alone brought the bishops £40 per annum. Towns were often founded in stages, as at Ludlow in Shropshire where five or six new planned extensions and suburbs were added to the initial foundation of about 1090 adjoining the castle. In a number of towns there would in effect be twin new towns, as a borough foundation by one lord would encourage a neighbour to foster urban development nearby – Chelmsford in Essex, for example, founded by the bishop of London in 1200, stimulated the growth of a suburb on the other side of the bridge over the River Chelmer at Moulsham, a manor of Westminster Abbey. Durham developed as a complex of four or five small adjacent boroughs founded at different times by two lords, the bishop and the priory.

Lords calculated that the growth of a town would add to the prosperity of their nearby rural manors by giving the peasants easy access to a market and allowing them to pay money rents. David, earl of Huntingdon on his Scottish estates achieved a notable success with the promotion of Dundee, but also founded a burgh next to his castle of Inverurie which brought an opportunity for exchange to the remote and thinly populated lordship of Garioch. A town also conferred a sense of importance on its lord. A castle or Benedictine monastery would have seemed incomplete without a town outside its gates, and a 'city' was an essential setting for a cathedral – a bishop's main church and throne were expected to be located in an urban place. Both Lichfield (Staffordshire) and Wells (Somerset) lost their standing as the seats of bishops because they were too rural, and had to be founded in the twelfth century as new towns in order to reclaim their old position against rivals at Coventry and Bath.

Every borough had a market and most were granted at least one fair, but many lords by acquiring a market charter from the crown founded these privileged occasions for trade in villages. Perhaps they hoped that the market would attract a permanent population of traders and the settlement would become a town. Some achieved this without acquiring borough status, such as Stowmarket in Suffolk. In most cases the place remained a village, and the lords had to be content to receive the tolls from the market, and presumably to enhance the prosperity of their rural estates. More than 1,000 market charters were issued in the thirteenth century, mostly to lords of all kinds promoting either boroughs or centres of commerce in villages.

In larger towns lords owned urban property, either exploiting the houses which had been attached to rural estates since pre-Conquest times, or buying houses as an investment. These were sometimes intended as bases, perhaps for warehouses and accommodation for officials trading on behalf of the lord; this explains, for example, why the bishop of Moray (in the north of Scotland) bought a house in the wool-exporting town of Berwick-on-Tweed. Lords also acquired houses which could be rented out profitably to merchants and artisans, and we can find lords like Coventry Priory, which already held much of the town at its gates, buying yet more property in the thirteenth century. New institutions founded after 1200, such as hospitals, chantries and colleges, were often located in towns, and depended for a high proportion of their income on urban property. For most lords, their rent from towns was no more than a useful supplement to their main income from rural manors. Urban revenues were appreciated because when agricultural profits were stagnating, expanding towns provided avenues for investment and profit. This was especially true of lords in the poorer regions. The number of boroughs in upland districts with low populations and restricted agricultural opportunities, such as north Devon, the Welsh marches, Staffordshire and south-west Scotland, reflects their founders' desire for a few more pounds of income. Presumably the concentration of fulling mills in western England and Wales can be explained in the same way.

v. *Knights and gentry*

To what extent did the lesser aristocracy, the knights and gentry, participate in economic growth in the same way as the bishops, abbots, earls and barons who have been our main focus of attention so far? They were

numerous, with perhaps 10,000 families in England in 1300, and at that
time they varied in wealth from rich knights on the verge of the baron-
age holding a half-dozen manors which yielded more than £100 per
annum, to freemen (they might be called franklins) with a single manor
or scattered pieces of land valued at £5 annually (see Map 8 above,
p. 117). Together, they held more land than the magnates, so that the
management of their estates is of great importance in the economy as a
whole. They were vulnerable to sudden changes in prices, bad harvests
and political upheavals, as their finances were fragile at the best of times.
Their manors often lacked servile tenants and customary labour services,
so rents tended to come from free tenants who paid fixed sums in cash,
which lost value in the inflation. Many small manors had a high proportion of their land in demesne, which allowed the lord to profit
from the sale of produce, but demesnes with less than 200 acres of arable
could not make a very large profit if most of their surplus grain was being
delivered to the household for consumption by the lord's family and
servants.

Another trap for the small landowner lay in the purchase of goods and
services, which also rose in price in the inflation. The gentry felt insecure
about their status as they aspired to be aristocrats on a modest income,
and so felt social pressure to consume at a high level, or even to increase
their expenditure. For example, in the counties north and east of
London, and in the north-western midlands, the standing of lesser lords
depended on surrounding their houses with moats, which were usually
linked with new building work, in all costing much more than a year's
income. A horse suitable for warfare could be bought for £2–£4 in the
early thirteenth century, but was more likely to cost £8 towards the end
of the century. Small and insecure incomes, the temptation to increase
spending, and family loyalties which persuaded families to provide for
non-inheriting children from meagre landed resources, all tended to pull
gentry families into debt. They could well have developed an optimistic
view of their circumstances after a run of good agricultural years, spent
too much, and then regretted their commitments when the crops yielded
poorly and disease spread among the sheep. They lived on credit at all
times, but a minority fell into serious debt, whether to Jewish moneylenders before the expulsion in 1290, or to wealthier aristocrats. 'In my
urgent need' as troubled small landowners would explain in their charters, they turned to a wealthy monastery or layman, and this 'friend' paid
off their debts, but in exchange would take over the land. Families ended
their days living on handouts from a monastery, having ruined the future
of their family. In 1219 Stephen de Fretwell came to an agreement with
the abbot of Eynsham whereby he surrendered his land (some hundreds

of acres) in the Oxfordshire village of Woodeaton, in exchange for which he and Sarah his wife were assigned a house at a low rent at Eynsham, and a corrody, consisting of a daily allowance of bread, ale, pottage and dishes of food from the monastery kitchen. The abbot would pay his debts in order to recover land in eight villages around Woodeaton which Stephen had surrendered to his creditors as pledges, after which the abbey would keep half of the land, and return the other half to the de Fretwells. Stephen and Sarah were clearly bankrupt (to use a modern term), and this was not a case of decline in old age, as they had daughters of marriageable age, one of whom would have her marriage arranged by the abbot, presumably at a profit. We can only imagine the humiliation of this once-proud aristocrat, who had been forced to move from his manor house to a modest dwelling in the town of Eynsham, specified in the agreement as 30 feet long, in the same street as tradesmen and abbey servants, and depending on food from the abbey.

Only a minority faced ruin, but some more general crisis must lie behind the rapid upheaval in status in the early thirteenth century. In the time of King John about 4,500 people were identified by the title 'knight', but in the following twenty years the title was restricted to a wealthy minority: only about a thousand individuals were dubbed knights by the middle of the thirteenth century, leaving thousands of lesser landowners, most of them holding land in fee, that is for military service, but without a specific title. This change must be related to advancing ideas about chivalry, which identified knights as an elite group with special qualities. It had an economic dimension, because it was expected that knights would have incomes from land of at least £20 per annum, and by the later thirteenth century £40: we know this because the government attempted to insist that all those with such incomes or above should be dubbed knights. Many relatively wealthy landowners preferred to pay the fine: not, we may suspect, because they felt themselves unworthy of the great honour, but because they knew that it would commit them to spending time and money on ceremonies and official duties. Each county's grand jury, for example, consisted of twelve knights, and as some small counties could barely muster a dozen, those who had been dubbed were expected to attend regularly. In time of war the knights would be required to turn out properly equipped with armour and weapons, riding a warhorse, which together could cost £20 in the 1280s and 1290s. They received pay, at a higher rate than other mounted soldiers if they were dubbed knights, but the initial expense was still formidable.

Despite all the difficulties of matching income and expenditure, fear of debt, and the problems of keeping their status, small landowners were given many opportunities in the twelfth and thirteenth centuries. They received grants of land from magnates, and were able to acquire land by purchase. Knights and gentry gained in two ways from the growth of state power, as the protection of the common law confirmed that they were no longer controlled by the magnates, and bigger government gave them employment opportunities as officials and lawyers. Initially the crown granted such offices as that of sheriff to trusted household officials, but during the thirteenth century these influential posts were occupied by the local landowners. At the same time, large numbers of gentry were employed in the direct management of magnate estates, and it became more common for magnates to recruit officials, advisers and supporters, sometimes by means of a written contract, and often with a regular payment of money as an annuity. The sums involved were not very large – but even a few pounds each year was a valuable addition to the £10 or £20 which most gentry received from their lands. Rewarding service with money rather than land has been called 'bastard feudalism', meaning not an illegitimate or disreputable version of feudalism, but a system of clientage resembling feudalism. As the law increased in complexity a legal profession emerged, and recruited many of its practitioners from the gentry. Already by the 1240s a group of sergeants of the Bench can be identified working in the royal courts, and by 1300 the local courts had their groups of professional pleaders, such as the fifteen who worked in the county court of Warwickshire.

Talented and well-connected administrators and lawyers could move between private and public office. Geoffrey Russell, from an obscure gentry family on the estate of Peterborough Abbey, became the abbey's steward in 1250–63, and then moved on to work for Isabella de Fortibus and other magnates. By the late 1270s he had been appointed a royal justice, and also steward of Wallingford on the estate of the earldom of Cornwall. The fees and perquisites of office gave him the resources to acquire land in the vicinity of Peterborough. Russell's contemporary, Sir Geoffrey de Langley, a royal official whose landed base lay in Warwickshire and Gloucestershire, expanded his property by purchases from lesser families suffering from debt. As a result of the failure of gentry families to manage their affairs, land did not flow just from them to the monasteries, but also to other more successful members of the lesser aristocracy. (Plate 6)

Office-holding and its profits gave some knights and gentry useful incomes in cash, but as the purchases of the successful officials show, their ultimate goal was to acquire land. Land provided a stable and enduring investment, and if well managed, could yield a high income. The gentry were committed to direct management of demesnes long before the magnates were converted by the circumstances around 1200. They often held a single demesne and lived nearby, so that leasing the land to farmers would have been unnecessary. Duties to superior lords or the king might take them away for long periods, but their wives could then take over the supervision of agriculture. Such was their interest in management that smaller landowners also became farmers of the manors of the great estates. So when the magnates went over to direct management, they were imitating the knights and gentry, and indeed a constant cross-fertilization between large and small estates continued through the thirteenth century as the new breed of officials brought to the manors of the magnates the experience they had gained on their own lands.

The management style of the small landowners would have differed from that practised on the larger estates. The structure of gentry manors, with their high proportion of land in demesne, forced them to rely less on rents, and put more emphasis on production. With few servile tenants owing labour services, the gentry depended on wage labour. A relatively small manor would need to spend a higher proportion of its income on investment in buildings and equipment. The lord would supervise all of these activities in person – he would practise hands-on management. There was no need to employ officials or keep a large archive of surveys and accounts, which is a loss for us, but probably made for greater efficiency as the lord knew exactly what was happening, and could conduct business orally. This might give the impression that the gentry were behaving like modern entrepreneurs, but there was still a great deal of direct consumption of produce, so the market had a limited influence, and there is not much indication that gentry manors used more advanced techniques than those found on the large estates. We can see a gentry manor at work occasionally, when accounts were kept by a wealthy knight. William de Curzon's sergeant, Hugh, presented his account for the manor of East Carlton in Norfolk in 1274–5. Rents, at £3 10s, were not very important compared with the sale of grain, which brought in £30. The lord derived little profit from his powers of justice, which produced only 2s 6d. The volume of sales was limited by the need to supply the household, which took half of the wheat, a third of the barley, and two-thirds of the oats. Few animals were sold: they were mainly used in the lord's kitchen. Curzon spent about 7 per cent of his receipts on farm buildings and equipment, a higher level of investment than would be found on many larger estates, and much of the labour, in the harvest for example, was hired. But this expenditure did not result in higher productivity, as the grain mostly yielded only two, three or four times the seed sown.

In a key respect, knights and gentry can be identified as innovative in their estate management, in their ability, like the new religious orders, to create new units of landholding. By a combination of land purchase, clearance of new land and exchange, the Segrave family built Caludon near Coventry into a new manor, with a 200-acre demesne, a small park and a few tenants, which gave the family an income of £20 per annum from the sale of produce in the mid-thirteenth century. This construction of new manors was especially characteristic of woodland regions, where gentry were numerous, and the assarting and fluidity of settlement and landholding gave them better opportunities. Minor lords had to use their ingenuity, because with their limited resources there were some projects that they could not envisage. They do not figure prominently in the lists of borough founders, for example, because they did not have enough land to attempt such large-scale ventures; but they established a good number of markets. Knights and gentry profited from the expansion of trade and other social, economic and political changes of the twelfth and thirteenth centuries. They took risks, and there were casualties, but these formed a minority. A sample of thirty-one families from Oxfordshire shows that five of them lost land, nine gained it, and seventeen remained in much the same position.

vi. *Aristocratic achievement?*

The overall impression must be that the aristocracy at all levels adjusted to the rapid changes of the period 1086–1300 and profited from them. They enjoyed high incomes in 1300, with perhaps 20,000 households living comfortably on between £10 and £100 per annum – that is the gentry and the beneficed clergy. At least 200 households – of the barons, earls, bishops and the greater monasteries – were equivalent to modern millionaires, with incomes of between £200 and £6,000.

But was their achievement so great? We can find estates which recorded leaps in annual income, like Bolton Priory which doubled its cash revenues, from £240 to £460 between the 1280s and *c.*1310, as a result of prudent investment and skilful management. But many of the estates with rising revenue, like that recorded for the Clare family, earls of Gloucester, between 1267 and 1317, came more from acquiring additional land than developing existing resources. Bishoprics and Benedictine monasteries, which tended not to add much to the size of their estates, increased their incomes in the period from the late twelfth century to *c.*1300 between two and three times – Ely bishopric from £920 to £2,550 for example, and the bishops of Worcester from

£330 to £1,200, while Westminster Abbey rose from £739 to £1,641. This was keeping pace with inflation, but only just. In the same period wheat tripled in price.

The aristocracy were held back in many ways. The magnates were not free agents: from above, the state was bleeding power away from their courts in the twelfth century, and setting limits on their franchises in the thirteenth. From below, their tenants in fee were wriggling out of their control in the twelfth century, and even the unfree peasants in the next century were able to limit their demands by defending their customs. Their demesne management was flexible and efficient, but they could not always exploit the resources of the land to the full. Better-off peasants and townspeople made more from the economic growth of the thirteenth century, but lords could not, for all of their bluster about their serfs owning nothing but their bellies, take away the full profits. Because they were inhibited in appropriating their serfs' wealth directly, lords resorted to indirect measures to make some money, like building fulling mills or founding boroughs in poor regions.

Most lords gave higher priority to war, politics and the government of church and state. The literature of the period, which presumably expresses their interests and concerns, has much to say about religion, courtly love and knightly prowess. The treatises on estate management were greatly outnumbered by books on these spiritual and chivalric themes. The cultural preoccupations of the aristocracy are reflected in the amount of land and resources they devoted to their hunting reserves. A few richer families held chases, or private forests, which could cover dozens of square miles. But more often the aristocracy, both churchmen and laity, and including knights and upper gentry, made parks, and most of the 1,900 known to have existed in the middle ages were created in the thirteenth and early fourteenth centuries. Parks yielded profits, as sources of venison, timber and wood, and grazing. But they were valued not for their economic benefits, but for the pleasure of hunting, the opportunity to make alliances with visitors who came to hunt, the chance to send gifts of venison, and as status symbols.

The wealth of the aristocracy cannot be measured entirely in acres or coins; they were not just money-grabbers. Status and reputation counted as well as wealth, but this reinforces the impression of them as a competitive and acquisitive group. They were not just rivals within their peer group: there was also a competition between the magnates and the lesser aristocracy, and between the churchmen and the laity. There was friction between the elites of different regions, particularly between the expanding rulers of the Anglo-Norman world and the chieftains beyond the frontiers. The aristocrats were not in complete control of the rest of society; they were inhibited by the power of the state, and did not always have their own way with the peasantry. The constant shifts within the aristocracy, and in their relations with others, provided one of the dynamic forces in medieval society and economy.

CHAPTER FIVE

Peasants, c.1100–c.1315

We rely on documents produced by peasants' superiors, and material evidence, to reconstruct their lives, because they did not write. They gained their education from the practical training given to them by their elders in house and field, which does not mean that they lacked intelligence. They were actively involved in the growth and innovations of the twelfth and thirteenth centuries. They perceived that some changes were to their advantage, and that others were against their interests, and behaved accordingly. For example, they cleared land, and sold produce, but resisted those technical changes which might involve them in more work for few benefits. In pursuing their interests they lacked power, especially as individuals, but in acting collectively they could have a significant influence.

i. *Families and population*

The growth in population in the twelfth and thirteenth centuries was largely the result of increases in the number of peasants. The population in towns expanded especially rapidly, but an important part of that growth came from migration from the countryside. We have seen that in England the number of people rose by between two and three times in the 200 years after 1100. The precise time scale is not clear, as twelfth-century surveys of manors record more tenants – sometimes twice as many – than were described in Domesday Book, but this was sometimes the result not of a real change but of under-counting in 1086. Some surveys of the 1160s, 1170s and 1180s show that recorded numbers had grown by a modest 50 per cent or by an even lower figure, which might suggest that the expansion came at the end of the twelfth century or after 1200, and in some places the most rapid acceleration seems to have occurred in the late thirteenth century. But regardless of its timing, the increase is plain to see from the growing ranks of tenants, or the many people who came before lords' courts, or the long lists of contributors to the king's taxes. The remains of hamlets in the Scottish Highlands and in isolated farms on the Welsh hills bear material witness to the extension of settlement. The process by which Britain had become as densely populated in 1300 as it was to be in the eighteenth century could be seen as the result of accidents in biology and the weather. The number of epidemics was reduced, and seriously deficient harvests became less frequent: for example, there were relatively few really bad years between 1260 and 1290. But changes in population are rarely the result of a single factor, and as well as the temporary easing in mortality, fertility rose as peasants were making decisions about marriage which had an impact on the birth rate.

Peasants traditionally approached marriage with great caution. For them, as for us, it was an event of great personal importance, but in the middle ages the alliance had profound implications for the two families, as transfers of property were involved: initially the goods given as a dowry with the bride, but in the long term the marriage and its offspring would determine the descent of land. Peasants assumed that marriage could be contemplated only if the couple had property of some kind, even if it consisted of no more than a cottage and garden on which they could establish a new household. The land might be obtained by inheritance, but it was often gained by purchase, or as a gift from a father or other relative.

In our period the legal basis for marriage changed. The church was especially active in the eleventh and twelfth centuries in defining marriage law. In the eyes of the church the consent of the marriage partners was all important, and if a couple agreed to marry, even if the exchange of promises (the troth-plight) took place in private, this was recognized as a binding contract which could be enforced in the church courts. In the real world the agreement to marry was often negotiated between the families. The parents weighed up the suitability of the intended partner, and the alliance was settled only after some haggling over the dowry. The families probably took some account of the feelings of the marriage partners, but their individual choice did not carry as much weight in practice as the church's doctrine might imply. The material implications of marriage are recorded only when the contracts went wrong and aggrieved parties brought actions to the secular courts. For example, some time before 1312 at Duffield in Derbyshire Avicia Maud married John Wade. John complained that Richard Maud, Avicia's father, had agreed to give with her a cow worth 10s and clothing valued at 13s 4d, and to build a house in which they could live at a cost of 40s, but this contract had not been carried out. Though not in dispute, and therefore not mentioned in the case in the manor court, a transfer of land may also have been involved, as the house was to be built on a plot belonging to John Wade.

Marriage, a public event, concerned not just the couple and the families, but the lord and the whole community. Servile women (and men too on some manors) needed a licence to marry from the lord, which was given in exchange for the payment of a fine. Women who were not married but who were sexually active had to pay leirwite (literally a fine for lying down) and childwite (a fine for giving birth out of wedlock). Lords were not just levying taxes, but had a real interest in the marriage of their serfs and their choice of partners, as serfs and their offspring contributed so much in cash and labour to the profits of the manor. Lords wished to see an orderly succession of heirs as tenants of the peasant holdings. They intervened in specific cases when on occasion they attempted to compel their serfs to marry, most often requiring men to marry widows, whose holdings they believed would be more effectively cultivated if they were in the tenancy of an able-bodied man. The lords even expected to gain a small benefit from wedding festivities, as on some manors they insisted that their farm servants (*famuli*) should be invited to the feast.

Neighbours kept a close eye on the marriage and the subsequent conduct of the partners. The more substantial householders and tenants had a direct interest in the marriage of their sons and daughters, and in the descent of land to the next generation. They also had a general concern for the maintenance of order and efficiency in the village – everyone cultivated land in the fields, and contributed to rents and taxes. A good marriage would ensure that these obligations were carried out effectively and would not put extra burdens on to other villagers, who expected stability and decency in the family life of their neighbours. No doubt they would bring informal pressure to bear on those behaving improperly, and if necessary would report such offences as adultery to the church courts. The loose behaviour of servile women would be made known to the manor court, where leirwite and childwite payments were enforced.

All of this demonstrates that peasants did not enter lightly or easily into marriage. Behind all of the restraints and regulations that surrounded the institution lay the practical principle that only couples with resources, and specifically some land, should be rearing children. This would help to prevent a population explosion, because those without land would remain celibate. Those who did marry had to wait, and this served as a mechanism by which the ups and downs of the economy affected the birth rate. If couples married in their mid-twenties, for example, rather than their late teens, the number of children born to them would be considerably reduced. Another influence on fertility, both outside and within marriage, may have been the contraceptive practices which were discussed in the writings of churchmen who heard the confessions of the laity. Through such non-mechanical methods as coitus interruptus and the deliberate prolonging of breast-feeding of infants, peasant couples could lengthen the intervals between births.

In addition to the favourable climate, economic changes in the thirteenth century may have had an influence on increasing the number of marriages, and encouraging couples to marry at a younger age. More intensive methods of cultivation or better storage of crops may have made people feel that the supply of food was more plentiful and secure. The better-off peasants lived in improved houses and enjoyed an adequate diet, which enabled them to bring up more children in spite of the hazards of disease. At Halesowen in Worcestershire in the late thirteenth and early fourteenth centuries the wealthier peasants had large families, with a mean of 5.1 children in each household, compared with the cottagers' 1.8 offspring. The 'average' peasant family therefore contained parents and two or three children, with a tendency for more families to have three or more offspring during the thirteenth century. The 'average' conceals many variations in family life and structure. There was much remarriage after bereavement, and many households included children from more than one union.

A major factor in raising the population was the formation of many new households provided with small quantities of land. In areas of partible inheritance, mostly in East Anglia and Kent, when a peasant died his holding was divided among his sons. Many families had only one son, but when subdivision took place a good number of sons evidently used their fragment of land as the basis for marriage. In harder times they might have accepted that a few acres did not provide a secure basis for married life, and sold the land, perhaps even to their brother in order to reunite the parts of the original holding. In the areas of impartible inheritance, where the holding descended intact to a single son, usually the eldest (primogeniture) but in a number of villages the youngest (ultimogeniture), fathers went to much trouble to provide the children who were not inheriting any of the main holding, both sons and daughters, with parcels of land acquired by clearing new land or by purchase. Again, sons who in earlier generations might have remained celibate were enabled by gaining a modest property to contemplate building a cottage and finding a marriage partner. Many young men, perhaps on their own initiative, were able to acquire land in the same village, typically by marrying a widow who had a holding. At Chesterton near Cambridge a sixth of sons obtained land during the lifetime of their fathers, demonstrating that the younger generation did not have to wait until their parents died before they were able to possess land.

The peasants' dilemma of choosing between loyalty to family and prudent notions about landholding as a precondition for marriage was shifted in the thirteenth century by the availability of an income from employment or a trade. These apparent opportunities tipped the balance in the argument in favour of allowing the setting up of married couples on smallholdings. There were more wage-earning jobs, both in agriculture and in crafts. Opportunities were growing for people without much wealth to enter into retail trade, such as brewing and selling ale. The wages of the male head of household would not have been very high, but his wife could add her earnings – from selling ale, for example, or spinning yarn – to the total income of the family. Children could contribute a little, and when they reached the age of twelve they could go into service in another household. Smallholders had various makeshifts to gain a little extra income: they practised a 'cottage economy'. Depending on the local custom, they could graze a cow on the common pasture, and gather fuel, bracken, broom and other useful materials from the commons. They could gain some profit from the growing market – they might sell rushes. Pieces of land might be acquired by subletting from neighbours, and livestock, such as a cow, could be hired. Such people lived on credit always, and could hope to borrow enough to survive in bad harvest years.

Peasant fathers were anxious to help their children without a customary right to land. They may have been aware that the cruel law of primogeniture had been forced on them by their lords, and they certainly knew that lords still resisted moves to divide holdings on the grounds that these were the tenurial units on which rents and services were assessed. Behind this family sentiment lay practical self-interest, because parents expected their relatives to help them in their old age. A kind gesture to a son early in life would be reciprocated in the parents' declining years. A typical arrangement was agreed at Cranfield in Bedfordshire in 1294, when Elyas de Bretendon granted his half-yardland (15 acres) to his son John, in exchange for a promise that John would supply Elyas and Christine his wife with a residence on the holding and 'suitable food and drink' for the rest of their lives. Such agreements were normal customs of the manor, but in this case the two generations distrusted one another, and the father felt the need of a formal contract and a special clause guaranteeing adequate quantities of food in case the relationship soured. Parents would wish to keep on good terms with all of their children, because the uncertainties of mortality might mean that when they needed help only one of their offspring had survived.

Peasant choice was always restricted. The size of some village populations did not increase in the two centuries after 1086. For example, Compton Verney in Warwickshire contained forty-eight households at the time of Domesday, and supported forty-five in 1280. Such examples of stability were not uncommon in the 'champion' country, the midland belt dominated by open fields and nucleated villages. A decision must have been made by the lord not to form any more smallholdings, which could only have been carved out of existing tenant land or the demesne as there was no new land to clear. The peasants, most of whom held full yardlands of 40 acres, may have accepted that their interests and their heirs were well served by preserving these larger holdings, which gave their tenants an adequate living and a saleable surplus. Smallholdings were created more readily in regions where new land was being reclaimed, or which came under strong commercial influence. For example, the numbers of tenants increased sixfold and more on such manors as Bromyard, Ross-on-Wye and Ledbury in Herefordshire, where towns grew and nearby woods and wastes gave opportunities for assarting, especially by smallholders. Even in these zones of opportunity, population growth slowed down at the end of the thirteenth or in the early fourteenth century as harsher times prevailed, though some communities continued to expand until the great catastrophe of 1348–9, the Black Death.

Having examined the rising population and the influence of the market, we can explore some of the ways in which peasants accommodated themselves to economic growth, and indeed encouraged it: the extension of cultivation and changes in the structure of landholding; and peasant contributions to the market in selling produce, technical innovation, and involvement in crafts and trades.

ii. *Peasants and their holdings*

Peasants played an important part in extending the quantity of agricultural land in the twelfth and thirteenth centuries. Some of the largest projects, such as the reclamation of a large part of the Somerset Levels in the thirteenth century, were funded by as wealthy a lord as Glastonbury Abbey. Some lords give the appearance of having cleared substantial areas of woodland, when they paid fines to the crown for offences against forest law, but this was often on behalf of their tenants who had carried out the work. They could also co-ordinate and encourage assarting by renting out parcels of uncultivated land at rents designed to encourage new tenants. In special circumstances, lords organized colonization on a grand scale, as with the new villages founded for English and continental immigrants in south-west Wales in the twelfth century. These settlements had a strong political dimension, and though they led to the land being occupied in a new way, with large villages and open fields which had been previously unknown in the region, the land had previously supported a native population, so cultivation was not greatly expanded.

Lords may have directed and orchestrated clearance of new land and the founding of settlements, but the initiatives taken by thousands of peasants cumulatively accounted for a much larger area of land. Peasants expended great effort to assart from woodland or scrub, because as well as cutting down trees, roots had to be dug out of the ground, and the land enclosed against animals. Often peasants could tackle an acre or two at most at a time. When they had brought the land into production, their lords required them to pay a rent – usually a few pence in cash. If the assart was located in a royal forest – which was often the case because in Hampshire, Wiltshire and Staffordshire, for example, forest law extended over a half of the county – a fine had to be paid to the crown: a typical record from the enquiry into assarts in Cannock Forest in Staffordshire in 1286 reads 'Robert Broun assarts and holds there one rood (a quarter-acre) enclosed with a ditch . . . sown twice with spring corn and twice with winter corn . . .' These small efforts accumulated into hundreds and thousands of acres – 1,286 acres in Rockingham Forest in Northamptonshire in the early thirteenth century, to take one example. Peasants' drainage schemes in the fenlands and marshlands provide a contrast with the individual clearings in the woodlands, because the only effective method was to build large walls or dykes collectively, in collaboration with lords and other villages. The village territories were extended progressively by a series of reclamations beginning before the Conquest and continuing into the thirteenth century, resulting in long strip-shaped parishes which stretched up to 16 miles towards the coast. Once protected from flooding and drained with ditches, the land was divided into small plots, so that individual peasants gained parcels on a similar scale to their contemporaries in the woodlands. On the uplands, too, the peasants were responsible for thousands of piecemeal encroachments and enclosures, by which hillsides and moorlands were taken into more intensive agricultural use. The expansion of cultivation was often accompanied by the foundation of new settlements, like the isolated farmsteads established next to areas of still visible plough ridges on the Lammermuir Hills in southern Scotland. In the Pennines of Yorkshire and on Dartmoor in the thirteenth century, both individual farms and small hamlets were settled among new fields.

The movement to convert woodlands, wetlands and rough grazing land into arable and improved pasture could be seen as evidence of peasant irresponsibility. The ecological balance of the countryside depended on the pasture, woods, marshes and moorlands on which animals grazed, and which provided fuel, building materials and other raw materials. If peasants, anxious to increase production of cereals for feeding their families, extended the arable, they would deprive themselves and their neighbours of valuable assets. Ultimately the arable would yield badly, as it was poor land at the outset, better suited for pasture, and because it was deprived of nutrients by the shortage of grazing for animals by which manure was produced. By their reckless assarting, it could be said, peasants displayed either short-sighted greed, or desperation.

Peasants were under pressure at this time, which may well have led them to make mistakes. But in general their assarting activity was pursued cautiously. The clearance of land might involve bold pioneering in remote places, but more often it resulted from gradual intensification of settlement and agriculture. In the uplands of Scotland and northern England, land was cultivated continuously in a small infield near the settlement, and occasionally in parcels of the much larger outfield, most of which was grazed. Assarting (or making a purpresture or encroachment) was often a matter of adding acres to the infield, or cultivating larger sections of the outfield, or pushing the boundaries of the outfield further into the moor. These regions remained thinly populated and with a limited area of arable, showing that the inhabitants sensibly chose not to endanger their livelihoods by over-ambitious expansion. As in the pre-Conquest period, some of the 'new' settlements were established on sites previously occupied seasonally as shielings, so again the changes were not as radical (or foolhardy) as first appears.

Communities practising more intensive arable farming in the midlands and the south were acutely conscious of the need for conservation of scarce resources. When the peasants of Oldbury in Worcestershire realized in 1301 that their lord was proposing to enclose and rent out an area of pasture, they paid a fine of 6s 8d and promised an annual rent for the land to be left as common grazing. In the 'champion' areas, where most land was already cultivated, a protective line must have been drawn around the surviving woods and pastures at a much earlier date. This was done through community action, but the peasants perceived their livelihood in terms of the balance of types of land in their own holdings. Each yardland, oxgang, wist (in Sussex) or other unit of tenancy combined dozens of arable strips scattered over the fields with rights in common meadows, pastures and woods, and the well-being of the whole unit would depend on maintaining enough grazing to complement the corn-growing land.

We have already seen that lords were willing to divide holdings into halves and quarters in their own interests, as more tenants meant more rents and services. This was in response to demand from the peasants, who wished to provide holdings for their offspring, and indeed would-be tenants were willing to pay substantial entry fines to gain access to such a newly created holding, even if it was rather small. By 1279–80, in a large sample of midland peasants listed in the Hundred Rolls, less than a quarter of peasants held full yardlands, and 40 per cent were in possession of half- and quarter-yardlands. In the north, tenants had often held double oxgangs, which broke down into single oxgangs and occasionally half-oxgangs in the thirteenth century. This meant that a diminishing minority of peasants belonged to the elite with about 30 acres, which gave the average family plenty of food, a saleable surplus in all but the worst years, and would need the labour of at least two full-time workers. A substantial minority of peasants held about 15 acres (a half-yardland or an oxgang) which would feed a family, provide a sufficient surplus to pay the rent, and could be worked by the tenant alone if he was able-bodied. Those with a quarter-yardland or half-oxgang would need to have an alternative source of income to supplement the produce of the holding, as it would not be fully sufficient for the family's food, let alone rent payments.

Some traditional units of tenure were fragmented. In East Anglia the old tenements survived as ghosts, because they were still used to levy rents and services, but in practice they were split up among many tenants. Throughout Norfolk, Suffolk and south Lincolnshire, and to a lesser extent in Essex and Kent, while a fortunate minority might hold as much as 20 acres of land, on many manors the majority of tenants had only 5 acres or less. Smallholdings had proliferated everywhere, as assarts, or fragments of demesne, cottage tenements carved out of yardlands or oxgangs, or parcels put on the market were joined to the already substantial minority of bordars and cottars recorded in 1086. Lords played a part in this, granting cottages to former slaves, encouraging small-scale assarting, or even changing the inheritance custom so that holdings were partible.

iii. *Peasants and the market*

Peasants changed the management of their land, and their way of life, in response to the growth in the market. They had moved away from simple self-sufficiency before 1100, and they were producing for sale on a considerable scale by the late thirteenth century. The landlords ran their

demesnes in order to take advantage of higher prices, but still a high proportion of demesne produce went to supply the household, or to feed
animals and servants on the manor itself. Peasants had small households
and few servants, and sold a high proportion of their crops. A yardlander
in the midlands in about 1300 could hope to harvest 23 quarters of grain,
and after reserving 6 quarters for next year's seed and 10 quarters to feed
his family and animals, was able to sell 7 quarters, for which he could
expect to receive a sum of between £1 and £2. The choice of crops was
partly influenced by the local soil and climate, and by the needs of their
families, but also by market opportunities. The people of the large woodland manor of King's Norton in Worcestershire in about 1300 paid tithes
which reveal that oats accounted for two-thirds of their grain. No doubt
they used some of this relatively cheap corn for brewing and baking, and
as fodder for horses, but they would also have sold a good deal, as there
was demand from the district immediately to the south which produced
few oats.

Niches in the market could be occupied by peasants. Demesnes tended
to concentrate on the staple, bulky products such as grain, wool and livestock. This left the peasants to cater for steady demand for the smaller
and troublesome items, such as poultry, eggs, fruit and vegetables, honey
and wax. Peasant gardens and yards were usually tended by peasant
women, and it is no accident that when we hear of the sale of these goods
in towns, they were often being hawked in the markets and streets by
women with baskets, like the fourteen women who paid a toll of a halfpenny each to sell beans, peas and apples in Bristol in 1282–4. Peasants
grew industrial crops in small plots and gardens, most commonly flax
and hemp, but also dyestuffs such as madder, all of it for sale. Demesnes
used most of their hay and straw for feed and litter within the manor, so
much of that sold in urban markets came from smaller producers.

Livestock were kept on peasant holdings mainly for the revenue that
could be obtained by selling wool, dairy produce and surplus animals.
Some of the cheese and bacon, and pieces of salt beef and mutton for
the wealthier peasants, went into the peasants' larders, but most wool
was destined for the commercial cloth industry, not domestic weaving.
The potential for surplus is most easily demonstrated for the more
pastoral regions. For example, when David Fychan of Marchros in Merioneth was assessed for the tax of 1293 (and no doubt was under-assessed)
he owned four oxen which he would have used for ploughing, and also
had six cows and twenty sheep. The 500 pounds of cheese and butter that
he could have expected to obtain from the cows would have been well in
excess of his family's consumption, and the cash (about 10s if he sold
half of it) was needed to pay rents and taxes. Fychan's flock of twenty

sheep was fairly typical in size, and throughout Britain there were many thousands of these modest flocks, an enormous number taken together. The scale of peasant sheep-keeping can be appreciated from the total of 46,382 sacks of wool exported from English ports in 1304–5, the peak year. If each sack contained 260 fleeces, the wool came from at least 12 million animals. We can estimate that at least two-thirds of wool production for export came from peasant flocks. At East Meon in Hampshire in 1302, the lord kept 1,300 adult sheep, which in the course of the year had produced 555 lambs. In the same year, the rector of the parish collected in tithes 150 new lambs, implying that 1,500 had been born in the parish. The peasant flocks in the parish therefore contained a cumulative total of about 4,000 adult animals.

Peasant producers were stimulated by rising prices. Wool from a dozen sheep (weighing a stone, that is 14 pounds) fetched about 2s in 1209. In 1302 the same quantity could be sold for almost 4s. In the same way a quarter of wheat (approximately the crop of an acre of land) was sold for 2s 7d in 1209, and 5–6s a century later (see Figure 1 below, p. 230).

Peasants responded to market demand by changing their farming practices. They worked within local farming systems, so there can be no generalizations which apply to the whole country. Each system varied in the proportions of enclosed and common land, and between private and public control of resources. They had different balances of arable and pasture, and cultivated with varying intensity, specifically the extent to which land lay fallow between crops. The choice of crops and animals also varied.

In western and south-eastern England were the districts sometimes called 'old enclosed', 'woodland' or 'wood/pasture', which often had areas of open field, sometimes with a dozen or more 'fields', combined with much land enclosed in crofts and closes (see Map 1 above, p. 16). Peasant holdings commonly combined both enclosed and unenclosed land. With the assarting movement the proportion of enclosures tended to increase, as newly cleared land was usually surrounded by a hedge and held initially by a single tenant. In the long run assarted land might be subdivided with inheritance and the sale of strips, and come to resemble an open field. The balance between different types of land often shifted towards arable in order to meet the subsistence needs of the cultivators, but peasants from these regions were able to sell surplus grain, dairy produce and livestock, such as pigs.

In the 'champion' or midland landscapes stretching from southern Scotland to south-west England the fields were under strict communal control, which maintained either a two-course or three-course rotation (see Maps 2 and 3 above, pp. 20 and 22). Every peasant produced both winter-sown crops (wheat, rye and maslin, a mixture of the two) and spring crops such as barley, oats and legumes. The fields were designed to provide adequate grazing for animals, mainly sheep and cattle. Changes included the rather rare conversion of a two-field to a three-field system, involving a new layout of the whole village territory in a single operation, but the much more common and more informal arrangement was that of inhoks, by which parts of the fallow field were temporarily fenced and planted. Both led to an increase in the planted area, and more frequent cropping. The cultivators intended to increase their output partly in order to send more surplus corn to market.

In hilly country, with its restricted area of arable, often in an 'infield', and extensive pastures, more land could be taken into cultivation by extending the infield or by cultivating the outfield more frequently. The quality of the arable was improved on uplands in Devon and Cornwall by applying sea sand (which contained lime) and beat burning (paring turf, burning it, and speading it on the land), but these methods, though recorded for the first time, may not have been new.

Some practices were adopted in a number of regions. Manure from the yard and animal houses of the peasant holding, as well as household waste and the contents of cesspits, was carried by cart to the fields, and was concentrated on the best land. Large quantities of marl, that is subsoil containing lime, was dug out of pits in the fields and spread on the land. Demesnes did this, but it was especially characteristic of peasant farming. The acreage under legumes expanded, to provide food for humans and animals and to benefit the next crop from the nitrogen in the roots. Peasant buildings, like those of the lords of the manors (see p. 131), were constructed with stone foundations and timber frames, which allowed crops to be stored in barns where they were protected from rats and damp, and byres, stables and sheepcotes also gave shelter to animals. Peasants increasingly used horses rather than oxen as draught animals. In the twelfth century most better-off peasants owned ox-drawn wains, which were effective, but were slow and best suited to carrying heavy loads around the fields. During the thirteenth century, mainly in the east of the country, peasants adopted horses and carts, which could be used for hauling around the village, but also were well suited by their comparative speed to carry sacks of grain or sides of bacon to market at distances of five or ten miles. (Plate 8) Horses were sometimes employed as plough beasts by peasants while the demesnes still relied on oxen.

The market encouraged greater intensity of cultivation. This trend was taken to extremes in north-east Norfolk, which was densely populated and came under strong urban influence. Peasant holdings were very small. In the manor of Martham in 1292, 220 of 364 tenants held an acre or two, and only ten had more than 10 acres. If the peasants followed the pattern of husbandry found on the local demesnes (see p. 127), which seems very likely, they worked their fragments of land with great care, cropping the arable with few or no periods of fallow. They prepared the land for sowing by ploughing (or digging in the case of the small-holders) the land repeatedly, and sowed the seed thickly. As the corn grew they hoed and weeded. They planted quantities of legumes. They used horses for ploughing as well as hauling. We do not know if the peasant land was as productive as the demesnes, with yields as high as 20 bushels per acre for wheat, but in order to support so many people on smallholdings they must have obtained better results than their contemporaries in the midlands. Throughout the country intensive methods were applied to the tiny plots used for horticulture, and although gardens accounted for a small percentage of total output, in some regions they made a significant contribution to peasant incomes. Again, in parts of East Anglia flax and hemp, though grown in small plots, contributed as much as 6 per cent of total agricultural production in the early fourteenth century, measured from the tithe revenues.

While capable of adopting new methods, peasants were understand-ably reluctant to make more radical changes. The Norfolk methods were appropriate to local circumstances: midland peasants would have been impressed by the grain yields, but would not have been envious of the amount of work that was expended to achieve them. Resistance to change was not necessarily the result of ignorance, but was based on rational calculations of advantage. For example, the Oxfordshire village of South Stoke, which had two fields, in about 1240, apparently on the initiative of its lord (the monastery of Eynsham Abbey), recast its fields to make three. The surrounding villages, which also cultivated their land in two fields, would have observed the results with great interest. South Stoke had trouble with its new third field, which proved too small, and the change led to a dispute over pasture. Even if the transformation had been better planned, the people of the neighbouring settlements would have been deterred from following South Stoke's example because the apparent increase in each holding's cultivated area by 33 per cent each year would not give them a proportionate increase in production. They would lose some grazing, and the new system tended to push yields down as the land was rested less often and deprived of some manure. The same reservation applied to the inhoks. The central concern of peasants throughout most of lowland England was their difficulty in keeping enough animals to bring high returns in the market and to maintain the arable in good heart. Many peasant flocks of sheep consisted of a dozen or two dozen animals, and many smallholders had none at all, judging from the inability of the lords' officials to find a beast which could be taken as a heriot when a cottager died. They would not have known about the deficiency in minerals, such as phosphorus, but they would have been fully aware from practical experience that extra cartloads of manure on the ploughed land made a difference to the subsequent harvest. Some of the technical changes which might be seen as far-sighted improvements seem to have been makeshifts in difficult circumstances. Peasants may have appreciated the speed and strength of the horses that they owned, but judging from the sums of money at which some of their old nags were valued, their chief virtue was their cheapness.

Although they were influenced by the market, peasants did not develop a fully commercial mentality. Very rarely did peasants at this time have sufficient confidence in the market to specialize in a cash crop and buy their main foodstuffs. The holding was expected to provide a proportion of the family's food, and most of the labour came from family members. They would make decisions on the basis of their needs rather than calculations of cash profits, expending much effort on a crop such as dredge, a mixture of barley and oats, which yielded well, was versatile in use, but did not fetch a high price. They were not free agents, but were bound by the rules of the village. For example, a yardlander could not in theory expand his sheep flock beyond the maximum fixed by the customary stint; in a typical village the limit was forty animals. Lords reduced their tenants' ability to invest in buildings, equipment or livestock by their rent demands, especially for high entry fines. And the lords enjoyed many advantages in the marketing of crops. Rents collected at Michaelmas (29 September) and the following months pressured peasants into selling corn when the price was low. Lords could keep their corn back until the price rose in the following spring and early summer. A modern economist would sum up the peasants' position by saying that at this time they were only 'partly integrated' into the market.

Agriculture had never been the sole source of peasants' incomes. In the early middle ages they had gathered and hunted around their settlements, and made their own utensils and clothing. In the twelfth and thirteenth centuries they continued to exploit the sources of food and raw materials that were locally available. On the coast they fished and made salt. In the Fens they caught wildfowl and fish, collected rushes, reeds and sedge, and dug turf (peat) for fuel. In woodlands they had access to fuel and timber, collected nuts and fruit, and when the opportunity came, poached deer for meat. But as market demand increased, peasants used these assets to generate a cash income, and in the woodlands burnt charcoal, made potash, and participated in a dozen crafts, from wood-turning to glass-making. Towns consumed ever-growing supplies of salt, fish and rushes. The population of London in about 1300 burnt about 140,000 tons of wood to warm their houses and cook their food, as well as to provide fuel for industries. This had repercussions for dozens of rural communities within easy reach by cart or boat (in practice 30 miles), especially those near to the Thames. In the Chiltern Hills on the north bank of the river, and Surrey to the south, peasants could exploit their common rights to woods, or cut wood in groves that they rented. Many smallholders found employment from the lords of the manor, or richer neighbours, in cutting wood and then carrying the faggots and 'talwood' (logs) to the river bank for loading on to boats.

The market not only intensified gathering activities, but also promoted a greater degree of specialization among peasant craftsmen and encouraged the spread of complex industrial processes in the countryside. Sometimes mining for minerals and smelting ore was carried out on such a large scale, like tinning in Cornwall and Devon, that most of those employed were full-time wage earners rather than peasants. Iron, lead and coal workings, which did not attract the same level of investment, gave opportunities for peasants to engage in mining as a part-time activity. Coal miners at Longdon on the edge of Cannock Chase in Staffordshire, for example, paid 6d per pick per week, in one case for seventeen weeks from May to September. These were small bell pits no more than 100 feet deep, which were sunk into the coal seam where it lay near to the surface; typically these were worked by two men using little equipment apart from a pick and shovel, and a windlass to haul the coal to the surface. Quarrying for building stone or millstones was another intermittent activity that could be fitted into the less busy times in the farming year.

A number of crafts which had been located mainly in towns in the early phases of urban growth spread into the countryside after 1100. It made sense to make pottery near to abundant supplies of clay and fuel. Villages gained such a reputation for pottery-making that their names changed, to Potters Marston (Leicestershire) and Crockerton (Wiltshire). Clothmaking continued as an urban activity, but was supplemented by an important rural industry. Lords noted the number of weavers on their manors, and from about 1180 built fulling mills in order to exploit the demand for mechanical cloth finishing. These are found especially in the south-west, the west midlands and the north-west, but judging from the distribution of occupational surnames such as Webb (weaver) and Walker or Tucker (fuller), the industry was also well established in the east in the thirteenth century, in such counties as Essex. A scatter of craftsmen are found in many villages. Smiths were often established by lords of manors, though they would also sell their services to their neighbours. Many leather workers (tanners in particular), and building workers (especially carpenters and thatchers) were widely scattered in the countryside. The number of tailors, one of the commonest non-agricultural occupations by *c.*1300, demonstrates the degree of craft specialization that had been achieved. The country tailors held land, but in order for them to make even a modest living from their craft a significant number of their peasant neighbours must have had their clothing made by a professional.

Cottagers and smallholders took up industrial employment because they could not make a living from their modest acreage of land. The whole landholding population of the Wiltshire potting village of Crockerton in 1234 consisted of tenants with 4 acres of land at most. But potting offered low status and rewards, and many other peasant-craftsmen had a stronger base in landholding. The manorial smiths were often tenants of a medium-sized peasant holding, a half-yardland or oxgang. Two charcoal burners who worked in Inglewood in Cumberland had goods (probably livestock) valued for tax purposes at between £2 and £3, which means that they formed part of the peasant elite. And peasants with their own carts were able to sell their services as carriers. As is so often the case, those who were already well off were in a better position to make the maximum from non-agricultural activities.

The same social and economic variety can be found among those, mostly women, who worked in the most widespread of medieval village trades, the brewing of ale. In every village in the late thirteenth century a high proportion of the women brewed for sale. Some were providing for their own households, and occasionally sold the surplus, perhaps only once or twice in a year. For others it was a more continuous, full-time occupation. The economic circumstances of these brewsters varied considerably. Some of them were the wives of wealthier or middling peasants, who used grain from the holding, while others were cottagers, widows and single women for whom brewing was their main source of income, based on malt that had been purchased. Of thirty-eight regular brewsters at Brigstock (Northamptonshire) before the Black Death, twenty came from settled middle-status peasant households, and eighteen were poor cottagers, recent immigrants and women on the margins of the community. Brewing is a well-known activity because it was regulated through the manor court, which enables us to calculate profits. The sale of 22½ gallons of ale brewed from 3 bushels of malt in about 1300 should have left the brewster with a surplus of 5d. On this basis, a brewster could have kept herself and her family if she brewed and sold ale from 6–8 bushels of malt each week. This was a feasible total, if she was working in a community with dozens of consuming households.

Peasants may have been only 'partly integrated' into the market, but this still enabled them to buy a wide range of goods and services. Everyone was handling money, whether it was gained from the sale of produce or earned in wages. A substantial proportion was earmarked for rents, taxes and church dues, but some could be devoted to consumption. A yardlander in southern England would have had £1 to spare in a good year, and wage-earning cottagers may well have spent more, though in their case the main call on the money would have been the purchase of foodstuffs. At least 40 per cent of rural families bought at least part of their basic supplies of grain, because they could not grow enough on their land. The middling and wealthier peasants tended to provide for their own food need from their holding, hence the strong regional traditions in diet, with wheat being the main bread corn in the south; rye and barley were baked in Norfolk. Ale was usually brewed from barley, but in Essex and the south-west malted oats were used. On the other hand, they did not rely entirely on their own crops for food and drink. Often they found it convenient to obtain ale from ale wives as we have seen, relying on the informal rota of brewsters within the village. Bread, joints of meat, cheese, puddings and pies were available from retailers in towns and often in the country too. For those who lived inland, sea fish, a regular item in their diet, came from the network of local markets.

The main calls on peasant cash, after food, came from their need for housing and clothing. To begin with their houses, modern commentators have sometimes assumed that these were built by the peasants themselves, using materials available in the locality at little cost. No doubt the peasants contributed to building work, by hauling materials and preparing the site, but they employed specialists, and in particular carpenters, to assemble the timber frame. Their handiwork can be seen in peasant houses that still stand, and indeed are inhabited at the present day, at Aston Tirrold and Harwell, both in Berkshire, which have been dated quite precisely, to 1282–4 and 1285–95 respectively. Many more houses have now gone, not necessarily because they were flimsily built, but because they became redundant in later periods. Their foundations have been excavated, and these show that between about 1180 and 1320 the rural building tradition went through an important change with the adoption of stone foundations. Builders used the local materials – granite, chalk, flint, limestone – or just set the timber frame on twenty or thirty padstones where stone was scarce. The stone added to the cost of construction, but helped to prolong the life of the timbers which now were raised above the damp ground. The dimensions of the foundations suggest that the timbers were assembled in frames in two or three bays, according to a convention that each bay measured about 15 feet by 15 feet, giving the houses a length of 30 or 45 feet. The use of standard sizes again points to the work of professional craftsmen, as do the distinctive local styles of building. Cruck construction predominated in the midlands and western and northern Britain, which meant that the main vertical elements in the timber frame consisted of pairs of curved timbers, often formed by splitting a single tree. In the south and east buildings the framing tradition was based on vertical posts.

Some materials used in peasant buildings – straw or reeds for thatch, and clay and dung to daub over the wattled walls – came easily to hand. But timber in sufficient quantity to build a whole house – at least twenty trees – and the timbers of the right size and shape to make crucks, were not to be found in every wood; they had to be carried from a distance, and often were purchased. The combination of paying craftsmen's wages and buying materials ensured that peasant houses were not cheap. We have seen (p. 157) that in 1312 in Derbyshire building a house, which may not have been very large, was said to have cost 40s. In the uplands, dwellings and byres were built in line under a single roof, which reduced total expenditure. Most houses, however, were specialized dwellings, which were divided between a hall and chamber. The dwelling was often accompanied by separate agricultural buildings, such as barns and byres, and as these could also be built with stone foundations and timber frames, the cost of an entire complex could have exceeded £6. The peasant demand for decent, secure and weather-proof accommodation, with adequate living space and shelter for crops, implements and animals, had repercussions throughout the rural economy. To afford the buildings peasants were stimulated to grow and sell more produce. Their expenditure encouraged the growth of a specialized and skilled labour force, and promoted trade in timber and other materials. Their houses also tell us something of peasants' attitudes to property and privacy. Often they lived close to neighbours in communities which enjoyed a collective identity based on shared assets, but the tenants of individual houses guarded their privacy. They were surrounded by hedges and ditches or walls, and their outer doors were secured with locks. Windows were small, barred, and protected with shutters. If outsiders penetrated into the house, they would find that clothing and other valuables were locked in stout chests in the inner private room, the chamber.

Clothing, like housing, was largely the work of specialists, and peasants bought their textiles: woollens for clothes, and linen for undergarments and household use, such as sheets and towels. A peasant from Walsham-le-Willows in Suffolk, William Lene, died in 1329, a little after our period, but his possessions were acquired earlier and are unlikely to differ from those of his predecessors in the late thirteenth century. He was a rich peasant, with 37 acres of arable, and he owned 10 yards of russet cloth valued at 9s, clothing worth 13s, four sheets and carpets (14s), two tablecloths (2s) and two towels (16d). His chests contained more textiles than most peasants had, but when thefts of clothing are reported, or reference is made to the provision of clothing in agreements to maintain old people, it is clear that there was widespread ownership of wool and linen cloth of some quality and value by peasants of all kinds. For example, when peasants on the Dorset manor of Sturminster Newton were summoned to have their Christmas dinner in the manor house, they were expected to bring their own tablecloths. These purchases created a mass market for relatively cheap textiles – William Lene had bought russet at 11d per yard, towards the lower end of the price range. Lene's inventory does not mention shoes, but peasants wore leather shoes and boots made mainly in towns, typically costing 6d per pair.

Even small-scale producers were also consumers of farming equipment, domestic utensils, furniture and objects for personal use. Most households contained dozens of manufactured items. Their number and quality varied with the wealth of the peasants, and there were great disparities between regions. One indication is provided by the objects found when peasant houses are excavated. At Cefn Graeanog in Gwynnedd, on a ridge between Snowdonia and the sea, a house, barn, stable and byre were occupied by a peasant family in the thirteenth century. The buildings, with their stone foundations and (probably) cruck frames, suggest owners of some substance, but they left behind for discovery by modern archaeologists only an iron spade, two knife blades, a horseshoe, a few pieces of scrap bronze and lead, seven stone objects, including whetstones, and four fragments of pottery. Perhaps they disposed of their rubbish away from the house, but more likely they based their domestic and farming activities on wooden and leather objects, and were careful to recycle any broken or worn-out metal tools or artefacts. A house at Upton in the Gloucestershire Cotswolds was occupied from the twelfth to the fourteenth century, but the thirteenth century marks the peak of occupation. The dwelling house and farm buildings were constructed with high-quality stone foundations, a timber frame and thatched roof. The twenty-one iron objects that were found included a billhook, a 'spud' for weeding, knives, horseshoes, door fittings, including a lock plate, latch and key. There were three bronze buckles from clothing, and a score of stone objects including pieces of hand-mills and whetstones. The pottery fragments exceeded 5,000 in number, and included pieces of cooking pots, jugs and bowls, which were mainly suitable for preparing and serving food and drink, but also were used in dairying and other activities on the farm. The contrast in their material possessions reflects the poverty and wealth of the two regions, partly because of their natural resources, and partly because of the unequal development of the market economy.

Small and quite cheap objects acquired by peasants were almost all produced at a distance, in specialist centres of manufacture, and a few were imported. Pottery at Upton came from rural industries 20 or more miles from the village, in western Worcestershire, north Warwickshire and Buckinghamshire. They reached their eventual owners through markets and fairs held in the local market towns, as did the hand-mills of German origin. The metal objects would have come from urban workshops, though some of the ironwork could have been made by country smiths. Urban craftsmen probably made the wooden and leather goods which are not preserved but are known from documents, such as ploughs, carts, harrows and harness for the farm, furnishings such as tables, benches and chests, and the tubs, troughs and vats used in preparing food and drink.

While they bought goods and employed artisans, peasants could ill afford luxuries, and often made do with old, worn-out and mended utensils. They were short of cash, so their purchases were usually based on credit rather than immediate payment. Nonetheless they had some spending power, and must often have faced difficult choices about whether to put their money into consumption, or to invest their limited funds in buildings, equipment and livestock on the farm. In general, even the most successful peasants did not opt for high levels of personal consumption. Their houses seem sparsely furnished, and their most valuable possession was a cart with wheels fitted with iron tyres.

The market for land was not always directly connected with the trade in produce and goods. Many transfers of land took place within the family, whether by inheritance after the death of a tenant, or by grants between family members, for example when an elderly tenant retired. In any peasant society there would be elderly people and widows who lacked labour and the need for large quantities of produce, and young and vigorous households which had more capacity to work and many mouths to feed. These inequalities could be resolved if parcels of land passed from one tenant to another. Such adjustments and exchanges had probably gone unrecorded in the early middle ages.

In the thirteenth century, with extended use of written documents and the growing value of land, transfers between peasants were more commonly recorded. In the case of free land the conveyance was made by charters or deeds. A typical deed concerns a grant of 2 acres of land in Elbridge in Kent which was made by Peter son of Nigel and Godeva his wife to William and Robert sons of Simon, in about 1200. The 2 acres of land were described in relation to the land of other tenants, and the rent specified as 9d. William and Robert gave 18s 6d for it. The grant was witnessed by a small group of local people.

Sales of customary or servile land were supervised by the manor court: a tenant would come into court and surrender a holding to the lord; a new tenant would then appear and be granted the land. In fact the parties had agreed the transfer before the day of the court session. This is made more explicit in the common procedure by which a tenant surrendered land to the lord for the use of (*ad opus* in Latin) another tenant. Sometimes the outgoing tenant paid a heriot to the lord, as this 'death duty' was often demanded on surrender of land as well as on the death of a tenant, and usually the incoming tenant paid an entry fine. A typical record in the court roll for King's Ripton in Huntingdonshire in 1294 reads 'Nicholas Hall in full court surrenders into the lord's hands for the use of Henry son of Simon a half-acre of land lying in Westcroft', for which Henry paid a fine to the lord of 6d. He would also have paid money to Nicholas Hall, but arrangements between tenants were no concern of the lord, and not normally recorded. The purchase price at that time of high demand for land would have been considerably higher than the entry fine. Such transfers were permanent alienations, in which the hereditary right to the land passed from one tenant to another. A short-term transfer could be made by means of a lease, which was handled by different lords in various ways. Some lords allowed leases, especially if they lasted for only a year or two, without insisting that they be registered in the court. Others attempted to forbid them, or required that they be reported to the court (at a price). Such controls encouraged the tenants to arrange them clandestinely, which created an illicit land market that was very difficult to police. The authorities sometimes discovered horrific examples of a yardland that had been divided among a dozen tenants, and in consequence had almost escaped from the control of the estate administration. When we have a systematic record of subtenancy, like the survey of the royal manor of Havering-atte-Bower in Essex in 1251, the normally hidden layer of subtenants is revealed to have consisted mainly of smallholders with a few acres.

A further area of controversy concerned the difficult border territory separating free and customary land, and between people of free status who held servile land and serfs who acquired freeholdings. Free land attracted the unfree, because it gave them more complete rights of ownership and carried light cash rents. They aspired to be able to buy and sell customary land in the same fashion as free tenants, without the oversight of the manor court, by means of charters and deeds. Lords like Peterborough Abbey would allow the serf to acquire free land, but only if the deeds were surrendered to the lord. On some estates the land was surrendered and granted back to the tenant by the lord, which allowed the lord to control the serfs' land acquisitions, and to make some profit from them. Lords would not compromise at all on attempts to hold customary land by charter, and communities that attempted this, like Barnet in Hertfordshire, met with stout resistance.

The changes in the land market in the thirteenth century extended beyond the introduction of better records. With the rise of market production, and a more lively commercial economy, successful peasants bought land, not in order to provide for the subsistence of their family, but as part of a strategy to expand their profitable agricultural production, or to gain rents by subletting land. A few entrepreneurs were building up their wealth at the expense of their less able, fortunate or ruthless neighbours.

A commercial land market developed most intensely in eastern England, where most manor court rolls contain dozens of records of land changing hands every year. Analysis of the manorial court records of Coltishall (Norfolk) and Redgrave (Suffolk) in the late thirteenth and early fourteenth centuries shows that 91 and 87 per cent respectively of the land transfers were made between people who were not related. Many of these transactions, like the example of a surrender given above, concerned small parcels of an acre or two. Larger holdings were more likely to be inherited or passed from one relative to another, so that if the quantity of land changing hands is being calculated, as distinct from the number of transfers, about half passed within the family. In the midlands and the west an active land market existed, but a higher proportion of land was kept within the family and a smaller proportion was sold to people who were not relatives. At the very well studied manor of Halesowen 63 per cent of transfers were between family members, and 80 per cent of the land was conveyed by inheritance or was granted by fathers to children, or from brother to brother, or between other family members.

Many motives lay behind the land market. We can be confident that some of those accumulating land were seeking to profit from the rents that could be collected from subtenants. An acre might be liable to pay the lord of the manor 3d annually, but could be sublet for 12d in regions of high land values. This is the most likely reason for townspeople penetrating the rural land market, like the burgesses of Dunstable in

Bedfordshire who held land in nearby villages in 1279. Active cultivators were probably acquiring land in order to maximize grain production. This is most likely to lie behind the marked tendency for land to be gathered by a few wealthy tenants from poorer neighbours during periods of bad harvests. At Hinderclay in Suffolk in the difficult years of bad weather and poor yields between 1294 and 1299, of the 112 people involved in transfers of land, thirty-nine were buyers, fifty-five were sellers, and another eighteen both bought and sold. Poorer people, who no doubt were already in debt, sold land in order to buy food, and a minority of better-off peasants took advantage and expanded their holdings. Cultivators with larger acreages were in a better position to produce a saleable surplus and to profit from the prevalent high grain prices.

If the number of sellers consistently exceeded the number of buyers, especially in the succession of bad harvests and cattle disease for thirty years after 1294, very large holdings would have developed and the small-holders would have lost their land. Such an extreme polarization did not take place, even in eastern England. The accumulations of land were rather fragile, and disintegrated soon after they had been created. To some extent this reflects the general economic instability of the times, with individual entrepreneurs who made some gains, but who failed to found dynasties of rich peasants. The lands were bought in an opportunistic fashion, and there is little evidence of a strategy by the purchasers to buy adjacent plots in order to cultivate with more efficiency. A further explanation of the breakdown of the larger holdings reflects the fact that their tenants were not ruthless economic men: often they divided their lands among their family. This provides further confirmation of the generalization that peasants were only partly integrated into the market.

Although East Anglia saw the most flourishing land market, it developed everywhere. In Wales, tenants were restrained by their lords from making permanent alienations of their land, but they found ways around these institutional obstacles, in the form of the pridd. By this device land was leased for a fixed term of years, but this was constantly renewable, so in effect the grant had been made for ever. The purchaser enjoyed considerable rights over the land, and could, for example, bequeath it.

The earliest document recording a pridd dates from 1286, and subsequently these arrangements multiplied until they became the basis for wealthy and successful tenants to build up considerable landed fortunes.

Those who bought and sold land were also involved in lending and borrowing money. The purchase price for a holding, and the entry fine, were often paid in instalments. In the same way, the purchase of goods or animals was invariably based on credit, in that the purchaser would not pay the full price for some months. Peasants would borrow from Jews, but Jewish communities were localized, and even before 1290 the main sources of peasant credit would be wealthier neighbours, the parish clergy, and urban traders, who might (for an advantage) pay money in advance for crops not yet harvested or wool not yet clipped. When creditors pursued those who owed them money in the manor courts, the 'pleas of debt' suggest that most debts resulted from sales of goods that went wrong, or non-payment of wages. But peasants did make loans of cash to one another, and in some cases a land transfer resulted from a failure to pay which forced the debtor to sell his or her holding.

iv. *Peasants and lords*

The growth in the commercial activities of peasants had important implications for their relations with their lords. We saw earlier the many ways in which lords increased their revenues from peasants (pp. 137–45), but how did these change the peasant economy? It would be easy to represent the period as a disastrous one for peasants, as their legal status was diminished by the imposition of villeinage, the new more precisely defined serfdom, making them liable to pay large sums in tallage, marriage fines and entry fines. The higher payments had the potential of milking the peasants of their profits in the market, and preventing them from accumulating money for consumption or investment. Servile peasants were restricted in a number of ways – in buying and selling free land, or in moving from their manor. The ability of their lords to behave in arbitrary ways, such as charging higher entry fines or imposing new dues, made serfs feel insecure. The growing rural population raised land values, allowing lords to increase rents and entry fines, and the shortage of land reduced the bargaining power of tenants.

In fact the tide did not always run against the peasants. The twelfth century brought an end to slavery, with the settling of slaves on landholdings by lords. Some holdings owing labour services were converted to pay cash rents, and freeholdings with no obligation but money rent multiplied with the clearance of new land. Once fixed, an annual free cash rent could not be changed, and the inflation around 1200 reduced its value to the advantage of the tenant. Free tenants accounted for the majority of the peasantry, and many of the most successful producers for the market were freemen (sometimes called franklins) who could accumulate large holdings without the expense of entry fines and without restriction from lords' courts. The most commercialized and prosperous regions, such as East Anglia and Kent, contained a high proportion of free tenants.

Even after the imposition of the new serfdom, lords exaggerated their arbitrary power over their villeins. When the lawyers claimed that an unfree tenant would not know when he went to bed what he would be doing the next day, this implied that the lord's officials could summon tenants to labour services as they pleased. Some boon works could be announced at short notice, but most labour services were fixed in terms of day and season. The conditions of tenure in many respects were defined in written surveys, and in unwritten customs that were declared and modified in the manor court. Lords could make increases in services or rents, but usually had to do so in indirect and subtle ways or they would provoke troublesome reactions among the tenants. Again, in legal theory, a servile holding was the property of the lord, and some lords would announce in a grandiloquent gesture in their manor courts that the villein holdings had been seized. In practice the holdings grew to resemble the property of the villein. Their hereditary rights were respected by the lords, who rarely interfered with the succession of land to heirs according to the local inheritance customs. Customary land could be bought and sold, providing that the transaction passed through the lord's court. Lords disapproved of peasants who made wills, but came in practice to accept bequests. For example, a device was used by which a tenant on his deathbed could surrender land to beneficiaries, preferably in the presence of an official of the lord, who could then report the transfer to the next court. Lords were always anxious to gain money, so that many of the rules that restricted serfs would be set aside for a payment.

Peasants achieved these advantages by vigilance and pressure. They were in continuous dialogue with their lords, employing a variety of strategies for defending their interests, from negotiation to outright rebellion. They had an opportunity to have an influence on the running of their manors because lords depended on peasant officials such as the reeve and the jurors in the manor courts. Peasants would use these positions in their own interests: for example, when they were asked to decide some disputed question of the custom of the manor, they would employ their collective memory selectively. The prominent peasants who occupied the responsible positions in the management of the manor negotiated directly with the lord. When labour services were commuted for cash rents, an agreement would be made for all of the tenants in a particular category (all of the yardlanders, for example) which must have resulted from some form of collective bargaining. Sometimes tenants found that they could buy a concession from the lord – they could escape from some irregular payment, or preserve their rights to a pasture, by offering a sum of money.

A characteristic clash between lord and tenants broke out at Bourton-on-the-Hill and Todenham in Gloucestershire. The customary tenants were supposed in the late thirteenth century to do labour services on certain days of the week. If one of these days coincided with one of the numerous religious holidays, their lord, Westminster Abbey, lost the day's work. A zealous abbot who came into office in 1315 insisted that they work on another day in compensation. The tenants resisted the change, and were charged money for the days' work that were lost, which they failed to pay. The abbot won, but offered in a gesture of reconciliation to cancel the money owed by the tenants. He imagined that this was a generous act, but the tenants thought that the money had been demanded unjustly in the first place. The abbot was enraged when the reeve of Todenham, Henry Melksop, 'of fair face but an ugly snout', 'did not deign to open his mouth to thank us'.

Tenants could register their resentment of customary works by not attending when summoned, sometimes in a co-ordinated withdrawal of service. Or they could work badly. They evaded the penalties of servility, most commonly by concealing the marriage of their daughters so as not to pay the fine, or by transferring land without going to the court (and paying the entry fine) or by illicit subletting. They showed their lack of respect for the lord by grazing their animals on his land, even in his corn, and by stealing corn and taking wood without permission. They took their corn to be ground at a mill other than the lord's, or used their own hand-mills. Lords responded to these offences by amercing (fining) them in the manor court, the revenues of which could provide a twentieth, or even a higher proportion of estate income. In Scotland lords took forfeitures from their tenants in compensation for offences, often in the form of valuable livestock, a cow or a sheep.

The protests and agitations of tenants could become purposeful and well organized. The men of Penrhosllugwy in Anglesey had suffered a harsh assessment of the obligations in 1294, in the aftermath of the English conquest of north Wales. A very heavy burden of labour services, which they had not previously owed, was valued for the whole community at £21, which came on top of payments for various dues and service worth £27. The tenants felt a strong sense of injustice, and mounted a legal campaign which lasted for forty years, including a petition to parliament in 1305.

Serfdom provoked the most consistent opposition from those who were judged to be of villein status after the legal reforms of the late twelfth century. Individuals defended their free status in both manorial and royal courts, and their actions led to the more precise definition of villeinage in terms of liability to pay specific dues such as marriage fines and tallage. More troubling from the lords' point of view were the collective actions brought by communities against their lord, alleging that if their manor had once belonged to the crown, as tenants of 'ancient demesne' they enjoyed a privileged status which allowed them to appeal to the king against any attempt to increase their rents or dues. These pleadings took place within the framework of the law, and show that the peasants believed that the king's courts would be capable of protecting them. Sometimes more direct action was involved, as lords would seize their tenants' animals to bring pressure on them, and tenants would sometimes become involved in violent confrontations, though rarely resulting in serious injury.

The tenants of South Petherton in Somerset in 1278–80 hired a lawyer to bring an action against their lord, Ralph Daubeny. They argued that their complaints had provoked the lord into seizing their goods to a value of £100, an exaggeration but indicating serious antagonism. These disputes raise key questions about the economic implications of serfdom. Tenants clearly resented the burdens that were imposed on them, but often their protests were directed against demands by the lord which appear relatively small-scale. The South Petherton tenants were upset because the lord attempted to seize the goods of widows who committed adultery – not an everyday event. In other cases the issue was pannage of pigs (a few pence paid to allow the pigs to eat acorns in the lord's wood), or some modest customary obligation. To remove these payments tenants were prepared to collect a large fund, £5 in the South Petherton case, in order to pay a lawyer. Usually the better-off peasants played a leading role and contributed most of the money. This was not a case of starving peasants who were being reduced to abject poverty struggling for their very existence. They were concerned with matters of principle – one arbitrary imposition might lead to other, more costly demands, which would be a particular concern for those with larger holdings who feared that their market profits would be lost to the lord. Behind some of the actions lay the belief among serfs that they had once been free, and that the king's power could restore their ancient liberty.

'Ancient demesne' pleas were usually unsuccessful. The courts were not impartial sources of royal justice, but tended to side with landlords. Small victories were registered, as in Battle Abbey's attempt around 1300 to declare the peasants who lived around the Sussex monastery to be serfs. John atte Doune, a tenant of customary land, brought a successful lawsuit in 1305 in the king's court which resulted in a declaration by the abbey that he was simply a tenant, not a serf. However, even in the cases that the lords won, their tenants had shown their solidarity, skill and persistence in fighting an unequal battle, and put their lords to great legal expense. The anger of the lords is displayed in the narratives they wrote about these conflicts. After they were over, both sides still resented the situation, and lords usually did not attempt any further imposition. In other words, the peasants had helped to draw a line on further extensions of their lords' power, and these messy and troublesome disputes served as a warning to other lords not to push their tenants to the limits of their patience.

Two other forms of direct action were used by peasants in conflict with their lords. One was flight, which is well attested in both Scotland and England in the twelfth century when legal measures were available to lords pursuing the escapees. The other was provoked by lords who sought to enclose land on common pastures, or to grant to tenants parcels of common land previously grazed by the whole community. The tenants sometimes attempted legal action, though the law favoured the lord, especially after the Statute of Merton in 1236 strengthened lords' rights over commons. Alternatively they might gather to remove fences and fill in ditches, like the 'malefactors and disturbers of the king's peace' who destroyed a hedge and ditch of Henry Baret's at Lydlynch in Dorset in 1279 'with force of arms, by night'. This could have served its purpose, either removing the enclosures or at least preventing any further encroachments, though the lord usually prevailed and the enclosures were restored.

Lords worked quite hard to increase their revenues from their tenants, but they were not able to extract as much money as they wished. The peasants paid more towards the end of the thirteenth century than they had a century earlier. Money rents were levied as labour services were commuted, and occasional payments such as entry fines could increase threefold. Nonetheless, the demands of lords rose less than the prices of primary products that the peasants sold. Lords could not override custom in order to make major increases in rents, and we have seen that they were slow to convert tenancies into leaseholds that would have reflected more accurately the value of land. The efficient running of estates was constantly held back by the surliness of their tenants. The better-off peasants were therefore able to keep some of their profits won in the market, though they still felt restricted by the ties of serfdom. At an earlier period the demands for cash from lords had helped to simulate peasants' trading by forcing them into the marketplace. By c.1300 the peasants had accepted the commercial habit with some enthusiasm, so were irritated by restrictions which did not drive them into poverty

1. Church of the tenth/eleventh centuries, Duntisbourne Rouse, Gloucestershire. This parish church stands as an example of the hundreds of its kind of this period, when the lords of the new small manors provided places of worship for their households and tenants. The walls are strongly constructed of large stones, so even such a small and plain church was built at considerable cost.

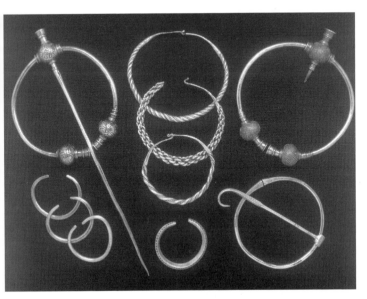

2. Viking silver hoard of the late tenth century from Skaill in Orkney. The objects shown here are large and ornate penannular brooches, together with neck rings and arm rings. These were worn as showy jewellery, but also served as stores of wealth. The chief who owned them may have concealed them when he left on an expedition, or at a time of danger, and did not return to recover them.

3. Reconstruction of an aristocratic house at Goltho in Lincolnshire, tenth century. A ditch and bank provided defence, with a gatehouse which is thought to have been high enough for a vantage point. In the hall, in the foreground, the household ate its meals. The long building near the gate appears to have been a weaving shed. The smallest structure was the kitchen, and nearer the hall stood the bower, or sleeping quarters.

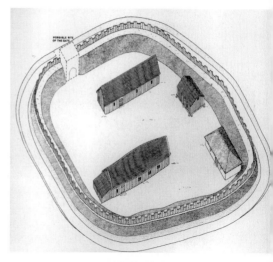

4. The White Tower in the Tower of London. The most impressive secular building from the late eleventh century, the White Tower demonstrates how the Norman conquerors from a site on the edge of the city observed and threatened the largest town in England. A building on this scale kept a labour force of considerable size employed for some years. The stone was brought by water from Caen in Normandy and from Kent.

7. (*facing page*) A windmill, from a fourteenth-century manuscript. These ingenious machines were invented towards the end of the twelfth century, and spread in the thirteenth. The mill and its machinery were mounted on a post firmly fixed into a timber framework. The pole to the left was used to turn the mill and its sails into the wind. In this illustration the miller is carrying a sack of corn, while a customer arrives by horse.

5. Tintern Abbey, Monmouthshire, from the south-east. A Cistercian monastery, founded in 1131, the site is typical of the order's preference for remote, wooded and hilly places away from the distractions of the secular world. The monastery was rebuilt in the thirteenth century, when its income was rising from the sale of wool. The monks sold 25 sacks of wool, much of it of the highest quality, to an Italian merchant in 1294.

6. A gentry house: Markenfield Hall, North Yorkshire. Built *c.* 1310 by John Markenfield, then chancellor of the exchequer, this opulent house reflects the profits of a royal official. Though surrounded by a moat, defence took second place to prestige and comfort. This view from the north shows the hall, lit by two ornate windows, with a chimney for a large hearth between them. The plain structure to the left of the hall contained the garderobes (lavatories).

8. A cart, from a manuscript of *c.* 1300. Carts were used in growing numbers in the thirteenth century. This is being loaded with sheaves of corn, and the artist accurately represents the construction of a light vehicle with two, well made, spoked wheels. The cart is being pulled by a donkey or mule in this mythical scene – in medieval England horses were invariably used.

9. Reclaimed land in the Somerset levels. This part of the valley of the Parrett was reclaimed as part of a large scale drainage scheme mounted by the monks of Glastonbury Abbey in the thirteenth century. In the foreground is the edge of a rhyne, a drainage channel, and behind the cows are shallow ditches dug across the field. All English landscapes are man made, but this was an especially audacious creation, showing technical expertise and an ability to think ahead.

10. A new town of the twelfth century, at Burford in Oxfordshire. The lord of the manor realized that this site, on the main road between London and Gloucester, had potential for making a town. In about 1100 his officials planned the main street, wide enough for a market place. They laid out rows of narrow plots on either side, and many of their boundaries are visible on this photograph. The venture was a success, settlers were attracted, and houses were built on the plots along the street, on the sites of those existing today.

11. The interior of a town house at Perth in *c.* 1300, reconstructed from excavated evidence. These small houses (often 25 by 12 feet) were built with wattle walls covered with clay, and the insubstantial upright timbers supported a roof of straw or heather thatch. Food was cooked over an open hearth in ceramic pots, and served on wooden bowls and plates. This living room would also have been used as working space by artisans.

12. (*right*) Abandoned fields on Bodmin Moor, Cornwall. The plough ridges and field boundaries stretched across this high moorland at Garrow show that arable cultivation extended, by the thirteenth century, over land which has not been ploughed since. The fields were worked from hamlets and isolated farms. Former fields on uplands in many parts of the country were abandoned at various times between *c.* 1300 and the late fifteenth century.

13. The Black Death cemetery at East Smithfield, London, during excavation. Two new cemeteries were opened in London in 1349 to cope with the sudden demand for burial space. The centre of the photograph is occupied by a long trench containing an orderly row of burials. It was later believed that 50,000 Londoners died in the epidemic, and this is not impossible. The well-organized burial arrangements do not support the view that panic led to social collapse.

14. A 'corner shop', at the junction of King Street and Broad Street, Ludlow, Shropshire, of 1403–4. This imposing three-storey building occupied a prime commercial site in the centre of Ludlow, the second largest town in its county. It was built very well of substantial timbers, both to fulfil its functions as a retail outlet and residence, and to impress. It was subdivided among a number of traders, including a mercer, fishmonger and a goldsmith.

15. Pottery from Southampton, c. 1490. The potters were using new techniques to satisfy consumer demand. A variety of wares were available in the port of Southampton: local products include the cooking pot and the 'Tudor green' drinking jug on the right, and the large bowl in the centre at the back. The other glazed and colourful vessels came from France, Spain, Italy, Germany and the Low Countries. The jugs and mugs reflect the importance of drink.

16. Sleeve of a fourteenth-century garment, found near the Thames waterfront at Baynard's Castle, London, preserved in water-logged conditions. It was made of wool, and was woven in a check pattern with some yarn dyed red and other yarn left undyed. The row of twelve buttons fastened into button holes in facings made of silk. This expensive garment demonstrates the skills of both clothmakers and tailors.

17. Ships of the late fifteenth century. These drawings, made in about 1485, show ships incorporating the new technical features of the period: the hulls are carvel built; two masts in the stern are fitted with lateen sails; and guns on the deck fired over the gunwale. These ships were designed to be efficient to build and sail, and were capable of crossing the Atlantic.

18a. A peasant house in the western, cruck tradition from Llanarth, Monmouthshire. The timber frame of Pit Cottage was based on four pairs of sturdy, curved timbers – crucks – of which one pair is visible at the gable end. This three-bay house contained a hall, a chamber and two small rooms. Hundreds of these houses, mostly dating from the fifteenth century, survive (and are still inhabited) in eastern Wales and western England.

18b. A peasant house of wealden type, from Plaxtol in Kent. Spoute House was built in two phases, dated from tree rings. The two-storey end to the right belongs to *c.* 1424, and the part to the left, containing the hall and the other end of two storeys, was built in 1445. One end is jettied – the first floor juts out. There are many surviving medieval houses in Kent – thirteen in the parish of Plaxtol alone.

19. The site of a deserted medieval village at Coates in Lincolnshire. Coates had about twenty households in *c.* 1300. It halved in size by 1377 and was not recognized as a separate village after 1428. The photograph shows the former village street as a long hollow running away from the camera. The figure stands on one of a series of platforms which mark sites of peasant houses.

but held them back from the full enjoyment of the fruits of their enterprise. A new dimension after 1275, and especially after 1294, came from
demands for taxation. The better-off peasants who were assessed for the
lay subsidy were often paying between 10s and 20s per annum in rent to
their lord, and were now presented with a demand for an additional 2–4s
to the tax collectors. It was not demanded every year, but it ate into their
disposable income.

v. *Individuals and communities*

The peasant economy contains many paradoxes. Peasants produced
for the market, yet practised self-sufficiency when possible; they made
technical innovations, while continuing with many traditional practices;
they were consumers, but on a modest scale; they developed a lively land
market, but avoided extreme polarization; they had to pay more to their
lords, but were still able to keep a proportion of their surplus. The final
paradox of the peasantry concerns the collective nature of their agriculture, while they retained a high degree of individual autonomy.

In many ways the rise in population and commercial activity
threatened to weaken the community. The village seems to have had an
egalitarian basis in the sense that the tenants were ranked according to
their standard holdings of yardlands, half-yardlands and oxgangs. Every
yardlander was treated equally by the lord, with the same services and
rents. However, individuals responded with varying degrees of skill
and talent to the opportunities of the market, as is demonstrated by the
varied tax assessments, based on the goods and especially animals that
they owned – one yardlander might pay 2s, and another 6s. Similarly,
when entry fines were charged they varied from holding to holding,
depending on how well they had been managed, fences repaired and
buildings maintained. Many of the changes of the period, such as the
growth of the land market, encouraged selfishness among a minority,
who took advantage of the weakness of their poorer neighbours. Even if
they were not always acting for their personal benefit, they were clearly
motivated by a strong attachment to their families and kin, and these
groupings could be seen as detracting from the unity of the community.

Even more damaging was the gap between those with holdings adequate to feed a family, and those with insufficient land who needed an
income from wages or non-agricultural activities. That divide had existed
for centuries, but population growth tended to swell the ranks of the
smallholders and landless. By the late thirteenth century an underclass had grown of workers without land, either servants living in the

household of their employer, or casual labourers leading a more precarious existence. A fifth of the population of some Wiltshire villages were called 'lads'(*garciones* in Latin) who were listed by the lord because they made a small payment to him. In eastern England they were known as *anilepimen*, and in Scotland *gresmen* because they were allowed to graze animals. In the period 1270–1320, when yardlanders could sometimes make good money from the sale of grain at high prices, the labourers were receiving miserable rates of pay, often 1d per day, which in the years of high prices must have made life almost impossible. They were in danger of spending periods in unemployment because there were few employers, and they had limited needs for workers. The better-off villagers benefited from this cheap labour, and indeed villages like Newton Longville (Buckinghamshire) in 1290 issued by-laws aimed at preventing harvest workers from earning more than 1d with food. Market forces, arising from abundant labour and scarce foodstuffs, had driven real wages to a low level, and the village community still sought to limit the one opportunity that these people had to earn a little extra.

Migration was encouraged by the combination of rising population and varied employment opportunities. Peasants' sons and daughters might need to leave if they had no inheritance of land, and the landless workers would always hope that better earnings could be obtained elsewhere. Successful towns, and rural areas that were industrializing or intensifying agriculture, would attract labour. In the villages of Weston and Moulton in Lincolnshire, where the lord, Spalding Priory, compiled lists of serfs and their offspring in the mid-thirteenth century, between a third and a half of adult children had left their village, and two-thirds of women married partners from outside the village. In Essex in the early fourteenth century, where males aged twelve and over were listed each year to pay a small sum to their lord, between 3 and 5 per cent of them moved each year. Villages were not inhabited by a static population, and migration is only one symptom of the wide horizons of peasants who knew a great deal about the outside world beyond their village.

In spite of this growth in individual initiative, self-interest and inequality, the community still showed signs of health. At its heart lay the management of the common land, especially when all of the arable in a midland field system (see pp. 21–4 and 165–6) was subject to common grazing. The pressure on land meant that rules had to be observed or neighbours would suffer. The village elite, acting through the manor court, issued by-laws especially to regulate the harvest. Animals trespassed in their grazing into forbidden places, such as gardens and cornfields, and tenants encroached on their neighbours' strips with the plough, but there is remarkably little evidence of flagrant indiscipline in cultivation at this time. Evidently everyone realized that there was a common interest in keeping agriculture running smoothly. The court records show that villagers were failing to pay their debts, or not returning animals and implements that they had borrowed. These were probably a minority of cases in which relationships had broken down, and there was a great quantity of co-operation which worked to mutual benefit, and was therefore unrecorded.

To some extent, village self-government was created by superior authorities, as it suited lords, the church and the state to have a system whereby local people collected their own rents and taxes, mended the roads, built the church, and maintained law and order. As government was becoming more complex, the functions of the village community were extended. But this was not always to the advantage of the authorities, as the people and the mechanisms that carried out official tasks could also organize petitions and lawsuits against their lords, as we have seen in the case of the pleas of ancient demesne.

The potentially divisive effects of the gap between rich and poor were bridged in a number of ways which helped to reduce tensions within the village. The harvest by-laws which bore down so heavily on the labourers were of course not observed, as can be judged from their constant repetition. Individual employers, anxious to secure workers at a time of peak demand, paid a higher rate. Wealthier peasants may have established long-term clientages among the cottagers, helping them out in hard times in exchange for guarantees of labour at peak times. At Redgrave in Suffolk in 1289–91, John Kyde, who held only an acre and a half, worked as a labourer for the relatively wealthy Oky family. Simon Oky acted as his pledge in the manor court. One way in which the poor came into contact with their richer neighbours was by living and working in the household as young servants, which must have made it difficult for them to express bitter resentment at their plight. The harvest by-laws included provision for the poor, who were allowed to gather beans and peas in the summer, and to glean ears of corn in the harvest field, providing that they observed regulations about the time and place of these activities. The community showed its interest in social security again when maintenance agreements for retired peasants were made in the manor court, inviting neighbours who were present when the contract was agreed to make sure that the old people were not subsequently neglected (see p. 159).

This period favoured individual initiative, but the peasants who showed these entrepreneurial and selfish tendencies were still contained within highly cohesive communities. No doubt some individuals were held back by the restrictions of common agriculture, but many more welcomed the security that came from belonging to a group with many shared interests. While small-scale enterprises took advantage of the market, under-employed smallholders lived in impoverished conditions. Those numerous villagers with a few acres or a cottage were dependent for their living on wage-earning. The increased numbers seeking work ensured a low level of pay, and the high price of grain reduced real wages. A calculation of the purchasing power of the daily wage – the amount of food that a worker could buy after a day's work – shows that a very low point was reached in the 1270s, and there was no sustained recovery until after 1320. The danger of the proliferation of families attempting to live on small amounts of land was becoming all too obvious by the 1290s.

CHAPTER SIX

Towns and commerce, c.1100–c.1315

The two centuries up to c.1300 transformed the urban scene in Britain. The total number of towns increased from 100 to 830; in England the proportion of the population living in towns rose from nearly 10 per cent to almost 20 per cent, and in Scotland and Wales from virtually none to more than a tenth. This chapter is concerned with exploring the significance of that urban expansion, and how it changed the lives and outlook of those who lived in towns and those who had contact with them. We have already seen the decisive contribution of the lords who founded many of the new towns as part of a policy of estate development (pp. 145–7). Now we can turn to examine the upheaval that led so many individuals to leave their homes in the country to swell the urban population. In order to understand that process of migration, we will need to define the anatomy of the towns, and the relationship they had with their rural surroundings.

i. Urban expansion

None of the hundreds of thousands of migrants has left a personal record of their move, but we can attempt to understand their motives. The rural economy could not give everyone an adequate living. The underprivileged, such as many young people and those with smallholdings, were faced with long-term impoverishment in villages already well supplied with labour, and in which land was scarce. A crowded countryside, occasionally threatened with food shortages, pushed its population into leaving, but towns also pulled in newcomers by offering them positive advantages. We define towns as permanently established concentrations of people, who were pursuing a variety of non-agricultural occupations, in which crafts and trades would predominate, but which also included administrators, clergy, schoolteachers, prostitutes and other specialists. To would-be migrants, the towns beckoned because they gave opportunities for different skills and talents.

Some towns that attracted immigrants at this time were brand new. David I of Scotland (1124–53) set up fifteen burghs in the first phase of Scottish urbanization, and encouraged traders and artisans to settle in them by offering the privileges of fixed cash rents and free disposal of land, which were based on the benefits enjoyed by the tenants of an English new town, Newcastle-upon-Tyne. The new arrivals who took up a plot in a burgh were given a five-year respite on paying their rent while they built a house and set up a business. The king and his successors founded most of their burghs in the eastern part of the kingdom where royal rule was firmly established. The burghs were associated with castles, and they were made the centres of new shires, thereby giving the towns political and administrative importance. Later they acquired religious houses, like the friaries founded in the larger towns in the thirteenth century. The towns also enjoyed the advantages of a region with a developed rural economy, and royal grants of the privileges of holding markets and fairs made them the commercial centre of their surrounding countryside. The most successful foundations were those best able to take advantage of overseas trade, notably Berwick, Edinburgh, Perth and Aberdeen. Permanent urban settlements, albeit small in size, grew across the west of the lowlands and in the borders, in places such as Renfrew, Lanark and Jedburgh. In addition to the royal foundations of David I and his successors, prominent churchmen encouraged and planned towns in the twelfth century at such sites as Glasgow and St Andrews, and lay aristocrats fostered towns on their estates, such as Dundee (Map 9).

The Scottish new towns of the mid-twelfth century recruited from scratch, so their settlers were real pioneers without experience of urban life, though some may already have been practising trades and crafts in the countryside. Most newcomers in the thirteenth century were not making such a leap in the dark, because towns were already familiar as centres for the surrounding countryside. They acted not just as hubs and meeting places where produce was sold and goods bought, but also often served as centres of administration, religion and entertainment. Country people would go to towns to attend courts, to participate in ceremonies, to watch a bull baited, or to hear musicians, and the move to live in towns often followed from such visits.

Contemporary attitudes and behaviour towards towns would have been influenced by their position in the urban hierarchy, which depended on their size, location and functions. At the top stood London, without

Scottish burghs in existence by 1300

N

- Cromarty
- Cullen
- Dingwall
- Elgin
- Banff
- Nairn Forres
- Fyvie
- Inverness
- Inverurie
- Newburgh
- Kintore
- ABERDEEN

- Brechin
- MONTROSE
- Forfar
- Arbroath

- PERTH
- DUNDEE
- Auchterarder
- St. Andrews
- Newburgh
- Crail
- Inverkeithing
- Stirling
- Kinghorn
- Kirkintilloch
- Linlithgow
- Dunbar
- Dumbarton
- Haddington
- Renfrew
- EDINBURGH
- Canongate
- Glasgow
- BERWICK UPON
- Rutherglen
- Lanark
- Peebles
- TWEED
- Irvine
- Kelso
- Prestwick
- Selkirk
- Roxburgh
- Ayr
- Crawford
- Jedburgh

- Dumfries
- Lochmaben
- Urr
- Annan
- Wigtown

● Burghs of the king

□ Burghs of other lords

⊡ Burghs passing between the king and private lords

BURGHS in capitals were important trading ports in the early 14ᵗʰ century

0   100km
0   100 miles

Map 9. Scottish burghs in existence by 1300. The larger towns were established mainly in the east, but smaller burghs were distributed across the central belt and to the south into the borders and Galloway.

Source: P. G. B. McNeill and H. L. McQueen, *Atlas of Scottish History to 1707* (Edinburgh, 1996).

any doubt the leading town in Britain, and indeed one of the largest and most important cities in north-west Europe. With a population by 1300 which may have been as great as 80,000, it was smaller than Paris, but probably exceeded in size any one of the great cities of Flanders or the Rhine valley. It towered over the main provincial capitals in England, and was at least three times as large as Bristol, Norwich or York. Norwich in the early fourteenth century may have reached 20,000. In the next rank lay the provincial towns, which could be as large as Winchester with its 10,000 people in c.1300, but most, like Canterbury, Gloucester, Oxford, Bury St Edmunds, Coventry and Lincoln, had populations in the region of 5,000. The major ports attained similar size, most of them on the east and south coasts, at Newcastle, Hull, Boston, King's Lynn, Sandwich and Southampton. Chester served the north-west of England and parts of north Wales. In all, about fifty English towns had 2,000 or more inhabitants, leaving the great majority, more than 600, which can be rated as market towns or small towns. The more important of these provided a living for a thousand or two, like Banbury, Chelmsford, Louth, Peterborough, Ludlow and Doncaster, but the majority, with populations measured in hundreds, like Tenterden, Petersfield, Lostwithiel, Lechlade, Newmarket, Bradford, Cockermouth and Alnwick, still contained a concentration of traders and artisans, and served as centres for the surrounding countryside.

The line between towns and other types of commercial and industrial community is sometimes difficult to draw. Hundreds of markets were founded, especially in the thirteenth century, in villages where the inhabitants were mainly peasants, and which did not build up a permanent population of people pursuing non-agricultural occupations. Some of these market villages provided useful venues for buying and selling, but these were just occasions on one day of the week, after which the community returned to the routines of cultivation. Some rural markets attracted a handful of butchers, smiths and carpenters, and began to resemble a town. Similarly, most industrial villages consisted entirely of weavers or lead miners or fishermen, and so lacked the variety of occupations that was so essential to a town, but again food traders and craftsmen might gather in the village, and create a community with town-like qualities.

The hierarchy had a different character in the less densely populated parts of Britain. In Devon and Cornwall, amid numerous very small towns, Exeter, the capital of the region, attained a modest size of about 3,000–4,000, smaller than the provincial towns 100 and more miles to the east. In the north-west of England, Carlisle served as a centre of administration, defence and religion, with its castle and cathedral, and provided an important channel of exchange across the border to Scotland, and yet was no larger than many market towns of the midlands and the south-east. In Wales a handful of towns, notably Cardiff, Carmarthen and Haverfordwest, rose a little above the 2,000 mark, and the great majority of Welsh market towns fell below 1,000. In eastern Scotland there was more of a hierarchy, with Aberdeen, Perth and Berwick probably above 2,000, and Edinburgh falling into the second rank. Western Scotland resembled the rest of western Britain in its very small towns.

The larger the population of a town, the more complex and varied its life became. The larger places provided a living for people pursuing numerous occupations, more than 100 in the case of a provincial capital. You would be more likely to encounter craftsmen making luxury or specialized goods in a large town – a bell founder or armourer, for example. Only large towns contained a group of really wealthy merchants, who traded either in luxury goods (such as wine), or in large cargoes for distant markets, such as wool being carried by the sack to Flanders. Small towns were full of artisans and petty traders supplying a limited range of relatively cheap and ordinary goods.

The larger towns were more likely to serve as centres of local administration, and to have powers of self-government. You would find in such towns institutions, like the half-dozen religious houses (mostly friaries) which were established in Newcastle upon Tyne, and two or three hospitals; the older towns were divided into many parishes, with a dozen parish churches in most larger provincial towns, and more than 100 in London. Many small towns could boast of no more than a chapel and a fraternity. Visitors would be struck by the large town's skyline dominated by impressive buildings – a castle keep, and church towers and spires. This emphasis on the vertical was continued by the houses in the main streets, which rose to three or four storeys, compared with the two- or even one-storey buildings and single church tower in market towns.

Every type and rank of town interacted in a different way with its rural surroundings. Each had an immediate hinterland extending for a radius of 6 or 7 miles, within which the rural population could easily and habitually travel to market. The towns formed a network, with market centres distributed over the land at regular intervals. This complementary system was to some extent the result of political decisions, as the lawyers said that neighbours might object if a new market was proposed within a radius of 6²/₃ miles. Markets (in towns and in villages) were held on different days, which reduced the amount of direct competition and allowed traders to move from place to place through the week. Large towns might have markets at the end of the week, so that a grain dealer, for example, could visit a succession of small town and village markets, buying up small quantities and then selling his accumulated purchases. In south Nottinghamshire, minor markets held at Wyssall on Wednesdays and Granby on Mondays could have fed into the large market of Nottingham. The even distribution of markets was often interrupted in the immediate vicinity of the larger towns, where both small towns and village markets were notably absent, whether through political influence, or recognition by would-be promoters that small ventures would not flourish in the shadow of a large town.

The larger towns had long-distance contacts for specific commodities and customers, and they dominated the smaller centres of trade within their spheres of influence. So London drew its grain supplies from ten counties, in some cases from a distance of more than 50 miles. Many small towns and markets served as collecting points for grain which would eventually reach the capital. Strategically placed small towns, notably Faversham in Kent, Ware in Hertfordshire, and Henley-on-Thames in Oxfordshire, were dominated by London traders, under whose control crops within carting distance were collected, stored in granaries, and loaded into carts and boats for carriage to the city. The dependent relationship worked in reverse when merchants from the larger towns supplied imported or luxury goods to small town retailers, like the wine from a Bristol vintner which was sold by the gallon in a tavern in the small Herefordshire town of Leominster. A large town's commercial reach crossed administrative and cultural boundaries. So Bristol had a strong influence on the towns of Glamorgan and Monmouthshire, just as those in north Wales looked to the merchants of Chester.

The traders of the large towns sold luxury items, or foodstuffs in bulk, direct to wealthy customers at a considerable distance. The bishop of Hereford, Richard de Swinfield, in 1289–90 bought wax and spices in London, and obtained most of his parchment at Oxford. The advantage of such dealings lay in the ability of the merchants of the major towns, especially in London, to supply quantities of luxury goods, to offer a wider choice, and to be able to sell in bulk at a good price, which did not include inland transport costs and the profits of provincial middlemen. Magnate consumers in the thirteenth century often bargained with the merchants at the great international fairs, where quantities of spices, wax, preserved fish and cloth were available at 'wholesale' prices. The merchants who sold these goods at such fairs as Boston and St Ives (Huntingdonshire) tended to come from the larger towns and especially London. The London merchants had the great advantage that as the city (together with neighbouring Westminster) emerged as the permanent seat of government, the magnates of church and state acquired grand houses in the suburbs of Holborn, Southwark and along the Strand, where they could stay on their visits to the royal household, the law courts and parliament. These residences contained storage space, and some magnates also set up separate 'wardrobes' in the city, where purchases could be kept for future use.

The size of the towns' trading zone varied from one commodity to another. Cheap and bulky goods could not be carried very far, or the cost became prohibitive, and so most towns, even large centres, obtained their fuel within a short distance, often 12 miles. Cattle, on the other hand, could transport themselves, with the encouragement of a drover, so herds came out of Wales to supply the butchers of major towns such as Gloucester, and some of them eventually made their way to London. Water transport enabled heavy goods to be carried long distances. The fine building stone quarried at Caen in Normandy was used for castles and churches in London and the south-east, and stone from Barnack in Lincolnshire, where the quarries lay near to navigable rivers, was taken by boat over much of eastern England. In the same way, metals such as iron and lead travelled many miles.

The hinterlands, with all of their variety depending on the town, the customers and suppliers, transport routes, and the goods being carried, had a considerable influence on the pattern of migration. A place that was already familiar from visits to market or carting journeys was likely to be the first choice of destination for those intending to find work in a town. In some cases the local rural population had more formal links with the town, because they paid a fee to have access to the market without paying tolls. In Wales, 'censers' who had attachments to such places as Caernarfon and Aberystwyth, often lived within 10 miles of the town. Half of Shrewsbury's 'foreign burgesses' in 1232 lived within a radius of 8 or 9 miles. Wealthier country people could also establish links by joining the town's religious fraternity. But most of the associations between town and country depended not on any institution but on the constant to and fro based on the weekly market.

Just as London had the largest hinterland, so it drew migrants from considerable distances, frequently from the east midlands and East Anglia, over 50 miles and more. Take an incident in a street in the capital on 11 November 1300. John de Bois, from Suffolk, was accidentally killed when a piece of wood, used to dry saddles during their manufacture, fell from the upper storey of a house in Cheapside, the busiest thoroughfare in the city. He was carried to the house of Adam de Drayton. The sudden death was investigated by the alderman of the ward, Walter de Finchingfield. Various people living nearby were required to give evidence, including Nicholas de Gotham, and among those appointed to ensure their co-operation in the investigation were William de Kent, William de Kemesing and William de Assington. De Bois came from Suffolk, and may have been a visitor to the capital, or a recent immigrant. The Londoners who became caught up in the events had names deriving from Middlesex, Essex, Suffolk and Nottinghamshire, with two from Kent. Names were becoming fixed at this time, and they may have been coined to identify the fathers or even grandfathers of those alive in 1300, but they still demonstrate past migrations; from this small sample of six, four had travelled more than 30 miles, and one had made a journey of about 100 miles. The larger towns often attracted immigrants from a distance of more than 20 miles. Exeter, which was an important place in its region, though of no great size, pulled in more than half of its population from within 20 miles, but 27 per cent came between 20 and 40 miles. Small towns drew most of their inhabitants within 20 miles, and commonly from a 10-mile radius.

Young people, including a high proportion of women, were most likely to make these moves, often in order to become servants in towns. An example is Emetina, daughter of John, son of Robert, of Moulton in Lincolnshire, who some time shortly before 1268 had moved 20 miles into the town of Stamford. Her father was quite prosperous, with a holding of about 22 acres, but her two brothers would have taken priority in the inheritance of the land. The family were serfs, so Emetina would acquire her freedom by leaving the control of her lord, the priory of Spalding. She showed her adventurous spirit in seeking her fortune in a relatively large town. Perhaps a friend or relative from the village had moved to Stamford earlier, and helped subsequent migrants to find jobs. She may even have been in contact with employment agents. The advantage of moving to a large town was the greater range of openings, both in service in households and in the cloth industry.

A different type of migrant moved into new towns, where the tenants of burgage plots were not penniless young peasant women, but mature men with the capital to build a house and set up business in such trades as smithing or tanning, and the skill to make a success of their trade. An example is Alexander de Hatton, who appears in the new town of Stratford-upon-Avon in 1251, just fifty-five years after the town had been founded. Either he or his father had moved from Hatton-on-Avon, a village within 4 miles of the town. Alexander's family in Hatton had some spare resources from their holding of a full yardland, and their servile status gave him a reason for migrating. The de Hattons in Stratford made a success of their new urban life. Already by 1251

Alexander had acquired a larger than average amount of property – a plot and a half – and his son thirty or so years later gained more land and joined the elite of the town, acting as bailiff and witnessing the deeds by which his neighbours conveyed property. Another type of relatively affluent migrant is represented by those who moved from one town to another. Having presumably acquired skills or capital, an artisan or trader might hope to make a better life in a different town. Often these men were seeking promotion by moving from a small town to a higher level in the hierarchy, which presumably explains the presence in Chester in the 1290s of Thomas de Manchester and William de Flint. Indeed, quite a high proportion of the migrants in the regional capitals and London had come from smaller towns. Those who had experience of a major centre would sometimes move down to a market town, like the people called 'de London' who lived at Baldock in Hertfordshire in 1185. Perhaps they hoped to play a larger role in a small place, or perhaps they failed to cope with the competition of the big city, or the move may have resulted from an accident of marriage or business.

A special case of movement between towns is found in Wales, where English influence was deliberately spread by town foundations. Recruits were gathered in western English towns, and so we find names like 'de Stratford' and 'de Warwick' in Carmarthen. Other migrant groups influenced by political events were the French colonists who moved into English towns soon after 1066. The most easily identified group, the Jews, came mostly from Rouen. They settled in dozens of towns, but formed especially strong communities in Lincoln and York, and by 1200 the Jewish population in England exceeded 5,000.

Towns attracted clergy, doctors, administrators and lawyers. The professionals were well placed to meet clients, or to travel out to them in the hinterland. The clergy were established in the towns from an early stage to serve the many parish churches, and as chantries and fraternities increased in number in the thirteenth century more chaplains were employed to say masses. By 1300 perhaps one in twenty of town dwellers was a clergyman, and many of them were migrants. Their economic contribution was mainly as consumers and as redistributors of wealth, as they took revenues from the laity in tithes and offerings and then often spent the money within the town. They contributed more directly as developers of church land. They also provided education, and wrote deeds and bonds. Towns could gain importance if the local church became a centre of pilgrimage. Every major church encouraged visitors to venerate relics or images, but a few pulled in large crowds, most notably Canterbury with its cult of the tomb of Thomas Becket, who had been murdered in 1170. Finally, some very well-heeled settlers are found in towns. The landed gentry did not acquire town houses just for temporary occupation or as bases for selling and buying, rather as the magnates did in London, but sometimes became almost permanent residents, like the knight John Sampson at York in the 1290s. And some successful merchants found it convenient to have houses and businesses in more than one centre.

Moving to a town was a risky venture. Some of the new foundations failed; migrants who moved hopefully into Skinburness in Cumberland found that not enough people followed them to make the town work, and so they had to move again, judging from the fact that the royal charter granting borough status in 1301 was cancelled only four years later. Not all of the large towns were expanding – Winchester was probably smaller in the early fourteenth century than it had been in the twelfth. One factor in its reduced size was the centralization of royal government at London, and another the rise of successful rivals such as Salisbury, which was founded in 1219. Political factors disrupted towns in Wales. Under English rule new towns were founded as part of the process of imposing alien rule, which damaged the existing towns set up by Welsh rulers. The population of the active port of Llanfaes on Anglesey was displaced when Edward I founded a new town under the walls of his castle of Beaumaris at the end of the thirteenth century. The Welsh directed their resentment against these instruments of foreign control, and Caernarfon, built under the walls of Edward I's castle in 1283–4, was burnt in the rebellion of 1294. Towns on both sides of the Anglo-Scottish border suffered in the fighting which began in the 1290s. The Jews encountered resentment in England, partly arising from hostility to their religion and culture, but also owing a great deal to their role as moneylenders under royal protection. The Jewish community endured periodic persecution, most savagely at York in 1190, and a century later the whole episode of medieval Jewish settlement came to an end with the expulsion of the Jews by Edward I.

But these setbacks and episodes of destruction were exceptional. Most migrants stayed, and hundreds of towns achieved some success. Behind the global increase in the urban population are many stories of growth in individual towns. Cowbridge in south Wales doubled in size between 1281 and 1306. Many of the larger English towns with 1,000 to 2,000 inhabitants in 1086 had 5,000 or more by 1300, and some had risen into the leading fifty towns after being founded in the twelfth and thirteenth centuries – Newcastle, Hull, Lynn, Boston and Salisbury all achieved success in a few decades of sustained growth. Migrants were needed in all towns, even those which did not grow very rapidly, because families in towns raised relatively few children to adulthood.

ii. *The urban environment*

The fabric of the town changed as the population grew, with consequences both for living conditions and the property market. The lords
made the initial town plans. Kings were the leaders before the Conquest,
and continued to take initiatives. Edward I, a great town founder in
Wales, also showed a personal interest in establishing Berwick-upon-
Tweed, Hull and Winchelsea, and indeed summoned a gathering of
advisers on town planning in 1297. In the twelfth and thirteenth centuries
the majority of towns were created by lords, with lay lords outnumber-
ing bishops and monasteries by a ratio of two to one. The purpose of
the planners was to establish a framework which would encourage trade
and crafts. At the heart of the town was the marketplace, often outside
the church or at the entrance to the manor house or castle. The market
was equipped with stalls, and a toll house or market hall. Often a separate cattle or beast market was established on the edge of the town, large
enough to take the animal pens. The planners would divert roads in the
vicinity to make sure that traffic passed through. They laid out streets
wide enough for carts to pass, and to provide space for overspill of stalls
and selling points from the main marketplace. The more elaborate plans
included side roads and back lanes so that deliveries could be made to
the rear of properties. (Plate 10)

Plots were set out with houses and shops fronting on to streets to make
contact with customers, sometimes with an entry from the street to allow
vehicles to have access to the plot behind, and a large enough plot (often
about a quarter-acre) for outbuildings, workshops and storage space.
The plan was flexible: if demand for premises increased, the plot could
be split down the middle, or even divided three or four times, with
narrower houses fitted end-on to the street, to maintain the vital direct
contact with the customers. If necessary the rear of the plots was used
more intensively, even to the point where these were filled with cottages
and workshops. Another response to growth was to add sections to
towns, with new streets and rows of building plots. These extensions
have left their mark on the modern town plans, and the successive phases
of growth can be reconstructed by close study of street plans and
property boundaries. Many of the 'New Streets' and 'Newlands' (to the
surprise of their modern inhabitants) date from the thirteenth century.
The planning could be the result of further initiatives by lords, or sometimes a neighbouring lord would set up a separate suburb (see p. 146).
The new phases of development could also come from townsmen who
had become landlords by buying up property, or from the urban community itself, like the rows of houses and shops, in effect a new street,

which were built on both sides of the first stone London Bridge when it was constructed between the late twelfth century and 1209.

The incentive to plan towns, extend them, and to build on the plots came from the money that could be earned from the renting and sale of urban property. Lords usually received an annual ground rent of between 6d and 18d, often 12d for each plot, which was many times the value of agricultural land, but did not reflect the full income generated by an urban economy. The burgesses or freeholders would sublet plots, or subdivide them and rent out a fraction, and if the demand for land was high could expect to make 20s from renting a house with its plot, and even 5s for a small cottage. A growing proportion of the subtenants would be leaseholders, and might pay their rents monthly. Such investments could provide acquisitive town landlords with large rental incomes, like the £22 per annum which a Bristol merchant, John de Cardiff, gained from property in the town in the early fourteenth century. Monasteries, which had in some cases founded the towns in which they stood, bought up land and houses in order to profit from the higher income that could be made by subletting. In Canterbury in 1199, houses and shops in the city worth £25 per annum belonged to the cathedral priory, but by 1300 it owned about a third of the town and enjoyed an income from rents of £110. As the urban economy expanded, and the demand for property increased, so the sale price and rent of urban land and buildings rose. The amount of money paid by buyers to acquire land in Coventry rose from about £1 in each transaction at the beginning of the thirteenth century to about £4 by the 1280s and 1290s. Urban landlords invested in buildings, and most of the houses in towns were rebuilt at some time in the thirteenth century. A minority of houses in the twelfth century had been constructed entirely in stone, and a few houses of this type were added after 1200, but most often stone was used in modest amounts to build a few courses for foundations to support timber-framed superstructures. A modest new house could cost £10, and landlords could certainly justify such construction costs, as they would quickly recover the money in rents.

Town houses incorporated workshops, and rooms where customers could inspect goods and make their purchases, but there were also premises given over entirely to commercial use. These were the stalls and shops built in marketplaces and along the busier shopping streets. In even the smallest market town the space set aside in the marketplace for temporary stalls was quickly covered with permanent structures, sometimes of two storeys, with a chamber above the shop where goods could be kept, or which came into use as accommodation for people. Some rows of stalls were dedicated to the use of a particular group of traders. The butchers would commonly have their 'shambles', segregated in order to keep the more unpleasant sights and smells away from other retailers and shoppers. A marketplace would commonly have a 'drapery' where woollen cloth was sold, or a 'mercery' for linen. To hold and build a stall could be very rewarding, judging from the rents they commanded; a stall covering only 100 square feet at a prime selling point could be rented annually for 10s, the same as 20 acres of good agricultural land. The busiest shopping street in Britain was Cheapside in London, where a shop in 1300 cost the tenant £3 per annum: this had doubled over the previous half-century.

The concentration of opportunities to make wealth, or at least earn a living, led people to be packed into the confined space where manufacture and marketing were focused. While in modern cities the rich live in the suburbs, leaving the central business district empty at night, with the poor living in other parts of the inner city, in the middle ages everyone, including the rich merchants, wished to live in the town centre, and the less fortunate were left on the outskirts. This created problems for those crowded in the densely built environment. It is true that even in large towns those at the centre could walk to fields and open spaces in a few minutes. At Ayr and Denbigh and many other places, most of the burgesses held some acres of land in the fields attached to the town. Larger houses often had gardens at the rear, even in the middle of London. But this access to space cannot alter the fact that most townspeople lived in cramped conditions. The less affluent often occupied houses with a floor area of 15 feet by 15 feet, though with two storeys to provide a sleeping room separate from the living and working space on the ground floor. Alternatively, labourers and servants lived in larger houses, but occupied only a room or two, commonly on an upper floor. These problems of overcrowding were not confined to the largest towns, as smaller places, such as Durham or Edinburgh, were often built on a restricted site. The inhabitants of Perth occupied very narrow plots, and their wattle-walled houses (revealed by excavations) lay near to cesspits, middens and manure heaps. (Plate 11) Here as in other towns animals lived close to people. Horses were essential for transport and many townspeople kept a cow or a few sheep on the land outside the town, but the typical urban animals were the pigs which were fed on household waste, though they also scavenged on rubbish. Trades such as butchery fouled the streets, and tanning put effluents into the rivers and streams. Almost every industrial process, from brewing to smithing, contributed to the smoky atmosphere, and some towns suffered from continuous fumes and air pollution, such as the salt-boiling centres of Droitwich in Worcestershire and Northwich and Nantwich in Cheshire. As coal production grew, the inhabitants of towns such as Newcastle and Nottingham experienced especially severe smoke problems.

The town authorities aimed to create a decent environment. The elite, after all, lived in the town centres, so there was an element of self-interest in their policy, but they were also concerned with the reputation and general well-being of their town. They were beginning to provide piped water supplies, and by *c.*1300 refuse disposal was changing so that less use was being made of middens and pits in the back yards of houses, and more rubbish was being carried to tips on the outskirts. The town governments were also concerned about the obstruction of the streets by manure heaps, stacks of firewood and building timber, and stalls jutting out of the front of houses and shops. In London these problems were resolved through the 'assize of nuisance'. For example, in 1301 William de Betonia complained that the cesspit of his neighbour, William de Gartone, lay so close to his cellar that the sewage dripped through the wall. This was investigated by the mayor and aldermen, who did not accept de Gartone's argument that he was a free tenant and that his predecessors had always had a privy. Instead, the offender was given forty days to build a stone wall $2^1/_2$ feet thick between the pit and his neighbour's cellar.

Those governing towns were also concerned about the hazard of fires, which occurred not infrequently when houses were closely packed and built of inflammable materials, especially thatch for roofs. A town with a healthy economy, like Boston which was burnt in 1288, could recover quickly enough, but Carlisle, in its vulnerable position on the Scottish border and in a relatively poor and thinly populated region, suffered a more serious setback from its great fire of 1296. One remedy adopted at this time was to insist that houses be roofed with slates, tiles or shingles.

Towns may have reached the limits of the size that could be sustained by about 1300. The proportion of the population living in towns, and therefore dependent mainly on the agricultural production of the rest of society, was nearing a fifth, which was not very different from the proportion in 1500 or indeed in the early eighteenth century. The urban population could be fed in normal years, though special measures had to be taken when harvests were severely deficient. One sign of strain was the difficulty in the supply of fuel, apparent in London at the end of the thirteenth century. The woods of the region were managed to provide a continuous flow of 'underwood' suitable for use in domestic and industrial hearths, but prices were high, and transport costs would not allow wood fuel to be brought from further afield. Some mineral coal was already being carried by ship from Newcastle, and the long-term growth of the capital depended on increasing use of this more efficient (if more polluting) fuel from the north-east.

iii. *Urban occupations*

People crowded into towns, in spite of the unhealthy living conditions, because they offered a means of making a living. At the bottom of the heap were the very poor with no stable source of income. Because they had no property and no formal role in society or government, we know little about them apart from the accusation in court records of their criminal or apparently anti-social behaviour. In London no 'whore of a brothel', according to an order in 1277, was allowed to live within the walls, and in York in 1301 it was stated that women living in the city and keeping brothels were to be imprisoned. Beggars were attracted to the cities by handouts of free food or cash from monasteries and wealthy households. The royal household fed 20,000 paupers at Westminster in 1244, suggesting the very large numbers of poor in and around the capital.

Most migrants hoped for a better life than was available on the fringes of urban society, and their first toehold in towns came from gaining employment as servants. These accounted for a high proportion of the population of towns in the late fourteenth century, when servants commonly made up 20 to 30 per cent of urban poll-tax payers. The proportion is unlikely to have been any less a hundred years earlier. The majority of employers would have no more than a servant or two in their houses, either carrying out domestic tasks or working in a par-ticular trade or craft. The servants usually lived in the household, and part of their pay consisted of food, drink, accommodation and clothing. Apprentices were rewarded in a similar way, but their masters had an obligation to teach them the skills of the craft, and could expect some reward from their parents for their instruction. At the same time they required a high standard of behaviour from the apprentice, and the master provided something resembling parental care.

While apprentices and some servants could expect to acquire a skill, many townspeople worked as labourers. This meant that they might keep their own household in a rented house or cottage, and walk to work each day. Many tasks in towns required little training, such as carrying water to houses, and removing rubbish. For every skilled building craftsman there were two labourers, digging foundations, hauling stone and timber, and mixing and applying daub to wattle walls. Their period of employment was often short-term and and precarious, and they might go in the morning to a meeting place to be offered a day's work, like those at Bedford who were said in 1305 to have 'stood at the Cross to be hired'.

As the labourers were ill-paid and their lives uncertain, those entering towns had the ambition to take up a craft, either in manufacture or retail trade, or in the service sector. The number of crafts increased with the size of the town, so that we know of 175 occupations practised in London, but no more than twenty in a small market town. The descriptions attached to an individual or group or used as surnames give an air of precision, as if people could be placed in a specific pigeon-hole. In practice their lives were more complicated. The male head of the household had a sideline, and his wife would commonly have her own trade, typically as a brewster. For example, Adam de Stretton, a butcher of Shrewsbury, who was assessed for tax payment in 1297, owned meat worth 20s, as would be expected, but he was also in possession of 5 quarters of rye, which was a greater quantity than his household would have eaten, and suggests that he dealt in grain. His supply of malt worth 10s could represent another part of his corn-dealing stock, or it might have been stored for use by his wife in brewing ale for sale. Material remains indicate a number of small-scale or part-time occupations. At Perth, the inhabitants of two adjacent plots on the High Street, in addition to working leather and metal, removed horns from cattle slaughtered by the town's butchers, in order to make transparent panels for lanterns, and skinned cats (there were many strays in towns) for their fur. We have already seen that many townspeople held some land, or at least a garden, which was not their main source of income but provided a valuable supplement. In spite of these dual or mixed occupations, the record of crafts and trades still gives a valuable impression of the range of activities to be found in each town.

In most towns the food and drink trades provided more employment than any other activity. Townspeople could produce only a fraction of their food needs, and in many cases their working lives allowed them little time to prepare meals. In addition, numerous visitors – travellers, customers, pilgrims, those attending courts – expected to eat and drink during their stay. In particular the sellers of food and drink catered for the country people who attended markets. In Winchester in about 1300, eight millers ground grain and malt for consumption in the town. There were twelve bakers, sixty brewers, eleven butchers and seven fishmongers. Counting the families and households of these traders alone, about 500 people were gaining a substantial part of their livelihood from preparing and selling food and drink, and this does not take account of the cooks and innkeepers who prepared and served meals, or the dealers in fruit and vegetables, dairy products, poultry, honey and salt. At the luxury end of the trade, vintners and taverners sold wine, and spicers and grocers dealt in expensive imports of condiments such as pepper and ginger, and dried fruits and nuts. A more basic living was earned by the hucksters, women with baskets of bread or eggs, vegetables and other foods, who obtained their supplies from the bakers and other well-established traders, and then sold their wares for meagre profit in the streets or from door to door. In a similar fashion, women called variously gannockers, tapsters or tranters would sell ale that they had obtained from the brewers. As in any branch of commerce, when demand reached a large scale in a major city, trade became more specialized, and a living could be made by a 'stockfishmonger' (dealing in dried cod from Norway) or a 'garlickmonger'.

Every town had some section of its workforce devoted to manufacture, which can be divided into branches depending on the products, and the materials used: leather (including sheepskins and furs), textiles (wool and linen), clothing, metalworking (iron, copper alloys, lead and tin) and wood. Building should be mentioned as an important sector of employment in towns as well as in the country. The balance between the different crafts depended on the supply of raw materials, local demand, the opportunities for wider distribution, and the traditions of skill that might develop in a town.

Making woollen cloth probably employed more people in towns than any other industry. The separate processes included combing and carding the wool, spinning the yarn, weaving and various stages of finishing – dyeing, fulling and shearing. It was well suited to larger towns where enough people were concentrated to practise the different crafts, particularly in the preparatory stages, when dozens of combers, carders and spinners were needed to supply a few weavers. The preparation of the wool and spinning of yarn were often carried out by women, who were paid relatively little for unspecialized tasks. The larger towns, such as Beverley, Leicester, Lincoln, Oxford, Stamford and York were important centres for clothmaking in the thirteenth century, and the presence of weavers' guilds in many of them suggests that the industry had become well established in the twelfth. Clothmaking was also a source of employment in smaller towns, such as Banbury, Cricklade and High Wycombe and, as we have seen, in many rural locations.

One element in the growth of clothmaking was the higher demand from a rising population. But the industry was very complex, and its ups and downs reflected fierce competition in both domestic and continental markets. The producers had to make difficult calculations about demand and customer preferences, because ultimately success depended on consumer choice. The very wealthy required a well-finished cloth, like Lincoln scarlets, the appeal of which depended on the quality of the shearing as well as the colour. The cloth producers of the English towns such as Lincoln and Stamford won continental customers, and exported large quantities of relatively expensive cloth in the thirteenth century. In the mass market, consumers demanded cheap textiles known as burrels, or cloths which were either undyed, or dyed grey or russet. Those who bought textiles were conscious of the price, so the producers might use coarse cheap wool, or they could economize on the wages needed to finish the cloth, with the danger that the consumers would notice the difference. There were always the continental producers, and especially the famous clothmakers of Flanders, waiting to take over the continental market, and indeed to make inroads among English customers.

Migrants into towns would find that opportunities for finding jobs depended on the amount of skill and training, and on the extent to which the craft required expensive equipment and premises. Yarn was often spun in the country, and a woman who moved into the town could continue in that activity. Finding an opening in the more skilled, and better rewarded, end of clothmaking was more difficult, not only because of the skill needed, but also because weavers' looms, or dyers' vats, or fullers' tubs and cloth shears cost money, and could only be used in a house or outbuilding with adequate space.

Other crafts were similarly closed to all but the well-prepared and properly funded. Tanners, for example, occupied yards with a series of pits lined with timber. They needed working capital in order to buy the raw hides (sometimes directly from the butchers) and materials such as oak bark from which the chemical tannin was extracted. Their investment was tied up in the long process of treating the hides to produce a supple and long-lasting leather. A similar scale of investment was normal in the metal trades. The raw metal was produced in the country: in forges for iron, in smelting furnaces for tin, and bole furnaces for lead, all located near the mines. The smiths, based in both country and town, worked the iron into implements, tools, weapons, nails and horseshoes, using bellows and anvils which again needed capital and extensive working space. Workers in non-ferrous metals – such as the pewterers who made tin into vessels, or the potters or bell founders who cast brass or other alloys of copper into cooking pots and bells, along with a range of smaller buckles and brooches – constructed furnaces and prepared moulds, requiring both considerable investment and a larger labour force than the two or three commonly working in an artisan workshop.

Other crafts were more open to newcomers in the sense that they needed very little equipment, but some of them depended on high levels

of skill which would normally be acquired, if not by a formal apprenticeship, certainly by spending some years as a servant to an established
artisan. The clothing trades belong in this category: shoemakers and
glovers, for example, could buy their raw materials in quite small quantities, and work them with cutting tools and needles and thread which
were not very expensive. The tailors had representatives in every town,
and dozens in the larger centres. They measured and cut cloth that
was often supplied by the customer, and stitched it, again without any
great outlay, though with considerable skill. In the building trade, the
materials and working space were generally supplied by those paying for
construction, so the workers provided a few tools – trowels and chisels
for masons, and saws, axes and augers for carpenters. The numerous
coopers who made wooden barrels and other vessels, or those who made
bows and arrows (bowyers and fletchers), or the ropers and stringers
who twisted fibres into ropes, cord and string, used quite cheap raw
materials and a limited range of equipment.

The variety of occupations gave towns their defining characteristic.
They did not usually specialize in a single craft or group of crafts, and
individuals and households were not tied to a single means of gaining a
living. Occasionally a town did gain fame for a particular product, and
a thirteenth-century list mentions a number which can be confirmed from
other sources, such as the 'knives of Thaxted' (Essex), the 'scarlet (cloth)
of Lincoln', and the 'cord of Bridport' (Dorset). These products provided
employment for only a minority of artisans, but they allowed small
towns like Bridport and Thaxted to sell their distinctive products over
long distances, beyond the limited hinterland in which their butchers,
tailors and shoemakers traded.

One of the specialities included 'herring of Yarmouth', a product
which employed a very large number of people and was widely traded.
The fish migrated seasonally, and so an intensive short-term effort was
required to catch them. The industry was typically small in scale, as the
fishing vessels, rarely exceeding 30 tons, cost between £3 and £27 in about
1300, and were often crewed by five men. The expeditions to the North
Sea usually lasted for a day or two, with intervals between voyages for
the catch to be unloaded, the crews to rest, and the boat and nets to be
prepared for the next sailing. Each vessel would make ten to fourteen
trips in a six-week season, making about £10 and £20 from its catches
of 10–20 last of herring (there were 12,000 fish in a last). The profit would
be divided between the boat owners (boats were often shared by a
number of investors) and the master and his crew. The fish quickly
decayed, and the bulk of them were cured, either by smoking (to make
red herring) or salting (white herring). They were traded in huge

quantities mainly at herring fairs, as the preserved herring were relatively cheap. They were eaten in great quantities in the households of the wealthy, but could be afforded at least occasionally by the mass of relatively poor consumers. Although this specialism was unusual in its concentration in time and place, it can stand as in many ways typical of medieval industry, with quite low levels of investment in a small enterprise that employed a handful of people in any one part of the production process (in this case both catching and curing) and sold quite cheap basic commodities to a large number of consumers, many of them of modest means. There were, however, profits to be made, and the people who became wealthy from the industry were not the seamen who braved the North Sea, or those who toiled in the smoky curing sheds, but the merchants who handled the barrels of fish.

Merchants contributed much to the economy of towns, and took their rewards in consequence. They traded over long distances both in expensive luxury goods, and in cheaper commodities in bulk. Without their management of the higher levels of the trading system, the larger towns in which they were based could not have existed, but they also had great influence on small towns and country markets, in which the commodities they handled were bought and sold. Merchants reduced risks by diversifying their activities, including the purchase of land, moneylending and holding office. They were the richest people in the towns, played a major role in municipal politics, and advised the royal government.

The wealthiest and most ambitious merchants had wide horizons. The twelfth and thirteenth centuries had been a period of globalization, in the sense that Europe's contacts with Asia grew in importance. This was not so much because of crusading and the establishment of a western Christian colony in Palestine, as through the growth of trade with the eastern Mediterranean and the Black Sea in spices, silks, cotton and other goods, which was mainly handled by Italian and Spanish traders. The Italians led the world in the business methods by which they raised capital in partnerships and companies, and then arranged profitable ventures in distant cities through their factors. The merchants of London and the other towns in Britain contributed to this trade mainly by acting as distributors of the luxuries, enabling rich consumers to indulge in a sophisticated Mediterranean culture. Even in the commerce of northern Europe, English and Scottish merchants took second place to those from Flanders, Brabant and France, with the Italians and the Germans rising in prominence towards the end of the thirteenth century. Nonetheless, native merchants still traded overseas, like Robert of London, who bought pepper worth £183 at Genoa in 1186, and exporters of wool like Lawrence of Ludlow from Shropshire, who went down with his ship in the North Sea in 1294 while taking a cargo to Holland. The English participated in this embryonic globalization when in the twelfth century they developed trade links with Spain, where merchants found an outlet for English woollen cloth, and brought back spices, gold and fine leather. Good-quality shoes were made from Spanish goatskins from Cordoba (cordwain), which gave English shoemakers, even if they worked mainly in locally produced leather, the distinctive occupational name of cordwainers.

When archaeologists excavated a rubbish pit in Southampton, in Cuckoo Lane near the quay, they found a seal bearing the name of Richard of Southwick, a merchant active in the 1270s and 1280s, who lived in a stone house nearby. The pit contained rubbish from Southwick's house, revealing his international contacts. He had business links with a merchant from Normandy called Bernard de Vire, whose seal was found, and he had bought decorated jugs from south-west France and lustreware from Spain, together with more valuable but perishable goods such as wine. The sheath for his dagger was made from Spanish leather, and he ate imported figs and grapes as well as local fruits. The pit also contained the skeleton of a small African monkey, brought to Southampton by a sailor from the Mediterranean and presumably kept by Southwick as an exotic pet.

Merchants aimed to earn maximum profits by handling the commodities which gave the best returns. This meant above all dealing in the most important export, wool. Merchants based inland bought up the fleeces from local markets, like the appropriately named Alexander le Riche of Andover in Hampshire, who in 1270 was buying wool over a range of 50 miles, from Wiltshire and Somerset. By an alternative method, merchants negotiated directly with the producers, and bought the wool in bulk. The celebrated Douai clothmaking entrepreneur, Jehane de Boinebroke, who obtained much of his wool from Scotland and northern England, contracted to buy seventy-two sacks from Newminster Abbey in Northumberland in 1270. The abbey acted as a middleman, and was able to add another twenty sacks to the bargain consisting of the *collecta*, that is wool bought by the monks from other producers, most of them peasants. Non-English merchants were then exporting two-thirds of English wool, but the share of native traders increased towards the end of the thirteenth century, and by 1304–11 the English handled 57 per cent. At this time Thomas of Coldingham of Berwick-upon-Tweed, applying the methods commonly used by foreign traders, negotiated to buy all of Durham Priory's wool. He drove a hard bargain because the priory wanted money in advance – he agreed to buy for the next three or four years, but at the very cheap price of £4 per sack.

He could sell these for £6 or £7 each in Flanders, and even after paying transport costs his profit margin must have been above 20 per cent. The advance of the English into this lucrative trade was helped by political troubles which had disrupted the trade in the 1290s, when Edward I had imposed an embargo on trade with Flanders in the course of his war with France.

Wool, together with wool fells (sheepskins), were the major export from the various parts of Britain in the period. Hides and fish figured prominently among the goods carried from Scottish ports, and metals were exported from England, notably tin from Devon and Cornwall, and lead from north Wales and the Pennines. Exports were closely linked with the import trade, as those who had carried wool to a continental port would have the money to buy goods and the space in their ships to carry them back. In the late thirteenth century when the Italian merchants played a key role in the wool trade, they also brought spices to London, which were then distributed by the London pepperers, later called the grocers. By the early years of the fourteenth century a higher proportion of spice was imported by the English traders. The expensive imported goods bought by wealthy consumers carried high profit margins. These included wine, which during the thirteenth century came increasingly from the English king's possessions in south-west France, the duchy of Aquitaine, and reached their peak in about 1308, when 20,000 tuns (5 million gallons) were imported. Manufactured goods included woollen cloth from Flanders, silks from Italy and Spain and linen from France. The north of Europe, Scandinavia and the Baltic, provided the furs which were used to line the clothing of the rich, and wax from which the best-quality candles were made for churches and the households of the wealthy. Merchants could also make profits by importing quite cheap and bulky goods which were in demand because they were not produced within the country, or obtainable in sufficient quantity. These included the alum, oil and dyestuffs, such as woad, essential for cloth manufacture; Baltic timber, especially in eastern England, for both houses and ships; and pitch, tar, iron and steel. Foodstuffs which were not especially expensive or luxurious, such as preserved fish, came from northern Europe, together with such ordinary domestic implements as whetstones and hand-mills.

Many merchants, especially those living in inland towns, did not trade overseas but transferred goods from one region to another. Some handled luxury commodities ultimately for aristocratic consumption, like the goldsmiths who sold plate and jewellery, or the vintners who distributed wine by the tun or pipe from inland ports such as Gloucester. The skinners were well established in Northampton in the thirteenth century, and from here they visited fairs at St Ives. In much of the inland trade the main opportunities came from the movement of grain, which was bought and sold by bladers and cornmongers acting as suppliers for the larger towns, and sometimes sending boatloads for more than 20 miles down the rivers to London, Bristol and King's Lynn. Raw materials for crafts included hides, iron and wool, which was being carried in quantity to industrial centres within the country, not just to the continent. Finally, manufactured goods were traded inland, notably woollen cloth from centres of the industry such as Lincoln and Stamford, and the linen which was made in Norfolk and sold through the drapers of Norwich.

The merchants traded from their houses, and just as artisans had workshops on the premises, so merchants' accommodation would include warehouses and counting houses where bargains would be struck and records of transactions kept. Merchants often travelled with their goods and negotiated deals in person, hence the occasional tragedy like the shipwreck in which Lawrence of Ludlow died. They also used agents or factors, often simply called 'servants', who represented their interests in remote places. This period marks the heyday of the English fairs, occasions when the maximum number of merchants and customers came together to conduct business for a few days of intense commercial activity. Almost every town acquired its chartered fair during the thirteenth century, and many changed the time of year when the fair was held, or added new ones, with the intention of finding the moment which would attract the maximum number of buyers and sellers.

The really successful fairs had established themselves by the mid-thirteenth century mostly in eastern England, and they followed each other in a sequence through the year, with the Stamford fair in Lent, St Ives at Easter, Boston in July, Winchester in September and Northampton in November. These were the fairs regarded in the 1250s by merchants in Douai and Lucca as especially important, though others such as those held at Bury St Edmunds, King's Lynn and Westminster attracted a great volume of trade. The fairground would be transformed temporarily into a small town as dozens of booths were erected, and within a few days hundreds of pounds' worth of goods would be sold. Agents from the great households attended and bought their supplies of wax, fish and cloth at wholesale prices. The archbishop of York, for example, regularly spent £60 per annum at St Ives in the 1280s. But most of the trade at the fairs was between one merchant and another. English drapers would lay in stocks of cloth from Flemish merchants at fairs, and sell pieces to customers from their town shops. A characteristic visitor to fairs was a Lincoln draper, Stephen of Stanham, who was especially active in 1299–1304. He bought goods at the fairs of Boston and St Ives, and held a shop in London. He was able to supply the king's wardrobe with spices, wax and cloth, and when parliament met in Lincoln in 1300, could provide the members with sugar and figs.

Those engaged in trade took the risk of losing their cargoes through fire, crime or shipwreck, or they might find that demand had slumped because of famine or war, or they could be defeated by commercial competition. They bought land most commonly to avoid risk and store some of their wealth in a secure asset. They may sometimes have gained capital from their rents from real property, but the amount that they owned does not seem adequate for that purpose – the landed assets of a leading merchant were commonly worth £10–£20 per annum, whereas they traded goods worth hundreds of pounds. Most were reluctant to tie up too much of their money in land. They may have included in their portfolio of interests the profits derived from leases on assets, such as mills or fisheries, or they acted as farmers, by collecting tolls or taxes, and paying a fixed sum to the state or the town government. So a late twelfth-century goldsmith, Terrice of Canterbury, in addition to his private trade in precious metals, acted as farmer of the royal exchange in Canterbury, where foreign money would be brought in to be changed for coin of the realm. He also purchased goods for the king. In addition he was a considerable property holder, with a rental income of £69 per annum. In a similar fashion, members of the Fortin and Isembard families in Southampton in the same period were put in charge of work on the royal castle and farmed revenues from the town.

As the larger towns became self-governing around 1200, merchants commonly occupied municipal offices, sitting on town councils and serving as chamberlains, bailiffs and mayors. These may not have been very profitable jobs, as they were often expected to pay for at least part of their expenses. But whether because of the indirect material benefits (which some contemporaries believed them to have exploited for private gain), or the status that followed from the exercise of public duties, merchants tended to fill the highest offices, and sometimes repeatedly, like the wealthy Selby family in York who served as mayor over three generations between 1217 and 1289.

Mercantile trade depended on credit. Goods were bought without immediate payment, and in selling goods the merchant advanced credit, allowing the purchaser to pay later. Merchants also had opportunities to accumulate cash, and lent money, for example to aristocrats who were incurring extra expenditure on a building project, or to kings embarking on war. In the twelfth century the moneylenders included Flemish and English merchants, notably William Cade, the great Flemish financier who died in 1166, and later in the century the Londoners, Gervase and

Henry of Cornhill. The Jews had come to England after the Norman Conquest as dealers in bullion: they bought and sold silver plate, which for the aristocracy served as the ultimate status symbol but was also a means of storing surplus wealth. Jews changed money, in support of the strict royal policy that foreign coins should not circulate in England, and they also lent cash. When Henry II in 1180 set up royal exchanges in eight selected towns, one of the functions of the Jewish community was lost, and they faced competition from English goldsmiths in the trade in silver plate. In increasing measure from the late twelfth century they made their living from moneylending. They could provide this service over a large area as Jewish communities developed in most of the larger towns in eastern England, in the most commercially active regions, and also extended to the west as far as Exeter, Hereford and Shrewsbury. The crown had always offered protection to Jews, who tended to live in towns near to the royal castle.

After a wave of anti-Jewish violence in 1190, which was especially savage at York where almost the whole community was massacred, the Jews were bound even more closely to the royal government. Chests containing records of Jewish loans were kept in selected towns under official supervision, and Jewish affairs were regulated by the Exchequer of Jews. Some Jews had become rich in the twelfth century, notably Aaron of Lincoln who died in 1186 with debts owing to him of £15,000. Under royal patronage they became even more wealthy in the early thirteenth century, when many aristocrats, unable to pay their way in the face of inflation, royal financial demands and expectations of a grander style of life, borrowed money on the strength of their landed assets. The Jews obliged, but at a cost. One type of loan imposed as a penalty on late payers an annual interest charge of 43 per cent. In 1241–2 the total amount owed to Jews can be estimated at near to £80,000, and the king, fully aware of the possibility of raising money from a vulnerable minority, collected £73,000 in taxes from the Jews in the years between 1241 and 1256. Not every debtor was aristocratic; indeed peasants and artisans figured more prominently among Jewish clients after 1260.

The Jews were a means by which the crown taxed landed society indirectly, as the Jews passed on to their clients the costs of the Jewish tallages and other financial burdens. The Jews declined in numbers and wealth in the 1260s and 1270s, through a combination of royal taxation and Christian prejudice, and were eventually expelled in 1290. The demand for ready cash continued, however, and the gap was filled partly by Englishmen with spare money, like the notorious government official, Adam de Stratton. Thomas of Coldingham, who has already been mentioned for his advance of money to Durham Priory on the strength of a guarantee of cheap wool (pp. 207–8), also lent money to landowners, and at one point in his career had taken over a manor from which he drew an income, which allowed him to profit from the loan. The greatest sums were advanced by the Italian companies, which were also taking over sections of the trade in wool. Edward I borrowed from the Riccardi of Lucca, but towards the end of his reign, after 1294, he developed a relationship with the Florentine company of the Frescobaldi, who were rewarded with trading privileges.

iv. *Techniques of trade and manufacture*

The growth in the population and in exchange increased the volume and value of trade with the continent. Records made in the course of assessing and collecting English royal taxation allow an estimate that in 1204 the combined value of exports and imports was worth between £55,000 and £75,000, and that the equivalent sum a hundred years later lay in the region of £500,000 per annum. Allowing for inflation, these figures suggest a threefold increase in overseas trade, and a growth in the quantity of exports and imports per head of population. The total value of inland trade cannot be estimated, but its growing importance is indicated by the higher proportion of rents paid in cash by 1300 and the section of the population which obtained most of its living from non-agricultural activities, which by c.1300 amounted to well over 20 per cent, counting those working in rural industries as well as the town dwellers.

Was this merely a growth in quantity, or was it accompanied by changes in technique and business methods? Perhaps those who made their living in manufacture or trade could expect to benefit from cheap labour and higher demand, and so were not impelled to make savings in labour costs or to improve the efficiency of their operations. No 'industrial revolution' can be identified at this time, but there were technological advances, designed to expand production and to increase profits. Water power was applied to a number of industries, notably clothmaking, with the first reference to a fulling mill in 1185. The water wheel operated wooden hammers which rose and fell rapidly on to cloth in a trough containing water and fuller's earth, a naturally occurring detergent. Traditionally the process had been performed laboriously by fullers agitating the cloth with wooden clubs, or more often by trampling it underfoot – hence the name 'walker' by which fullers were commonly known. By the end of the thirteenth century about 800 fulling mills had been built in England. The main motive for investing in the mills, as we have seen, was the local lord's desire to make some profit from a local

industry, and as fulling represented only one operation in the many stages
of cloth manufacture, these mills cannot be compared with the textile
factories of the eighteenth and nineteenth centuries in which a number
of processes were mechanized. On the other hand, the mills would not
have been built unless the local clothmakers could have been persuaded
to use them. Lords' attempts to use compulsion had limited effects, and
the main motive for people to bring their cloth to be fulled was the labour
and money that could be saved. It was said that fulling by foot produced
better results than the new machinery, so efficiency seems to have been
the main consideration.

Water mills could also be used to power heavy metal shod hammers
to forge iron after it had been smelted, or to work up wrought iron
into implements and tools. At Bordesley Abbey in Worcestershire, for
example, a triangular pond was constructed in the valley of the River
Arrow in about 1175 to provide a flow of water for machinery housed in
a timber-framed mill. The first mill burnt down, but was soon replaced,
and the building and machinery went through a series of alterations and
rebuildings throughout the thirteenth and early fourteenth centuries.
It was clearly regarded by its monastic builders and owners as a good
investment that repaid its heavy initial costs and the expense of maintenance. The operation of the mill resembled a small factory, because a
number of metalworking processes were carried out, including bronze
casting, as well as the central activity of forging iron. In a fashion typical
of the Cistercian monks who funded the mill, a venture which may originally have been designed to serve the internal needs of the monastery
and its estates became a commercial enterprise satisfying the local
market, producing a variety of implements and equipment, including
weapons and armour as well as nails and the tenterhooks on which cloth
was stretched after fulling. Human smiths wielding hammers would have
done this work more slowly and, one suspects, less thoroughly, than the
water-driven machine. The adoption of this technology undoubtedly
advanced productivity.

In most industries the new methods were not as expensive or as far
reaching as mill-powered machinery. Instead, modifications were made
to the process or the product which aided the artisan or the consumer.
In building, the adoption of stone foundations and improved methods of
timber framing created structures with a high degree of durability. Construction cost more initially, but maintenance and rebuilding expenses
were greatly reduced. In towns, the replacement of thatched roofs by tile
or stone slates was similarly expensive, but saved in the long run as the
roof did not require such frequent renewal, and was less likely to burn
down. The fact that houses built in the early fourteenth century for

renting to the lower grades of artisans in York have survived and are still in use is a remarkable tribute to the technical accomplishment of medieval builders.

In the English pottery industry, glazed jugs were made in a few kilns before 1100, but by the late thirteenth century almost all of the dozens of centres of production were making these vessels, often in attractive designs. They were bought in large numbers for wealthy households, but peasants and artisans served ale in them. In Scotland, pottery manufacture was introduced in the twelfth and thirteenth centuries, and while the ownership of decorated jugs was more restricted than in England, locally manufactured cooking pots were in widespread use, especially in towns.

The techniques of trade were also being adapted to make the process easier and less costly. Inland transport was improved by building bridges and roads. Fords, which took many roads across rivers, were replaced by bridges; timber bridges were rebuilt in stone; the roads approaching bridges were built on causeways to raise the traffic above the level of river valleys that were liable to flood. A high proportion of bridges were sufficiently wide to allow carts to cross – they were not mere pedestrian or pack-horse bridges. By 1300 bridges had been built on the main crossing points, and on many rivers no new bridges were added until new routes were developed and new demands made of the transport system in the eighteenth century. On the River Severn below Montford Bridge, for example, eight bridges had been built by the early fourteenth century, compared to ten after a passage of another 400 years. Edward I had new roads made for his armies when he invaded north Wales in 1277, from Chester to Diganwy through Flint and Rhuddlan. Throughout England, road-building was being carried out by town governments, or by landlords and village communities, mainly on short stretches, but cumulatively this work helped the passage of traffic over long distances. Some roads were rerouted, and new sections – of the Great North Road, for example – constructed. At a local level, roads and tracks were more numerous than they are today, serving every field or house, so that even a small parish would contain 20 miles of road.

Traders who were organizing the transport of goods often chose to use pack-horses, which could negotiate steep and narrow paths but carried relatively small quantities of goods. We have already noted the gradual replacement of the ox-drawn wain by horses and carts for transporting bulky goods. Cart journeys over longer distances seem painfully slow to us: it could take eight days for a loaded cart to cover the 150 miles between Gloucester and London. Anyone contemplating carrying goods over such a distance had to allow for the expenses of feeding the horses, shoeing them and repairing the cart, as well as the hire and living expenses of the driver. Costs for transporting wheat from Huntingdon to London in 1305 amounted to $1^1/_2$d per mile for each ton of grain. If corn prices were high, then the expense was worth it, but if wheat was selling for 5s per quarter, a quarter would gain $7^1/_2$d in cost if it was carried for 20 miles, which might not be profitable. On the other hand, a tun of wine which was worth £5 could be transported many miles without an unacceptable addition to its price. Land transport was dependable, and even long journeys were made in the winter, contrary to modern myths about impassably muddy and potholed roads.

Carriage by water was much cheaper, at a halfpenny per ton/mile, but England's inland waterways served only a small proportion of the country. A network of rivers in the east midlands and East Anglia, such as the Trent, Nene, Witham, Welland and Great Ouse, supplemented by the Foss Dyke (a canal originally built in Roman times to join the Witham to the Trent), served such inland towns as Nottingham, Lincoln, Stamford and Cambridge, joining them and their hinterlands to the ports of Hull, Boston and King's Lynn. The south was served by the Thames, the west midlands by the Severn, and Yorkshire by the Ouse and Hull. Coastal shipping often provided a cheaper and more convenient alternative to roads, which allowed Cornish tin, Purbeck marble from Dorset, and coal from Newcastle upon Tyne to make the journey to London relatively cheaply. But these important and useful arteries for commerce left large parts of the country dependent mainly on roads.

Among seagoing vessels, bulky cargoes were carried by the hulk and the cog. The advantage of these vessels was their carrying capacity rather than speed, so they were wide in relation to their length. The larger cogs were 65 to 100 feet long, with a capacity of 200 tons. In the ports, the town authorities built timber-faced waterfronts where ships could be loaded and unloaded, and sometimes docks were constructed, as in Hartlepool in the thirteenth century. Cranes were being used at the larger ports before 1200.

The business methods of English merchants lagged behind those employed by the Italians, but they were developing partnerships as a means of raising capital and extending the scale of their trade. We tend to hear about their arrangements when they went wrong, which led to revealing court cases. One such deal was made in 1304 between John Chigwell and William de Flete, both Londoners. This was not an isolated alliance, as the two men, and their relatives, had been trading in partnership for many years. Both men employed servants to travel to foreign ports, to collect goods and pay for them. The two merchants agreed each to put up £40 as trading capital for a year, and then to divide the profits equally. Although the partnership agreement mentioned sums of money, they invested goods rather than cash, which were actually worth more than £40. De Flete contributed a consignment of wine, beans and salt, which was carried to Scotland and sold, probably to supply the castle garrisons in the area of English occupation. The profit on that transaction, once transport costs and other expenses had been allowed, gave a return of 25 per cent. Chigwell was offered a consignment of wool and hides by a Scottish magnate, John Comyn. To raise the money, the London merchant made another partnership with an Italian who had travelled with him to Comyn's castle. They paid £220 for the goods, and £125 to carry them for sale at St Omer, and they were sold for £396. After other expenses this transaction made a profit of £51. Meanwhile some mishap overcame a cargo of woad from Picardy which was Chigwell's contribution to the partnership, and the two fell out, mainly because de Flete thought that he had contributed all of the capital, but had to share his profits with Chigwell.

Most partnerships and business transactions are not recorded in any detail because they were conducted successfully, even though one suspects that they were just as complicated as the Chigwell/de Flete arrangements. They bore some resemblance to Italian practices of their day, in the sense that, like the Italian *commenda* contract, the parties agreed to share the investment and the profit. In the Chigwell/de Flete case the parties both contributed capital and personal participation in trade, but some partnerships involved a 'sleeping partner' who put up the money and an active merchant who did the negotiations. In England, groups of traders were known in the Latin phraseology of the documents as a 'society', but there were no large companies of the Italian type. Those embarking on complex business ventures needed some assurance that money would be paid and debts recovered. A common way of recording a debt was to use a bond, in which the borrower promised to pay by a certain date. These documents were often linked to a gran of land which provided some guarantee that the creditor could recover something of value. Recognizances recorded an obligation, and this method was standardized and given the backing of the state in 1283 when by the Statute of Acton Burnell certain towns were given the authority to maintain an archive in which the documents could be kept. In 1285 the Statute of Merchants clarified the earlier law, and strengthened the measures for forcing the debtor to pay.

Much medieval business was not recorded in writing. Bargains were made between the parties directly, and promises to pay were mainly oral. Written accounts were not apparently kept, and were certainly not preserved. The whole system depended on word-of-mouth communication and informal agreements. Traders had reputations which were made by personal recommendation and could be damaged by gossip. Successful trading decisions depended on the spread of intelligence, whereby news would be conveyed from one town to another on which decisions would be based. In 1319, for example, the price of wheat in England was quite low, at about 4s 6d per quarter, but for some reason, probably a harvest failure caused by bad weather in the south-west, Exeter wheat prices rose to 6s. Ships arrived within a few months from eastern England and northern France loaded with grain, proof of the rapid and accurate flow of information.

Many of the commercial techniques were developed to aid 'business to business' dealings, but the end of the process involved traders selling goods to customers. Here the main object was to bring as many consumers as possible into direct contact with the commodities and the sellers, and to tempt them with a wide range of goods at competitive prices. To some extent this aim was achieved by the proliferation of markets, fairs and towns in the twelfth and thirteenth centuries, so that no one needed to travel for more than a few hours to find a place to trade. It was important there should be plenty of space for marketing, and numerous stalls and shops. The rational arrangement by which trading was fixed for particular days and times, and the stalls in the marketplace, or the shops in the streets, were grouped so that all of the butchers, drapers, ironmongers and shoemakers could be found together, was a convenience for customers and traders alike. Trade was not restricted to market days, and medieval people could 'shop' throughout the week. Efforts were made to maximize the concentration of retailers. One strategy was the seld, the medieval version of the shopping mall, which reached its most developed form in Cheapside in London. In this central street dozens of selds were built, which consisted of rows of stalls or even chests from which goods could be displayed and sold; by 1300, 4,000 shops, stalls and other points of sale were operating there. Selds were introduced on a smaller scale into many provincial towns.

An especially high density of shopping outlets was provided in Chester, which was almost the regional capital of north-west England and north Wales, and a port for the Irish trade. It expanded within a confined space, as its walls were essential for security in a border area, and there was limited land for suburbs. The Chester townsmen devised a means by which the number of shops could be doubled by building houses along the four main streets with the usual shops on the ground floor, but also with galleries at first-floor level. Shoppers could move along the streets to see the wares below, and by flights of steps at frequent intervals gain access to covered walkways along which were ranged a further row of shops. The successful planning of the 'Rows' depended on compromise between the private interests of the individual owners and builders of each house, and the public authority of the town government which regulated the arrangement.

v. *Urban government*

The reduction of 'transaction costs', the modern economist's phrase for measures to make trade more convenient and efficient, took place within a framework of security provided by the state and town governments. Townsmen were normally of free status, so their lords could not make arbitrary demands of them, and their rights to landed property were protected in the king's courts. The English legislation of 1283 and 1285 ensured that credit arrangements could be officially recorded, and aided the recovery of debts. Criminals would steal goods and merchants could be waylaid on the road, but the state kept some control over disorder, as much as was possible in an age before a professional police force.

The English government maintained a high-quality currency. Admittedly the silver pennies, struck at a rate of 240 to the pound of silver, were a rather clumsy means of conducting both large and small transactions. If a merchant wished to pay £100 at once he had to assemble a bulky collection of 24,000 coins; if a consumer of modest means wished to buy a loaf of bread or a quart of ale for a farthing, small change was in short supply. Kings like Edward I made some effort to answer the demand for small denominations by minting halfpennies and farthings, and pennies were often cut into halves and quarters, but there were never enough. However, the inconvenience of the penny coinage was of small account compared with the problems on the continent posed by debasements and manipulation of the currency by states pursuing short-term profit. The weight and the silver content of the coinage were usually maintained by English governments through their financial crises. There were problems of price inflation, as we have seen, occasioned at the end of the twelfth century and in the early fourteenth by influxes of silver from the continent, and there were periods when coins were in short supply, notably between the 1070s and the 1160s. Edward I had to cope with an influx of foreign coins (crockards and pollards) in the 1290s, which he finally resolved by a major recoinage, but in general the principle that only English coins could circulate was maintained. The English kings were continuing a long tradition, while the Scottish royal coinage began, together with the burghs, in the twelfth century, and from the first striking of pennies in 1136 until 1367 the Scottish kings maintained a standard of coinage closely linked to that south of the border. The majority of coins circulating in Scotland were in fact English, and the two currencies seem to have coexisted: unlike any other 'foreign' currency, Scottish coins were tolerated in England.

Medieval people seem rather inconsistent in their recognition of towns, as the words 'town' and 'toun' in both English and Scots had a very general meaning, and could be applied to a wide range of rural settlements as well as the larger non-agrarian places that we regard as towns. The Latin word *villa* ('vill' in English) was equally ambiguous, and the term *villa mercatoria* (market town) was coined in the thirteenth century to identify settlements with a trading function. 'Borough' in England and Wales and 'burgh' in Scotland, *burgus* in Latin, meant a place where the tenants enjoyed the privileges of paying fixed cash rents and free disposal of land – in short, holding defined plots by burgage tenure. Modern historians compile lists of English boroughs on the basis of references in documents to burgage tenure, burgesses or burgage plots, but contemporaries seem less precise about the whole notion. When officials were deciding on the taxation of boroughs, or selecting places to be invited to send borough representatives to parliament, they made some very unpredictable judgements. A number of 'boroughs' were summoned to Edward I's parliament in 1295 where there is no evidence for burgage tenure, and only 221 places with such tenure, out of a total of about 600, paid tax as boroughs in any of the lay subsidies between 1294 and 1336.

Perhaps remote officials were uncertain about the status of a place, and those who lived in towns were more conscious of the rights and privileges which affected their daily lives. Lords granted tenants burgage tenure because they believed that a borough provided the right institutional framework within which a town could develop. They would offer packages of privileges based on those enjoyed by other towns, such as Newcastle or Hereford. The 'laws of Breteuil', deriving from an obscure town in Normandy, were widely conceded to new boroughs throughout England and Wales. Many lords continued to encourage their new towns – having granted burgage tenure in one charter, they might offer new privileges in a second. Lords were often ready to co-operate with the urban elite; for example, the leading townspeople would fill the offices of bailiff, or serve as jurors in the borough court. The townspeople farmed the market tolls, which in effect gave them the management of the market. High Wycombe in Buckinghamshire paid a fee farm of £30 for all of the revenues from the town to its lord by an agreement of 1226, an important step towards running its own affairs. The same end was achieved at Burford (Oxfordshire) when it was allowed to have its own guild merchant, that is, its traders were able to regulate the commerce of the town. In general, judging from the absence of any evidence of friction, the inhabitants of towns ruled by their lords were willing to go along with the arrangements made, which often involved some practical compromise between the interests of the lord and of the most influential townspeople.

The tenants in some towns were freeholders, but lacked the special privilege of burgage tenure. This did not prevent the development of an urban economy. In the west, towns which were not boroughs tended to be relatively few and small: they included places like Bridgend in Glamorgan and Rugby in Warwickshire. But in the east they were numerous, and included large market towns like Wymondham in Norfolk, and as important a place as Westminster, which in spite of its prominence in servicing the great abbey and royal palace had the status of a 'vill', no different from any rural community. The implication of these 'informal' towns is that they began from initiatives taken by traders and craftsmen, who created their own town without a lord's active patronage. On occasion a town struggled for its lord to recognize its borough status. Burgesses were acknowledged at Cirencester in Gloucestershire when the town was ruled by the crown, but after it was handed over to the new abbey which was founded in 1131, the canons treated its tenants as if they were villagers. At Bury St Edmunds the monks accepted that the settlement at the gate of their monastery was a borough, but resisted the townspeople's foundation of a guild merchant which would have allowed them to control access to the market. A number of monastic towns resembled these two places in their long-term disputes with their lords, at Abingdon, Dunstable and St Albans, and towns under the lordship of bishops were capable of occasional outbursts of discontent, notably at Wells in Somerset. Townspeople who were unable to run their own affairs found ways of meeting and working together by forming their own institutions, often a religious fraternity, which would acquire property, employ chaplains, and exercise at least some influence over the government of the town. At Henley-on-Thames by the 1290s the fraternity which maintained the vital bridge over the Thames had become a *de facto* town government, appointing a warden, two bailiffs and two bridge-wardens, who collected and spent a considerable annual income.

The form of self-government which townspeople desired was usually only acquired by the larger royal towns, which by charters granted between around 1189 and 1216 were allowed to pay rents, tolls and other financial obligations by a fee farm. They managed their own affairs through a mayor and council, they held their own borough courts, and expressed their separate legal identity by holding a common seal. Their right to hold a guild merchant meant that the townspeople decided who could trade toll free. All of these institutions, but with some different nomenclature – feu ferme, provost and bailies, guild merchant – were acquired by the leading royal burghs at rather later dates in Scotland. Those who received these rights clearly valued them, as towns were willing to pay substantial sums of money for their charters of privilege. Lincoln, for example, gave King John £200 for its charter in 1200. The townspeople, above all the elite, felt that they would enjoy economic advantages from self-government. They could decide how to levy the money to pay the fee farm; by-laws could be framed to advance the common good; the borough court would be run by people who understood trade and the disputes that might arise from it; the guild merchant would be able to make and enforce regulations for the general economic well-being of the town.

We can see the importance townspeople attached to controlling their space. They resented the existence of separate jurisdictions, like the precincts within the walls that belonged to cathedrals and religious houses. At Norwich a section of the city belonged to the cathedral priory, and it was suspected that criminals could escape justice by hiding there. The economic interests of the townspeople were thought to be damaged because the monks did not enforce strictly the rules of trade, such as the regulation of the price of bread and ale. And those who lived in the priory's enclave did not contribute their fair share to the municipal budget. These suspicions and grudges came to a head in 1272 when, after a dispute in the marketplace of Tombland adjoining the priory, a servant of the monks shot and killed a townsman with a crossbow. In the ensuing riots part of the priory was burnt. The list of rioters shows that they included the whole Norwich community, from the civic elite to craftsmen and servants.

Perhaps people at the time were right to think that their towns would prosper if they achieved the special status of a borough, or gained the more advanced rights of self-government. The opposite is almost impossible to prove, but we can only point out that places which were not boroughs – three-quarters of the towns in the highly urbanized county of Norfolk, for example – seemed to flourish in spite of their supposed disadvantage. Lords often gave borough charters to places where economic opportunities were uncertain, to give an institutional stimulus to a new town in a region like north Wales or Cumberland, where the population was rather thinly spread and the agricultural surplus meagre. Towns like Attleborough or Aylsham in Norfolk could grow without the need for such artificial stimuli.

The same reasoning can be applied to the higher stages of self-government, because for all the grumbling and rebellion of the people of Bury, their town was the second largest and richest in the county of

Suffolk at the time of its most bitter conflicts with the monastery in the early fourteenth century, and indeed it ranked twenty-fifth in the country as a whole, ahead of places like Northampton which had all of the desired privileges. Boston in Lincolnshire was ruled by officials appointed by its lord, yet it was placed in the top four provincial towns by wealth. The suspicion must be that contemporaries did not distinguish between the political advantages of self-government and the economic gains. Political autonomy allowed a section of society to order the affairs of the town in ways that favoured themselves, and this was the most pressing reason for campaigns for independence. We think that a charter of liberties freed those who received it from restrictions, but freedom in the middle ages meant privilege in an exclusive sense: charters often gave the recipients the right to rule over others.

The same problems of assessing the ideas and attitudes of contemporaries are apparent when we consider competition between towns. In the twelfth and thirteenth centuries new towns were founded which carved out hinterlands from the commercial territory of existing centres. This caused no great problems in the early stages, when towns were still widely spaced, but by the mid-thirteenth century the rivalries became more acute. Some newcomers faded rapidly back into obscurity, but some old established places were damaged, such as Hedon in east Yorkshire, founded in *c.*1170, but overshadowed by Beverley and Hull, and temporarily eclipsed by the mushroom growth of Ravenserrodd, a town which was built on a narrow peninsula of temporary dry ground off Spurn Point in the mouth of the Humber estuary. Towns which felt threatened searched for legal and political remedies. The law allowed English market holders to object to a new market which might damage their trade, and the lawyers adopted the rule that markets should lie $6^2/_3$ miles apart. The monks of Bury St Edmunds in 1201–2 resisted a newly founded market at Lakenheath, which was more than 15 miles from Bury, and sent a band of its supporters to demolish the stalls, in effect claiming a monopoly.

Welsh towns were granted monopolies like Carmarthen's privilege of selling wax and tallow in its vicinity. Transactions of all kinds within 15 miles of Cardigan had to take place in the town. In Scotland, towns also claimed monopolies, like the exclusive right of the inhabitants of Lanark according to a grant of 1285 to buy wool and skins in Lanarkshire. Guild merchants attempted to extend their powers beyond their own town. Lincoln, for example, campaigned against the traders of Louth, and Leicester objected to the purchase of local wool by traders from Melton Mowbray, Loughborough and Lutterworth, all of them towns within

Leicestershire. Guild merchants more often brought pressure to bear on their own members, prohibiting them from trading outside the town, or requiring them to discriminate against outsiders. The butchers of High Wycombe were ordered in 1313 to offer hides firstly to their fellow townsmen, and only then to sell them to 'foreign' traders. Occasionally it is possible to show that these regulations were enforced, but even then we suspect that those who were fined for trading, for example within 15 miles of a Welsh town, or the member of a guild merchant who was punished for selling forbidden goods to outsiders, were unlucky. Medieval governments did not have the resources or police force to protect monopolies or supervise markets, especially over long distances. In the same way, townsmen expressed prejudice against their rivals from overseas. The Lombards (Italians) and Hanseatics (Germans) probably attracted more hostility than any other groups, though like the Jews they received royal protection. More general regulations sought to restrict traders from overseas by insisting that they be 'hosted' by an English merchant, and foreign merchants were forbidden to trade retail. These restrictions in practice did not prevent the foreign trade on which the towns depended.

Attempts to control the economy were more likely to succeed within the town, where the powers of self-government gave wealthy minorities the ability to manipulate the regulations and the borough courts in their favour. The town authorities often used the rhetoric of the common good, but self-interest had a strong influence on their actions. The general privileges granted to burgesses or freemen or citizens were confined to a minority. In a borough governed by a lord, only the tenants of the burgages were eligible; in a town with a guild merchant, entry into the guild was by inheritance or apprenticeship, or by purchase. To join one of the fraternities which acted as unofficial town governments a fee was usually required. Entry fees alone excluded many artisans from full membership of the urban community. Discrimination against weavers in particular was a feature of the regulations governing trade in the larger towns. At Winchester, the guild merchant forbade weavers from dyeing or selling cloth, and Leicester weavers were ordered not to work for country employers except when no one within the town had work for them. Here we clearly see the influence of the drapers, whose main interest was to secure for their warehouses a steady supply of cloth, of reasonable quality and at the lowest possible cost.

Often regulation was used by the merchants to secure their control of commodities and exclude competition. At Southampton only members of the guild merchant could sell herring or millstones, or keep a tavern, or sell retail outside the marketplace, in their shops, on days other than market day. The big London companies emerged in the thirteenth century, and some of them performed the apparently innocuous and public-spirited function of inspecting and checking the quality of goods for sale. We can be sure that as the fishmongers inspected the fish markets, and the goldsmiths made sure that silver and gold plate were of good materials and workmanship (by a rule of 1238), defective goods were most commonly identified on the stalls of rivals or on those of members of their own companies who were not co-operating with a ruling faction. Opponents of the ruling groups alleged that they managed the tax system so that the poor paid a disproportionate share (at York in 1305, for example), and lists of assessments show hundreds of taxpayers contributing a few pence who, if the payments had been made under the officials of the royal government, would have been exempt.

Elitist manipulation of urban government was not always effective. Towns sought to curb excessive profiteering, especially by food traders. Perhaps this was a further example of self-interest, because those who sold cloth, leather, ironware and other products of urban artisans, or who employed labour themselves, did not wish to have the cost of living of workers pushed up to the point where they demanded higher rates of pay. But town governments had some commitment to good government, and were also anxious to avoid the trouble that might be caused by blatant exploitation of consumers. Accordingly they attempted to prevent forestalling and regrating, that is the purchase of goods, especially grain and fish, before they entered the public market, so that middlemen could create scarcities and sell at a higher price. The assize of bread and ale was enforced everywhere, but was particularly contentious in towns where the volume of sales was much greater and a higher proportion of the population were dependent on the market for prepared food. This regulation fixed the weight of a penny, halfpenny or farthing loaf of bread on a sliding scale which depended on the price of grain; similarly the price of ale varied with the cost of barley. Although this restricted the free market in food, and allowed a fixed amount to the bakers and brewers for the cost of production and profit, the regulation respected the market price, as the key variable was the price of grain, which depended mainly on the quality of the harvest. The town governments seemed to believe that in an ideal world consumers of foodstuffs would buy direct from producers, without the intervention of middlemen, at a price fixed by supply and demand. In the real world corn dealers and other entrepreneurs sold much of the food, and a number of traders, such as the cooks, lived by buying food and selling it at a profit.

vi. *Towns in a feudal economy*

The special status of towns gave many of their inhabitants privileges. Burgesses and citizens had their own courts, and many were governed by local laws. Their involvement in the market set them apart from the traditional agrarian economy. Among them lived groups even more distant from the mainstream of society, such as the Jews, communities of foreign merchants, and the mendicant friars. Historians have understandably regarded medieval towns as an alien growth within a feudal society and agrarian economy. Indeed, the urban economy can be seen as the economy of the future, a modern, capitalist implant, and even a subversive force, spreading ideas about freedom, individualism and the participation by citizens in government.

This conception of the modernizing role of towns in medieval society is of limited value. Towns were fully integrated into the political and social structure. Kings certainly gave them special treatment, valuing them as sources of tax revenue and appreciating the expertise of merchants. At times of war, the towns were called on to make extra efforts, above all in their financial contribution, but also to provide practical assistance, such as the ships of the Cinque Ports which aided Edward I's campaigns in Wales. They recognized their political strength, especially that of the Londoners, who at a number of crucial moments gave support to the king's baronial critics. The towns were supposed to rule in the king's name, and if they were ineffective, for example in maintaining order, their governments were suspended and the king took over direct rule, as happened in London in 1285–98. When parliaments were developing in the late thirteenth century, representatives of the boroughs formed an important part of the commons, primarily because their consent was necessary for the acceptance of the taxes to which towns contributed such a large share.

Feudal lordship and urban life were also fully compatible. Lords of all kinds founded towns, promoted them and invested in urban property. They appreciated that towns added to their revenues directly from rents and tolls, but also had a beneficial indirect influence on the revenues from their rural estates. They and their tenants sold rural produce in urban markets, and lords enjoyed the good things that could be bought from merchants. The elite in seignorial towns co-operated with their lords' government by serving as officials. Leicester showed deference to its lords, the earls of Lancaster, by greeting them with gifts on their visits to the town: they obviously regarded them as patrons as well as overlords. Monastic lords were more likely than others to quarrel with their towns, but that reflected their conservatism as landlords, and the townsmen were not generally opposed to lordship on principle, or to organized religion. Indeed, the towns were the scenes of exceptional devotion, with their processions and well-attended sermons. Town dwellers gave a great deal of financial support to the religious institutions which were especially attuned to the towns' needs, such as parish churches, friaries, hospitals, and of course fraternities.

Both the countryside and the towns were dependent on money and trade. There were many parallels between the urban and rural worlds, in both of which the household served as the main unit of production. The values of the town dwellers were not markedly different from those found in landed society. The aristocracy provided role models; they set the style for dress, and heraldic devices were in widespread use in decorating metalwork, floor tiles and textiles. Towns were not democratic, as the rulers, like the London aldermen, emphasized hierarchical distinctions, and kept the majority of townspeople out of elections and municipal office. The political and social ideas found in towns tended to favour authority, by maintaining that decisions should be made by the 'greater and wiser part', that is, the wealthy minority who ran the larger towns. Even the urban rebels aimed at nothing more revolutionary than a share in the privileges enjoyed by those in power. The respectable merchants who led the agitations against the abbey of Bury St Edmunds suppressed a movement of hot-headed youths calling themselves the 'bachelors' in 1264, but these young people did not wish to overthrow the existing social order, merely to replace one guild with another. The peasants who in the thirteenth century were inspired by an imagined ideal past of universal freedom were expressing more radical ideas than those put forward by many rebellious townsmen.

The aristocracy looked down on mere traders, who did not appreciate the finer points of chivalry or courteous behaviour, and the church condemned the avarice of the urban rich. But the landholding elite knew that towns represented civilization and provided an appropriate setting for their castles and cathedrals. In Wales, new towns were part of the process of colonization, which brought a wild countryside and its unruly inhabitants into the mainstream of Christendom. The shape of the town mattered as well, as a regular plan projected a rational image, reflecting in its geometrical forms the symmetry of the divine order. The church's teaching on economic matters reflected the accommodation between Christian values and the urban way of life. Rather than the traditional belief in the sinfulness of personal wealth, which presented an obstacle to salvation, theologians showed that private property and moderate affluence, if accompanied by charitable giving, accorded with the law of nature. Trade and exchange were socially useful, providing they were not exploited for greedy and selfish ends. The just price at which goods should be sold was the market price. Workers should be rewarded for their efforts. Money was a useful means of exchanging and storing wealth, so long as its acquisition did not become an end in itself. Usury was a serious sin, because the lender profited from the passing of time, and time belonged to God. Lenders found legitimate ways of gaining interest, such as taking the income from a piece of land surrendered by the borrower as a gage, or seeking compensation for the damage caused by the temporary loss of the money.

A more numerous and affluent aristocracy, a peasantry involved in the market, and urbanization were all linked together, and developed simultaneously. The urban sector was not competing with 'feudal' society or undermining it, but formed part of the feudal order. The interactions of town and country developed their own momentum and the lords became less important players in the market economy, which they sought to manipulate, but could not control.

CHAPTER SEVEN

Crisis, c.1290–c.1350

Those who experience turning points in history are not always fully aware of the great movements around them. This is especially true of changes in economy and society, which tend to develop inexorably but gradually. An exception to this rule was the first half of the fourteenth century, which was punctuated by two sudden natural disasters: the Great Famine and agricultural crisis of 1315–22, and the epidemic of 1348–50, usually known as the Black Death. The famine affected the whole of northern Europe, and the plague spread over virtually the whole continent. These disruptions of economic and social life coincided with momentous political events, when two English kings, Edward I (1272–1307) and Edward III (1327–77) fought wars within Britain, in an attempt to subdue Scotland, and also against France, the year 1337 seeing the beginning of the Hundred Years War. Edward II (1307–27) faced a number of episodes of opposition from the aristocracy, and in the last of these he was deposed and killed. Scotland was disrupted by disputes over the succession to the throne and the wars with the English. This was also a troubled period in religious life, when the papacy left Rome and settled at Avignon. A general sense of unease throughout western Europe may have been expressed in the persecution of minorities. The notion of a 'general crisis' of the whole social and political structure may help us to see the developments in Britain on a broader canvas, but our first concern must be to establish when economic expansion came to an end, and in particular to identify the turning point – did it come after the Black Death, or in the decades before 1348?

i. *Great Famine and Black Death*

A first question must be to ask if the Great Famine was a really momentous event, or just a transient episode. It began with the poor harvest of

1314, succeeded by two years of wet weather and disastrous crops. The good harvest of 1317 did not bring the level of prices back to normal until 1318. Another bad year, especially in East Anglia, followed, in 1321–2. The deficient grain harvests coincided with disease among sheep, and an epidemic affecting cattle in 1319–21. The shortfall in cereal crops can be calculated very precisely from the yields recorded in manorial accounts. On the bishop of Winchester's manors in the southern counties, from Somerset to Surrey, wheat yields fell to 60 per cent of average in 1315, and 55 per cent in 1316. This meant that the bishop's officials were taking into their barns in the autumn about twice as much corn as they planted, not four times as much, as was normally the case. After they put to one side the seed for the next year, this left them with very little to spare for feeding animals and servants on the manor, or for supplying the lord's household, or for sale. The harvests on the estates of Bolton Priory in Yorkshire suffered more acutely, with rye crops on the land adjoining the monastery in 1315 and 1316 down to 28 per cent and 11.5 per cent of normal. The north generally suffered more severely than did the south. Parts of East Anglia, and Cornwall were spared the worst effects. The same problems of low returns affected peasant crops, reflected in the amount collected in tithe. A number of chroniclers reported that wheat prices reached a high point of 40s per quarter (instead of the normal 5s or 6s), and that they remained at 26s 8d per quarter for two and a half years. This was an exaggeration, but a quarter of wheat on average over the whole country cost a very high 16s during the two worst famine years, and a quarter of barley 10s to 11s instead of its usual price of 3s or 4s (Figure 1).

Cereals were not the only foodstuffs affected. The rain spoiled the supplies of peat and reduced salt production, and high salt prices affected the supply of butter, cheese, and preserved meat (such as bacon and salt beef). Hay production was also damaged by the weather, which in turn affected the health of animals. The only reductions in price were for oxen and cart-horses in 1316–17, but that was another symptom of crisis, because peasants were selling their draught animals to obtain cash to buy grain, and few people could afford to buy them. The peasants who reduced their ploughing capacity presumably suffered further hardships when the time came to prepare the land for the next year's planting. Their difficulties continued after the bad harvests when cattle died of disease in large numbers in 1319–21.

Everyone lost income as the famine cut into production. The large cultivators, the managers of the lords' demesnes which ran to hundreds of acres, could profit from poor harvests if they could sell their smaller surplus at a very high price. But a really bad harvest left some manors

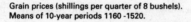

Grain prices (shillings per quarter of 8 bushels).
Means of 10-year periods 1160 -1520.

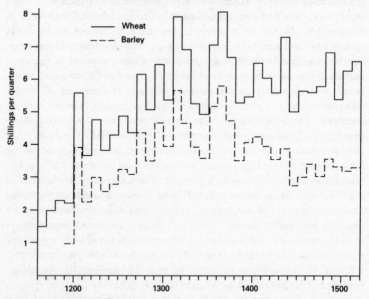

Figure 1. Grain prices in England, 1160–1520. Prices in shillings per quarter of 8 bushels. Means calculated in ten-year periods, for wheat and barley.

Source: AgHEW, vols 2, 3 and 4.

without much to sell, and so they made no money out of the shortages. Some smaller monasteries had to reduce their food consumption. The lords and their companions would not starve, but workers on the manor were sometimes deprived of their payments of corn, and lords, such as Bolton Priory, dismissed servants. The wage earners were doubly hard hit: grain prices were very high, and peasants as well as demesnes cut down on their employment of labour. Traders and artisans found that demand for their products fell as household budgets at all social levels were squeezed by the high price of food, which left little to spare for clothing, building or manufactured goods. Brewing and selling ale, one of the most widespread of commercial occupations, declined as malt shortages pushed up the price and most consumers saved their money to buy bread. In terms of a household budget, enough barley (a cheap grain) to feed a family for a year cost 60s, but a labourer would be lucky to gain in wages as much as 30s. The earnings of wives and children contributed something to family budgets, but even small-scale casual employment became hard to find.

The famine caused much social and economic stress. The chronicles exaggerated, or rather reached for the literary clichés which were commonly used to describe extreme hunger, when they reported that the poor ate dogs, cats, horsemeat and even human flesh. More objective evidence reveals less lurid but still significant symptoms of hardship, in that peasants were selling land in great quantities. In most years at Redgrave in Suffolk before 1315 no more than sixty-five transfers of land were made between one living tenant and another, but in 1316 there were 188 transfers, and in 1317, 135. Small amounts of land – less than an acre on average – were being sold on each occasion, and there were more sellers than buyers. Relatively poor peasants sold parcels of land to their richer neighbours. It could be simply said that the smallholders were selling land in order to buy food, and that the better-off peasants were able to take advantage of their poverty to acquire more land. A more complex sequence of transactions may lie behind the sales of land, suggested by the large number of debts that peasants were attempting to recover through the manorial courts. Many of those selling land had probably borrowed money or grain, and had been forced to surrender the land when they could not repay the loan.

On the Yorkshire manor of Wakefield the court records of the famine period are filled with references to the acquisition of new land by tenants through assarting. In a typical entry of July 1316, Richard, son of John Bete of Sowerby gave the lord 5s for permission to take an acre of new land, paying thereafter an annual rent of 6d. This wave of land clearance appears to show peasants expanding the size of their holdings in the hope that they could produce enough to feed their families at the next harvest. It reveals another dimension of the social stress arising from the famine, as the lord's officials, realizing the profits that could be made from the desperate plight of the peasants, charged high fines for the new land. They may even have been discovering a backlog of land clearances made over many years and were charging retrospective fines for them.

The records of manor courts and royal courts throughout England during the famine years contain the names of thousands of people accused of crimes, especially the theft of foodstuffs. Hungry people were turning to crime as the famine reduced their ability to make an honest living. Another factor may have been a shift in the attitudes of those in authority. As their incomes diminished, they felt threatened by the poor, reduced their charitable giving, and were not prepared to tolerate or condone misbehaviour by the lower orders. The famine strained the normal social bonds by which poverty was alleviated. For example, in April 1316 at Wakefield, John, son of Adam Bray, who had previously been accused of stealing 14s in cash, was said also to have taken a bushel of oats worth 12d from his father. The information about the new (petty) crime must have come from the father, who in normal years would surely have helped his son, or at least turned a blind eye to a member of his family 'borrowing' some grain.

The links within communities, as well as family ties, were tested at this difficult time. For example, the lord of Eldersfield in Worcestershire in 1316 heard sympathetically the complaint that the wealthier villagers, when they gathered money to pay collective fines imposed by the lord's court, insisted that those without land should contribute more than their fair share. Whether this was a new abuse provoked by the famine, or an old practice which attracted complaints only at this time of stress, is not known, but in either case relations between the upper and lower ranks of village society had deteriorated. Illegal gleaning posed a more widespread problem. In normal years village communities (according to by-laws which were approved and enforced by the manor courts) allowed the genuine poor to collect ears of corn left in the fields after the sheaves had been carried. The able-bodied were not permitted to glean, and care was taken that it did not serve as a front for sheaf-stealing. In the famine years complaints multiplied that the various rules governing gleaning were being broken, perhaps because the hungry poor were stretching the rules to the limit, and also reflecting the intolerance with which the better-off regarded their less fortunate neighbours.

Lords in general seem to have made some profit from the plight of their tenants, as the increased business in their courts and above all the fines paid on land transfers gave their revenues a temporary stimulus. Occasionally the difficulties of tenants were recognized, and they were let off payments, like the labour services at Ibstone in Buckinghamshire which Merton College did not demand 'on account of the poverty of the tenants'. The royal government reacted to the threat of famine in 1315 by making an ineffective attempt to regulate the prices of animals, and by collecting a lay subsidy in 1316 which it was thought the taxpayers could afford. More constructive efforts were made to encourage the carriage of grain from areas less severely affected, such as Cornwall.

A test of the severity of the famine must be the extent to which it led to an increase in mortality. A rising total of deaths can be observed in manorial court records of the tenants who died, the reduced numbers of males over twelve years old who were liable to pay an annual head penny, or the gaps in the lists of landless, unmarried wage earners, the *garciones*, found on the manors of the Glastonbury Abbey estate. From places in different regions come estimates of mortality of 10 per cent, 15 per cent, and in the case of the *garciones* of Longbridge Deverill in Wiltshire, 17–18 per cent. An unusually high death rate is not found everywhere – for example, Coltishall in Norfolk, in a region which escaped the full effects of the famine. Not all deaths in the famine years were caused directly by the food shortage, as there was also an epidemic of disease. This may have been typhus, which spread from those deprived of food to the more affluent: parish clergy and members of the gentry died, though not in the number found among peasants and wage earners.

The troubles of 1315–22 disrupted social and economic life, and were associated with severe mortality which affected much of Britain, together with a large section of northern continental Europe. Analysis of tree rings shows that unusual climatic conditions prevailed beyond Europe, which suggests that the events recorded here formed part of some major natural disaster. For England this was the worst famine in recorded history.

The impact of the Black Death of 1348–9 will be discussed in more detail below (pp. 271–81). It caused much higher mortality than the Great Famine. Peasants died in very large numbers, varying from 40 per cent to 70 per cent of the observed population, and it would be reasonable to estimate the death rate in 1348–9 at about half of the English population. Its effects were universal, and no village, town or region for which records exist escaped. If the total population stood at about 5 or 6 million, there were $2^{1}/_{2}$ or 3 million casualties. As we will see, lesser but repeated later epidemics, and underlying shifts in fertility, reduced the population for the next two centuries, so there was no sustained recovery from the Black Death.

We are faced with the evidence of an almost unimaginable catastrophe. The Black Death on a global scale exceeded in mortality any other known disaster. By the standard of the events of 1348–9, the deaths in 1914–19 from war and the Spanish influenza, in relation to the total population affected and in long-term consequences, seem of lesser significance. The case for regarding the Black Death as a momentous episode seems stronger than can be advanced for the Great Famine. By the rather macabre yardstick of the number of corpses, the famine was responsible in England for no more than a half-million dead, a mere fifth or sixth of those who died in the plague. Yet in identifying turning points, we ought to search in the decades before 1348. The famine may not in itself have been the key factor, but the Black Death's role seems to have been to confirm, deepen and emphasize tendencies which had begun earlier. The expansion that had been such a pronounced feature of the thirteenth century came to an end in the first two decades of the fourteenth century, and contrary tendencies of contraction in important areas of the economy had at least begun in the period 1320–48.

We cannot appeal to contemporaries' comments to confirm this view, so the argument must be based on the information gathered together from year to year in administrative documents, and the unspoken testimony of the physical remains.

If the Black Death had been a turning point for the population of England, we would expect to find that the population growth of the thirteenth century, after an interruption in 1315–17, continued up to 1348. In some cases this seems to have happened. At Halesowen in Worcestershire, for example, the number of males mentioned in the manorial courts stood at 331 in the five-year period between 1271 and 1275, and increased to 485 by 1311–15; after falling mainly because of the famine to 412 in the early 1320s, the total climbed back to 470 by the late 1340s. After the famine at Halesowen much land came into the hands of young people who were able to marry and produce children, and these children in turn were of marriageable age and adding another generation in the 1340s. At Coltishall in Norfolk the number of tenants increased from 141 in 1314 to 198 on the eve of the Black Death, without mortality in the famine. But these places experiencing growth are outnumbered by the examples of falling population after the famine, notably in Essex, where the total of males aged over twelve fell, at Chatham Hall, from seventy in 1320 to fifty-five in 1346, while at the much larger manor of Great Waltham, the peak of 320 in 1306 was reduced by the famine to 254 in 1319, and then was further eroded to only 200 in 1340. On the Northamptonshire manor of Brigstock the number of adult males resident in the manor can be estimated at about 500 before the famine, and was reduced to about 400 on the eve of the Black Death. A similar tendency to decline after the famine can be observed among the *garciones* of Longbridge Deverill in Wiltshire.

Harvest failures and epidemics both before and after the Great Famine help to explain the population decline. The severity of an episode can be judged by the rising cost of grain, in which prices which were 25 per cent above the average can be regarded as a significant threshold, or by low yields, especially those 15 per cent or more below the average, or by signs of social stress such as an increase in mortality, a peak in the sale of land by peasants, or an increase in illegal gleaning cases. These hard times affected different regions unequally, reflecting the variety in the climate, soils and local economy. Bad harvest years were concentrated between 1293 and 1296, followed by an episode of high prices and a rising death rate in 1310–11, and after the famine, in 1321–2, 1322–3 and 1331–2.

There were also epidemics when the death rate increased in years when the harvest was not especially deficient, in 1304 for example. Sometimes an abnormal number of deaths is found in a particular locality, such as Downham in Cambridgeshire in 1327–8. In east Sussex there were fourteen deaths among the townspeople of Battle in the late autumn of 1331, and six tenants of Beddingham died in the same year. The numbers seem small because it is only the deaths of tenants that were recorded – for every adult landholder who died, there could have been four deaths among relatives and dependants, as young people, women and the elderly are consistently under-represented in the documents. We should not assume that they were the only factor behind the fall in population, as changes in the birth rate are likely to have played their part. We have noted that the famine could have stimulated long-term population growth by giving young people the opportunity to acquire land, and to marry, at an early age, but it would be over-optimistic to think that every mortality peak was followed by a compensatory baby boom – the troubled times of frequent harvest crises and epidemics cannot have created the confidence and optimism to encourage early and universal marriage.

In the light of the successive short-term food shortages and bouts of mortality, the episode of famine and disease of 1315–22 appears to form part of a pattern, and a longer period, beginning in the mid-1290s, can be identified as bringing to an end in most regions the thirteenth-century growth in population (Figure 2).

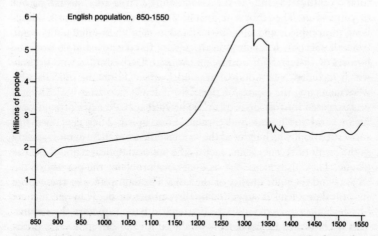

Figure 2. English population, 850–1550. A speculative reconstruction. The figures from 850 to 1086 are pure speculation. The subsequent figures are based on Domesday (1086), the Poll Tax (1377), the subsidies (1524–5) and the military survey (1522), and by extrapolation from manorial records of tenant deaths and payments of headpennies and common fines.

Sources: J. Hatcher, *Plague, Population and the English Economy, 1348–1530* (1977); R. M. Smith, 'Human Resources', in G. Astill and A. Grant (eds), *The Countryside of Medieval England* (Oxford, 1988); E. A. Wrigley and R. S. Schofield, *The Population History of England, 1547–1871: a Reconstruction* (London, 1981).

ii. *Contraction and change*

Both peasants and lords were reducing the scale of their farming operations in the early fourteenth century. There had been earlier threats to
agriculture, such as the outbreak of sheep scab in the 1270s and 1280s,
but significant reductions in the area under cultivation came after 1300.
The heroic phases of large-scale reclamation in the fens and marshes
were over. Small-scale drainage projects continued after 1300, such as
those in the Isle of Axholme in Lincolnshire. In the 1330s and 1340s
throughout the country thousands of acres were lost to agriculture from
flooding. Such episodes as the tidal surge in the Wash in 1338 played their
part, but this was a long-term deterioration in the whole system of water
management, not just a series of accidents. The extension of cultivated
land by the clearance of woodland and scrub, and by breaking up
pasture, had accounted for a large proportion of the new land of the
twelfth and thirteenth centuries, and again in some regions this assarting had come to an end by 1300. Clearances can still be found in the early
fourteenth century, like the inroads into the Weald in the south-east as
late as the 1330s and 1340s. But these assarts were not raising the global
total of cultivated land, as at the same time a large area was falling out
of cultivation. The reports of uncultivated or 'frisc' arable, of holdings
lying unoccupied, and of houses abandoned by their inhabitants come
from all parts of the country in the 1320s. To take an example from the
borders of eastern Staffordshire and western Derbyshire, a wooded area
which included Needwood Chase and Duffield Frith, the officials who
were managing the estates of the earls of Lancaster, after Earl Thomas
was executed for treason in 1322, reported that 6,000 acres of land were
vacant, and 167 houses and cottages unoccupied. They explained this
sorry situation, which reduced the rent income from these manors, partly
as the result of recent events, such as the political upheaval and the cattle
plague. They also mentioned as long-term problems the poverty of the
tenants and the poor quality of the land. The importance of these more
structural problems is suggested by three phases of decay in rent income
of which they gave details, which stretched back to before the famine.
This is confirmed by documents produced for the earl nine years previously which mention falling rents and abandoned land.

The tax assessors in 1340–1 listened to complaints which showed that
parts of England were experiencing widespread decline in cultivation.
The parliament of 1340, in order to provide money for Edward III's
French wars from an already tax-weary country, experimented with a
grant of the ninth lamb, fleece and sheaf of corn, in effect an extra tithe

of agricultural produce after the church had taken its normal share of a tenth. The grant met with much opposition, and the reasons given for non-payment (recorded in the 'Inquisitions of the Ninth') might be dismissed as the usual excuses of reluctant taxpayers. We would expect to find that taxes were disliked in equal measure over the whole country, but the grumbles are found in particular places, and mentioned appropriate local problems. For example, in coastal parishes in Sussex they blamed flooding for the loss of productive land. In inland counties they complained of sterile and infertile soil and sheep disease, all of which caused land to fall out of cultivation, the inhabitants to become poor and on occasion to leave their homes, even to go off to beg. More than half of the villages in Buckinghamshire were said to have suffered shrinkage in arable land. In that county, and in Bedfordshire, Cambridgeshire, Gloucestershire and Oxfordshire, the villages that were affected were in the main corn-growing belt of the midlands, not precarious upland settlements which might have been vulnerable to changes in climate. There were reports of poverty and declining cultivation also on higher ground, in Shropshire and north Yorkshire. It therefore appears that the abandonment of land was widespread, both on the sandy soils of Bedfordshire and on the clays of Buckinghamshire, land that had been cultivated for many centuries, and on recent assarts. (Plate 12)

Perhaps the complaints of 1340–1 were a temporary episode, after which cultivation resumed and the villagers returned and prospered? When individual cases are examined in detail, it can be shown that the assessors of 1340–1 were reporting events which belonged in a sequence of long-term changes with permanent results. For example, when they came to Aston Blank in the Gloucestershire Cotswolds they found that the full amount of tax could not be paid because seven families from the hamlet of Little Aston had given up their holdings and left the parish. As Little Aston contained fewer than a dozen households, this meant that it had lost most of its population, and indeed soon afterwards it ceased to exist. The landlord, a small nunnery, lost all revenues from the place for a time, and eventually received 40s per annum from Little Aston instead of its normal income of 66s 8d. The arable fields belonging to the hamlet were turned into pasture, and were not cultivated again for centuries. The remains of peasant houses can still be seen on the site of Little Aston, and deserted farms and hamlets are also found on much more exposed and difficult soil on Dartmoor. One of them, Hound Tor, had developed in the thirteenth century, when new settlers ploughed up some of the moor and kept livestock on the rough pasture, but in the early fourteenth century the inhabitants retreated down into the valley. A similar upland site at Cefn Graeanog in north Wales was probably abandoned at this time, and a settlement on the south Wales coast at Rhossili was covered with blown sand, though it was probably abandoned because of agricultural problems before the sand took over.

The compilers of estate surveys in the early fourteenth century described the deficiencies of the land that they were valuing in the same language used by the enquiries of the tax assessors in 1340–1. They said that the soil was stony or sandy, or simply poor or infertile. The fields did not acquire these characteristics suddenly, so these criticisms must have come to the minds of officials because they were conscious that land was not giving sufficiently abundant or consistent crops, and needed to justify valuations as low as 2d per acre. The concern about soil fertility is difficult to verify. Although the accounts kept by manorial officials contain many thousands of figures from which yields can be calculated, they vary so much from year to year that long-term trends cannot be easily identified. On the estate of the bishopric of Winchester over the period 1209–70 the average bushel of barley that was sown produced 4.32 bushels of grain at the harvest, after the tithe had been deducted. This ratio declined to 3.36 in 1270–99. This downward movement was not continued; in the early fourteenth century the ratios increased slightly, to 3.57 in 1300–24, and 3.74 in 1325–49, though still remaining well below the pre-1270 figure. Yields may not have recovered after 1300, however, because the amount of land cultivated by the bishopric was reduced, as the lord leased parcels of demesne land to local tenants. The estate officials, it has been suggested, probably selected inferior plots of land to be rented out, in order to concentrate the lord's crops on the better soils, hence the apparent recovery in yields. Had the information on the missing acres been available, the yields would have remained at a low level or even deteriorated. At Cuxham in Oxfordshire, where the area of demesne was reduced only slightly, an underlying downward movement in productivity can be detected between 1298 and 1348, which did not affect barley and oats, but which reduced yields of wheat per acre by about 18 per cent. This has been explained as a result of the gradual loss from the soil of the essential mineral phosphorus, caused by the annual removal of crops without an adequate return of nutrients to the soil.

Information about yields derives from demesnes, which covered perhaps a quarter of the cultivated land, and the crucial question is whether the peasant cultivators, who managed most of the land in the country, experienced similar changes in the productivity of their crops. Occasionally a lord's officials harvested a tenant's grain, when he died or left the holding. The crops on tenant holdings at Bourton-on-the-Hill (Gloucestershire) which were harvested after the plague in the autumn of 1349 suggest peasant yields of less than 8 bushels per acre, well below demesne production, but this was a year of unusually bad weather as well as plague. It can be argued that each acre of peasant land would produce less than an acre of demesne, because it was likely to receive smaller amounts of manure, and peasants would have inferior equipment, buildings and draught animals. Lords had greater control of their land, and were not always bound to follow the routines of common field farming. Peasants would be taken away from vital seasonal tasks such as harvest by labour service.

There were some advantages for the peasant in compensation: the labour force, consisting largely of the peasant family, was committed and hard-working, in contrast to the unenthusiastic spirit in which labour services were performed (see p. 134). Peasants could afford the time to carry out those jobs requiring close attention to detail, such as weeding. Demesne managers, conscious of labour costs, were tempted to reduce the amount of time spent on such tasks. Estates may have been managed by men who had read the books which gave farming advice, such as *Walter of Henley*, and the reeves and bailiffs who ran the manors knew that the auditors would make them pay for any errors. But peasants had the advantage of the accumulated wisdom of many generations, and intimate knowledge of their holdings. Above all they knew that their well-being and even survival depended on their decisions. The advantages and disadvantages of peasant cultivation probably cancel each other out, with the result that their yields were rather similar to those of the demesnes. They probably followed the same tendency to stagnate or even decline in the first half of the fourteenth century, as suggested by the many reports of poor tenant land and abandoned holdings.

Total cereal production declined in the period 1300–48. The acreage under the plough diminished, and the productivity of the land that remained under crops stagnated or fell. The prices of grain were declining in the long term: wheat was sold on average for 5s–6s per quarter in the period 1270–1310, but had dipped to about 5s in the 1330s and 1340s. The change in the same period took barley prices from 3s 6d–4s 8d in 1270–1310, to 3s 6d–3s 11d in 1330–47 (see Figure 1 above, p. 230). There are many ways of explaining that downward tendency, one of them being an improvement in the weather. An underlying influence could have been the reduced number of consumers. That this was a factor is supported by the apparent rise in wages at the same time. A carpenter's daily wage before the famine (1280–1310) moved around $2\frac{1}{2}$d to $2\frac{3}{4}$d, but between 1320 and 1347 the average wage rose just above 3d (Figure 3).

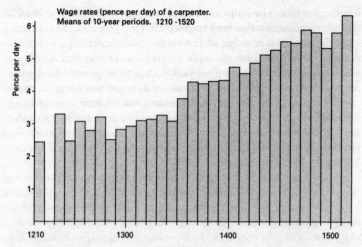

Figure 3. Wage rates in England, 1210–1520. Wages, pence per day, of a carpenter. Means calculated in ten-year periods.

Sources: AgHEW, vols 2 and 3; J. E. Thorold Rogers, *A History of Agriculture and Prices in England*, vol. 3 (Oxford, 7 vols, 1866–1902).

The increase in cash wages was slight – less than a halfpenny per day – but when combined with the reduced cost of grain, the purchasing power of a skilled worker's wage rose by about 15 per cent. Real wages can be measured directly, confirming that the rising wage was not just a statistical illusion. When estate officials in Norfolk and other counties gave food as part of the wages of harvest workers in the late thirteenth century, bread, often baked from cheaper grains such as barley, bulked large in the diet. For each pound of bread, the workers received only a half-ounce of meat, which was often bacon. In the early fourteenth century a higher proportion of the bread was baked from wheat or rye, more ale was allowed, and the amount of meat increased. More fresh meat was included in the meals. The most likely explanation of the tendency for rewards to workers (both skilled and unskilled) to rise must be that a decline in population, combined perhaps with the broadening opportunities for employment created by industrial expansion, was making labour a little more scarce.

These were harder times for some lords and for those who managed their estates. The era of 'high farming' was coming to an end. The policy of maximizing demesne production, with land purchases, reclamation, marling, new building and other improvements, often gave way to different strategies, especially after the famine. Since the late thirteenth century some estates had been making calculations of the 'profit of the manor'. They must have become aware that the prices of grain (and also those of wool and livestock after the diseases of the 1320s), were in decline, and labour costs were beginning to rise. The estate officials introduced further accounting devices to allow them to monitor grain yields, and to recover some money if poor performance could be blamed on the mismanagement of the reeve. These involved setting targets for yields – it would be stated that wheat should have returned four times the seed planted, and the reeve would be required to pay the difference if the crop fell below that level. Sometimes the auditors' target became a quota, and the reeve who was required to produce 300 eggs would then return that figure each year, selling any surplus for his own profit. When they adopted this method of securing a minimum fixed income, the estate managers were starting on the road to leasing their assets.

Lords, no longer believing that profits would increase, were beginning to focus on reducing their losses. The next stage was to rent out an acreage of the demesne to peasants, who were anxious to acquire parcels of land and would pay good rents. Lords were strongly attached to direct management of their demesnes, and in East Anglia they often kept them intact and under cultivation throughout the early fourteenth century. In the midlands and the south, estates such as those of Westminster Abbey, the bishoprics of London and Worcester, or the lay lords of the Welsh marches, in addition to renting out piecemeal parts of demesnes, also leased out the whole demesne of a few manors. These were often selected because they were small, or detached from the main estate. In the south-west and north-west directly managed demesnes were scarce even in the late thirteenth century, and leasing of demesnes was far advanced by 1320.

As lords began to doubt the value of land, they stopped buying it as an investment. Some, like Quarr Abbey on the Isle of Wight, acquired little after 1300, and others went on into the 1320s and 1330s, such as the Lincolnshire abbeys of Crowland and Thorney, which had bought a great deal in the thirteenth century. Church estates had been restrained in buying lay land by the Statute of Mortmain in 1279, but they could still acquire land legally if they bought a licence from the king. Church estates ceased to grow mainly as a result of economic calculations rather than legal restrictions. Lay magnates who bought a great deal of property, such as the Beauchamps, earls of Warwick, also acquired less in the early fourteenth century. Some lords continued to buy urban property, suggesting that it was agricultural land in particular that was seen as unprofitable.

The scaling down of demesne production changed the relationship between lords and peasants. A movement from labour service towards rent is found in all parts of the country, on the scattered manors of the Abbey of Bec, the estates of the monks of Westminster, which were mainly near London, and the lands of Ramsey Abbey in the east. A different story is found in Kent, where labour services were limited in number, and those few were demanded by such lords as Canterbury Cathedral Priory.

In general, peasants in *c.*1320 were paying more cash to lords than ever before: they owed leasehold rents for parcels of demesne and cash payments in lieu of labour service, as well as the usual assize rents, entry fines and other dues. Lords attempted to make as much as they could from tenants, especially as their demesnes seemed less profitable. The variable payments such as entry fines and marriage fines which were negotiated by individuals offered the best chance of profit, and they are also helpful to us in understanding the rise and fall in demand for land. They rose on the Ramsey Abbey estate until the monks' officials could collect 66s 8d for a yardland, and 40s for a half-yardland in the 1310s – though the fines were lower in the 1320s. Thanks to the long series of documents compiled for the bishops of Winchester, the successive fines paid for individual holdings can be traced over long periods. A yardland at Bishop's Waltham was acquired in 1227 for 20s, and when it changed hands in 1328 cost 80s, but then fell back to 40s in 1331 and 20s when it was sold again in 1333, 1338 and 1341. This suggests that the would-be tenants of this holding were making a pessimistic calculation of the profits of land after 1330, and were unwilling to pay the higher sum which was no doubt sought by the bishop's officials. A similar insight into changes in the market for land comes from Cornwall, where the estate of the earl of Cornwall adopted conventionary tenancies in 1333. This was a form of leasehold by which tenants paid a fine for a seven-year term, after which the whole tenancy was renegotiated. The first payment of these 'assessionable' rents in 1333 yielded a large increase in revenue, which was partly the result of the introduction of the new system, but partly an indication of the high demand for land. There was, however, no increase in the 1340s, suggesting a levelling in the demand for land as tenants recognized the limits on their profits.

The peasants were not entirely gloomy about their circumstances, however, judging from the continued liveliness of the land market. Lords could lease out parts of their demesnes profitably because peasants were anxious to acquire extra acres. The decline in cultivation did not leave land derelict, but gave the peasants the chance to acquire more animals:

individual flocks of a hundred sheep were reported in a number of midland and southern manors.

The aristocracy had problems in managing their expenditure as well as their incomes. They began to experience the 'price scissors', as the price of the goods which they sold, such as grain and wool, tended to fall after about 1320, while their cost of living began to edge upwards. We have seen that wages were rising slightly, making building in particular more expensive. Wine from Gascony, a major item of household expenditure for the magnates, was sold commonly for 3d or 4d per gallon at the turn of the century, but by the 1330s and 1340s the price had risen to 4d and 5d. Lords were concerned to control their spending, and household accounts were compiled with more care and sophistication. From about 1310 the more complex accounts included in their calculations not just the money spent each day, but also valuations of the goods used from stock. An unusual budget compiled in 1346 for Thomas III, Lord Berkeley, summarized the expenditure for a year (which probably took up too high a proportion of his income) and noted various savings which had been made by substituting cheaper meat and malt. Monasteries, especially smaller and poorer establishments, were prone to overspending and indebtedness, and reports of monastic debt are concentrated in the period 1329–48.

Towns, trade and industry were naturally caught up in the crisis as they were so closely integrated into the rural economy. Commercial life had its own dynamic forces leading both to decline and new growth. The foundation of new towns had already begun to slow before 1300, and it virtually ceased in the first half of the fourteenth century. New markets and boroughs were still founded, but in reduced number, and with diminishing chances of success. New Eagle in Lincolnshire is an example of the fate of optimistic hopes in an unfavourable economic climate. Its founders, the Knights Hospitallers, obtained a charter in 1345 which justified the creation of a new town because of the lack of stopping places for travellers on the Fosse Way between Newark and Lincoln. The charter authorized the building of a chapel, the planning of plots for houses, and the holding of a market and fairs. The site is now marked by a single inn and empty fields, and there is no evidence that anyone ever settled in the new town. The economy of older and larger urban centres was evidently slowing down. Rents were reduced in the centre of London, and in its suburbs of Southwark (after 1320) and Westminster (in 1317–41). Falling rents are also found in the provinces, at Oxford for example. At York, which enjoyed some economic advantages in the early fourteenth century, new rows of houses were being put up in the 1330s, but new building slowed in some towns, and some old properties decayed. There are hints of a scaling down of food and drink production at Colchester, where one of the eight mills went out of use after 1311, and the number of ale wives was reduced. There were some disasters, as towns as well as arable fields were subject to flooding and the inroads of the sea. Dunwich on the Suffolk coast lost 209 houses, a quarter of the town, between 1278 and 1326. But in general the signs of urban decay before the Black Death were on a modest scale.

Underlying the waning fortunes of many towns were reduced levels of trade and industrial production. Wine imports probably reached their highest point in the whole medieval period in 1308. Wool exports peaked, at 46,382 sacks, in 1304–5, and remained at between 20,000 and 30,000 sacks in 1315–30 (see Figure 4). The mining of tin in Cornwall had been in the doldrums in the first decade of the fourteenth century, but then increased to a remarkable total of more than 1.6 million pounds of metal in 1332, followed by a decline which became a serious slump after the plague. Major building projects on cathedrals and large monasteries seem to have reached their highest level of activity in the 1270s, and had entered into pronounced decline by 1320. Each product had its own momentum, and its own special reasons for expansion and contraction. All goods which crossed the English Channel in time of war were subject to embargoes, piracy or new taxes. But there were also underlying long-term economic rather than political influences, such as aristocratic need to check spending which damaged the wine trade.

Clothmaking was an important English activity in the late twelfth and thirteenth centuries. Weavers, fullers, dyers and other specialist artisans

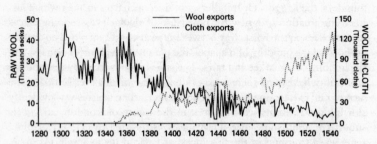

Figure 4. English exports of wool and cloth, 1279–1544 (cloth exports are only consistently recorded from the mid-fourteenth century).

Sources: E. M. Carus-Wilson and O. Coleman, *England's Export Trade 1275–1547* (Oxford, 1963); E. M. Carus-Wilson, *Medieval Merchant Venturers* (1954).

are found in many towns, notably in the larger towns of eastern and central England. Their products, such as 'stanforts' (probably referring to a distinctive weave rather than the town of Stamford), 'haberget' (made at Stamford among other towns), and Lincoln scarlets were well known on the continent. The English made light, quite cheap cloth which sold well in the Mediterranean world. A list of cloths compiled in Portugal in 1253 mentions 'Northamptons'. Between about 1290 and 1320 various complaints are heard that the numbers of weavers and looms in such major centres of the industry as Leicester and Oxford had declined drastically, and continental documents make no mention of English cloth.

Town-based clothmaking may have collapsed because the guilds and urban governments were too restrictive, and the high costs of urban life, such as taxation, pushed up the price of English cloth. Part of the industry relocated in the country, and a large share of the cloth market, it is said, was seized by the Flemish who outdid their English rivals in both quality and price. This cannot be entirely accepted, because the number of cloths from Flanders, Brabant and other parts of northern France and the Low Countries imported each year in the early fourteenth century amounted to 10,000–11,000, but many of these were quite expensive, and were clearly aimed at the wealthier consumer. To replace their worn-out clothing, each year the English needed at least 200,000 cloths (each measuring about 25 yards in length). The Flemish industry was going through its own troubles, and was not in a position to supply the English market with more than a fraction of its requirements. The bulk of England's cloth must have been supplied internally, and its manufacture continued in places such as Winchester and York and was growing in towns like Colchester and in the countryside. The worsted industry in Norfolk, based in villages and small towns, notably at Worsted and Aylsham, expanded at this time. Native cloths, both cheap and more costly, gradually and almost imperceptibly took over the domestic market, helped by the taxation of wool exports which made English wool much more expensive for the clothmakers across the sea. By 1347–8, 4,000 cloths were being exported, and the industry was entering a new phase of growth as English cloth became an article of international commerce. The industry had gone through severe problems, but had emerged even before the Black Death in a healthier state.

Lords, peasants and townspeople were caught up in the complex and inconsistent movements in the economy of the early fourteenth century. In parts of East Anglia the upheaval was not so pronounced, but generally the trends, not merely of a few decades but of the previous two or three centuries, were checked, and went into reverse. A similar pattern of events is found over much of continental Europe. There was indeed a crisis of the fourteenth century, which had profound effects before the Black Death.

iii. *Historical debate*

Such a remarkable change in direction demands an explanation which takes into account the long-term as well as the immediate symptoms of crisis. An ambitious model was created by M. M. Postan, and received support from the continental historians W. Abel and E. Le Roy Ladurie. Postan's interpretation emphasized the changes in population as the main dynamic force in the economy, and the impact of expanding agriculture on the ecology of the countryside. He saw all of the changes as inter-connected, and all flowed from the great expansion, which had to stop because it was unsustainable. The premise of Postan's thinking was that in a peasant society the balance between the cultivators and the land pro-vided the crucial variable factor. At the level of the individual and the family, he saw landholding as being adjusted to suit the needs of larger and smaller households. As a young family grew, its food needs and labour capacity were satisfied by transfers of parcels from the holdings of the elderly or disabled. This was a 'natural' land market, with the sub-sistence requirements of each household being met by the exchange of land between neighbours. In the same way, whole populations depended on land for their living, and any movement in population would have an impact on the use of land. In England, by 1200 the population was quite high and the land extensively cultivated. Yet the numbers of people more than doubled in the following century. At Taunton, where each male over twelve years old paid a penny to the lord of the manor, the numbers rose from 506 in 1209 to 1,359 in 1311. Almost every local calculation based on the recorded tenants or taxpayers reports different rates of growth, but the same upward trend.

As more people crowded on to the limited areas of cultivated land, holdings fragmented, leading to the proliferation of cottagers and tenants living on small parcels. Postan put together a collection of estate surveys, mostly of the thirteenth century, from different parts of the country, and found that 45 per cent of tenants had a quarter-yardland of about 8 acres, or smaller amounts of land. This substantial minority of smallholders could not feed their families from their land alone, and sup-plemented their crops with earnings, at inadequate rates of pay which reflected the abundance of labour. The demand for land increased in the late thirteenth century, and the lords could sometimes demand very high entry fines for their holdings – as much as £40 for a yardland on church estates in Somerset. Rising land values and high corn prices encouraged the extension of cultivation at the expense of woodland and grazing land, which created imbalances between arable and livestock husbandry. The high rents paid for pasture and especially meadow indicated the shortage of land for feeding animals. Peasants did not own enough animals to keep the land well manured. For example, the tax records of a group of Wiltshire manors from the year 1225 show that a countryside ideally suited to sheep farming suffered from a shortage of sheep. The total number of peasant animals, according to tithe records, was diminishing in the late thirteenth and early fourteenth centuries.

These imbalances helped Postan to explain why grain yields, such as those on the estates of the bishopric of Winchester (see p. 238), were so low, and were becoming even lower in the course of the thirteenth century. The 'metabolism of the field system' had been disrupted by the misuse of land. The cleared woodland and ploughed-up grassland did not benefit the cultivators in the long term, because the land was often of poor quality and had been left unploughed by previous generations of farmers for good reason. Comparison of the yields of crops on 'colonizing' manors with those from old cultivated manors shows that the recently assarted marginal lands gave poor returns. Eventually these newly won lands were given up: there was a 'retreat from marginal land'.

As growing populations were trapped on their limited holdings of land which produced ever smaller quantities of crops, Postan considered their inability to make technical changes, such as those introduced in the eighteenth century. He concluded that peasants were too poor to innovate, partly because of their subordination to lords, and because the lords themselves were too preoccupied with impractical learning and with expenditure on display. The lords were unwilling to invest capital in their manors. The population was, in the view of Postan and his supporter Titow, poised on a knife edge of subsistence. Every time a deficient harvest pushed up the price of grain, peasants died in unusual numbers, as is reflected in the extra heriots recorded in the accounts of the bishopric of Winchester. The famine period was merely the worst among many years of high mortality. The expectation of life among peasants declined from an already low level. In the late thirteenth century, at the age of twenty a peasant could expect to live for another twenty-four years; in the early fourteenth the figure sank to twenty years. In short, according to this account of events, the fourteenth-century crisis was man-made. Too many people produced too many children in the thirteenth century, the population outstripped resources, and the land could no longer feed everyone. Death and economic contraction followed as night follows day.

This coherent theory, made plausible by supporting evidence, has been a valuable stimulus to thought about the period, and alternative interpretations of it have been developed. These lead us to question both Postan's underlying assumptions, and the evidence that underpins them. If we begin with the growth in population, this was thought by Postan to be the normal pattern in a peasant society, especially in the absence of epidemic disease or serious famine. As we have seen, from an early date there was an inbuilt restraint against rapid population growth, in peasants' acceptance that marriage should be based on the possession of land. These restrictions were modified by the land market and the growth in non-agricultural employment. An increased rate of marriage, perhaps with a reduction in the number of celibates, a lower age for marriage, as more young people were able to acquire a cottage or parcel of land, and a subsequent rise in the number and frequency of births all helped to promote population growth. Children had a better chance of survival as the quality of houses improved, and as food became relatively plentiful in the middle decades of the thirteenth century. Population growth was a product of economic change, not an independent factor which caused other developments.

Nor should the population increase be seen mainly in a negative light. People were assets: they could make a positive contribution to their own well-being and that of society as a whole. We have noticed, for example, the small landholdings and high density of population in north-east Norfolk, which led not to immediate mass starvation, but to the careful and thorough application of labour to the land, from which came higher productivity. Smallholdings had been numerous long before the population growth of the thirteenth century – Postan's calculation of the high proportion of those without adequate quantities of land included figures from surveys of the Shaftesbury Abbey and St Paul's estates of the late twelfth and early thirteenth centuries in which smallholders accounted respectively for 33 per cent and 48 per cent of tenants. This substantial minority of wage earners and craft workers provided a flexible labour force that was essential for lords' demesnes, larger peasant holdings, and industrial workshops. They were often a disadvantaged group with meagre earnings, but the economy would not have functioned without them. They were not a miserable underclass acting as a drag on the rest of society. To be specific, they brought in much of the harvest, as both demesnes and larger peasant holdings lacked a permanent labour force capable of handling the intense work pressures of August and September. They also gathered the fuel necessary for domestic and industrial use: wood-cutting, charcoal-burning, peat-digging and coal-mining were largely carried out by the smallholders.

The intense demand for land was a significant feature of the thirteenth-century economy. The very high entry fines found in Somerset were rare elsewhere, but many lords charged as much as £3 for a yardland. Tenants were willing to offer a great deal of money to acquire scarce and valuable land, but they must have made the realistic calculation that the returns from cultivation would enable them to pay back the moneylenders. The lenders must also have judged that the cash they advanced could be repaid. Entry fines give us evidence for the squeezing of the resources of peasants by lords and moneylenders. But in the scale of fines we can also find some positive signals about the state of the peasant economy.

Postan was aware of the dangers of formulating reliable statistics about village livestock on the basis of tax records from which so many peasants were omitted, and which were subject to a great deal of evasion and manipulation. Although the figures are questionable, no one would argue that peasants in general had an abundance of animals, because many fragmentary sources, such as heriot payments, lists of animals straying on to lords' demesnes or feeding in royal forests, and lists of stock seized by lords from rebellious or absconding tenants, support the general proposition that peasant holdings were under-stocked in lowland England. The balance between arable and pasture was an ever-present problem, going back to the origins of the open-field village. Peasants had limited access to fodder, both from grassland and from crops such as beans and vetch, because they had to give priority to producing crops for human consumption. But were they trapped in a deepening spiral of expanding arable, manure shortages and lower productivity? The existence of some open-field villages with much the same population and cultivated area between 1086 and *c.*1300 suggests that the inhabitants had found some sustainable agricultural system with limited amounts of pasture, which did not lead to disaster over many generations – though such villages often encountered difficulties in the fourteenth century.

The 'retreat from marginal land' can certainly be observed in the abandonment of hamlets and farmsteads on Dartmoor and Snowdonia. But its importance was exaggerated by Postan. Much of the land that fell out of cultivation in the early fourteenth century lay in good corn-growing districts such as mid-Buckinghamshire, which suffered from no major physical disadvantage apart from the heavy soils which were by no means confined to that county. In districts with more severe limitations on cereal crops, such as those on high ground, or which were densely wooded, or surrounded by marshes and fens, peasants had devised means of balancing resources, cultivating a limited area and taking advantage of the pasture, wood, turf, reeds or fish to supplement their income from cultivation. In the Breckland on the borders of Norfolk and Suffolk, for example, the sandy soils were cultivated occasionally, not continuously. Much use was made of the extensive heathy pastures, and of the nearby fens. The concept of 'marginal' land varies greatly with such human factors as the level of rent and proximity to markets. A moorland field was worth cultivating for its meagre crop of oats if the rent had been set, as was often the case, at 2d per acre. Poor land could be profitably cultivated as a garden, provided that it lay near to a large town where fruit and vegetables were in demand.

The methods of making productive use of different soils and landscapes were just part of the range of technologies applied to agriculture at this time. This was a period of innovations, such as the extended use of horses as draught animals and the planting of legumes (see pp. 166–7). Peasants lacked capital, and their lives were insecure, so they were limited in the techniques that they could use. But they should not be regarded as trapped and unable to adapt.

Peasants were vulnerable to disease and hunger, but not to the extreme degree that Postan suggested. The calculation that peasants died in every poor harvest, and that their expectation of life sank to twenty years at the age of twenty, was based on the evidence of heriots, but heriots were sometimes paid on the surrender of a holding, that is a sale of land, as well as on death. In years of scarcity peasants felt hardship, but sold land to survive. Their life expectation, based on tracing individuals through the series of Halesowen court records, can be estimated for the early fourteenth century at 30.2 years at the age of twenty for better-off peasants, and 20.8 for the smallholders. These are higher figures than those calculated by Postan, but are still much lower than those found in the era of parish registers, in the sixteenth and seventeenth centuries. Halesowen's adults were dying young, and of course we know nothing about the deaths of those aged under twenty, but we suspect that they suffered great losses. If the population of Halesowen was rising at this time, as seems to be the case after the famine, to compensate for the heavy mortality there must have been a very high birth rate. This leaves us with a further unsolved problem, as one view of the demography of this period represents it as a 'high pressure' system, in which people married young, produced many children but also suffered high rates of mortality. This has been identified at Halesowen, and might support the view that this was a period of overpopulation and careless reproduction. Another interpretation suggests that the demographic system of the fourteenth century resembled that of the early modern period, in which marriage was delayed until both partners were in their mid-twenties, and a proportion of people remained celibate. Such a system meant that levels of population followed changes in the economy: in hard times people married very late, or not at all, and the size of the population was reduced through the mechanism of the birth rate rather than mortality. We simply do not have enough information about marriage and births to know which of these best describes the behaviour of the population before the Black Death.

iv. *Crisis in Scotland*

The early fourteenth century in Scotland is not so well documented as in England, but it still provides a helpful comparison. Scotland seems to have gone through the same sequence of growth and contraction as occurred in England and the rest of Europe. In the thirteenth century there is a recognizable pattern of expanding cultivation, increase in the size and number of towns, growth in the export trade in wool and hides, and a rise in the amount of coinage in circulation. Monastic foundations, some of them new, built up respectable incomes, so that by about 1290 Newbattle Abbey was worth at least £267 and Holyrood near Edinburgh £774. The secular magnates, numbering about fifty families, prospered, and the earl of Fife, for example, was worth £500 per annum.

Between 1296 and 1328, and again in 1332–5, the economy was disrupted by war with the English, but in addition we can detect underlying problems. Long-term economic changes in Scotland are signalled by three documents which valued the property of the church for taxation purposes. From the early thirteenth century comes the 'ancient assessment' (*antiqua taxatio*); Bishop Halton's assessment dates from about 1300; and the 'true value'(*verus valor*) of 1366 reflects the situation after the Black Death. The valuations recorded in the 'ancient assessment' doubled by the time of Bishop Halton's survey: in the diocese of St Andrews they rose from £8,000 to almost £14,000, and for the Glasgow diocese the increase was from £4,000 to a little more than £11,000. After 1300 came a collapse in values, with the 'true value' recording much lower figures than in Halton's survey, even below the level of the 'ancient assessment'. A local survey of the bishopric of Moray allows us to trace the decline in a little more detail: the value in about 1300 of £2,496 was cut to £928 in the mid-fourteenth century, and then sank to the very low £559 in 1366.

In interpreting these figures, the effects of the fighting, the plague and any longer-term economic malaise cannot be disentangled. Tithe revenue contributed a high proportion of these church valuations, and the ups and downs in tithe are a good indicator of the fluctuations in general economic activity. It was therefore not just the Scottish church, but the whole country which apparently suffered from a profound recession in the fourteenth century. This is confirmed by the royal accounts of the 1350s which refer to waste and lost revenues on a more damaging and widespread scale than would be expected from the plague epidemic alone. Settlements in the countryside were abandoned in the fourteenth century, such as farms and fields on the Lammermuir Hills, and a hamlet at Springwood Park on the edge of the burgh of Roxburgh. The economy of the towns suffered a setback, if we consider the way in which a site in the centre of Perth, where there was plentiful craft activity in the thirteenth century, shows little sign that goods were being manufactured there in the early fourteenth century. Some of the new burghs that were founded in this period, such as Tarbert and Staplegorton, initially failed to develop as towns. The export trade in wool and hides in 1327–32, of 5,700 sacks of wool and 36,100 hides per annum, declined to an annual 2,450 sacks and 17,900 hides in the early 1340s. Both sets of figures probably reflect a period of depression, judging from the known productive capacity of the great estates, and the larger amounts, which were traded in the early 1370s – 7,360 sacks and 39,500 hides.

The Scottish economy contracted in the fourteenth century, though there is little direct evidence of the effects of the Great Famine or the Black Death, and the date of the turning point remains uncertain. The country could have experienced some problems resulting from the over-exploitation of land. Settlement and cultivation were unevenly distributed, with much of the population living on the best agricultural land in the east. In the south-east, nucleated villages cultivated open fields and displayed a bias towards arable farming similar to that found in much of England and continental Europe. Yields would have fallen in the Isles if there had been a reduction in the regular spreading of manure such as seaweed on the infield. In addition, fields were cultivated on hillsides at altitudes in excess of 1,000 feet which were especially vulnerable to episodes of bad weather. Some wheat was grown in the south-east, but much of the Scottish population was dependent on oats and barley to a dangerous degree. In times of bad harvests consumers in more favourable climates could switch from wheat and rye to barley, oats and other inferior corn, but if the spring-sown crop failed, many Scots had no alternative cereal. Disputes over grazing rights between monasteries and other lords with rights to upland pasture suggest some pressure on land, and overstocking may have contributed to the outbreak of sheep disease, like that in 1294.

In spite of these disadvantages and weaknesses, it would be hard to maintain that this was a countryside in which an excessive proportion of the land was under the plough, or where grazing had been reduced to the point that the arable was deprived of manure. The *sourning* (allowance of animals allowed to landholders, called a stint in England) for an oxgang of about 15 acres of arable on the estates of Arbroath Abbey was fifty-two sheep, five cows, two oxen and a horse, which does not suggest any shortage of pasture – a peasant in the English midlands would have been allowed half of this. Much of the arable lay in outfields which were cultivated occasionally. The suggestion that land was over-exploited, or that the pressure of population damaged the rural ecology, would be difficult to apply to Scotland, which even after the growth of the thirteenth century must be regarded as a thinly populated country.

Many medieval peasants were compelled to hand over a high proportion of their surplus production in rent, which deprived them of their potential capital and sometimes of their food, and contributed to the crisis. Again, there is little evidence that this was a serious problem in Scotland. Lords did not usually cultivate large arable demesnes, so it was unnecessary for them to demand heavy labour services from their tenants. Many lords kept extensive flocks of sheep, but these did not require much peasant labour. Peasants often paid a rent in cash by the early fourteenth century, and while these could be as high as 18s for a husbandland on the Kelso estate, they were not usually so burdensome. The extra dues that were extracted in cash and kind do not seem very heavy, judging from the earl of Fife's revenue from his whole estate of 40s from marriage fines, 33s from heriots and 16s for forfeitures. Scottish lords were oppressive, in their restriction on their peasants' freedom of movement, for example. Tenants were not allowed hereditary succession to their holdings, which led them to petition Edward I in 1305 (when he was occupying the country) to allow them the same rights of inheritance as their counterparts in England. Scottish peasants often lacked material possessions, as can be seen from the finds from excavations of rural sites, and sections of the peasantry were servile in status, but they did not apparently suffer increased privations at the end of the thirteenth century which might have precipitated the crisis that overtook the Scottish economy.

If Scotland went through a turning point in the fourteenth century without an ecological crisis, this must create doubts about whether the imbalance of arable and pasture, the shortage of manure, and the 'metabolism of the field system' in England and elsewhere were the main reason for the economic setbacks of the period.

v. *Explanations*

The crisis may have been caused by some external change (an exogenous factor) which jolted the economy and turned it downhill. One of these could have been the climate, which played an important part in the harvest failures, the flooding of reclaimed wetlands, and the Great Famine. The climate went through a period of instability between 1290 and 1375, which was particularly damaging to cereal production because a number of wet summers prevented the ripening of crops. The hay harvest was disrupted, which affected livestock, and damp ground could encourage diseases such as foot rot and liver fluke in sheep. Wet conditions created a favourable environment for pests and plant diseases. However, although the climate undoubtedly contributed to the crisis, its role was surely to expose economic weaknesses. Today, third world countries are vulnerable to natural disasters such as flooding because they do not have the capacity to repair the damage, while more advanced economies can shrug off these problems. In the history of western Europe the most adverse weather conditions in the last 2,000 years created the 'little ice age' of *c.*1550–1850, in which the economy sometimes went into recession, but also entered the first stages of the industrial and agricultural revolutions. Bad weather does not necessarily lead to disaster and recession. In the later middle ages, the climate returned to stability and allowed a succession of good harvests after 1375, but the economy did not resume the growth patterns of the thirteenth century.

In a similar vein, another disruptive influence came from fluctuations in the supply of money. The later middle ages saw a long-term decline in the amount of silver in circulation throughout western Europe, partly because the mines did not produce enough to compensate for the loss of precious metal which was hoarded, used to make plate and ornaments, or sent to the east in the course of trade. In the first half of the fourteenth century, silver was liable to move from one country to another because of changing government policy on monetary matters. In 1305–10, for example, the authorities in the Low Countries temporarily ceased minting in silver, and the king of France overvalued his gold coins, which caused continental silver to flow into England, leading to a temporary sharp inflation in prices. Much more serious was the loss of bullion in the late 1330s, when Edward III taxed the country heavily to pay for the opening of the Hundred Years War, and specifically to make gifts to rulers to persuade them to become his allies. At that time there were complaints that goods could not be sold because of the shortage of coin, and the tax granted by parliament in 1340 was to be levied in kind. These episodes were disruptive, but the troubles of the period must have had deeper roots, because they continued in times of monetary stability.

Perhaps the crisis began because of stresses and strains in the social and political structure? The power of lords over peasants has already been mentioned as an explanation for their poverty. The number of demands made by lords seem particularly high, and little reduction was made during the critical years in the Welsh marcher lordships, which enjoyed relative independence from the crown and could exploit inhabitants ruthlessly. The marcher lords – that is, aristocrats such as the earls of Arundel, Gloucester and Hereford, who also held extensive English lands with conventional rights as lords of the manor – gained a small proportion of their income in the Welsh march from demesnes and labour services. They also exploited their powers as lords, such as their right to revenues from mills, and in particular their judicial authority, to extract money. The courts were used to levy large quantities of cash. For example, in 1321–2, 700 people in Caernarfonshire were fined a total of £27 for failing to attend the lord's court. The right of tallage was also enforced in an arbitrary way – a 'gift' could be raised if the lord incurred some unusual expense, such as serving with the king's army in France. In 1324 in the lordship of Chirk the tenants paid 1,600 marks (£1,066) for a charter which gave them hunting rights, access to pastures and woods, and exempted subtenants from the obligation to pay heriot. The suspicion that this bargain benefited the lord more than the tenants is confirmed by the issue of another charter ten years later confirming the first, and allowing free tenants to build mills, again for 1,600 marks.

Arbitrary exactions, however, were confined to particular regions and particular types of tenant, and the fourteenth-century crisis was universal. A high proportion of English peasants, probably the majority, were free, and for many customary tenants increases in dues had not kept pace with thirteenth-century inflation. A more intangible influence arose from the aristocracy's position of social leadership. They provided the lesser ranks with role models, and their example did not set much store by thrift and industry. But peasants were capable of forming their own ideas, and were by no means uncritical admirers of the aristocracy. The conclusion must be that social inequalities and lordly power were a contribution to, but not a prime cause of, the crisis.

The disruption and draining of the economy by war played some part in precipitating the crisis. Wars were being fought in Britain or by the rulers of England or Scotland for at least forty of the years between 1290 and 1350. Armed conflict was a normal activity in the middle ages, and it usually made no extraordinary demands on the economy. But in this period it was organized more systematically, on a larger scale, and on a long-term basis. Edward I's campaigns in Wales had established new methods of war, in which the armies received wages and which aimed at the systematic and permanent conquest of territory. Roads and harbours were constructed, and the troops were kept supplied with food and weapons by land and sea. Once the enemy had been defeated, massive castles were built at strategic points to control the population, and colonies of English settlers established. All of these activities cost money, and when English aggression was turned on Scotland and France, the long lines of communication, the large armies (some containing 20,000 men), the support of ships and sailors, and the complex diplomacy, added still more to the expense of war.

The most direct economic impact of war was the destruction of the countryside and towns by armies, which was not an unforeseen accident of campaigning, but a deliberate policy to damage enemy resources and to force opponents to abandon the conflict, or to accept a settlement favourable to the attackers. The Scottish borders were especially badly devastated. The country around Carlisle was attacked by the Scots in 1297: mills and barns were burnt, and peasants killed and driven away. Another raid led to the burning of villages and seizure of cattle in 1314, and more raids followed in 1315, 1316 and 1322. In 1345, after more incursions in the same district, sixty-four villages were judged to be unable to pay their taxes in full. The Scots found that the eastern side of the border offered richer pickings, and penetrated in a series of attacks into Northumberland, Durham and northern Yorkshire. The revenues received by Durham Priory from churches on the eastern side of the border, in south Tweedsdale, came mainly from tithes, and their fluctuations indicate general changes in agricultural production. Before 1297 the priory received above £400 per annum from these churches, but in 1297–8 the figure sank to £35, as a direct result of Scottish destruction. After full recovery, from 1318 with the Scots back on the offensive, revenues fell back to £20, but in the subsequent period of relative peace they failed to climb higher than £269, in 1338–9. English pillage of the Scottish countryside is not recorded in such detail, but this was not confined to the border area, and in 1337 a destructive invasion reached as far north as Aberdeen and resulted not just in the burning of that town, but also in the ravaging of some of the best agricultural land, such as the Mearns to the north of Montrose. The threat of raids caused distress to the border population, because they had to pay for fortifications, and the English were sometimes able to pay the Scots not to attack. The presence of English soldiers supposedly defending the border was a dubious benefit, as they tended to rob the local population, and even to turn to brigandage. The events at Flint in 1294 indicate the vulnerability of towns. The English authorities, fearful of an attack by Welsh rebels, themselves burnt the town which had been built next to the castle, to prevent its use as a shelter for a besieging army. The seventy-five burgesses were paid £521 in compensation for the loss of their houses and goods, which probably did not cover the full value of their property. Towns in the south of England were raided in 1338–40 by the French, which caused not just much damage to property, but afterwards the expense of building a more effective town wall at Southampton. In general, as in the case of Flint, a programme for reconstruction followed the destruction of war, and no permanent setback necessarily resulted. More serious economic consequences followed repeated attacks, especially in districts like the Scottish borders or north Wales which were not agriculturally rich, and where town life was still rather precarious. The most northerly counties of England changed their character in the early fourteenth century: the atmosphere of insecurity became a dominating feature for centuries.

Armies destroyed specific localities, but war affected everyone who paid taxes. Direct taxation in England was raised only in time of war, and the almost continuous series of campaigns between 1290 and 1348 resulted in the levying of successive lay subsidies, which brought to the government a total of £1,055,300. Additional measures to swell government coffers included the taxation of the clergy, which yielded £551,000 in the same period, the taxation of international trade, from which the king obtained an income in most years in excess of £10,000, and a number of measures such as purveyance, by which the king's agents made compulsory purchases of supplies for armies or the royal household, for which the 'sellers' received a poor price only after long delays.

Was this of real economic significance? It could be said that the total wealth of the country was sufficient to provide these sums without undue strain. If the king took £80,000 (beyond his regular income of about £30,000) in a year of active campaigning, for example in 1297, this amounted to just under 2 per cent of the estimated Gross Domestic Product. It was a small sum compared with the total of rent that lords collected: for example, each year the lay aristocracy and the higher clergy and monasteries received incomes totalling £600,000. The money was not taken away completely – much of it was used to pay English soldiers, or to buy food, equipment and weapons with benefits for the English producers. The administration of taxes, it might be said, was not harsh or oppressive. The taxes were granted by parliament, so that consent had been given, and unlike the French, the English taxpayers did not usually rebel on a large scale. All social classes were included within the tax system, including the aristocracy and clergy. The only exempt categories were those of tin miners in Devon and Cornwall, the men of the Cinque Ports, and the inhabitants of Cheshire and Durham, who paid taxes in a different form. No one could have had a strong sense of resentment that some wealthy groups were not paying anything. The assessments, based on valuing moveable goods (for most peasants this meant livestock) were carried out by local people who did not include every item, and who used some generously low valuations. The rules allowed the poor to escape, by stating that those with goods worth less than a certain sum (commonly 10s) would be exempt. Large numbers of people with goods worth much more than 10s were given a sympathetic low valuation which took them below the tax threshold. The tax was administered with some sensitivity to the feelings of the taxpayers, so that although the rate, that is the fraction of the value of goods, could be as high as a ninth or as low as a thirtieth, the amount collected did not change greatly, suggesting that officials turned a blind eye to large-scale evasion and under-assessment.

In spite of these reservations, we must accept that some people suffered from war taxation. A great lord like Canterbury Cathedral Priory paid so much in the mid-1290s that it sank into debt and was forced to reduce wine purchases and cease building operations. The better-off peasants, who paid a high proportion of direct taxes, were required to find 2–4s in many years, which was a considerable sum on top of their obligations to their lord. A peasant born in 1270 and acquiring a holding of about 20 acres by 1293 would find himself contributing for the first time in 1294, followed by further payments to the taxes granted in rapid succession in 1295, 1296, 1297 and then in a further nine years between 1301 and 1322. If his son succeeded him in the mid-1320s, during a brief respite, he would pay in 1327, 1332, 1334, 1336, and contribute to three subsidies in 1337–40. In all, the two generations of this family paid about 60s to the lay subsidy, which may not seem very much, considering that their saleable surplus over forty-six years would have amounted to at least £40, and their rent payments to more than £20. The tax demands would have been a nuisance because they appeared unpredictably – they fell in the years that suited the king, not the peasants, and they tended to come in concentrated groups, notably in 1294–7 and 1337–40. Nor did the grants take much account of adverse circumstances, such as the bad harvests of the mid-1290s, and we have seen that a subsidy was collected in the midst of the famine in 1316–17.

The official records tell us of the payments that were returned to the central government, but other sources show that tax collectors were bribed. Those who were making their contribution would also be liable to purveyance, which fell unequally across the country, with counties such as Lincolnshire bearing more than their fair share. On occasion the king also demanded quotas of foot soldiers from the shires, which under the system of array meant that each large village, or groups of smaller ones, would find and equip a recruit and pay him until he reached the main army, towards the cost of which again our better-off peasant would have had to pay a few more pence. In addition, the taxes on wool, which helped to push down the price to the grower, would reduce the profit of many peasants' main cash crop. The smallholders may at first sight seem to have slipped through the tax net, but we should take account of interdependence in the village economy. If money was taken from the wealthier peasants, they had less to spend locally, which reduced the employment opportunities of smallholders, or diminished the market for such non-essentials as ale. When, in response to complaints of corruption and mismanagement, the administration of the subsidy changed in 1334, tax collectors no longer assessed each individual, but instead each village and town was given a quota of taxation to raise as it saw fit. The peasant elite passed some of the burden on to their poorer neighbours, who had previously been exempt. So hard-pressed smallholders did feel the effect of taxation, both indirectly and directly. Finally, the king's taxes were alleged to have caused such poverty among peasants that they left their holdings. This was said during the collection of the ninth in 1340–1. In Shropshire at Clungunford the existence of waste land was blamed on the king's many taxes, and all but two of the inhabitants of the hamlet of Cold Weston, on the slopes of Clee Hill, were said to have abandoned the settlement for fear of taxation.

Having weighed up the arguments for and against regarding direct taxation as a major influence on the economy, the conclusion must be that it had a considerable impact, but not on a scale sufficient on its own to have precipitated the crisis of the fourteenth century. War and taxes had universal effects. Most other changes, such as those in the policies of landlords, or the climate, or the long-term consequences of land clearance, varied from place to place and region to region, whereas government demands were felt everywhere – and this applies in particular to taxes on international trade. The wool export trade attracted the attention of government because its high profits could be tapped without immediate economic damage, and as the wool was carried through a small number of ports there was limited scope for evasion. In addition, the clothmakers of Flanders depended on supplies, and therefore political pressure could be applied by cutting off the trade, or directing it elsewhere. The 'great custom' on each sack of wool from 1275 stood at 6s 8d (sacks varied in price from £4 to £8). In the time of Edward I's wars, and in later episodes, a *maltolte* ('bad tax') was imposed which in some years brought the level of tax up to £2 per sack. The most ambitious scheme to allow the king to enjoy the full profit of wool sales was that launched in 1337, when a consortium of wool merchants advanced a loan of £200,000 to Edward III in return for a monopoly of the bulk of the wool trade. The operation was over-ambitious and badly organized, and it ended in tears, with royal officials selling the wool cheaply in 1338 at Dordrecht in the Low Countries and paying off the merchants with bonds that would enable them to recover money – eventually. The government continued to intervene in the wool trade in the 1340s, and in 1343 a 'company' of thirty-three merchants, who may have been representing a much larger group, took over the whole customs system on wool in exchange for grants of money to the crown. One explanation of their move was that this removed the provision in an earlier law that wool merchants had to bring back bullion from the continent for each sack sold.

The government's manipulation of the wool trade – with its taxation, embargoes and monopolies – was bad news for the producers of wool, because it disrupted the marketing of their product to varying degrees. The high levels of taxation could not be passed on entirely to the foreign customers, so taxation probably contributed to the long-term drop in the prices that the producers received. Trade in general suffered from the emergency measures of wartime, such as the requisitioning of merchant ships to carry armies, and the increased danger of piracy, which forced ships to carry an extra crew of soldiers and to sail in convoys. Fear of the loss of ships, and of the unpredictable shifts in politics, cannot have helped business confidence.

Warfare is often credited with some positive economic benefits, for example, the acceleration of technical innovations. Some people did benefit from the military expeditions of 1290–1350. The traders of York, for example, enjoyed prosperity because the city at times served as a temporary capital of the whole kingdom. The urban and industrial life of north Wales was transformed by Edward I's conquest, to the benefit of the new urban colonists. Even the coal mines of Flintshire experienced a boom as fuel was needed for the smiths making the tools, nails and other ironwork used in castle-building. Members of the aristocracy expected to profit from war. They would contract to bring a contingent of troops, and make a small surplus from the pay for the men under their command. The general expansion of government activity and expenditure increased the number of official positions; those who performed well were rewarded with titles and the lands and grants of money to support them, like the new crop of earldoms created by the youthful Edward III. The campaigns in France in the 1340s brought plunder and ransoms for those on active service, and the earlier conquest of southern Scotland resulted in English nobles enjoying temporary profits from confiscated Scottish lands.

The indirect effects of war deserve our attention. Taxation on wool exports pushed up the cost of the raw materials used by continental manufacturers and made their cloth more expensive. The taxation was applied only to exports, so the wool available in England was relatively cheap. Cloth made in England was cheaper than that produced by its continental rivals, which helped it to capture the home market and begin to make inroads once more among the consumers across the sea. English commerce also gained from the growing proportion of trade handled by English merchants. Aliens paid a higher rate of tax on wool exports, and various protectionist measures, such as a prohibition on foreign merchants buying wool directly from the producers, helped local traders. From 1313 a staple was introduced, by which all wool was supposed to be carried to a single continental port. The choice of town depended on diplomatic considerations: the staple was initially located at St Omer, and then moved to Antwerp and on to Bruges, but later in the century was fixed at Calais. The staple policy was primarily meant to keep control of the trade for political and fiscal reasons, but it also had the effect of favouring English exporters, as the whole system was sponsored by the government and managed by an English mayor. The wool trade was closely connected with substantial loans to the crown. All three Edwards had used as their bankers big Italian companies: the most prominent names were the Riccardi, then the Frescobaldi, and finally the Bardi and Peruzzi, and these hard-headed businessmen gained trade privileges, and especially access to wool exports, as a reward. The last two firms failed in the 1340s – not entirely because of the inability of Edward III to honour his debts. Increasingly the king relied on loans from English merchants, such as William de la Pole who came originally from Hull and acquired a large landed fortune from the profits of trade and financial dealings with the crown and the aristocracy. In Scotland, by the 1330s a staple had been fixed for wool at Bruges, which was linked with royal taxes, including higher rates for alien merchants. In the thirteenth century most Scottish wool had been exported by continental merchants, but now 85 per cent of the wool trade was in the hands of Scots.

In general then, the wars of the period had a profound effect on the economy, resulting both from the disruption of agriculture and trade by military operations, and from taxation, but some of the positive developments of the period in the cloth industry and the advances by native merchants also owed something to short-term government policy. Perhaps this was intended, but it is more likely to have been an accidental by-product.

The crisis of the fourteenth century cannot be given a simple cause, any more than we can easily explain other turning points in history, such as the fall of the Roman empire or the decline of the European colonial powers in the twentieth century. The economy and society of *c.*1300 had become complicated and interlocking, and growth had added tensions and pressures. We cannot unpick the complexities and identify a single internal problem, such as population growth, or a single external change, such as climate, and give these a privileged place in our interpretation of the period. We can indicate a number of points of weakness in the structure that had been assembled in the period of growth before 1300. Each area of achievement had its limitations, or its negative repercussions. Such was the success in agriculture that in most years there was sufficient food for everyone, including the substantial minority of town dwellers and country people employed in industry. In times of stress, townspeople did not necessarily suffer most hardship, as the urban authorities were able to secure supplies, in which case the rural poor went hungry. Migrants into towns were often looking for chances to better themselves, and many succeeded, but at this time a migration of the desperately poor in search of charity or casual work was of no benefit to the town or to the migrants themselves.

The size of the towns created ecological difficulties, as we have seen in the case of London's fuel supplies. But towns also had economic problems if the demand for traded and manufactured goods was levelling off soon after 1300. The spiral of demand, and of interaction of the urban and rural economies, was flattening at this time. Country people who sold food and raw materials to the town found that as demand for these goods declined, they could not spend so much on urban manufactures. The turning point in the cycle of trade may have come in the years before the Great Famine, and the economy was certainly not recovering after that event. The many peasants' sons and daughters who had founded new households on the basis of opportunities in the non-agricultural economy were experiencing difficulties in the 1290s and were among the casualties in 1315–17. Perhaps it is not just the population that had grown as far as was possible by the early fourteenth century, when Britain was as populous as it was to be in about 1750. The whole commercial economy and level of urbanization – in the relatively thinly populated parts of Scotland, Wales and northern and western England, as well as in the south and east – had reached their upper limits.

The aristocracy had been drawn into participation in the trading system when they took their demesnes into direct management in the early thirteenth century, and in the next hundred years they improved both production methods and administrative techniques. By the early fourteenth century, having specialized to some degree, and made some technical innovations, they realized that their profit margins were not very high. After the instability of 1295–1332, they experienced a fall in grain prices and a rise in labour costs which discouraged them from continuing with high farming. They could not squeeze more out of the peasants, because these small producers were affected to some extent by the same problems, such as low prices, and could not afford to pay any more rent. They also resisted demands, or suffered hardship from royal tax collectors. The lay aristocrats welcomed the opportunity of war and royal service as an additional source of income, but not all of them made great gains, and the general extension in the authority of the state tended to close off avenues of profit for the landlords, such as their powers of private justice. The aristocracy cut back on expenditure, with further dampening effects on trade and manufacture.

The surge of economic activity which had begun in the tenth century was losing momentum. The nucleated villages, the open fields dedicated to extensive grain production, the manorial structure based on binding peasant rents and services to demesnes, the magnate estates, the larger towns, were all running into stagnation or decline after 1300. But even at this decisive moment when these organizations reached their peak and began to falter, we can see signs of growth in the reviving cloth industry, especially in the countryside and small towns, greater confidence and more trading activity among English merchants, and a rise in the import-ance of London and some provincial towns such as Coventry. The peasant land market and peasants' larger sheep flocks are signs of vitality. The crisis of the early fourteenth century, like the period of 'recession' that followed, had its dimension of innovation.

PART THREE

Making a new world, c.1350–c.1520

In this period the sources change, as those who once dominated the economy lost their active role. The manorial accounts kept by reeves and bailiffs, which tell us so much about agriculture under the management of the lords, become less informative after 1400, and are quite rare by the late fifteenth century. This was because lords, and especially those with large estates, pulled out of direct involvement in growing corn and rearing animals. We know something about the new activists of the economy, especially the wealthier peasants and entrepreneurs, from the growing number of wills. Some documents are informal and full of insights into human reactions, notably the letters in English written by the gentry. The English language, newly emerging from its inferior status in relation to Latin and French, was the vehicle for much social and political criticism in the half-century after the Black Death, when poets such as Chaucer, Gower and Langland, together with many writers whose names are not known, expressed their perceptions of a shifting, often troubling world. Their depiction of the age supports modern historians' view that the crisis that began before 1348 continued and deepened, to the point that articulate observers thought that the old order was threatened.

Contemporaries realized that they lived in a material world that was contracting, because most villages and towns bore the scars of collapsed buildings, and settlements as a whole or in part were abandoned. A fifteenth-century book of school exercises, in which commonplace comments were to be translated into Latin, refers casually to a hazard of urban life: 'The roof of an old house had almost fallen on me yesterday.' At the time, it was not known that the population of England had been reduced from about 5 million on the eve of the Black Death to 2.5 million in 1377, and it was to remain around that level until after 1520 (see Figure

2 above, p. 235). But employers and landlords were fully aware of the scarcity of labour and tenants, and there was much disquiet in the early sixteenth century about the shortage of manpower for the armed forces. After the mid-fifteenth century, the changes in population in parts of the continent, notably France and Italy, where numbers were growing quite rapidly, contrasted with the persistence in England of low levels of population until about 1540.

Those who lived through these years were very conscious of the short-term fluctuations from year to year in the quality of the harvest, reflecting the patterns of weather, and they would refer to 'good' and 'bad' years on the basis of the price of corn, though sellers and buyers had different views on shortage and plenty. Prices were mainly low, as our school-book suggests when it sets passages for translation such as: 'All manner of white corn, as wheat and barley, was never sold better cheap [cheaper] than it is now . . .', and 'there is no man now alive who can remember that ever he saw wheat or peas or other corn or any other foodstuff that is brought to the market to be sold cheaper than we see now . . .', leading to the comment put into the schoolboy's mouth that he is sorry for the peasant producers ('poor husbands') who 'sell much things for little silver'. In terms of average prices, wheat in England retained or even surpassed in most decades between the 1380s and 1490s the figure of 5s per quarter at which it settled after the Great Famine. But barley declined to only 3s to 3s 6d per quarter in the same period and oats fell below 2s for much of the fifteenth century (see Figure 1 above, p. 230).

Contemporaries also commented on the shortage of coin, and especially on the lack of coins of small denominations. This reflects the 'bullion famine', as it has been dubbed by historians, which meant that the outflow of silver to the east was not matched by new supplies from mining. Governments were faced with hard decisions on how to keep the economy running on diminishing quantities of silver. In England, the mint which had been accustomed to producing coins worth at least £1,000 in a year was striking £182 in an average year in the early fifteenth century. The authorities supplemented the silver currency with gold coins from 1344, the most frequently minted being the noble, worth 6s 8d. Gold accounted in the late fifteenth century for half of the total amount of cash in circulation. Debasement, in which coins were minted with a lower silver content, was another option, though by the standards of other countries the reduction of the silver content of the penny in the 1340s, again by one sixth in 1412, and in 1464, was on a modest scale. The amount of silver available for minting increased after 1465. The English government showed some concern for the needs of those using coins, and introduced the groat (worth 4d) in the 1340s, and then the half-groat, which were quite convenient after the Black Death because rises in wages meant that employers needed to pay 4d per day to skilled workers, rather than the 3d that prevailed in the 1330s and 1340s, and in the fifteenth century craftsmen commonly earned 6d per day. But, as in earlier periods, the mintings of halfpennies and farthings were insufficient to meet the demand for small change.

In Scotland, which had a sterling currency closely matching that of England, the debasement route was followed from 1367, after which Scottish coins were no longer accepted in England, and English pennies were driven out of use in Scotland. The initial decision was taken for the profit of the state rather than in response to the shortage of bullion, but further reductions in the quality of the coins were encouraged by the lack of silver. In the late fourteenth century, an English pound sterling was judged to be worth 26s 8d in Scottish money, but by 1483 was equivalent to £5. Gold was minted in Scotland, and in the late fifteenth century low-denomination coins made from base metal were issued. The fluctuations confused those who used the coins, leading to formal statements of rent payments or other obligations as being payable in 'the usual money of Scotland', a phrase which acknowledged the changeable nature of the currency. Rents and prices were affected by the shifts in the money, and to further confuse the issue there were changes in the measures, such as the 'boll' in which grain was sold. Prices of grain, of which oats were the most important, rose in the long term, while lower prices were paid in the fifteenth century for the ever-plentiful livestock.

The conventional historian's view of the period is one of contraction, a trough between periods of growth in the thirteenth and sixteenth centuries. A concern of those alive at the time was the moral and social deterioration that followed the Black Death. John Gower wrote in the 1390s that:

> The world is changed and overthrown
> That it is well-nigh upside down
> Compared with days of long ago.

He was ostensibly contrasting the world of antiquity with his own times, but when he went on to refer to former wealth and plenty, and to an age when knights were honoured, aristocracy received proper respect, and cities were not divided by contention, he clearly had in mind the changes of the previous half-century. Gower and other poets of the late fourteenth century made much use of the 'three orders' idea, which explained that society could function in peace and harmony if each order – those who fought, those who prayed and those who worked (aristocrats, clergy and peasants) – pursued its God-given duty, while receiving services from the

268

Making a new world, c.1350–c.1520

other two orders. Workers should carry out their tasks and pay their rents, confident that they would be protected by the military skills of the aristocrats, and benefit from the prayers of the clergy. Everyone agreed, however, that each order failed in its obligations, and threatened the unity of society. Another member of the elite, the Norfolk esquire John Paston, complained in 1462 that tenants 'hoped to have a new world', referring to their reluctance to pay rents. The estate officials of the bishop of Worcester in 1450 gloomily compared the 'ancient' rents and servile dues of the thirteenth century with the lower sums prevailing 'in modern times'.

The long-term trends of the period worked against the interests of the aristocracy. The low population reduced the numbers of tenants and the demand for land, and therefore rent income declined. The price of primary products, especially grain, fell because of slackening demand, while the costs of scarce labour rose, together with the prices of manufactured goods, to which wages made a considerable contribution. So the incomes of lords decreased while their cost of living increased: they were caught in the famous 'price scissors'. But these tendencies are apparent only when we survey the evidence over fifty or a hundred years, while the lifetimes of individuals were often influenced by short-term movements sometimes in one direction, sometimes in another. The period between 1349 and 1375 was one of generally expensive grain, so the picture of falling prices applies after 1375, and even then was interrupted by periodic shortages, notably in the late 1430s, the early 1480s and in 1519–22. The commercial economy was subject to fluctuations, the most significant being the quite high levels of trade around 1400, the depression of the middle years of the fifteenth century, and the new expansion after about 1470. In addition there were sudden shocks like the slump in the early 1520s. The end of the period saw the first stage of the inflation in prices that was to become such a dominant feature of the sixteenth-century economy.

The contractions in the period should not dominate our view of it. The lower orders of society have left us no accounts or letters to inform us of their experiences, but we can appreciate that high wages, reduced rents and cheap food may not have done them great harm. Also, while it is important to understand the ups and downs of the economy, structural changes in the control of production and the distribution of wealth deserve our attention. The old cliché that this period saw 'the rise of the middle class' has no validity, as no middle class existed. If the phrase refers to townspeople, they multiplied in number, and some of them became prosperous, before 1300, and after the Black Death they recovered, but were scarcely 'rising'. But different social groups were repositioned, with a weakening of those sections of the aristocracy dependent on traditional manorial revenues, the decline of some towns, and the greater prominence of new social and occupational categories, such as gentlemen, yeomen, farmers and clothiers.

Regions had varied fortunes, with the densely populated grain-growing, village-dominated English midland claylands falling behind the more dynamic industrializing pastoral areas, such as southern East Anglia, Kent, the south-west, and west Yorkshire (see Map 11 below, p. 359). The position of England in relation to the continent of Europe also underwent a transformation. Large towns, international trade and intensive agriculture had been located in north Italy and Flanders, and these regions remained key points in the European economy, but in the fifteenth century the centres of gravity shifted to the north and west, with the rise of Castile and Portugal, Holland, the port of Antwerp, and England. England became an industrial and maritime power, as its woollen cloth was exported in quantity all over Europe, and a growing proportion of overseas trade was organized by English merchants and carried in English ships.

The political upheavals of the period have been seen as providing the appropriate setting for economic contraction. In England, dynasties of kings were overthrown when Richard II, Henry VI and Richard III were forcibly removed from their thrones, and the Wars of the Roses broke out sporadically in the period between 1455 and 1485. Scotland has also been seen as dominated by 'over-mighty subjects' who caused so much insta-bility that James I was assassinated in 1437 and James III deposed and killed in 1488. Nonetheless in both countries an underlying community of interest between aristocracy and monarchs has been identified, and recent writing has emphasized the desire for peace which prevented anarchy. For example, the contracts between aristocrats secured by the bonds of manrent in Scotland, and the alliances between English magnates and gentry based on 'bastard feudalism', aided cohesion and harmony rather than disorder and civil conflict. The Wars of the Roses had a limited direct impact on the economy, and they were brought to an end because aristocrats were reluctant to continue with disruptive internal warfare. The rulers at the end of our period – the Tudor dynasty in England and the Stuarts James IV and V in Scotland – brought stability, albeit using increasingly autocratic methods.

For contemporaries, the main impact of the state on the economy came from demands for taxation, which in England were heavy in the 1370s, and in the early fifteenth century, when Henry V resumed aggres-sive policies towards France. Taxes ceased to be a serious burden after the English defeat in the early 1450s and English rulers gave up the war.

In Scotland money had to be raised to pay David II's ransom in the period 1357–77. The heaviest incidence of direct property taxes, the 'contributions', lay between 1358 and 1373, and in 1424–5 to pay another ransom, this time after the capture of James I by the English.

CHAPTER EIGHT

The Black Death and its aftermath, c.1348–c.1520

i. Plague and population, c.1348–c.1520

The epidemic of plague which spread from Asia into western Europe reached Britain in 1348. It was in effect a new disease, as an interval of six centuries had passed since the previous major epidemic. The plague moved through the population of black rats, colonies of which surrounded human settlements, even in remote places. When the rats died, their hungry fleas moved on to human beings and infected their new hosts when they bit them. The bubonic plague was a warm-weather disease, so it was most active in the summer, but in the winter it developed a pneumonic strain which could be spread directly from person to person by coughing. Most of those who contracted bubonic plague died after a few days, but almost all of those who caught the pneumonic form succumbed very quickly.

Plague spread inexorably from its entry point in south-west England in the late summer of 1348; it reached the midlands in 1349, and probably did not end in northern Scotland until 1350. Its movement to villages and hamlets indicates the completeness of the commercial network, as every place was visited regularly by travellers, cartloads of grain or hay, and packloads of goods, all of which might contain infected rats or fleas. Once the disease had begun, its passage through the community was aided by the sociable and charitable impulses of a society in which neighbours entered afflicted houses in order to visit the sick, mourn the dead and comfort the bereaved. The official procedures of will-making, and the distribution of bequests of grain and clothing, would help to maximize the number of contacts. The mortality among the privileged sections of society could be quite low – 27 per cent in the case of the tenants-in-chief of the English crown (earls, barons and some knights and gentry). They lived in stone houses and at a distance from the rats. Among the parish clergy, who were also relatively affluent, between 42 and 45 per cent died. The proportion of peasants who died, according to manorial court records, was usually above 40 per cent, and could reach 70 per cent, which gives the basis for an estimate of a 50 per cent mortality overall. A very high mortality, admittedly from a small sample, is provided by the twelve tenants of the demesne lands of Llan-llwch near Carmarthen, eleven of whom died.

Those who survived the epidemic had to struggle with appalling problems. Most families lost at least one member. Others came near to being wiped out. For example, the monks of Stoneleigh in Warwickshire, when they recorded in the 1390s the histories of different properties on their estate, recalled that a substantial freeholding, amounting to about 50 acres, had belonged to Robert le Heyr, and 'in the first pestilence' Robert, both of his sons Henry and Richard, and Robert's grandson all died, leaving the land vacant. The first task facing those who still lived was to bury the dead. The tradition that 50,000 corpses had to be buried in London may not be an exaggeration, and two new cemeteries were opened, with communal graves. Then came the legal problems: proving wills, arranging for the transfer of property, and providing for widows and orphans. The task was complicated if, as in the case of the le Heyr family, the succeeding generation had died as well. Faced with such horrors and difficulties, the economy and system of administration might have broken down, but with remarkable resilience people returned to work, and the whole system held together.

At Longdon in Worcestershire, the manor (which belonged to West-minster Abbey) was being managed in the year before the plague by the reeve (a tenant of the manor), Andrew Eyloff. He continued in office for another term, beginning in September 1348, but he died halfway through the year, on 14 April 1349. Seventeen other tenants also succumbed to the epidemic, and the manorial officers collected their heriots, the death duties of the best beast on each holding, amounting to two oxen, five cows, two horses, two sheep and two pigs, the others being too poor to contribute. A superior official, a sergeant, was appointed to fill Eyloff's place in the emergency. He had to cope with an acute labour shortage on the manor. The dairymaid died, as did the carter, and a ploughman left his work through illness after six months. Another ploughman temporarily took over carting jobs 'because no one could be hired to carry (corn) this year because of the pestilence'. In spite of the difficulties, there are only a few signs that the routines lapsed, for example, when we are told that a payment was made 'by a certain man, whose name the clerk does not know'. At the end of the year, in October or November 1349, the written account was compiled as usual, showing that the agricultural work had been completed, and the rents collected. Everywhere officials, clerks and tenants died, but substitutes were usually found. In the surviving documents the handwriting may abruptly change, as a new clerk takes over. The royal courts resumed their work after a brief interval, and the number of cases was understandably reduced. The institutions were clearly sufficiently robust to withstand the stress of the epidemic. The mass graves of the London plague cemeteries revealed by modern excavations provide an excellent demonstration of this ability to cope. 'Plague pits' in our lurid imaginings suggest corpses being tipped hastily into great holes, but instead the authorities dug long trenches, and the bodies, some in coffins, were laid in an orderly and dignified fashion side by side. A body may sometimes show signs of decay before burial, perhaps after lying unnoticed for some time after death, but the main impression is of a civilized and organized society doing its best to make decent arrangements in desperately difficult circumstances. (Plate 13)

Having dealt with the immediate effects of the plague, people returned to their usual tasks. Some activities were temporarily halted. Lead mining in Denbighshire stopped in 1349; building operations on the parish churches of Ashbourne in Derbyshire and Patrington in east Yorkshire, and on the west front of Exeter Cathedral, all seem to have ceased, either because of deaths among the workforce, or a sudden shortage of funds. These interruptions lasted for some years, but work was eventually resumed. All of the potters at Hanley Castle in Worcestershire were reported to have died in 1349, but the industry flourished again later in the century. Cornish tin mining did not apparently cease, but it suffered a severe setback, as in 1338–42 more than a million pounds of the metal was presented annually for taxation (coining), but in 1351 less than a quarter of that amount, 237,408 pounds, were recorded. Production climbed back to pre-plague levels by 1386.

On many landed estates, peasant holdings were left vacant in the 1350s, lying, as the court records say, 'in the lord's hands', but over the years they were rented out, if only on short-term lettings. The new tenants were in many cases the younger generation who acquired their inheritance more quickly than expected. Some previously landless labourers and servants took advantage of the situation to rise into the more substantial peasantry, but these opportunities were limited, because capital was needed to acquire the land, and to buy equipment and livestock. Many holdings were taken by tenants who survived, who were given the chance by the death of their neighbours to expand their acreage. In these circumstances, houses surplus to the tenants' needs were neglected, and the countryside was dotted with even more ruined houses and empty plots. These decayed holdings were distributed over all settlements, however, and very few whole villages or hamlets were abandoned as a direct result of the first plague. Quob, a hamlet in Hampshire, was reported deserted immediately after the Black Death, as was Tusmore in Oxfordshire, but the latter was in severe decay in 1341, so the epidemic did no more than seal the fate of an already declining village. Some parts of the economy seem to have proceeded almost unscathed, such as wool exports, which, at 35,000 sacks in 1350–1, were at much the same level as in the 1330s and early 1340s (see Figure 4 above, p. 244).

Perhaps the statistics of production and landholding are taking too cold a view, and we should suppose peasants, miners and shepherds continued their tasks in a traumatized state? Contemporary witnesses, such as the chroniclers, do not suggest that society was paralysed by the loss of life. The writers worked within the conventions of their age, which meant that they tended to express stock moral judgements. They linked the plague with the sins of mankind, and exaggerated the effects, claiming in some cases that the mortality rate was 90 per cent, that there were scarcely sufficient survivors to bury the dead, and that many villages were deserted. They also remarked on the disruption of the social hierarchy. The Rochester chronicler noted the inversion, whereby those formerly at the top could only afford to eat bread and pottage, while labourers whose wages had risen could buy more expensive food. In addition, he claimed that there were so many funerals at which free bread was distributed (a normal show of charity on such occasions) that the poor did not need to work. 'Those who were accustomed to have plenty', he said, 'fell into need', and 'those accustomed to suffer want' experienced abundance. There may have been despondency after the plague, but the survivors appreciated the new opportunities.

In the next one or two generations people referred back to 'the first pestilence' as a landmark, but reactions to that event are difficult to disentangle from responses to changes over a longer span of time. The fall in population and the continued low numbers into the early sixteenth century were part of a process rather than a single event. A catastrophic epidemic need have had no more than temporary effects as the young survivors married and replaced the losses. But the Black Death came after a period of declining population, and was followed by more obstacles to growth. A series of plagues after the first outbreak, in 1361–2, 1369 and 1375, caused fewer deaths than the epidemic of 1348–50, in the range of 10 to 15 per cent, but they were severe and frequent enough to cut back any recovery after 1350. They were succeeded by more localized episodes of disease, which visited most parts of England once in every ten years from the 1390s until well after 1500. In a very similar pattern, chroniclers recorded eight plague years in Scotland between 1349 and 1420, and in Wales there were nine in 1361–1415, and again they continued into the late fifteenth century. Plague became an endemic disease, which was liable to appear sporadically and locally.

Terms used by observers at the time, like 'pestilence', are difficult to identify precisely, but the number of episodes of mortality in the late summer suggests the presence of bubonic plague, the warm-weather disease. In 1473 the chroniclers describe an epidemic with the symptoms of dysentery, and in 1479 this was followed in many places by the worst mortality of the fifteenth century. From 1485, the 'sweating sickness', perhaps a form of influenza, caused further rises in the death rate. Towns may have suffered more frequently and severely than the countryside, though rural populations also experienced regular epidemics. These were dangerous times, when people understandably feared for their safety; those who could afford to do so kept clear of large towns in times of plague. Everyone would have been endangered by infectious diseases, both those which killed large numbers in a few months, and ever-present threats such as tuberculosis.

The expectation of life can be calculated by investigating the length of adult active existence. Lives were shorter than they were to be after 1540 (when parish registers provide abundant evidence) and life expectation tended to fall during the fifteenth century. Monks at Westminster lived after the age of twenty for twenty-nine to thirty years in the early fifteenth century, and in the later part of the century for only twenty years after reaching twenty. At Canterbury Cathedral Priory the comparable figures were thirty-two at twenty, falling to twenty-four at twenty. These monks were privileged people, with an ample diet and comfortable accommodation, but they lived in unhealthy towns. The townspeople of Westminster, for example, experienced very high mortality at the end of the fifteenth century, so their infections evidently spread into the monastic community. Peasants of the late fourteenth century, who were poorer but had a healthier lifestyle, judging from Essex examples, could expect to live for forty-two years after they reached the age of twelve. Those born in the early fifteenth century had an expectation of life of thirty-nine at twelve, and later in the same century of thirty-six years at twelve.

The general health of the population should have been improving at this time. Few should have died of starvation, as cheap bread was available in most years after 1375. The last great medieval famine, from 1437 to 1440, caused hardship as yields fell and prices rose, just as they had done in 1315–17. But unlike the earlier episode, there was no great increase in mortality, except in regions where a plague epidemic coincided with the food shortages. In normal years, not only were basic foodstuffs cheap, but more people enjoyed a balanced diet with a higher proportion of meat and fish. Diseases associated with a poor diet, such as leprosy, were in decline. Rural housing improved in quality; in the south-east, for example, a house would commonly have a chamber at first-floor level, which gave living space separated from the dirt of the street and the farmyard. In the towns, the authorities often provided piped water, and rubbish was carted to communal middens. Disease seemed to have an independent ability to kill a higher proportion of the population, regardless of their improved standard of living.

Was mortality the main cause of the low population which prevailed from before 1348 until about 1540? Changes in population usually arise from a combination of the death rate and the birth rate, but in our period deaths were more carefully recorded than births. Fifteenth-century families were small – they often contained no more than four people, that is, two adults and two children. It would have seemed an ageing society, which lacked an abundance of children and young people. This may reflect high rates of mortality among children, though these are not known precisely. Disease could also influence the birth rate by creating a 'gashed' age structure, in which potentially fertile age groups were reduced in number by epidemics. So the first plague tended to kill older people, but still caused some mortality among those aged between twenty and forty. Twenty or thirty years later there would have been a reduced number of births because of the 'missing generation' who would otherwise have been born in the 1350s and 1360s. Still more serious for future generations was the tendency for the epidemic of 1361–2, the 'children's plague', to kill young people, and therefore to have a negative effect on the birth rate in the 1380s and 1390s. Towards the end of the period the numbers of children recorded in a sample of Kent wills declined from 2.08 in the fifteenth century to 1.90 in 1501–30. Did this reflect a rise in mortality affecting children, or did changes in the age of marriage reduce the number of births?

The main cause of the lower birth rate could have been late marriage. If it became customary for couples to marry, say, at the age of twenty-six rather than twenty-two, then this would reduce the number of children surviving to make up the next generation. A further influence would have been an increase in the number of those who did not marry at all. A feature of the population history of England in later centuries is both late marriage and the significant proportion of celibates, but for our period there is not enough evidence to reconstruct marriage patterns with any certainty. The period of servanthood which often preceded marriage for those in their late teens and early twenties may have been prolonged. It has been argued that this was partly a choice of employers, because in the countryside the move from arable towards pastoral farming created an increased need for full-time shepherds, cowherds and dairymaids. It may also have been a decision made by the young employees. Women in towns, for example, had better job opportunities and greater earning power after 1348–50, so they may have spent more time in employment before they married. This is not entirely convincing, because while it is true that young servants were an important part of the labour force in both town and country in this period, employees expressed a strong preference for short-term employment, and women had no great incentive to remain single as they could continue to earn after they had married. Women seem to have valued marriage: quite apart from emotional and other intangible benefits such as enhanced status, it offered them security and access to property.

An alternative approach is to note the changes in the peasant family at this time. These did not follow immediately after the plague, but developed over a number of generations. The rising rate of migration, and the loosening of bonds of kinship, meant that land was less likely to pass from one generation to another. At Halesowen in Worcestershire in the two or three generations after 1349, land stayed within the family because relatively remote relatives, such as nephews and cousins, took on the inheritance in the absence of sons. In the long run, by the early fifteenth century, not even these heirs came forward, and high proportions of land passed from one family to another. Even when sons did inherit their parents' land, they immediately sold it. The old family solidarities no longer worked. Fathers did not acquire land for the benefit of sons, and old people could no longer be sure that their children would look after them in their declining years. This greater individualism might have encouraged early marriage, as young men could find cheap holdings of land very easily, especially if they were prepared to move from village to village, and the possession of land gave them the basis for marriage and starting a family. But perhaps early marriage did not follow automatically. This became a restless and rather unstable society, with its lack of kin solidarities and with a reduction in family support. Social pressures to find a partner may have been relaxed, and the negotiation of marriage more difficult.

In terms of economic logic, there should have been an era of early and youthful marriage in the early fifteenth century, and easily available land and jobs would have led to a high rate of fertility and population growth. Something of this kind did happen in parts of continental Europe, suggesting that an English family culture had emerged which prevented population growth. Whether by accident or some hidden and presumably unconscious design, the English peasants avoided a repeat of the rapid increase that caused problems around 1300.

ii. *Low population,* c.1348–c.1400

While the explanation of the long period of low population is uncertain, its consequences are better understood. Here we will focus on the late fourteenth century. After the Black Death, all of those 'accustomed to suffer want' (to quote the Rochester chronicler) expected improvement in their conditions. This was a time of liberation, when old restraints were removed and new freedom of choice opened. Scottish serfdom seems to have faded away, though an occasional reference to fugitive serfs, for example from the estates of the Bishop of Moray in the 1360s, suggests its persistence if only on a small scale. The lack of evidence for unrest suggests that serfdom ended without great contention. Servile peasants in England could not easily persuade lords to give them their freedom, but an increasing number of them left their lords' manors, especially in the 1380s and 1390s, and were able to acquire employment or land on manors where their servile origins were either unknown or quickly forgotten. At Hemmingford Abbots in Huntingdonshire in the 1370s, Simon Duntyng, a serf, had moved to the small Northamptonshire town of Daventry, while the daughter of Thomas Clarell had gone to London. The lord of Hemmingford, the abbot of Ramsey, ordered their relatives who still remained to bring them back, with threats of financial penalties, but serfs who had departed stayed away and became free by the fact of their separation from their lord. Peasants negotiated reductions in the costs of tenancy, with a continued move towards the conversion of labour service into money rent, and some reductions in rents and entry fines. They avoided some servile and occasional payments by concealing marriages or land transfers. This process was very uneven and partial, however, and in many cases rents did not fall as much as might be expected in view of the sudden reduction in the ranks of would-be tenants.

A second liberated group were the wage earners, who to some degree were freed from low wages and poor conditions of employment. Their behaviour was described at length by employers who resented their new-found freedom. They would not accept a contract to work for a year, as had been normal before 1348, but preferred shorter terms such as three months, or insisted on working by the day or by the task. Richard Tailor of Legsby in Lincolnshire chose freedom, when on 31 July 1374 he was required to continue to serve William Lene of nearby Lissington as a ploughman for a whole year. He refused the offer, and left to work 'in the district' (moving from job to job) for higher wages. Short-term employment was preferable because it was abundant, with dozens of employers anxious to hire labour, and work by the day was much better paid. In the harvest season, when Richard Tailor significantly made his decision, the going rate in Lincolnshire was 4d per day, that is the same wage as a skilled craftsman (a carpenter, for example) earned. His total reward for his work in August and September could have been 15s. A ploughman would have been lucky to receive 13s 4d for the year, together with an allowance of grain worth twice as much, and a few minor perks equivalent in total to less than 2d per day. Workers also insisted on increases in rewards in kind: the grain allowance for servants contained a higher proportion of wheat, and harvesters received meals with bread wholly or mainly baked from wheat, as well as ample supplies of fresh meat and ale.

Wage earners gained more freedom to choose their occupation. As the gap between skilled and unskilled workers narrowed, a common result of an overall labour shortage, it sometimes paid a skilled artisan to move into agricultural work, especially in the harvest. Likewise, less skilled workers took up specialized work, like the ploughman who became a carpenter, and another who went to sea as a mariner. Skills, training and experience were evidently not being given a high value. Workers also chose for whom to work, and frequently moved from one employer to another. Above all, they sometimes took breaks from work, for example in order to travel to a new workplace. They took more holidays, worked shorter hours, and insisted that they should still be paid – the old custom was discarded that winter work (limited by the hours of daylight) received less pay than summer work.

A third dimension of the liberation of the disadvantaged after 1348–50 was the freeing of many of those afflicted by poverty. The numbers of smallholders were drastically reduced, as heirs did not take up vacant cottages and some tenants acquired extra land or moved to larger holdings. We have already seen that wages, especially the wages of less skilled workers, rose, and real wages increased decisively after 1375, when grain prices fell. The area cultivated with cereals did not shrink as much as the population, so that when the run of bad harvests ceased, corn became abundant, and the purchasing power of agricultural wages expressed in bread, meat and cheese increased by 40 per cent between the 1340s and the 1380s. The unemployment and under-employment prevalent in the early fourteenth century no longer blighted the earning capacity of the poor, which helped to exasperate social commentators, who saw no excuse for begging by those capable of work. Charity was not withdrawn because of the criticism of the idle poor, but instead was focused on those thought to be in genuine need.

After the plague, individuals found that they were no longer tied so closely to the social groupings which had previously been so powerful.

The family was a less dominant influence, as young people were able to find work and land away from their homes, though the peasant family was too strong to crumble even under the shock of the first pestilence. Similarly the village community had rallied to protect the interests of its members during the hard times of the early fourteenth century, and had acquired new powers in 1334 when it became responsible for the assessment and collection of the king's main form of taxation, the lay subsidy. Again, it was too firmly founded to break apart after the plague, but it was put under some strain as individuals sought to claim their independence in such matters as the use of the common pastures. Thomas Baldwyn of Shuckburgh in Warwickshire, for example, refused to accept by-laws drawn up by his neighbours, and defied them for thirteen years until his death in 1400.

The Black Death liberated the women who asserted themselves in a male-dominated economy. Many still worked in the less skilled and less well paid preparatory processes in clothmaking, such as wool-combing and spinning. They seem to have expanded their role in the better-rewarded craft of weaving. For their traditional tasks, such as weeding and harvesting, they demanded higher pay, like the male labourers who closed some of the gap between their wages and those of skilled craftsmen. Women improved their rewards, but rarely received pay equal to that of men. Women also entered occupations from which they had traditionally been excluded, even such heavy tasks as metalworking. Joan Edwaker, a married woman of Eynsham in Oxfordshire, was driving a cart pulled by two horses in 1389. We know that she was doing this 'man's job' because she was killed by a fall, and her death was the subject of a coroner's inquest. Towns had always provided more economic opportunities for women, sometimes to carry on their own trade, notably in preparing and selling food and drink, and sometimes as participants in their husbands' craft or trade. Their role in the 'family' business became apparent when widows took over when their husbands died, showing that they had acquired the necessary skills and experience. In the 1360s Margaret Hogg of Edinburgh went on trading expeditions abroad with her merchant husband, and was involved in the business. When he died, she continued by marrying his business partner. As wives, they negotiated with customers, sold goods and managed the servants; as widows they took over credit negotiations, purchase of raw materials, training of apprentices and production. Emma Erle had established herself as a major dealer in cloth in the Yorkshire town of Wakefield by 1395–6, when she sold forty-eight cloths in a year, worth at least £50.

Women gained more rights over property, not just as widows entitled to their traditional 'free bench' (the right to hold all or part of their dead husbands' land for life, providing that they remained single), but also as joint tenants with their husbands, which gave them more extensive rights to land in widowhood. In this period we find that more women made wills; they reveal themselves from their bequests as owners of much moveable property. Women were still at a great disadvantage in a man's world; for example, they were excluded from political office, including positions of authority in fraternities and guilds, and found it difficult to gain full trading privileges in towns. The achievements of women tended to be gained informally. They acquired skills by experience, often without serving an apprenticeship. They traded on their own account, but their husbands appear in the records, as when men paid the routine penalties for selling ale at too high a price when it was their wives who were brewing and managing the alehouse. An all-female craft, silk-weaving, was developing, and though the silk women had a collective organization in London, they did not form a guild of the kind found in male-dominated crafts.

These new freedoms were not acquired without cost, and those who felt threatened by them struggled against the changes. The poet William Langland represents one point of view, that of a cleric of strong religious convictions who was offended by the immorality of the new social order, but he also reflects more widespread prejudices. Langland spent his adult life writing and then rewriting his great poem, known to us as *Piers Plowman*. The second version, the 'B' text of about 1380, brings his social and economic views into sharp focus. Piers, the central figure, is presented as an ideal peasant, diligent, frugal, dependable, loyal, honest and blunt in speech. The poem shows this admirable worker on a spiritual quest for salvation, and the poet puts into his mouth plain and virtuous comments on the sinful world. He is depicted within the conventions of the 'three orders', as a hard worker who is committed at one key point in the poem to the cultivation of a half-acre of land. He makes a contract with a knight, promising to work for the benefit of his superior, providing that the knight upholds law and order and hunts harmful animals. This model of mutual obligation was depicted in order to underline the failings of the real world. Piers had to remind the knight not to oppress his tenants, and while he could arrive at an agreement with the knight, he was unable to make a contract with a priest. Langland steps outside the conventions of the three orders by introducing a fourth estate of wage earners, beggars and petty criminals. Piers attempts to set this unruly labour force to work on the half-acre, but they soon stop. Piers criticizes them harshly, and the poem argues that only the threat of hunger will drive the idle back to work. Elsewhere in the poem Langland comments on the greed of labourers, who insist on the best food and drink, and makes especially harsh comments about beggars, both the secular vagrants and their clerical equivalents, the friars.

Piers Plowman was a bestseller in its time, in that numerous manuscript copies were made and many people heard it being read. Peasants knew of its contents, and naturally appreciated the favourable picture it gave of them, though of course Langland also portrayed a greedy and envious peasant, who criticized his neighbours behind their backs. Members of the social elite, both laymen and clergy, read the poem, because they could agree with many of its sentiments. In particular they shared Langland's belief that the social order had been dangerously undermined by the bargaining power of labourers, who demanded too much, used their newly acquired wealth in excessive consumption, and did not contribute enough to taxes. Beggars made the problem worse, because they lived on alms and refused to work.

Prejudices (formed well before Langland expressed them) led to legislation and changes in government policy, as they informed the thinking of the king's advisers, and of the landed magnates, gentry and wealthier townspeople who attended parliament. The Ordinance of Labourers (of 1349) and the Statute of Labourers (of 1351) made it illegal to demand or to offer rates of pay above those prevailing before the Black Death; it was also against the law to refuse to work, for example for a servant to decline an offer of a year's employment, or to break a contract by leaving before the term of employment was completed. Prices were also fixed. The Ordinance prohibited giving alms to those capable of work, 'so they may be compelled to labour'. The law was redefined by the Statute of Cambridge in 1388, which paid particular attention to those wandering in search of work, who were expected to carry documents, and beggars, who were supposed to stay in their place of origin. The laws were enforced by the local gentry, the specially appointed Justices of Labourers in the 1350s, and then by the Justices of the Peace, who had a general responsibility for law and order in the localities.

The labour laws have a superficial air of fairness in the sense that employers as well as employees were liable to prosecution, and the cost of foodstuffs was supposed to be regulated as well as wages. Enforcement was not just carried out by the gentry, as local people were drawn into the process. The constable of each village or town (mostly peasants or artisans, serving part-time out of duty) were expected to make workers swear an oath to observe the laws. The juries which gathered information for the courts and reported wrongdoers contained leading peasants, and some of the complaints must have come from peasant employers. Villagers were encouraged to bring offenders to the notice of the justices because the money collected in fines would be deducted from their quota of taxation for the next lay subsidy. The village of Beauchamp St Paul in Essex, for example, owed 75s in tax, but when the lay subsidy of 1352 was collected the 'fines of workers' came to 60s, which meant that the better-off villagers who normally paid the tax had to find only 15s. The tax burden was being shifted on to dozens of small-holders and labourers without land.

Despite the participation of those below the gentry in the courts, the law was used in a very one-sided fashion to defend the interests of the employers, and in particular the larger employers, such as the lords of manors and their bailiffs. In a court session held at Braintree in Essex for the administrative district of Hinckford Hundred in June 1378, the bias of the court is obvious. Only three cases were brought against employers, and in each case they were described as 'labourer' and 'mower', so they were leaders of groups of workers, subcontractors as we would call them, who carried out a task such as mowing a meadow for a lump sum, and then paid individual workers out of the proceeds. Not a single member of the gentry, lord of the manor or bailiff came before the court, yet we can be confident that they were paying wages above the legal rates. Instead, twenty-six labourers and other workers, such as a ploughman, a disabled carpenter and a roofer, were accused of taking high wages, especially in harvest time, or were said to be wandering from village to village 'for excess'. A typical case was Nicholas Thressher, labourer of Halsted, who 'takes 2d per day, both in winter and summer, and 4d in the harvest'. Gilbert Rougge of Sturmer was fined 5s for refusing to take the oath and therefore being 'a rebel against the constables'. No food traders were pros-ecuted in this session. The gentry justices who presided over the court were punishing a selection of workers from the hundreds of men and women who regularly broke the law each year. They may have hoped that their actions would help to depress wages, and therefore reduce the costs of production on their own manors. But they were probably not acting so directly in their own interest. They resented the earning power of the lower orders, and wished to make an example of some of them.

The Sumptuary Law of 1363 was not enforced, but it indicates the frustrations of those represented in parliament. The law complains of the 'excessive apparel' (extravagant clothing) that was being worn, and sets maximum levels of expenditure on cloth and accessories. Agricul-tural servants (ploughmen and shepherds, for example) were not allowed to wear cloth worth more than 12d per yard. This piece of unenforceable legislation was prompted by the rising price of manufactured goods, which those in parliament believed was being pushed up by demand from the lower orders. Another motive, however, clearly expressed in contemp-orary literature, was that as the visible symbols of social rank ceased to have their former meaning, the whole hierarchy of society was being threatened. If silk clothing, silver buckles and fur linings had previously been worn only by knights and great lords, it was feared that aristocratic privilege as a whole might be compromised if merchants or minor gentry wore such finery.

The aristocracy's role was to fight, and this became a serious problem in the 1370s, when the war with France was resumed after a truce in 1360–9. In the late 1340s and 1350s English armies had been successful, winning famous victories at Crécy and Poitiers, at modest cost for the taxpayer because the soldiers to some extent paid for themselves by living on the French countryside and making profits from ransoms. After 1369 the victories were elusive, the war came to England with raids on coastal towns, and the taxpayer was required to pay for the ineffective military effort. In the opinion of those in government, the tax system was not tapping effectively the wealth of the country, and an unfair burden fell on the contributors to the lay subsidy, including the peasants with middling to large holdings of land. After an experiment with an ill-planned parish tax in 1371, the poll taxes of 1377, 1379 and 1381 were seen as a useful supplement to the lay subsidies. They brought into the tax system a large section of the population previously exempt, that is wage earners without large quantities of livestock or other goods, both servants living in the households of their employers, and labourers who had their own cottages or smallholdings. The first poll tax of 1377 expected everyone over the age of fourteen to pay 4d, without any attempt to match income to payment. The second assessment of 1379 showed some awareness of criticisms, by raising the age to sixteen, and by using a sliding scale by which the rich paid more than 4d. The third, granted in 1380 but collected in 1381, demanded 12d from each person over fifteen, but within each village and town the rich were encouraged to help the poor.

The tax was clearly motivated by the belief that the wage earners whose rate of pay had risen since the 1340s should contribute to the national war effort. The labour laws may have failed to prevent wage increases, but at least those who broke the law could pay a part of their extra earnings to the state. The new tax was bitterly resented by those who had to pay for the first time. It was thought particularly unfair that young servants, including females, whose modest rewards reflected their limited productivity, should have to pay. In practice, their employers or parents must have found the money. The taxpayers' response was to evade payment, mainly by concealing young people, whether servants or children, and especially females. This could be done by denying the presence of adolescents in the household, or more commonly by claiming that young people were under fifteen or sixteen. The number of those paying throughout the country fell from 1,355,201 in 1377 to below 900,000 in 1381. These figures alone point to a high level of discontent. As often happens when groups do not speak to each other and nurse grievances, rumours spread which helped to poison the atmosphere. After a rash of lawsuits mounted by peasants in forty villages in southern England to claim the privileges attached to 'ancient demesne' (see p. 181), a petition in 1377 from the knights in the lower house of parliament claimed that if the French invaded, the peasants would support them. This accusation was not justified by later events, when peasants, even those exasperated with the government, remained fiercely loyal to the crown.

Such measures as the Statute of Labourers meant that the government was intervening in the economy in a new way. Before the Black Death the state had an interest in maintaining law and order, which lay behind laws regulating merchant debt, or in rewarding the king's supporters with such economic benefits as market charters, or in economic measures that would raise revenue, such as Edward III's wool monopoly. After the Black Death the ruling groups temporarily closed ranks, and used the power of the state to defend the interests of the rich in a blatant manner. Members of landed society (both laymen and churchmen) made up the personnel of government, as civil servants and members of the king's council and household, and their membership of parliament allowed them to bring their influence to bear. One of the most important developments strengthened the role of the local gentry as the agents of the state by giving the JPs more responsibility and power. The ranks of society below the gentry felt that the state was losing any claim to impartiality as it became so closely identified with the landed interest.

Landlords influenced state policy, and at the same time took measures in their private courts. While the local justices enforced the labour laws, a 'seigneurial reaction' was being mounted in the manors. Manorial courts had always provided useful profits, but after the Black Death their revenues increased, a remarkable development as the numbers of tenants had fallen drastically. Lords whose income from rents was tending to diminish stepped up pressure on local officials to search out breaches of manorial discipline, such as peasants who allowed their animals to stray on to the demesne land, or who failed to carry out their labour services. Each offender was charged an amercement of 3d, 4d or 6d for the offence, and the totals on a large manor could amount to £5 or £10 by the end of the year. On some manors each peasant was paying on average twice as much to the courts as his predecessors had done before 1348. The lords' courts also clamped down on those who evaded payments or broke the rules governing tenancy or servility. If servile women married without paying a fine, or if customary tenants sold land without informing the court and paying an entry fine, or if they allowed their buildings to fall into ruin, the court would eventually catch up with them, exact the payments that had been avoided, and make them pay extra in amercements. Take the case of John Hamond of Earl Soham in Suffolk, who was attempting to build up a larger holding by buying land, keeping this secret so that his lord would not interfere with his activities or charge entry fines. In 1379 the manorial officials discovered that he had acquired a servile holding in 1377 and was failing to repair the buildings. For ten years he had held 7 acres by free tenure, but had ingeniously assigned them to a trust to avoid the difficulty of a serf acquiring free land. It must have been well known in the village that he was in possession of the land, but his neighbours kept quiet. In such cases, the peasants who were supposed to report such matters to the lord's court, the chief pledges or the jurors, might be made to pay an amercement for the offence of 'concealment'. The peasants or artisans who had been pushed into accepting offices in the manorial administration felt divided loyalties, as they were members of a community and wished to remain on good terms with their neighbours, yet they had an obligation to serve the lord and present to the court 'well and faithfully' those who broke the rules. It is not surprising that substantial peasants like Thomas Gardiner of Little Barton in Suffolk refused in 1380 to take the oath as chief pledge, even when ordered to do so four times. On some occasions in Essex and Suffolk, the friction between lords and tenants reached such a pitch that all of the tenants boycotted the court.

iii. *Revolts*

The rising of 1381 (the 'Peasants' Revolt') shows that the ordinary people of south-east England sought political solutions for their grievances, but their complaints were rooted in economic and social problems. The rebellion was provoked by official enquiries into the evasion of the third poll tax in Essex and Kent. The poll tax was not the cause of the rising, but it served to highlight the whole issue of taxation and misgovernment. The burden of taxation was already heavy: it amounted to £382,000 collected from the laity in the ten years before 1381. The taxpayers, that is mainly the more substantial peasants and artisans, were each contributing more than their predecessors had done before the Black Death. The quotas of the lay subsidy had been fixed in 1334, and these sums now had to be shared out among fewer villagers, who by the 1370s were no longer benefiting from the fines paid under the labour laws. Many households were having to find 4s for each lay subsidy, which meant that a middle-aged couple with two children in their late teens would have paid 8s in 1378 (when parliament granted a double subsidy), 6s in 1380 (a grant of a subsidy and a half), as well as 1s 4d in 1377 for the first poll tax, rather less in 1379, and a threat of another 4s in 1381. Their dissatisfaction was provoked partly by the amount to be paid, but also by the suspicion that the money was being wasted through incompetence and fraud within the government. There had been widespread support for the faction in the 'Good Parliament' in 1376 which persuaded the assembly to refuse a grant of taxes, and to prosecute corrupt officials. That wave of enthusiasm turned to bitter disappointment when subsequent parliaments, influenced by the richest and most powerful magnate, John of Gaunt, Duke of Lancaster, reverted to a policy of futile military campaigns funded by more taxes, including the poll taxes.

The rebellion was directed initially against local government officials, such as the sheriffs and escheators, and against the local properties of the 'traitors' in central government who were held responsible for the failure of policy. These included John of Gaunt, Simon Sudbury (the chancellor, who was also archbishop of Canterbury), and Robert Hales (the treasurer, also prior of the Knights Hospitallers). Such was the level of political consciousness in the south-east, and the rapid spread of news and rumours, that the rebels were sufficiently well informed to know the name of a relatively minor figure in the government, John Legge, who had proposed the enquiries into tax evasion. The rebel bands assembled at meeting points in their counties, and then converged on London, acquiring on the way a leader, Wat Tyler. They presented themselves as agents of the king, calling themselves the 'true commons', that is the king's loyal subjects, seeking to replace the 'traitors' who had misled him. They recruited men and collected money as if they had taken over the government, and they advanced under banners and pennons like a legitimate army.

When the rebels reached London they demanded to see the king, and met him on 14 June at Mile End to the east of the city. The young Richard II issued charters of freedom, and appeared to agree to the removal of the 'traitors'. The rebels had already attacked property belonging to their enemies in and near London, such as Gaunt's palace of the Savoy and the headquarters of Hales's Hospitallers at Clerkenwell, and now they captured Hales, Sudbury and others and killed them in what they believed was a judicial execution. On the next day Tyler met the king at Smithfield, presented a list of demands which appear to have envisaged the removal of aristocratic privilege and the church hierarchy, and the creation of a popular monarchy in which the king ruled over self-governing village communities. Shortly afterwards Tyler was killed and the rebel bands dispersed. Rebellions in Cambridgeshire, Norfolk and Suffolk continued for some time after the collapse of the Kent and Essex risings, with gatherings at Bury St Edmunds, Norwich and Cambridge. The whole country was brought under control after fights at Billericay in Essex and North Walsham in Norfolk. Dozens of rebels died in those confrontations, and in a flurry of executions.

The political actions of the rebels reflected their perception that the government and the landlords were bound together in the same corrupt system. They resented the dual role of the king's justices, such as John Bampton, whose enquiries in Essex set the revolt in motion, and Sir John Cavendish, the Chief Justice of King's Bench, both of whom lent their legal expertise to major church landlords for profit. We understand the rebels' thinking better when we can identify them as individuals and examine their lives before the revolt. They included every type of person, from servants to a few gentry and clergy. Townspeople joined in, from London, Bury, Canterbury and St Albans within the central region of the revolt, but also in pursuit of their own specific quarrels at Beverley, York and Scarborough in Yorkshire, and at Bridgwater and Winchester in the west.

The majority held land, often with middling holdings of between 5 and 20 acres, and owned herds of cattle and flocks of sheep. The majority in Essex, Suffolk and Norfolk were customary tenants. William Smith of Ingatestone in Essex can serve as an example. He was accused of joining the revolt at the beginning, of attacking John Bampton the justice, and also of taking part in the killing of the escheator of Essex. He was a serf and a customary tenant, and owned at the time of the revolt at least six cattle, five calves and some pigs. The rebels included a significant number of craft workers, such as carpenters or tailors, or those who were involved in trade, though these people often held land as well. Many who attracted the attention of the authorities, that is the local leaders of the revolt, had served in official positions in their manors or villages, as chief pledges, jurors, reeves and constables. William Smith of Ingatestone served as an ale taster, and as his daughter was married by 1387, he must have been at least in his late thirties at the time of the revolt. The rebels were middle-aged, responsible people, who were moved to rebellion not by poverty or despair, but by hope. They had observed the changes in the world since 1349, which potentially benefited them, in terms of cheaper land, the opportunity to increase their livestock, and an expanding market for ale, meat and manufactured goods. Individuals who joined the rebellion are known to have acquired extra land before the rising. These better prospects were opening for peasants and artisans everywhere, but the south-eastern counties seemed to offer particular advantages, as London's economic influence was strong, towns like

Colchester were prospering, and rural industries flourished. Yet in parts of this commercial and mobile society the old institution of serfdom was still strong, and both lords and the state found ways to take their cash. The leading peasants and artisans who served as local officials felt acutely in 1350–80 that their lords were pushing them one way, and their neighbours pulling them in another. They knew something about law and the working of local government, so they could criticize lawyers and government officials on the basis of experience.

The rebellion drew strength from the ability of the local elites to organize contingents from each village and co-ordinate their movements. The bands made rapid progress across the country because they were riding on their own horses, a further indication that they were not desperately poor. The letters which circulated encouraged the rebels to stick to their cause and complete the task by emphasizing the solidarity and loyalty of the rebel bands: 'stand manly together in truth'. The rebellion was a serious matter, and those who took part must have realized that they were risking their lives, but an air of festivity emerged, perhaps because the time of the revolt coincided with summer games when village communities normally celebrated and drank ale.

The leading rebels' aims flowed from their experiences and frustrations as subordinates in a world that offered a prospect of improvement. Their ideas were well established. Some of them, such as the people of Harmondsworth in Middlesex or Mildenhall in Suffolk, came from villages which had a long history of resisting serfdom, especially by appealing to the king for protection as tenants of former royal estates. The strategy of the 1381 rising was based on the correct assumption that only the authority of the state could set aside the property rights of lords and free the serfs. These convictions were encouraged by the message of the renegade preacher, John Ball, who reminded them of the Christian doctrine of the equality of all men, and the injustice of aristocratic privileges. The letters that were sent out by Ball or like-minded associates urged the moral justification for rebellion: 'do well and better, and avoid sin'. In the localities rebels burnt manorial records, an act which symbolized their rejection of serfdom and the authority of lords, but which also had the practical effect of removing the written evidence for their unfree status.

When the rebels met the king, they did not mention the poll tax, but instead demanded their freedom. At Mile End they declared, according to a chronicler, 'no man should be a serf, nor do homage or any type of service to any lord, but should give 4d for an acre of land'. The sum of money mentioned was quite low, but not absurdly low. They also insisted that service should depend on contracts that had been agreed freely (a reference either to labour service, or to the compulsory contracts under the Statute of Labourers). Other demands that are reported to have been made at Mile End included free buying and selling. The central importance of serfdom for most rebels is suggested by their willingness to return home once they had been granted the royal charters of liberty which were issued at Mile End. Other rebels remained, realizing that they had scored a notable victory and could press their opposition to the power of lords yet further. When they met the king again at Smithfield they repeated their demand for freedom, and added that 'no lord should have lordship in the future, but it should be divided among all men'. They were envisaging removing the lords as intermediaries between king and people, and empowering themselves to run their own affairs. Their demand that there should be no law except the law of Winchester would have dismantled the royal courts, removed the lawyers and deprived the lords of their jurisdiction, placing the maintenance of law and order in the hands of each village community.

Many of the local actions and demands of the rising pursued this hostility to lords. At St Albans and Bury St Edmunds the rebels insisted that ancient royal charters of liberty had been hidden by the monks who ruled over those towns, and at St Albans they claimed common rights to pasture animals and to take game in the local woods and pastures. One chronicler reports the extension of hunting rights as a rebel demand in London, which would show the rebels envisaging the removal of lordly privileges in a concrete and practical form. The rebels generally focused their attacks on individuals who oppressed them, either particular agents of central government, or specific lords. They did not assault or kill lords in general, perhaps because this would be unnecessary as they expected to abolish their powers as a group. The reasons for their choice of victims sometimes remain a mystery, and in particular we do not know why they hunted and killed Flemish immigrants in London and the provinces. The rebels were not 'anti-foreigner': they caused no problems for German merchants, so clearly they had some grievance against the Flemings, perhaps because they competed with English textile workers.

Was the revolt of any significance in the long term? The first impulse must be to regard it as a transient episode. The revolt's collapse was complete and sudden, after only two months. Many rebels were killed or put to flight, and the charters of manumission were declared invalid. Lords held courts in the late summer or autumn of 1381, sometimes headed 'the first court after the rebellion', which had to cope with the practical problems caused by the destruction of the records. The tenants made their submission to their lords, after which their names, holdings and terms of tenure might be written on the court roll, and a fine demanded. The lords were anxious to reimpose their discipline, and to resume normal life and the routines of rent collection as soon as possible. The crown granted rebels who had escaped initial capture the chance to buy a pardon, and lords allowed them to return to their holdings. William Smith of Ingatestone, the typical rebel mentioned above, returned to his manor and was serving again as ale taster by 1386.

Although the rebellion was short-lived and normality swiftly returned, it left a profound sense of shock. The chroniclers who wrote about the revolt all reacted strongly to an event that seemed so sudden and unprecedented. Some of them emphasized the sinfulness of the rebels, who had offended against the divinely ordained social hierarchy by refusing to accept their role in the three orders. Some observers compared the rebels to animals; like mad dogs and unnaturally fierce oxen they behaved savagely and without reason. Others did not condemn the rebels only, but blamed the errors of government and the sins of the aristocracy. The severity of the shock made the royal ministers abandon the poll taxes, and the expensive campaigns against France. Among the peasants, artisans and wage earners, the ideas expressed in the revolt could not be erased. William Smith, our Essex rebel, continued to cause trouble in his lord's manor, refusing to pay a common fine in 1386, and in the following year he had to be bound over to be well behaved towards the lord's bailiff. New small-scale rebellions broke out throughout the 1380s, 1390s, and into the following century. They raised the same issues of freedom and the power of lords, as for example at Barnet in Hertfordshire, where tenants of the monks of St Albans rose in 1381, and in 1417 renewed an old demand that they be allowed to buy and sell customary land by charters, rather than having to take such transactions to the lord's court.

When peasants between the 1390s and the 1440s came to negotiate with lords for conversion of labour service to money rents, or for rent reductions, or the removal of archaic servile dues and collective payments such as tallages and common fines, their hand was strengthened by both sides' memories of 1381. They did not need to use violence, but merely had to show their determination by refusing to pay, or by threatening to leave the manor to find land elsewhere. The lords' officials usually gave way. Serfdom withered away in the fifteenth century, together with high and unpopular rents, partly because the economic realities made it essential for lords to make concessions to keep tenants, but also because the 1381 rising had demonstrated the potential strength of the peasants.

Twenty years after 1381, a revolt shook Wales even more profoundly. It was led by a member of the gentry, Owain Glyn Dŵr, and its objectives were overtly political: the end of English rule. The rising attracted much support from peasants and artisans, and an important reason for their participation was the extreme 'seigneurial reaction' in the Welsh marches. The marcher lords did not feel inhibited by the restraining power of the state or by local custom. When their rents began to stagnate or decline in the fourteenth century, the great lords were able to compensate themselves with other sources of revenue. While every English manor's revenue was shrinking after the Black Death, the Arundels increased their income from the lordship of Chirk in North Wales from £300 to £500 per annum in the sixty years after 1322. They pushed up leasehold rents, which were partly based on their power as lords, as mills were one of their main assets and they profited by maintaining a milling monopoly. They could also, like the other marcher lords, impose collective fines, aids, tallages and 'mises' on the inhabitants. At Chirk, the lords demanded a collective payment of £500 because the tenants failed to carry timber as a labour service. These impositions caused distress to tenants because they were unpredictable both in their timing and in the amount of money levied. There was a particular concentration of demands at a time of political instability when a number of marcher lordships changed hands after Richard II confiscated the estates of his opponents in 1397. Henry, duke of Lancaster used the occasion of his succession after the death of his father John of Gaunt in 1399 to force the people of Cydweli to pay £1,575. The tenants could respond by paying slowly or not at all, and by 1400 arrears at Chirk, mainly caused by unpaid fines and rents, had built up to £663.

Relationships were made more difficult because the lords were English and the peasants Welsh, and differences in customs caused dispute and resentment. For example, under English law, if a line of hereditary succession to a holding died out (as tended to happen after the Black Death), or if a tenant failed to pay his rent, the land would escheat to the lord, but under Welsh law it went to the kin. Naturally English lords favoured their own custom. A good deal of native Welsh resentment was focused on the towns, which had been founded as English colonies and were given rights and monopolies. As late as 1399 a charter to the Flintshire town of Hope stated that Welsh brewers could not sell their ale within a radius of 3 leagues (4½ miles). These discriminatory measures were still imposed, although they were becoming irrelevant as more Welsh people moved into the towns and the English acquired land in 'Welsh' areas.

Glyn Dŵr rose in 1400, and the war continued for seven years. The attacks of the rebels, especially on towns, and the movement of English armies against them, caused much destruction. Even a century later, the decay of dozens of towns was blamed on the revolt, but there were probably deeper economic problems, as some places burnt by Glyn Dŵr's armies, like Carmarthen, recovered quite quickly. A positive development after the revolt brought more Welsh people into towns, so that they came to dominate even in such a colonial borough as Caernarfon. In the marcher lordships, tenants commonly refused to pay rents, and arrears built up to very high levels. Lords had to accept the situation, and in doing so they were acknowledging the danger of offending tenants to the point that they would again rebel.

To sum up, the Black Death liberated the lower ranks of society; the elite were stimulated into a reaction, which soured relations and provoked rebellion. The revolts established a new balance, in which the authorities adjusted to the reality that the peasants, artisans and wage earners had improved their bargaining power. The fall in population created the environment in which these changes took place, but reduction in rent and the freeing of serfs did not happen 'naturally'. The entrenched institutions would crack only if the lower orders developed ideas which contradicted those of their rulers, and asserted themselves in a coherent and organized way.

iv. *The economy, c.1348–c.1400*

The general economic aftermath of the Black Death and the reduced population was neither simple nor predictable, partly because of other impersonal influences, and partly because people reacted to their new circumstances in unexpected ways. The long-term impact of a smaller population, as we have seen, was to reduce the demand for basic foodstuffs, which depressed corn prices, lowered rents and encouraged the shrinkage of the area of land under cultivation. As the labour force became smaller, wages and the cost of manufactured goods increased. The period 1349–75 does not, however, fit this pattern. Corn prices remained at a high level, probably because unstable weather conditions reduced yields. Real wages, that is wages expressed in terms of the prices of food, were in consequence depressed, and indeed cash wages did not leap forward as much as we would expect after a halving of the workforce. The labour shortage should have been acute, not just because many workers died in the epidemic, but because many smallholders who had been part-time workers acquired enough land to live without needing to earn wages. Wages rose rather gradually in the late fourteenth century, and did not reach their highest level until twenty or thirty years after the first epidemic. Mowing an acre of meadow, for example, cost 5d in the 1340s, between 6d and 7d in the twenty years after the first plague, and 7½d in the 1370s and 1380s. In many parts of England the daily wage of skilled building workers such as carpenters, which had been 3d before the Black Death, hovered between 3d and 4d in the 1350s and 1360s, and only in the last quarter of the century reached a plateau of 4d (see Figure 3 above, p. 240). The slow rise in wages may reflect the large number of under-employed people in the 1340s, who took the place of the plague casualties. The labour laws may also have had their effect, both by keeping wage rates down for fear of punishment, but also by distorting our evidence, so that higher wages were really paid, but the illegal rates were concealed in the manorial accounts which provide most of our information. Plague mortality was also playing a part in making workers more scarce in the 1380s, as the cohort of young people who then entered the labour market had been depleted by the death of their parents' generation in the 'children's plague' of 1361–2. In addition, urban and industrial growth in the 1380s and 1390s was creating more competition among employers.

In the countryside the persistently low population should have halved the size of villages, and therefore put double the amount of land in the hands of the surviving tenants. The impact on landholding varied from region to region and from village to village. In general, the number of tenants did not fall as much as would be expected. At Alveston in Warwickshire, where there had been eighty-five tenants in the thirteenth century, the number had reduced to fifty-five by 1385. It was not until the next century that the numbers fell to only thirty-two. At Alveston and in the midlands generally lords and tenants kept to the old yardland or oxgang units, but it became increasingly common for two half-yardlands or two yardlands to be put together, or a smallholding or a cottage to be added to a yardland or half-yardland. A rental of the Dalkieth estate of the Douglas family made in 1376–7 shows that the standard holding had become four oxgangs, double the normal substantial tenements of the early fourteenth century. A higher proportion of holdings reached 30 to 60 acres, but very large accumulations of land, containing 100 acres or more, were quite rare. At the south Devon village of Stokenham, the main landholders (as distinct from cottagers) reduced in number between 1347 and 1390 from 147 to 120, and the average amount of land held by each tenant rose from 31 to 45 acres. These relatively modest changes came about because a higher proportion of the rural population acquired land. Young people could gain a holding at an early stage of their lives, and the landless workers, like the *garciones* recorded in the south-west, almost disappeared. Evidently, acquisitive peasants did not pursue the accumulation of very large holdings, perhaps because they had difficulty in finding labour either from within their own families, or by hiring workers. In central Essex a high proportion of smallholders persisted, with nearly half of holdings (both before and after the plagues) containing less than 5 acres, perhaps because so many tenants were employed in industry.

At the other extreme, while relatively few villages were abandoned at this time, a minority went into severe and terminal decline, as tenants left, or died without successors. A handful of small villages in the Cotswolds disappeared, and in many parts of the midlands villages lost more than half of their population. In these cases the land was sometimes acquired by ambitious villagers, and so holdings could grow as large as 5 yardlands. Alternatively, no tenant wished to take it, and it was left 'in the lord's hands'.

Lords took various steps to prevent the loss of tenants, such as drastically reducing entry fines, or converting the former servile land into leasehold, so that tenants could take on a term of perhaps six or nine years with a fixed cash rent, with the reduction or abolition of the uncertain and variable extra payments which caused so much dissatisfaction. There were still tens of thousands of tenants in the 1390s who held their customary land on hereditary tenures in much the same way as their predecessors fifty or even a hundred years earlier. In west Suffolk and Cornwall, some rents were as high towards the end of the fourteenth century as they had been before the first plague. Labour services were mostly being commuted, but that was a continuation of a trend that had begun well before the Black Death. Lords might still be able to charge a few pounds' entry fine for a yardland. The really decisive and universal change through much of lowland England was the leasing of lords' demesnes, which had begun before 1348. The first plague did not push lords into wholesale leasing. Direct cultivation of large acreages paid quite well while the high grain prices lasted, and it was the combination of falling prices and rising labour costs after 1375 which forced lords to accept that it was better to let a tenant worry about the profit margin. In the 1380s and 1390s, one large estate after another embarked on the process of handing over the demesne of each manor as a block to a farmer for a fixed annual rent.

The economy of towns might have been expected to suffer severely from the loss of population: the number of inhabitants should have fallen by a half, partly because of the general decline, but also because of the notorious tendency for towns to harbour disease. Trade and industry could well have contracted after the fall in the number of both workers and consumers. We have seen that industries were disrupted in the 1350s and 1360s, but the general level of commercial activity reached a very high level around 1400. Wool exports were certainly reduced, from about 35,000 sacks annually in the mid-fourteenth century to about 18,000 in the 1390s, but this was partly offset by the increase in cloth exports, from about 2,000 cloths just after the first pestilence towards 40,000 in the 1390s (Figure 4 above, p. 244). Overall production must have been at least four times this level, because most of the cloth from English looms was bought within the country. It is therefore not surprising that clothmaking became widespread in the countryside and in small towns, as in Essex, Suffolk, Wiltshire and Somerset. Towns which specialized in woollen textiles, Colchester and Coventry, brushed aside the effects of the Black Death and actually increased in size from 4,000 to 6,000 in the first case, and from about 5,000 to 9,000 in the other. Larger towns, which subsequently declined, such as Bristol, Norwich, Southampton and York, experienced a phase of prosperity at the end of the fourteenth century, and small places like Chelmsford were growing, with new shops being built in 1384–1417. Scottish wool exports stood at a high level in the 1370s, and merchants like John Mercer of Perth (who died in 1380) and Adam Forester of Edinburgh (who died in 1405) made fortunes at this time.

The tin industry, after going through a trough in the middle of the century, was booming in the years 1386–1416. Cornish tin miners and smelters produced more than a million pounds of the metal in a year, comparable with output in the 1340s. Lead and iron mining were prospering, and imports of wine from Gascony climbed to a peak in 1403 that came near to returning to pre-war levels.

Why did trade, industry and towns do so well when they should have been depressed? A partial answer might be that the landlords did not suffer a catastrophic fall in income, and were able to maintain quite a high level of expenditure. England, notably through its cloth exports, was producing goods previously made in continental Europe, and so was prospering at the expense of its rivals. But home demand was all important, and here the developing consumption of the mass of the population accounts for much of the health of trade. People who had previously spent most of their food budget on basic cereals for bread and pottage could now drink more ale and eat more meat, so the trade of brewers and butchers was growing at this time. Consumers were also able to spend a higher proportion of their incomes on non-food items, such as clothing, houses, utensils and furnishings. They could replace their clothes more often, and could own a number of garments. Fashion was influencing the choices of peasants and wage earners, who adopted the shorter and more closely fitting styles which had been taken up by the aristocracy in the mid-fourteenth century. The new ideas were encouraged by the many tailors who worked throughout the country in towns and villages. (Plate 16) The fashionable lined garments used more material, and ordinary people wore more colourful clothing, which was expensive because of the cost of dyeing. In their households, consumers began to replace their cheaper utensils with more durable and attractive materials. Wooden plates were supplemented with pewter, and cups were made from glazed pottery as well as wood. Peasants kept more horses, and probably spent more on ironwork for their shoes and harness, and on the iron fittings on carts. Town-based craftsmen provided cast brass cooking pots, which were now in universal use, and also mass-produced inexpensive buckles, and small metal ornaments for a large market.

The first pestilence confirmed and deepened a downward trend in population which became a characteristic of the next two centuries. The plagues and the low levels of population did not have the immediate consequences that would be expected. Wages, rents, prices, lords' incomes and the fortunes of towns all failed to rise or fall in line with predictions. This was partly because of the manipulation of the economy by those in power. Social tensions built up as the poor glimpsed better opportunities, and the rich resisted. Once the air had cleared after the explosion of revolt, the economy settled down. Lords gave up their role as direct producers, and the peasants cautiously accumulated larger holdings. As the masses, including those depending mainly on wages, spent their new wealth, the urban and commercial economy regained some of the lost ground and grew once more. The low population also failed to produce predicted effects because there were many other forces for change, such as innovations in the organization of production. We will now turn to these developments in both town and country between 1350 and 1520.

CHAPTER NINE

Towns, trade and industry, c.1350–c.1520

In 1462 John Paston remarked in exasperation that his tenants looked forward to a 'new world', but could that phrase be applied in general to economic and social changes in the century and a half after the Black Death? Those who made their living from commerce and manufacture, whether they lived in town or country, encountered difficulties in a time of recession. Yet towns retained their importance, some grew and new ones emerged. There were changes in the flow of trade, and from industry came new methods of production.

i. Urban fortunes

Towns, and large towns in particular, in the fifteenth and sixteenth centuries provided limited opportunities for enterprise, because many were shrinking in population, and their trade was reduced in volume. This was sometimes stated by the inhabitants, at length, when they asked for release from the burden of taxation. The north Lincolnshire town of Grimsby, which supported near to 2,000 people before the Black Death, contained 1,500 in 1377 and fewer than 900 in the early sixteenth century. In the 1450s the town was unable to pay to the crown in full, and on time, the fee farm of £50 per annum which had been fixed in 1256. In 1461, the royal government had been informed that the town was 'greatly impoverished' by the excessive charges laid on it. The complaints do not suggest that the inability to pay was merely a symptom of economic troubles, but imply that the high fee farm was in itself a cause of the town's ills. The annual payment was reduced to £30 in 1464, yet the towns-people still complained, and in 1490 asked for the fee farm to be reduced to £20, giving as an explanation the problem of supporting three parish churches and four religious houses, in addition to the payment to the crown. They claimed that newcomers were discouraged from settling in the town by the financial responsibilities imposed on them. Buildings were falling down, and the number of wealthy people had diminished. Trade had 'gone down', and the harbour was 'wrecked and stopped'. If the fee farm was not reduced, the town would be 'utterly destroyed'.

Taxpayers have always pleaded poverty to justify reductions in their assessments, and Grimsby's claims, like similar excuses made by other towns at this time, were exaggerated. The harbour, though silting up, was still in use, and some trade was continuing. The leading burgesses of fifteenth-century towns in general, though they made much of their troubles, had no difficulty in justifying their arguments, and we can confirm their complaints to some degree. Houses were falling into ruin, and their empty sites were converted into gardens or rubbish dumps. At Oxford, colleges could be built near the town centre because land there was either vacant or cheap. When Robert Cole compiled a rental in 1455 for one of the main landlords in Gloucester, the priory of Llanthony, he found that six houses were decayed or ruined, twenty dwellings were being used as stables, there were twenty-four vacant plots and sixty tofts and curtilages, many of which had previously contained houses and cottages. In many towns, even when houses were still occupied, the diminishing demand for property forced landlords to accept lower rents. The vicars choral in York, a major landowner in the city, received £122 in 1371, but that figure was almost halved, to £68, by 1500. Individual houses in many towns were rented for about 20s before 1350, but these were typically reduced to 15s or 13s 4d after 1400. In Canterbury, the slide in rents began in the 1420s and 1430s, and in Oxford in the 1440s and 1450s, and in both places low rents then prevailed in the late fifteenth and early sixteenth centuries. Rent collectors in Newcastle upon Tyne had difficulties in persuading the tenants to pay, and could not prevent reductions, in the second half of the fifteenth century.

Public buildings were liable to decay. Town walls, which served as much as symbols of civic identity as practical means of defence, were everywhere neglected. At Aberystwyth, where the fee farm had been halved, by the early sixteenth century the walls had fallen into ruin. Parish churches were abandoned in Winchester. There had been fifty-four of them in 1300, but twenty-one had decayed by 1400, and another seven went in the fifteenth century, leaving less than half, twenty-six, that were still in use in 1500.

The physical decay of public buildings could be seen as a symptom of a deterioration in civic loyalties. Towns complained that those eligible for office in the town government refused election, fearful of the personal expense. Finally, some towns could point to the changes in the coastline and the sea level, which caused part of Dunwich (in Suffolk) to fall into the sea, but at Yarmouth and Saltfleethaven, as at Grimsby, silt was being deposited in the harbour.

These problems were by no means universal, and even in the towns which were affected the complaints give only one side of the picture. For almost every apparent symptom of decline there are reasons for doubting the evidence. The fee farm was not such an enormous burden for places which contained many people and much wealth. Often when towns said that they could no longer afford to pay, they meant that specific revenues which had been earmarked for the fee farm (such as rents on particular properties) had diminished. Leading townsmen did not lack a sense of civic duty – individuals had always declined election to such time-consuming jobs as that of chamberlain or bailiff, and some councils nominated candidates who they knew would refuse, in order to collect a fine. The decay of some houses removed overcrowded and cramped cottages, and left space for gardens, which improved the quality of life for those who remained. The rents which decayed were often being collected on behalf of remote institutions, and some of the collectors may not have tackled their work with much zeal or efficiency. Townspeople were sensible not to maintain the walls, which often served no useful purpose. While they saw no point in maintaining parish churches for which there were inadequate congregations, even in shrinking towns they lavished money on the embellishment or even rebuilding of the churches that remained in use. Many towns either rebuilt or added substantially to their parish churches in the fifteenth and early sixteenth centuries, and not just the 'wool churches' of the Cotswolds, or those in the clothmaking districts in Devon or Suffolk. There were many complex motives for church-building, among which local prosperity was one important dimension. But if we take the presence of a large new church as evidence that people had cash to spare for expensive building work, then it reflects not just the wealth of a few individuals, but of the whole community, as fundraising was frequently a collective effort, to which many parishioners contributed.

Towns had to adjust to reductions in the size of their populations, especially after the period of relative prosperity around 1400. Winchester suffered more than most, when its 10,000 to 12,000 people in *c.*1300 dropped to below 8,000 in 1417, and to about 4,000 in 1524–5. Places which lost about half of their populations between 1377 and 1524–5 include Boston, Lincoln, Lynn and York, while Beverley, Leicester and Grimsby shrank severely. They probably fell more catastrophically between 1300 (before the plagues) and the 1450s, when trade reached a low point. The larger east coast ports were especially vulnerable to decline, as were both large and small towns in the east midlands, such as Stamford in Lincolnshire and Brackley in Northamptonshire.

The towns which ceased to be towns entirely, either because their inhabitants deserted them or because those who remained turned to agriculture, tend to be found in the west and north of Britain. In Wales, at least nine boroughs were completely deserted, and a dozen others, like Caerphilly, ceased to have an urban economy. Failed boroughs are also found in north-west England, for example at Greystoke in Cumberland. At least twenty Scottish burghs, like Auchterhouse and Scrabster, either failed to develop, or by the early sixteenth century had relapsed into rural settlements or fishing villages. Failures are also scattered over the midlands and the south, like the Warwickshire borough of Bretford, and Newton in Purbeck in Dorset. With many of these places we cannot be sure that they had ever been flourishing towns. Often they were granted a market charter, or burghal privileges, but in the fifteenth or sixteenth centuries the burgage plots were vacant or occupied as agricultural holdings.

Changes in the size of towns came about because of inhabitants' decisions about where to establish their homes and businesses, and how to make their living. In towns which did not offer a good income or future prospects, landlords or tenants neglected to carry out work on houses, or allowed them to fall down, or could not see any benefit in building anew. Potential immigrants were discouraged, or moved to a place which promised more jobs and higher rewards.

Towns suffered setbacks when the trade in basic commodities was reduced in volume. The Scottish trade in wool and hides was doing quite well in the late fourteenth century, when 9,000 sacks of wool were exported in 1372, and more than 70,000 hides in 1381, but in the 1460s exports had fallen to 2,000 sacks and 15,000–18,000 hides. Exporters were carrying from England 18,000 sacks per annum in the 1390s, about half of the figure earlier in the fourteenth century, and this slipped to 15,000 annually in the early fifteenth century, and after a period of volatility in the 1440s and 1450s, settled down to 8,000 to 9,000 sacks in a typical year between 1460 and 1520 (see Figure 4 above, p. 244). This damaged the prosperity of east coast ports, from Aberdeen to Yarmouth. A higher proportion of exports went through London, so ports like Boston and Hull were handling a diminishing share of a declining trade. Wool exports were organized by a small number of merchants, but it was not just a handful of rich men who suffered from the loss of trade. The merchants employed labour to cart, load, unload and ship the wool, and the returning ships would bring merchandise into the town. An active port kept the food and drink trades busy, as ships were provisioned before each voyage. The wool merchants spent some of their profits on local goods and services. The recession in trade had effects on the whole supply network, and might help to explain the decline in population of such inland centres as Melton Mowbray in Leicestershire, where wool had been collected for transport to the east coast.

The traders of the east coast ports also suffered because of the decline in their access to the commerce of the Baltic. The merchants of Lübeck, Hamburg and the other north German ports belonging to the Hanseatic League struggled with the English government over reciprocal trading rights. The Hanseatic merchants were able to operate from English ports (where steelyards were established as depots), and the English could trade in Germany. One of the success stories of the late fourteenth century, in addition to the general advance made by English merchants in gaining a larger share of the country's trade, was their expansion into the Baltic. A period of friction in the early fifteenth century was only temporarily settled by treaties in 1409 and 1437, and open hostilities broke out in 1468–74. The English lost in this struggle, and although twenty-one Scottish ships were able to pass through the Sound into the Baltic in 1497, English vessels were absent.

The decline in the Scottish wool exports set back that kingdom's overseas trade: no major substitute commodity could compensate for the loss of the country's most abundant product. The kingdom's customs revenues, which had been running at an annual £9,000 in the 1370s, had fallen to £2,500 in the 1450s, and picked up again, but only to £3,000, in the late fifteenth century. For England, cloth exports filled at least part of the gap created by the fall in the wool trade, but this did not come to the aid of all of the ailing towns. The cloth trade as a whole was subject to ups and downs. The number of cloths going out of English ports between the 1390s and the 1440s expanded from about 40,000 per annum to almost 60,000, but then fell back to 40,000 or even below that figure, and did not recover fully until the 1470s (see Figure 4 above, p. 244). A high proportion of the cloth was exported through London, so that Bristol, for example, did not handle all of the cloth from Somerset, Wiltshire and Gloucestershire. And the manufacture of cloth, which could bring much employment and wealth to individual towns, was subject to fluctuations depending on unpredictable changes in fashion or competition. So Colchester and Coventry based their fourteenth-century success on textiles which did well in continental markets, but went into decline during the fifteenth century. At Coventry, cap-making provided employment as textile manufacture declined, but that did not last. By 1523 Coventry's population had fallen to about 6,000, having reached 10,000 at its peak in the early fifteenth century. York had been famous for its cloth, but its industry declined before the Black Death. After a revival towards 1400, it suffered loss of business and employment during the fifteenth century when demand fell and production was cut back.

Merchants who did not necessarily handle a great deal of cloth could still make money from the import trade in raw materials used in textile manufacture, such as oil for treating yarn for weaving; woad and other dyestuffs; alum which was used in dyeing; soap; and Spanish iron which had the right properties for making the wire used in cards for preparing wool. Many of these goods were imported through London. Individual wealth diminished because of these changes in the pattern of trade. At York, 83 per cent of merchants left less than £50 in their wills after 1460; before that date the figure had been 65 per cent. Five York merchants (for whom we have records) who died in 1379–1415 thought that their estates could afford to pay £300 or more to beneficiaries. In the period 1468–1514 only two could dispose of so much.

In some degree the difficulties of the ports – especially those on the east coast, but also including Bristol and some of the larger inland towns – can be explained by the decline in wool exports, the fluctuations in cloth manufacture, and the growth of London as a channel for exports and imports. But why did the smaller towns, especially in a belt running from east Yorkshire through the east midlands to the western fringes of East Anglia, lose population? This was not so much an example of urban decline as a case of the whole population of the region shrinking, in villages and towns together. This part of England had been devoted to arable cultivation, which brought less prosperity as the grain trade stagnated. Wool was a leading product of the region, but not much of it was made into cloth locally; most was carried into other parts of the country, such as Suffolk. Elsewhere towns stood on the frontier between contrasting landscapes, and their markets would provide a point of connection between different rural economies. In the east midlands there was less variety in landscape, with less need in consequence for local exchange. The towns did not collapse, but continued to serve as useful market centres (see Map 11 below, p. 359).

The successes among towns outweighed the failures, probably leaving the urban sector as large as it had been before the Black Death. The proportion of the English population who lived in towns, according to the tax records of the 1520s, stood at about 20 per cent. This is very similar to the proportion of town dwellers in 1377, and the situation had probably not changed greatly since the late thirteenth century. In other words, England had achieved quite a high degree of urbanization by about 1300, and the towns retained their relative importance two centuries later.

This must mean that the commercial outlook which had been established before the Black Death did not revert to a more primitive economy based on self-sufficiency. The rural population still produced a surplus to feed the townspeople, and still spent money on the goods and services that towns had to offer.

The most successful city in England was London. Badly hit by plague epidemics, in 1377 it contained about 50,000 people, which represents a drop from the estimated 80,000 at the beginning of the fourteenth century. By the 1520s about 60,000 were living in the city, with 3,000 in Westminster and 8,000 to 9,000 in Southwark (much more than in 1300), which together with lesser suburbs made a formidable conurbation. Londoners enjoyed great advantages over the traders and artisans of the provinces. The city lay at the centre of the kingdom in every sense, which drew the magnates to establish town houses, numbering 75 by 1520. Every year hundreds of provincial gentry came to stay at London's inns, to attend parliament and the central law courts, but also to enjoy the social and cultural life of a metropolis. The Thames estuary gave London an excellent port, with easy access to the hub of continental trade in northern France, Flanders, the Low Countries and the Rhine. Coastal trade connected London with Exeter, Yarmouth and Newcastle, the Thames provided a convenient route by boat between the capital and the south midlands, and the radiating network of roads brought trade and travellers from every part of Britain. London merchants, in addition to superior communications, had more capital and more political power than their provincial rivals. Talented and ambitious people in the provinces moved to London because they expected that their aims could be achieved there. Richard Whittington, for example, did not arrive penniless in the city, though as the third son of a Gloucestershire knight he had little prospect of inheriting much land. In the 1380s and 1390s he became a rich mercer, selling silks to the royal household and to landed magnates. Later in life he was lending money to Richard II and Henry IV, and traded in wool on a large scale. He became mayor of London three times, and left money at the end of his life to fund charitable work in the city. The story grew up that he became rich through the intervention of his miraculous cat, because people felt the need to explain how such great wealth came from small beginnings.

Whittington was just one of many London merchants who gained a large share of exports, both in wool and cloth. Sarplers of wool (each containing two sacks) and packs of cloth were brought in growing quantities by road or down the Thames to London. Imports came into London rather than other ports, and were distributed over the country by London merchants. The grocers of London, for example, handled a great variety of goods, including wool and cloth, but their distinctive trade was in spices, dyestuffs and alum: goods that were sold by weight. They visited fairs to sell these commodities to provincial traders, or made direct contact with the spicers of the towns who would sell the goods retail in their localities. Chapmen also played a part in distribution, some of them small-scale traders who bought packs of spices from a grocer and then travelled round the country hawking them in penny parcels. Whatever the method of distribution, we can be sure that the largest profits were made by the Londoners. The major consumers, even those from the northern counties, like the bishop of Carlisle or Durham Priory, bought spices from London grocers, because they had a better choice if they selected their goods from the large quantity on offer, but also because a bulk purchase of pepper, ginger and dried fruits could be obtained more cheaply directly from the wholesaler (see Map 10 below, p. 306).

London was a centre of manufacture, with the range of workers in cloth, leather, metal and wood that would be found in any large town, many of them serving local needs. Consumers came to London from a distance, however, particularly to buy luxury goods, because London craftsmen had a reputation for high-quality workmanship, and the presence of so many specialists in one place gave the purchaser some choice. A provincial town would often have only a single goldsmith, but the London company had a membership of 180 in 1477, and 210 in 1506. If a rich aristocrat wished to buy jewellery or silver plate, or to have a seal engraved, or if a church was seeking an ornate processional cross or chalice, they would go to a London goldsmith. Church bells could be cast in a number of provincial towns, such as Leicester and Nottingham, but the reputation of the Londoners meant that their bells were hung in churches more than 100 miles from the capital. Richard Hill, who flourished between 1418 and 1439, made bells for parish churches at Tixover in Rutland and Shipton Moyne in Gloucestershire. The quality that London craftsmen brought to their work can be appreciated from the brass plates on tombs engraved with figures by London marblers. Those made in the late fourteenth and early fifteenth centuries show a sensitivity, sense of proportion and elegance of line which few provincial rivals could achieve. London brasses were still chosen throughout the country when their quality was not quite so high, so the memorials to gentry such as Robert Eyr at Hathersage in Derbyshire (1463) and Sir Robert del Bothe of Wilmslow in Cheshire (1460) were commissioned from craftsmen in the capital.

The extension of London's dominance over many branches of the commercial economy was partly achieved, as has been suggested, by the advantage of price, choice and quality that the merchants and artisans

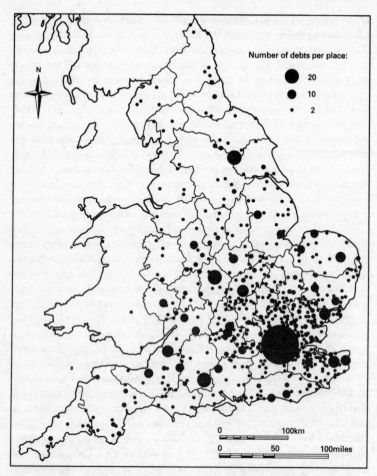

Map 10. Debts owed to Londoners, *c.*1400. The debts recorded in the royal courts, arising from sales of goods, or business dealings that went wrong, demonstrate the extent of London's trading connections.

Source: J. Galloway (ed.), *Trade, Urban Hinterlands and Market Integration c.1300–1600* (Centre for Metropolitan History, 2000).

could offer. But they also drew benefits because of their superior organization and political influence. The London fishmongers, for example, controlled the sale of fish in the city, and excluded the Yarmouth men. The merchants from London were fully represented in the two organizations that oversaw the trade in wool and cloth, the Staplers and

Merchant Adventurers, and they used their position to the disadvantage of provincial rivals. There were Merchant Adventurers in Newcastle and York, but the Londoners were given effective control of cloth exports to the Low Countries, and in 1497 northern merchants were forced to join the London fellowship, in spite of strong protests. In 1478 they complained that at the cloth fairs the Londoners took the best stalls, and left them points of sale on the periphery.

Although the rise of London weakened the ports and the larger provincial towns by drawing away their share of trade, some towns in the south-east gained from the association. Southampton and Sandwich served as outports for the capital, so that Italian ships *en route* to Flanders would load and unload at Southampton without making the longer journey up the Thames estuary. Some small town traders in the vicinity of the capital learned that they could profit from the great concentration of consumers in London, and so High Wycombe (Buckinghamshire) bakers produced as their speciality simnel bread which was sold in the city; Walden in Essex grew saffron in gardens around the town, much of it for London consumption. The inns at Newbury in Berkshire and St Albans in Hertfordshire did a busy trade because they provided convenient stopping places for travellers on two of the busiest main roads into London.

Edinburgh expanded its commerce as well as its role as the centre of government. It became the permanent centre of administration under James III (1460–88). A relatively small town in the fourteenth century, overshadowed as a trading port by Aberdeen and Berwick, it developed as the principal exporter of wool in Scotland, handling 57 per cent of the total in the 1440s, partly because it took over much of Berwick's trade after that town was lost to the English. It became Scotland's largest town in the sixteenth century. Another successful Scottish town, Dundee, overtook Perth and Aberdeen. In Wales the largest towns before the plagues were in the south and west, at Cardiff, Carmarthen and Haverfordwest. They were joined by expanding centres in the east and north-east of the country, at Brecon, Denbigh and Wrexham. From relatively small Welsh towns, these moved towards the upper rank with populations near to 1,000. A smaller Welsh town also in the north-east, Ruthin, did well at this time from its cloth industry. Brecon and Wrexham were helped in their rise by their strategic positions on the routes taken by cattle drovers into the English midlands.

Some towns were able to prosper because they replaced another centre within their region. Wrexham increased in size while Holt shrank, just as Reading in Berkshire flourished while Wallingford declined. In southeast Wales, Trellech and Usk went downhill, while Abergavenny and Monmouth improved their relative importance. Sometimes the reasons for these shifts are not easy to explain, but Abergavenny was given an advantage by its clothmaking, while Trellech had depended excessively on an uncompetitive iron industry. Many towns which maintained their position or even expanded were relatively small market towns, and their traders attracted custom away from the small village markets which must always have offered a very limited choice of goods, and may not have given the best prices for those selling agricultural produce. The village markets, which had received charters in such numbers in the century and a half before the Black Death, had mostly ceased to operate by the sixteenth century. In Staffordshire, forty-five markets are known to have been founded, of which twenty were still in use after 1500, and all but one or two of these were located in towns.

An active role in clothmaking undoubtedly protected the vulnerable larger towns from shrinkage. Some revived, or new cloth towns peaked early, as we have seen in the cases of Coventry, Colchester and York, which had all fallen back by 1520. Others benefited from a steadier and more sustained growth in their textile industry. Salisbury, with many weavers and fullers in the town, maintained its position throughout the period. Exeter, at the centre of the dynamic south Devon clothing district, with a population of only 3,000 in 1377, grew to 7,000–8,000 in 1524–5, mainly in the previous fifty years. Worcester also expanded during the fifteenth century and became a major centre of clothmaking, while cloth enabled Kendal to grow in the early sixteenth century to become the largest town in the north-west. These changes meant that in the hierarchy of English towns Exeter moved into the top ten, while an old cloth town which had failed to find a new role, Lincoln, dropped into thirteenth position.

Some traders in the large towns, such as Exeter and Salisbury, prospered because of their association with the spinners, weavers and fullers who lived in the hamlets, villages and small towns in the vicinity. Small towns in these districts based their success on providing goods and service to country clothmakers as well as their own industry. This helps to explain the presence among the fifty wealthiest and most populous English towns in the 1520s of Crediton in Devon, Hadleigh in Suffolk and Newbury in Berkshire. Others with the same basis for their growth include Halifax, which had a cloth hall for the sale of locally made textiles in 1500, and Leeds, where three new fulling mills were built between 1455 and 1499. Tiverton and Cullompton in Devon were the homes of the wealthy clothiers John Greenway and John Lane, both of whom left permanent memorials by paying for lavish additions to their parish churches. At Lavenham in Suffolk, the clothing Spring family, who converted themselves into landed gentry, contributed 37 per cent of the town's taxes in 1524; its many timber-framed buildings and its large and ornate church show how much money came into the town in the fifteenth and early sixteenth centuries. These small towns, founded in the phase of urban expansion before the Black Death, took on a new lease of life in the fifteenth century. Some new towns grew almost imperceptibly at this time, without charters or encouragement from lords, such as Stroud in Gloucestershire and Pensford in Somerset, both housing numerous cloth workers in the heart of busy textile districts.

The traders and artisans of other small towns also took advantage of local industries which were practised in the town and its surrounding countryside. Birmingham by the early sixteenth century was a flourishing centre of a number of crafts, including tanning, but its blades, including scythe blades, were traded over a wide area. Stourbridge, a new town at this time, benefited from the iron industry and pastoral agriculture in its north Worcestershire neighbourhood. The distinctive industries in some towns were directly connected to local resources, like the marble quarried near to Corfe in Dorset. Sometimes the initiative came from an entrepreneur or group of entrepreneurs who, realizing the potential of a particular product, encouraged the skills of manufacture and devised a system of distribution. Walsall in Staffordshire, for example, had nearby resources of fuel, limestone and iron, but so did a number of other towns in the vicinity. The human factor must explain why it became a supplier of lime in its region, and also produced horse bits which were traded beyond the midlands. Nearby Burton-on-Trent was also famous for two products, beer and religious statuary carved from the alabaster quarried nearby.

Most new towns in England are associated with the period of urbanization before 1300, and the concept seems to fit uneasily with the shrinkage and even extinction of towns in the two centuries after the Black Death, but three examples have already been mentioned, and on the coast Brighton and Minehead both seem to have become urban settlements towards the end of the middle ages. In Scotland, again, most of the towns which became important centres of local government, trade and manufactures had been founded before 1348, but between 1350 and 1520 another fifteen burghs, ten of them royal, were created, and a remarkable fifty-nine burghs of barony and burghs of regality were founded from the early fifteenth century onwards, especially in the period 1488–1512. Each was granted a weekly market and annual fair, and the inhabitants acquired trading and legal privileges, but not the monopoly over trade in their district which was enjoyed by the burghs. The burghs of this new generation were speculative ventures, and about half of them failed, but others met with some success as commercial centres, as at

Alloa, Paisley and Hawick. The Scottish burghs received formal grants
of privilege, unlike the unofficial and therefore poorly documented
English new towns of this period.

The expansion of a few of the larger towns, the growth in many of
the smaller towns, especially in the industrial districts, the foundation
and emergence of new towns, all deserve our attention when they take
place against a background of an overall stagnation in population. Most
townspeople, however, lived in existing urban centres which lost varying
proportions of their population. These towns still performed their functions as centres of exchange, production and administration. Coventry,
for example, after the apparent disaster of losing almost half of its
people, in 1520 was still the capital of its region, with trade links extending overseas through the ports of London, Bristol, Chester and Boston.
Even after its shrinkage, it was still larger than it had been in 1300,
and numbered some very rich individuals among its citizens, including
Richard Marler, one of the wealthiest merchants in the whole country.
The experience of living in such towns was by no means one of misery
and poverty. They still attracted immigrants. These are especially visible
in Wales when so many people of Welsh descent settled in towns, even
those formerly regarded as English colonies, that their language and
culture became a dominant influence. High earnings encouraged people
to move to towns. With wage rates at 6d per day in the fifteenth century
for many skilled building workers in the south, a fully employed skilled
mason or carpenter could hope to earn £6 in a year. The profits of artisans who ran their own businesses, as shoemakers or tailors for example,
are difficult to calculate, but they regarded carpenters as their inferiors.
Workers paid by the day would have their earnings limited by the dis-
continuity of employment caused by the search for work, as well as by
illness and bad weather. Those with longer contracts would earn less
but be guaranteed continuous employment, so journeymen cappers in
Coventry were supposed to receive 44s per annum, with meals. The food
would have taken the total remuneration above 60s, and as the regulations were seeking to prevent excessively high wages, the journeymen
presumably received more than the legally defined maximum.

In spite of problems with the flow of trade, mercantile profit could
still be high; this enabled the Cely family, merchants of the staple around
1480, to receive about £100 per annum. Even in Aberdeen, which was
well past its peak as a port for overseas trade, a merchant like Sir John
Rutherford flourished between about 1467 and his death in 1528. He had
a good start as the third generation of his family in the town. Like
merchants everywhere he diversified, protecting himself against failure.
He dealt in cloth, oats, meal, salmon, salt and wine – both luxury goods

and more basic commodities for a broader market. These goods were sold in Aberdeen, in other Scottish towns such as Forfar and Dundee, and overseas to Dieppe. Rutherford invested in property in both town and country as a means of storing wealth, as security for raising future capital, and as a source of income from rents. He rented peat cuttings, fisheries and sheep pastures. He bought jewellery and silver plate, and was accepted in aristocratic society: his first and second wives were both the daughters of local lords.

Artisans often seem to have been a particularly underprivileged group in Scottish towns, but this does not mean that the lesser ranks of Aberdeen did not enjoy some of the fruits of the town's trade. Tax assessments from 1448 and 1472 suggest prosperity among smiths, shoemakers and dyers. Individual craftsmen held property in the town, and owned such prestigious goods as silver spoons. Throughout England and Wales, good-quality timber-framed houses of this period, including both large merchants' dwellings, and many modest two-storey houses appropriate for artisans, are found in towns of all sizes, with different economies and in varied regions, at Salisbury, Stamford, Ludlow, Hadleigh, Winchcombe, and dozens more. The buildings are still used because their original construction and materials were of a high standard, and the successors of the medieval owners did not demolish them and rebuild. The urban property market was less lively than it had been around 1300, but landlords, such as monasteries, found it advantageous to buy up houses and plots and to pay for new buildings for rent. This happened in the vicinity of Westminster Abbey, where the monks developed the town in the interests of increasing their rent income, and enterprising laymen were following suit, behaving in the style of modern speculative builders by acquiring an empty plot and running up a row of houses.

In their house designs the landlords, or indeed the many tenants who also rebuilt their own properties, were following the established tradition of urban building, but they added a little to their expense with a greater number of separate rooms, even to the extent that in Stamford the main public room, the hall, was eliminated and replaced by a more comfortable and intimate parlour. A growing proportion of houses were roofed with tile and slate rather than thatch or shingles, and instead of open hearths, rooms were heated with fireplaces and chimneys. Builders were paid by their clients to make some show of status on the street frontage, with 'close studding' in which a great quantity of timber was displayed, with decorative carving, and jettied upper storeys towering over those passing by. (Plate 14)

Townspeople aspired to increase their domestic comfort by purchasing internal fittings such as wainscoting, as well as painted cloths for the

walls, and soft furnishings such as carpets and cushions. Artisan households would be equipped with a range of metal cooking and table ware,
and plentiful ceramic pots, cisterns, jugs and cups. One small town
artisan, John Symond of Wickham Market in Suffolk, when making his
will in 1481, described himself as a barber, but he also traded as a wax
chandler. He does not seem to have had very much cash, as he left £2 10s
mainly to the church, and allowed his wife, as well as the use of his house
and land, an income of 13s 4d each year for five years. However, in his
life he had bought a range of household goods, as he bequeathed twelve
silver spoons, a feather bed and bedclothes, six pewter plates and at
least two pewter salts, a brass pot, fire irons, a chest made of spruce
wood, four candlesticks of latten (an alloy of copper and zinc), rosary
beads and a saddle and bridle for his horse. These were only the goods
that Symond thought worthy of mention. Other wills and inventories
show that a prosperous artisan's possessions would have included furniture, household textiles such as towels and tablecloths, and many
garments. In addition to increasing their purchases of consumer goods,
townspeople also enjoyed an improved diet, with greater quantities of
meat, fish and ale.

Towns attracted the poor, who could obtain casual employment there,
and because surplus food was handed out both by religious institutions
and by better-off private households. The most generous doles were provided at funerals, when townspeople making their wills assumed that a
large crowd of paupers would assemble. For the indigenous poor, that is
the townspeople who were unemployed, ill or old, the arrangements for
social security probably improved at this time. The number of places in
almshouses and hospitals grew, certainly in relation to the population,
and private charity, some of it channelled through the churchwardens or
religious fraternities, was directed at the 'deserving poor', that is widows,
sick, old and poor householders with children.

The urban scene changed significantly between 1350 and 1520, but not
out of all recognition. The numbers of towns throughout Britain probably fell from 800 to 740, but then a handful of new towns pushed the
figure up again above 750. The population of towns fell overall, though
at different rate, and some places were larger in 1520 than they had been
in 1300. The urban share of the whole population did not change. Towns
moved up and down the urban hierarchy, but the leading towns of 1300
were still quite highly placed in 1520. The shifts in trade and industrial
output had a significant influence, especially on the east coast ports and
the clothing towns. The stability of the network of towns in some regions
is suggested by the way that the same market towns served the same hinterlands as in the early fourteenth century, and indeed were strengthened

by the disappearance of the village markets. The clothing districts saw some changes, as small places became more important; some new towns even grew up. But the pattern that had emerged before the Black Death, both in terms of the proportions of large and small centres and in their geographical distribution, stood the test of time (see Map 11 below, p. 359). In parts of England the urban system had reached maturity. Wales and particularly Scotland were not so stable, with a crop of new burghs in Scotland at the end of the period, and more casualties than can be found in lowland England. Of course, individual town dwellers went through hard times as their town shrank or their trade failed, and they fell into poverty or moved out, but most townspeople were enjoying a higher standard of living than their predecessors.

ii. *Urban economies*

Did the quality of town life and the character of the urban economy change? Townspeople seem more articulate and assertive in this period, partly because there are more records and more of them were written in English. But the creation of documents, and the use of the vernacular, was part of the desire to reflect the importance of their town, and to communicate positive messages to fellow townsmen and to outsiders. A characteristic statement of civic pride and responsibility was the 'Mayor's Calendar' written by Robert Ricart, the town clerk of Bristol, in 1478. The book celebrated the liberties of the 'noble and worshipful town of Bristol', which were the same as those enjoyed by the city of London. Ricart provided a history of Bristol, including a myth of the town's foundation, and then went on to describe civic ceremonies, and to give the text of the oath to be sworn by a new mayor. The mayor's duties included holding courts, meeting with the masters of the guilds, supervising the bakers and brewers, and regulating the markets. The ideas expressed in the 'Calendar', which were shared in varying ways in all of the larger towns, emphasized the duty of officials to provide good government and celebrated the unity of the town, which suggests a closing of ranks in times of uncertainty.

The leading townsmen, which in large towns usually meant the merchants, aimed to exercise close economic control. They accepted the aspirations of the artisans and small-scale traders to have some representation in the government of the town through the common council. But the key decisions were usually made by a group of councillors (in most towns numbering twelve or twenty-four), together with a small group of officials: the mayor, sheriff, recorder, bailiffs and chamberlains in England, or the provost and bailies in Scotland. They represented the town's interests in the outside world by sending burgesses to parliament, petitioning the crown and pursuing cases through the courts. They sought patronage from aristocrats who might help them in their political and legal negotiations. In Scotland, towns would enter into formal agreements to gain the influence of local lords through bonds of 'manrent' (see p. 269). Their concerns remained much as they had been before 1350, such as disputes with rivals, as when Brechin, Forfar and Montrose worked out their conflicting interests in the late fourteenth century, or Yarmouth at about the same time pursued its quarrel with Lowestoft. Towns still resented the enclaves of jurisdiction held by the church; Exeter, for example, unsuccessfully challenged the power of the clergy to rule in their cathedral close in 1445–8. Londoners were exercised by Southwark's independence, which they thought allowed criminals and rogue traders to carry on their dishonest practices south of the river. And foreigners were distrusted at best, and occasionally persecuted, as when a wave of violence was directed against the Italians in London in 1456–7.

The elites who ran the towns were concerned to maintain peace and order. They used the traditional system of courts to do this, but also sought to extend their control over society in a manner reminiscent of the later puritans, as they passed laws against prostitutes, eavesdroppers, gossips and night walkers, and made desultory attempts to forbid the playing of illicit games, from football to dice. In a more positive spirit, they founded or refounded hospitals as shelters for the poor who were (as they saw it) genuinely in need. They were also concerned to follow social policies that would prevent unrest, hence their legislation against forestalling and regrating, the rule in the markets that corn be sold for the first few hours to the consumers, not the grain dealers, and the enforcement of the assizes of bread and ale (see p. 224). At Aberdeen, oatmeal could not be bought in bulk, and the sale of oat bread was forbidden. The bakers could produce wheat and rye bread for the better-off, but the basic food of the poor was to be kept out of the hands of the dealers and processors. There was concern about the creation of monopolies by the linking of crafts, so that, again at Aberdeen, butchers were not allowed to make candles for sale, as they controlled the supplies of tallow. In many towns the poor were expected to be able to buy cheaply the brewers' dregs and the butchers' offal. The rules were not kept, but they must have had some effect when the town took determined action. At Aberdeen, the butchers (fleshers) were constantly before the courts between 1505 and 1509 for selling meat at an excessively high price, and the authorities decided in 1511 to expose the fleshers to competition by allowing anyone within the burgh or the countryside to sell meat as they wished in the town.

Their food policies might suggest that the governing minority ruled in a public-spirited fashion, upholding the common good against profiteers. However, in many ways they protected their own interests. The freedom of the town was restricted: it could be acquired only by inheritance, apprenticeship or purchase. The cost of buying the freedom, which carried with it full access to the market, was often fixed at a high level which excluded many artisans. At Dunfermline, the fee was set at 40s, which meant that only about a third of the burgesses enjoyed the privilege. The artisans in larger towns belonged to fraternities, or 'craft guilds' as they are now known, which gave them the chance to hold social gatherings for those in their trade, and discuss matters of common interest. But these organizations were regulated by the town's government, which took a close interest in their internal affairs. The authorities supervised the craft's rules, which were approved by the mayor and copied into the town's archives.

The ordinances of the Bristol cobblers were drawn up by eighteen named masters of the craft in 1364. These limited the wages paid by the master craftsman to the servant or servants (journeymen) who worked in his shop to 6d for sewing and 'yarking' (finishing) a dozen pairs of shoes, with more for boots. If a servant was contracted to work for a master, he could earn no more than 18d per week with a bonus of eight pairs of shoes each year. Masters were forbidden to poach workers from other members of the craft. This is a typical example of wage regulation after the Black Death, supporting the restrictions of the Statute of Labourers. It was in the interests of the employing masters to keep down wage costs, but the wider body of consumers would be protected from paying more for their shoes, and the governing elite of the town, who were all employers, would welcome measures to limit wages. The mayor approved the regulations, and may have played an active role in framing them.

The influence of the Bristol merchants is readily apparent in the dyers' rules of 1407, which were focused on the problem of shoddy workmanship and the lack of proper training among the dyers' craft. The regulations allowed for inspection of dyed cloths by two masters approved by the mayor, and the exclusion from work of those who lacked the right skills. The craft was clearly difficult to discipline, and the rules were being imposed against the will of some of the masters, as it was ordered that 'all the masters of the said craft of dyeing . . . ought to come before the mayor to hear the said ordinances, and whether they will assent to and grant the same or not'. The initiative behind this measure came from the merchants, who had seen Bristol's cloth exports fall in the period 1399–1407 and, searching for an explanation, blamed the dyers for giving Bristol cloth a poor reputation.

The authorities wished to have well-ordered towns, where everyone knew their place in the hierarchy. The 'craft guilds' played their role as disciplinary organizations. The contribution of each craft, and its place in the civic body, was symbolically displayed each year in the plays performed on Corpus Christi day, when each craft was assigned a biblical episode, often appropriate to their skill: so the carpenters performed the story of Noah's ark, and the smiths (who made nails) the crucifixion. The plays cost money, for the costumes and props and pay for professional performers, which led to grumbling, and some of the smaller crafts clubbed together. In Scottish towns, artisans were not allowed to form associations in the early fifteenth century. Their 'customary congregations' in 1427 were described in an Act of parliament as conspiracies. They still met, although they were not supposed to trade while pursuing their craft occupations. After 1469, guilds of craftsmen were formed.

Unskilled workers were not allowed to associate. For example, at Coventry the daubers and rough masons were forbidden to form a fraternity. The government of London also clamped down on illicit fraternities of journeymen. Nicholas Symond and eleven other journeymen spurriers were found in 1381 to have been meeting each month in St Bartholomew's church in Smithfield for the previous nine years. They swore an oath to support the fraternity, contributed money to a common box, and made ordinances, which had been written down. The members no doubt saw their organization as a legitimate religious and social body, so much so that when a member failed to attend meetings he was reported to the church court for perjury (an offence under canon law, the church's legal code), which brought the fraternity to the notice of the authorities. The mayor and aldermen of London regarded this little group as a sinister conspiracy to raise wages – they had apparently fixed the minimum reward for making twenty-five spurs at 20d. The city elite reacted strongly to this serious threat to the common good, and ordered them to disband.

Townspeople came together in religious fraternities more often than in any grouping outside their households. They had developed in the thirteenth century, but after 1350 became more numerous, prestigious and prosperous. In self-governing towns the fraternity gave the elite the opportunity to organize a collective chantry, employing priests to pray for the souls of the brothers and sisters. They would arrange ceremonial funerals for members of the fraternity, and they gave alms and founded almshouses. They employed schoolmasters and built schools, and often paid for local facilities, such as bridges and roads. Their annual feasts and other gatherings were important social events for the leading townspeople. In larger towns the management of the religious fraternity provided valuable training in the skills of government, and the master of the Corpus Christi Guild or Holy Trinity Guild would often progress to become mayor a few years later. In smaller towns the fraternity became the primary collective body, which in fact if not in name governed the town. The exclusive and opulent character of some small town fraternities is indicated by the Holy Trinity Guild of Wisbech in Cambridgeshire, which was reputedly founded in 1379, and flourished in the fifteenth and early sixteenth centuries. Its membership was restricted to the more substantial townspeople (the 'better and wiser part', as they were called elsewhere) who numbered sixty-six in 1453. The alderman who presided over them was elected by a jury of twelve to eighteen leading members. The property which the fraternity accumulated was worth £40 annually in the mid-fifteenth century, which was ample to pay for a priest, a schoolmaster and the upkeep of the guildhall. At the splendid annual dinner venison and veal were served, and minstrels provided the entertainment. By a rule announced in 1506, the poor were allowed to eat the leftovers.

These organizations were intended to have an impact on the town's economy. They encouraged co-operation among the elite, by bringing them together at social events and by providing a forum for settling disputes. They gave the leading townspeople pride in their community and opportunities for informal government. Often members were recruited from the surrounding countryside, or other nearby towns, which helped business dealings. If the local gentry could be persuaded to join, they gave useful political and legal advice, added to the prestige of the fraternity, and brought trade to the town. The fraternity provided some measure of social security, especially for the relatively affluent who feared for their future when they became old or ill. The spending of the fraternity's funds on building the chapel, guildhall, school and almshouses, but also on bridges and roads, and on repairs and replacement of the houses in the town with which it was endowed, offered employment and represented investment in the urban fabric. Towns were made more civilized and dignified places by the fraternity's activities. Small towns in particular owed their impressive public buildings, schools, colourful processions, and their standing in the region to the efforts of their fraternities. But, like many other aspects of the collective life of towns, these facilities were devised by elites for the benefit of elites.

Town governments and the lords of seigneurial towns, and individual townspeople, contributed along with the fraternities to town buildings. They realized the need for roads, bridges, quays, marketplaces and stalls for the easy flow of trade, and there are many examples of substantial and useful public works taking place at this time. Occasionally these involved not just the replacement of existing facilities, but new ventures which helped the town's economy, as when the leading townspeople of Abingdon in Berkshire, acting through their fraternity, paid for a new bridge over the Thames at Culham, which brought new trade and helped to seal the fate of Wallingford. As in earlier periods, the authorities were much concerned with public health, which led them to legislate for street-cleaning, and more towns were provided with a public water supply. The battle with the butchers continued, to force them to clean up the squalid mess that they left in the gutters and to carry their waste to some approved dumping ground well away from the town centre.

An ambiguous example of an initiative which changed the public face of many towns was the provision of clocks in church towers or purpose-built 'clockhouses'. In some ways these can be seen as civic ornaments, showing that the town appreciated technical novelties, and often they had no more practical purpose than ensuring that religious services took place at the right time. Eventually they were adopted for measuring the working day, and a journeymen capper at Coventry in 1496 was enjoined 'to come to his work at 6 of the clock in the morning, and to leave at 6 at night'. Working hours had previously been defined with reference to light and dark, which left room for debate, but now precision could enter into a central aspect of work discipline.

Civic elites were skilled image builders, who were capable of creating a sense of community by fostering legends about the early history of the town. They used high-flown rhetoric about the good government they claimed to be practising, praising their predecessors (at Wells in Somerset) for the 'convenient ordinances' which they had made 'worshipfully and discreetly'. If we accept that urban economies were closely regulated by town governments we are in danger of believing their propaganda. The stream of local legislation gives the impression that the town was run with an almost military discipline, and this has led historians to argue that they created a strait-jacket of regulation, levied heavy taxation to pay for civic building and ceremonies, and helped to drive business away.

In fact, many of the attempts at control were not very successful. The food traders habitually bought grain before it reached the market, as this was an essential part of the long-distance grain trade which kept town populations fed. Direct sale of corn or fish by producers to the consumers was a utopian idea, inappropriate to a complicated market system with its many middlemen. The regulations were not enforced in such a way that they would change the behaviour of the offenders. In small towns we often find that the assizes of bread and ale, or the regulations to restrict profit on the sale of meat and fish, were being broken by members of the leet jury or other officials. Ale tasters presented themselves (or their own wives) for breaches of the assize: they paid the fine, and continued as before.

Attempts to control rates of pay or to ensure that workers were properly trained were no more successful than the Statute of Labourers, because they were attempting to hold back the tide of the labour market. Artisans could not be pigeon-holed into occupational categories. Nor could their journeymen and other wage workers be entirely prevented from forming their own small fraternities. The artisans resented the elitism of the town governments, and voiced their dissent. In London the tailors gave their support in 1438–44 to Ralph Holland when he led an agitation against a city government that was biased in favour of the drapers. They even questioned the assumption that merchants should dominate the city's affairs, and remembered that one mayor, Walsh, had been a cordwainer, and he was said to have been the best mayor that the city had ever had! Individuals, like a series of dissenters from the fraternity which governed Wells, including William Webbe and Thomas Chynnok, were expelled and had to make a humiliating submission to their superiors.

Some towns were managing without much government. Alongside very closely regulated small towns were Bromsgrove in Worcestershire, or Buntingford in Hertfordshire, where there is very little evidence for an active controlling hand, whether from the lord of the manor or a fraternity. Towns had sometimes developed in a number of manors and parishes, so that no single conventional authority could dominate them. Others escaped close supervision because they grew up in a corner of a much larger manor. Those places with small and weak fraternities, and an inactive lord, were also free from much formal regulation. The large suburb of Southwark, which grew to the size of a large town in its own right, had no central government – different parts of the sprawling settlement came under the jurisdiction of a number of lords, none of them very assertive. Modern advocates of the free market might point to these places as 'enterprise zones' which flourished without economic controls. But while it is true that Southwark grew rapidly, many of the smaller towns like Buntingford succeeded only in the sense of serving usefully as a small market town.

In a parallel development traders tended to ignore the formal network of markets. In theory, the royal government had either issued charters to enable lords or towns to hold markets on set days, or had accepted that some markets were old and well established. The country was dotted at regular intervals with these chartered markets, and almost everyone lived within a short distance of one. We might be led to expect that the bulk of buying and selling took place in designated marketplaces on the appointed day, under official supervision and with tolls paid. In practice much urban trade was conducted on days other than those of the official market, in shops or warehouses. Bulk purchases of agricultural produce such as wool and corn were agreed at the farm. Inns, in both town and country, were much used for bargaining over these unregulated sales. There were also unofficial trading places, where small groups of traders, artisans and innkeepers formed embryonic towns, such as Knowle in Warwickshire, at the junction of roads joining Warwick, Birmingham and Coventry. There were markets and fairs which took place without official recognition, but were so well established that their marketplaces were incorporated into the plan of the settlement, and are still visible. Perhaps the general lesson that can be learned is not that regulation was harmful and stunted economic growth, but that it did not make a great deal of difference. The flow of commerce was more powerful than the efforts of government to control behaviour.

Crafts and trades became more specialized. The unit of production remained the workshop based on the household, which normally consisted of a handful of workers: the master, his wife, a child or two if they were of working age, and one or two servants or apprentices. Occasionally a master in the metal trades employed a larger workforce, the greatest number known being the eighteen servants and apprentices employed in Thomas Dounton's pewter workshop in London in 1457. Some official records might suggest that the number of specialisms was increasing. In London, for example, 111 organized crafts were listed in 1422, and the occupational labels used to identify people coming before the courts in the fifteenth century suggest minute subdivisions of skill. For example, among those preparing animal skins, as well as tanners and skinners we find curriers, pelterers and tawyers. But the suspicion must be that these descriptions result from the official desire to fit artisans into categories, rather than real changes in the work they did. In the fifteenth century, as in earlier periods, an individual would pursue a number of occupations, like John Symond, the barber/wax chandler of Wickham Market.

Specialization came about when many people in the same craft settled in one place and dominated its economy. This on the whole had not happened at the time of the poll tax lists of 1379 and 1381, and if we classify the occupations of the taxpayers into the categories of food and drink, leather, textiles, clothing, mercantile, metal, building, wood and transport, we find that in most towns all are represented, but none predominate. The main function of a town was to provide its hinterland with a full range of goods and services, hence the diversity of crafts and trades. An exception is found in the case of the food and drink trades, which, for example, account for 27 per cent of the taxpayers in Oxford and Southwark, reflecting the response of the towns' traders to demand from those attending the university in the first case, and the travellers entering and leaving London in the other. Among the manufacturing crafts, specialists sometimes gathered in small towns, like the 25 per cent of the population of Sheffield who were listed as metalworkers in 1379; already the town was becoming a centre of knife-making. Usually the share of the population in any one branch of manufacture did not rise above 15 per cent.

During the fifteenth century, concentrations of particular crafts in individual towns became more common, especially those producing cloth. At Salisbury in 1421 the numbers of cloth workers attending a meeting to discuss the industry suggest that, with their families, they accounted for about a quarter of the population. By the sixteenth century Worcester's textile workers made up about 40 per cent of the inhabitants. Those acquiring the freedom of larger towns were recorded in registers, which are biased sources because of the exclusion of the poorer workers and other categories. It is still worth noting that the proportion of textile workers among the new freemen at Wells increased from 19 per cent in the late fourteenth century to 31 per cent in the late fifteenth. In another clothing district, the occupations of those assessed for the military survey at Long Melford in Suffolk in 1522 show that clothmakers, weavers, fullers and others in the clothing trades accounted for 37 per cent of those with specific occupations. In the same survey, eighty-three cappers and hatmakers were listed for Coventry, and two years later there were fifty shoemakers in Northampton: together with fifteen tanners and thirteen glovers, this suggests that the town's modern reputation as a centre of leather-working was already beginning.

This trend towards specialization in such small towns as Tiverton, Stroud, Saffron Walden, Walsall and Burton-on-Trent has been mentioned (see pp. 308–9). Its economic importance lies in the implication for the distribution of goods, which were being produced in these centres for distant markets, in greater quantity than would be needed in the immediate vicinity of the town. The products must have been given distinctive qualities which customers would recognize. The workers are likely to have gained in skill and efficiency through working in large numbers in close proximity.

iii. *Consumers*

The flow of trade and manufacture was strongly influenced by the high level of consumer demand, in spite of the reduced size of the population. Trade in some luxury goods, such as wine and furs, was in decline, reflecting the reduced spending power of the aristocracy and the difficulties of supply in wartime, which in particular pushed up the cost of wine from south-west France. The very wealthy altered their choices because they were concerned that the new rich after the Black Death were buying goods once affordable only by the aristocracy. Squirrel fur linings for clothes, for example, were now being worn by the wives of artisans. The response of the elite was to stop wearing so much squirrel and to buy small quantities of scarce furs such as marten, which maintained the distance between them and the social climbers. In the same spirit they drank expensive sweet wines from the Mediterranean, such as rumney and malmsey. If the volume of international trade declined, especially in the middle of the fifteenth century, so did the population, and traded goods per head had a higher volume than in the thirteenth century.

The sustained demand for textiles from the majority of consumers kept the economy of some towns buoyant, which meant that clothmakers, as well as making quite expensive broadcloths and such high-quality brands as Bristol reds, were also producing relatively cheap woollens at 1s or 2s per yard. Their production of these affordable cloths helps to explain the large output, especially from Devon, west Yorkshire, Kendal and Wales. Scotland did not produce cloth for export on a very large scale, but its cheap products served not just customers of modest means at home, but also gained markets among the poorer sections of Flemish society. Peasants and wage earners who had previously bought minimal quantities of very cheap cloth were now able to afford more of a better quality. This tendency provoked the Scottish Sumptuary Law of 1447, which forbade husbandmen and labourers from wearing dyed cloths on working days; they should wear only grey and white (undyed) cloth. It was ignored, like all such regulations, to the benefit of clothmakers. Linen was produced in many parts of the country, and in quantity in Norfolk, but we can only guess how much. In order to keep households of all levels of society supplied with shirts, underwear, sheets, towels and tablecloths, imports of the cloth were recorded at 462,000 ells in 1390 and 420,000 ells in 1480–1. Only the trade of alien merchants is known. If estimates for the imports of natives are included, the total imports in these years could well have exceeded a million yards.

The increase in meat-eating ensured that butchers were an important group in the urban economy. Their supplies were maintained by the long-distance cattle trade from Wales and from northern England into the midlands and London, in which a number of Welsh and midland towns played a part. The higher consumption per head of ale and beer encouraged major changes in the urban brewing industry, with a concentration of the trade into fewer hands: this forced out of the trade some of the women who brewed occasionally for sale. At Oxford, for example, the numbers of those brewing and selling ale declined from over 250 in 1311 to about twenty-four in the early sixteenth century, but the total amount brewed probably increased. At the end of the fourteenth century, beer (which contained hops) was introduced from the Low Countries. The spread of this drink in eastern towns had far-reaching consequences, because the hops not only gave a distinctive flavour, but also acted as a preservative. Now, instead of brewing a few hundred gallons of ale which had to be sold and consumed within a few days, before it deteriorated, breweries could produce beer on a larger scale, store it, and carry it considerable distances. It could be used, for example, to provision ships. A domestic industry was being industrialized, with investment in more expensive equipment (the brewing vessels often cost in excess of £20) and larger quantities of raw materials. A rather similar change affected the herring fishery, again under Dutch influence. A new technique for gutting and preserving fish on board the boat made the whole operation more efficient, and gave the consumers a product with a superior flavour.

In the metal industries, the growth in demand for pewter table ware made the pewterers one of the leading London companies, with fifty-six masters, thirty-four journeymen and ten others working in the city in 1457. Among traders, the period saw the rise of haberdashery, which emerged as a specialized trade out of mercery; the specific role of haberdashers was the selling of small items such as hats, purses, pins and buckles, inessential but desirable accessories which a large number of consumers could afford. Some of these items were made by urban craftsmen who were developing techniques for turning out large numbers of buckles and other metal ornaments, not all of them well designed or finished, but cheap enough to enable labourers and lesser artisans to decorate their belts with showy fittings. Such goods were also imported in quantity. When William Mucklow, a clothier from Worcester, exported cloth in 1511 to the Low Countries, he brought back for sale in England hundreds of bells, spectacles, pins, girdles, silk ribbons, sheets of brown paper and pouches.

Demand from individual consumers stimulated industries in the countryside. Rural industries were well established in the early middle ages, so the novelty in the period after 1350 lay in the scale of the operations. In the extractive industries, such as mining for iron, coal, tin and lead, or stone quarrying, the presence of the minerals determined the siting of the industry, but other crafts could be located either in town or country, and the reasons for preferring a rural setting seem to have been the convenience of being near to raw materials and fuel, the presence of water, both for industrial processes and as a source of power, and the relative cheapness and flexibility of the labour force, many of whom were part-timers who also held land or worked in agriculture. The industries often developed in districts with a bias towards pastoral farming, which needed less labour than arable, and left workers with free time for industry. Labour costs were especially important, as they constituted one of the main expenses. In clothmaking, for example a 12-yard piece of cloth in 1391 which was sold for 24s cost 12s 5d in payments to a succession of artisans to do the spinning, weaving, fulling and dyeing, with materials accounting for much of the remainder. Consumers may have had more money to spend, but they still counted their pennies, and the success of an industry in competition with its rivals often depended on providing goods more cheaply. This encouraged the concentration of production, to turn out goods on a larger scale (we have already seen this happen in the urban brewing industry) or to gather producers in specialist centres.

Pottery manufacture was scattered in *c.*1300 over hundreds of mainly rural kilns. By the fifteenth century many of these had gone out of production, and instead potting was focused on a smaller number of centres with a larger output. In Oxfordshire, for example, lesser kiln sites like one at Ascott-in-Wychwood seem to have gone out of use, while the larger industry at Boarstall and Brill, which supplied Oxford as well as much of the north of the county, survived. But a large and enterprising pottery centre outside the county, in Surrey, came to supply an ever-increasing proportion of Oxfordshire consumers together with those through much of the south-east region. English potters competed with the accomplished products from the continent, such as German stoneware, and were successful in producing hard, well-glazed pots, which could be used as table ware instead of wood. There was less emphasis on local variety; kilns in different parts of the country produced similar types, such as 'Cistercian ware', which was light, thin-walled, and finished with a distinctive metallic glaze. (Plate 15)

Consumers demanded more iron, which peasants and artisans used for tools, implements, horseshoes and cart fittings, and in the house for knives, hinges and pothooks. Iron purchased by Durham Priory came mainly from Spain in the mid-fifteenth century, but from the 1480s the bulk was produced in local ironworks, especially in Weardale. Before the Black Death, iron was smelted in many small country bloomeries, which individually had a limited output – one at Tudeley in Kent in the early fourteenth century made between 2 and 3 tons of iron in a year. Water power was being applied to smelting at this time, but its use spread, for example in Yorkshire, where mills powered both hammers and bellows. The machinery and the pond and channels to control the water all required a heavy investment, but the works could produce much more iron, such as the operation at Byrkenott in Weardale (County Durham) which in 1408–9 yielded more than 18 tons of forged iron in less than a year. Mechanization of the most labour-intensive processes increased the output per worker. The next stage down the route to more efficient production came when English ironmasters followed the example of continental smelting processes, and introduced the blast furnace, which depended on a water mill to power the bellows. This made more metal, but also generated high enough temperatures for a new product – cast iron. The first blast furnace was operating in Sussex in 1496.

Capital was invested in clothmaking in a different way. Mechanization had arrived before 1200 in the form of fulling mills; these, as we have seen, spread through some of the clothing districts in the thirteenth century. Mills were built to serve the new needs of the industry in the fifteenth century, with a series, for example, in the stream valleys of Stroudwater in Gloucestershire. A total of 202 are known to have been built in Wales by 1547. Fulling, however, was only one process in making cloth, and some cloths, such as the worsteds made in Norfolk, were not fulled at all. Otherwise clothmaking used much the same equipment as in the thirteenth century, except that there was a spread in the use of the spinning wheel, which made yarn more quickly than the distaff method. The impact of new capital came through the organization of the industry by country clothiers. Entrepreneurs in the industry were not new – urban clothmakers before 1300 had used the putting-out system, by which the merchant or draper controlled the various stages, providing the raw material and selling the finished cloth, sometimes lending money to the artisans, or supplying the weavers with their looms, and therefore making them virtually his employees. Artisans in both town and country were often able to maintain their independence. Half of the weavers in York in 1456–7 owned their own looms, and in the cloth villages of Essex and Suffolk around 1400, most of the weavers made cloth on their own account. Some customers would pay a weaver, fuller and dyer separately for their work, rather than buying the cloth ready made.

In the fifteenth century the clothiers extended their control of sections of the industry. We have already noted the prosperity of John Greenway and John Lane in Devon, and the Spring family of Lavenham. Other figures include Thomas Horton of Bradford-on-Avon in Wiltshire, who owned four fulling mills and whose fine house was admired by visitors to the town. Thomas Paycocke's grand timber house still stands at Coggeshall in Essex, and in his will of 1518 he indicates the extent of his patronage over the local artisans when he asks for 12d to be given to each of his weavers, fullers, shearmen, combers, carders and spinners. No doubt the previously independent artisans lost money when they fell under a clothier's control, but the industry as a whole expanded under their influence. They were able to achieve the 'vertical integration' of which modern economists speak by acquiring sheep pastures, flocks of sheep, fulling mills, looms, dyeing establishments and warehouses, and by dealing in wool, dyestuffs, alum and oil, as well as the cloth, and therefore controlling the flow of materials and products through the various processes, and profiting from every stage. They came near to introducing a small-scale factory system when they built next to their dwellings spinning houses and dyehouses, and employed directly some craftsmen, such as shearmen who trimmed the nap from cloth. They had contacts with London merchants and knowledge of customers' requirements which individual weavers would acquire with difficulty. Their wide horizons enabled them to spot the best markets for buying wool cheaply and selling the cloth for a good price. For example, the Wiltshire clothiers at the end of the fifteenth century found that there was a demand in Flanders for 'white' cloth, which was taken to London to be carried across the Channel, where the Flemish drapers could have it dyed to their own requirements and then exported to Italy.

Coal mining also attracted entrepreneurs, such as the Newcastle merchants who profited from the coal trade of the north-east, with a good deal of investment from landlords such as the bishops of Durham. In the thirteenth century most coal had been dug in small bell pits, in which two men would work, often as part-timers. As demand increased, from domestic consumers but mainly from those in other industries, such as lime burners, brewers, brickmakers and blacksmiths, the scale of production rose. At Coleorton in Leicestershire, miners were working underground using the 'pillar and stall' technique by the late fifteenth century, and elsewhere deep mines needed expensive drainage adits. A horse-powered pump was removing water from a mine at Finchale in County Durham in 1486–7. The labour force of the larger collieries consisted of a dozen men. The scale of operations rose to the extent that Railey in County Durham was producing annually 8,000 tons in the mid-fifteenth century, and Wollaton in Nottinghamshire yielded 9,000 tons in one year in the 1520s. In 1508–11 Newcastle was sending out annually 40,000 tons, much of it to London. Workers at Whickham in

Northumberland and Railey in Durham were achieving productivity comparable with that of the early nineteenth century, with a hewer (underground worker) producing each day between 1.2 and 2 tons.

iv. *Old and new*

We have discussed the influence on the medieval economy of unregulated trade, consumer demand, entrepreneurs' responsiveness to markets, capital investment, mechanization, specialization of production, increased scale of production and productivity of labour. Does this mean that commercial and industrial activity had by about 1520 gone through a transition to capitalist methods of production, and had medieval people adopted a modern economic outlook? Significant change had occurred, but in many ways the traditional economic system still had a powerful influence. The great merchants were not as willing to innovate as the country clothiers or the enterprising artisans who changed the brewing or iron industries. Export of wool and cloth lay in the hands of powerful associations of merchants who were concerned to secure markets and maintain a profitable routine, by which wool was carried to the staple port of Calais, and a high proportion of cloth exports were sold by the Merchant Adventurers in the Low Countries, and increasingly at Antwerp. Their business partnerships continued the type of *commenda* arrangements developed over the previous two centuries (see pp. 215–16), though we can see larger groupings of merchants resembling later joint stock companies launching genuinely adventurous trading initiatives, like the Hull and Lynn merchants who pioneered a new trade with Iceland in the fifteenth century. It was from another port in contact with Iceland, and also with Ireland, Bristol, that an expedition set out in 1480 to explore the west Atlantic, and Cabot made his voyage to Newfoundland in 1497. English merchants visited a wider range of ports than they had in c.1300, for example in trading regularly with Spanish ports, but they did not penetrate far into long-distance markets, such as in the Mediterranean. Even in 1500 about 40 per cent of English overseas trade was in the hands of continental traders.

Raising money for capital may in the long run have become a little easier, as interest rates in the fifteenth or sixteenth centuries, at about 5 to 7 per cent, seem to have been rather lower than the 10 per cent prevailing in the thirteenth century. Merchants' credit arrangements still consisted mainly of allowing buyers to pay late, so that everyone involved in business was bound into an endless chain of informal debt. Not uncommonly, when a merchant died, the bulk of his assets consisted of unpaid debts, and his estate was heavily encumbered with commitments to others. Formal recognizances, used as a legal assurance that debts would be paid, which had developed in the thirteenth century, declined in number, perhaps reflecting the recession after 1400. There was a growing use of the bill, by which a simple promise was made to pay, and this could change hands, so that a purchase of goods could be made on the basis of an earlier obligation to pay. The debt could therefore be assigned from one merchant to another, without cash changing hands. The merchants of the Calais staple would receive for their wool letters of payment, by which a continental merchant would give them written authority to receive the money from a third party, often in London. Again, the document could be used in further transactions, and in this respect resembled paper money. English merchants in general depended on verbal agreement and mutual trust to make their bargains. Their account books, of which very few survive, consist of memoranda of transactions with notes of money paid, which were primitive instruments compared with the more precise methods of the Italians.

The ships in which goods were carried abroad underwent major structural changes after about 1410. Until then, ships were propelled by a square sail attached to a yard on the single mast. The hulls were clinker built, from overlapping planks, in the same technique as that used by the Vikings. During the fifteenth century, Mediterranean carracks and caravels were imitated in English shipyards, and vessels were given two or three masts, with a lateen sail on the mizzen (rear) mast; the hull was 'skeleton built', with planks fitted on to a framework, edge to edge in the carvel method. The new techniques allowed the ships to make more efficient use of the wind, and the hulls were rather cheaper to build, requiring less skilled labour and smaller quantities of timber, while gaining in strength. All of these features were being employed by English shipwrights in the 1460s, and the vessels which made the first recorded Atlantic crossing in 1492 used essentially the same design. (Plate 17)

Much else in 1520 maintained the traditional medieval economy. The small artisan workshop and the unspecialized town still predominated. But we cannot dismiss as resistant to change a period which saw the invention, introduction or much wider dissemination of brick buildings, paper mills, drinking glasses, guns, gunpowder, the printing press (innovations that space has not allowed us fully to discuss) as well as blast furnaces, deep mining, beer brewing and carvel-built, three-masted lateen rigged ships.

New attitudes to the economy are demonstrated by public efforts to control disruptive and idle behaviour, and by discriminatory policies adopted towards the poor. This early puritanism applied to personal as well as public life, with more emphasis on privacy in the home and a new value placed on thrift. A work ethic was widely influential: idleness met with disapproval. Ordered working lives began with training and experience in youth, and led to retirement for those with even small amounts of property. Wage earners did not all choose to work fewer days when their pay increased, but maximized their earnings in order to buy better food and desirable goods. Household incomes were increased by the ability of men, women and children to contribute, often undertaking a number of activities during the year. Employment contracts based on lump sums for the completion of a task, such as 20s for the carpentry of a building, encouraged hard and purposeful work. When apparently low rates of productivity are recorded, such as the Hull tiler in the late fifteenth century who laid 300 tiles in a day, compared with 1,000 for a modern roofer, this may reflect the conditions of work and the range of tasks expected of the medieval worker, such as fixing laths as well as tiles, rather than his lack of commitment to the job. Those working on the land also changed their way of life and economic outlook.

CHAPTER TEN

The countryside, c.1350–c.1520

The prejudice that new ideas come from towns, and that country people are slow and conservative, was held to be true in the middle ages, as it is now. The superiority of the towns does not survive close examination. The rulers of large towns clung to old values and attempted to preserve their prosperity by preventing change, while the country and small town clothiers contributed a new energy and expertise to industrial production. Here we turn to the the rural economy, to see how those who made their living from agriculture stood up to the tests of the long-term changes after the Black Death.

i. Landlords

After 1348–50, the higher aristocracy had to make hard decisions about the management of their lands in altered circumstances. We have seen that they hoped that the fall in population, with all of its damaging implications for wages, agricultural profits and rents, would be a temporary problem, and they believed that they could hold back the economic tide until normal times returned. This was not a stupid response. They had experienced setbacks before. They were given hope by the high grain prices for more than twenty years after the Black Death, and the rise in wages that was less rapid than expected. By the late 1350s, holdings were tenanted and peasants were still paying substantial rents and dues. The 'seigneurial reaction', helped by circumstances, worked, and over the generation after the first plague epidemic the revenues of some estates fell by as little as 10 per cent. In some places, such as the Welsh marches, they even increased.

The estate managers in the late fourteenth and early fifteenth centuries continued to make decisions about which crops to grow and how much land to cultivate, just as their predecessors had done. More barley was grown on demesnes, often instead of oats, because of the rising demand for ale, which drinkers preferred to be brewed from barley malt. Many manors also expanded their acreage of beans, peas and vetch, in order to feed these crops to animals, which were being kept in greater numbers. The managers responded to the labour problem by reducing the scale of arable cultivation, so the gradual shrinkage of arable demesnes which had begun before 1348 continued. On a Devon manor belonging to Tavistock Abbey at Werrington, for example, 128 acres had been cultivated in 1298, but this fell to 80 acres by 1350 and 50 acres by 1420. Some of the land that was no longer cultivated by the lord was rented to tenants, but some was used as pasture for the manor's livestock, because lords appreciated that greater profits came from animal husbandry. This was not a response to rising prices; although animals such as oxen fetched more money after 1360 than they had in the 1330s and 1340s, wool slipped down after 1380. The great advantage lay in the relatively small number of workers who could look after flocks of sheep and herds of cattle, compared with the many hands needed to cultivate cereals, and above all to harvest them.

The large estates had to make choices about the use of the crops that they produced. Selling as much as possible could be the right decision if the manor lay a long way from the household, or if the lord did not find it convenient to visit a manor in order to consume its produce. Manors near large towns, where prices would be high and transport costs low, would also sell their grain. Lords were quite ready, even if in earlier times they had become accustomed to buying grain, to provision their households directly from their demesnes. This decision was made by a small and quite remote monastery, Owston Abbey in Leicestershire, which in 1386 was entirely self-sufficient in grain, and also by a large metropolitan establishment like Westminster Abbey.

The magnates had to decide how much of the income from their estates they were prepared to put back into agriculture by paying for new buildings, or fencing, or other productive investments. Routine repairs cost more because of rising wages, but in addition estates which contemplated leasing out their demesnes judged it prudent to offer to the lessee buildings in good repair, in order to obtain the highest possible rent.

Manors derived more income from tenants than from their demesnes, and those assets had to be managed as well. At their most extreme, lords were seeking to keep intact servile obligations, to keep rents as high as possible, and to push up court revenues. They attempted to prevent the migration of serfs, and to compel those left behind to repair their buildings. However, the more realistic estates had to compromise by reducing rents and entry fines, and converting tenancies from customary tenure to leasehold. The demand for land did not usually collapse, so that the influence of the market as well as coercive pressure helped to prevent rents falling immediately and disastrously.

As the years passed, the old conditions showed no signs of returning. The good harvests after 1375 reduced the price of grain and therefore the profit of cultivation. Wages rose in the 1370s and 1380s. Tenants showed by their concerted efforts in 1381, and their truculence as individuals throughout the period, that there were limits to the lords' options in bullying their subordinates to stay put and pay the old rents and dues. The officials of the earl of Warwick decided in about 1400 that labour services on one manor should be commuted into cash rents, 'until the world is restored', which they must have realized was becoming a faint hope. Lords in growing numbers decided to lease sections of arable demesnes, or whole demesnes on individual manors through the fourteenth century, but the movement became an overwhelming tide between about 1380 and 1410. A businesslike monk of Canterbury Cathedral Priory, Thomas Chillenden, taking over as prior from the otherworldly John Vinch, acted decisively and leased all of the monastery's demesnes in 1391–6. A more typical caution was shown by their neighbours, the archbishops of Canterbury, who leased eighteen of their thirty demesnes between 1381 and 1396, more of them in the next few years, and were left with six still under direct management in 1422. The great lords were putting their demesnes into the hands of lessees or farmers, in return for a fixed cash rent.

The end of direct management of agriculture by the great estates represented a sharp break with a long tradition. The decision to lease was made after detailed calculations by the estate's receiver and auditors. These financial experts working for the bishop of Worcester decided in 1393–4 that the profit on cultivating the arable on the manor of Bibury in Gloucestershire amounted to 11s 4½d on a cash outlay of £6. The amount of profit was not the only consideration, as the managers also weighed up the advantages of a guaranteed regular annual income from a farmer against the unstable returns from direct management. The demesne was farmed out two years later. The change on this manor and thousands of others was much more than just a financial technicality, because it was often accompanied by the final conversion of all labour services to money. The two parts of the manor, demesne and tenant land, which had been held together by the bond of labour service for centuries, were being separated. Occasionally the farmer took on the whole manor, tenant holdings as well as demesne, but usually the demesne alone was rented out, and the lord continued to collect tenants' rents and hold the manor court. Nonetheless the link between lord and peasants was weakened by the break, as the manor would receive less frequent visits from officials, and lords' residence might cease entirely if, as often happened, the manor house fell into disuse. A more remote and impersonal lordship contributed to the long-term decline in rent income.

The break with direct management occurred on many manors before 1410. Sometimes when the arable was leased, pastures were separated from the manor and kept under the control of the lord. This was another blow to an old tradition, which was based on mixed farming with a balance between different types of land. The duchy of Lancaster kept more than 1,000 sheep on its pastures detached from the manors of Aldbourne, Lambourne and Berwick on the Berkshire and Wiltshire downs in the 1430s. The flock was expensive to maintain because, while the old manorial system kept breeding ewes to replenish numbers, the duchy owned only wethers, mature wool-producing animals, and maintained their numbers by purchase. The profits on this operation were reduced by falling wool prices, and in 1443 and 1445 most of the sheep were sold and much of the pasture leased. Many estates gave up their sheep flocks in the middle of the fifteenth century. Some estates continued to manage some arable demesnes directly until the same time, and after that kept one as a home farm for supplying the household. Tavistock Abbey unusually kept four arable demesnes under its own management until 1497. There was less change in the northern counties of England and in Scotland at this time, because they had either not developed large arable demesnes, or they had leased them out before 1350.

The transition of the magnates' estates into organizations for collecting rents did not mean that they were relieved of the problems of management. Without constant vigilance, rents would diminish or even disappear. The great estates continued to recruit talented officials, some of them clergymen but mainly members of the gentry with a training in the common law. As in the days of direct management, receivers, auditors and stewards collected money from reeves and bailiffs, checked accounts, and held courts. The lord's council met to discuss such matters as legal disputes over land. Some lords were constantly in the royal courts, even bringing lawsuits against household and estate officials who owed money. A new official was the supervisor or surveyor, who was charged specifically with negotiating leases and new tenancies. The estates, challenged with the problems of collecting rents, required new types of document, and officials compiled valors, which attempted to show lords how much each manor was worth, together with lists of arrears to identify reluctant payers, general surveys to investigate lost revenues, registers of extracts from court rolls which contained useful precedents, and books of leases to ensure that tenants' obligations were remembered. The documents had a defensive tone, as they focused on preventing losses. Estate management was not just a question of poring over the archives to catch tenants evading rents, nor were the offices of the great estates staffed entirely by grey bureaucrats and lawyers. One of the most engaging characters and original minds of the period was William Worcester (1415–85), who served Sir John Fastolf, the self-made Norfolk knight, as secretary and surveyor. Worcester had been educated at Oxford, which would normally have led to a career in the church, but he remained a layman, and has been described as a gentleman-bureaucrat. He kept a notebook designed to help his master profit from his manor of Castle Combe in Wiltshire, which had become one of the most prosperous centres of clothmaking in England. Worcester anticipated the gentry antiquarians of later centuries in his interest in topography, architecture and local history, and his notes on Castle Combe, in which he analysed revenues over the previous hundred years, bear some resemblance to economic history.

Worcester and his contemporaries devised the most advantageous method of leasing the demesnes. Should they be rented out as single entities, often 200–400 acres at a time, or would there be more money for the lord in breaking the land into parcels? Would the demesne yield a higher rent if livestock and equipment were included in the lease in addition to land and buildings? The officials had to search out farmers, individuals or groups, who would take on the lease and stay the course as reliable tenants. The exact terms of the lease had to be negotiated: the rent, the length of time (usually in years), and detailed conditions such as the responsibility for building repair. Sometimes a lord, concerned that a farmer might neglect the land, would insist that it be returned in good condition, with a minimum area manured and under the plough, for example. The rent would usually be in cash, but some lords might ask for part to be paid in kind, and monasteries such as Coventry Priory required the farmer to send specified quantities of grain, animals, cheese and so on to feed the monks through the year.

Once the indenture recording the agreement had been written, and the farmer installed, the negotiations did not stop. The officials would have to cajole the tenant to pay his rent in full and on time. The tenant in the early phases of leasing would have taken the land for a term of between seven and twelve years, but later in the century this increased to twenty or forty years. He would complain that a rent agreed in 1430, for example, did not take into account declining prices in the 1440s, and would argue for a reduction. Farmers would drive a hard bargain by paying only part of their rent, like Nicholas Poyntz, an assertive member of the gentry who leased the unprofitable demesne at Bibury already mentioned. In the 1430s and 1440s Poyntz successfully pushed his lord, in some years by paying nothing at all, into reducing the rent from £6 16s to £4 16s, and then he paid £4 per annum as if he regarded that to be the just rent.

Most leases required the tenant to repair buildings, though the lord would agree to help with timber or stone. In practice the tenants would complain that they could not afford repairs, and persuaded the lord to take over the work. Lords found it difficult to refuse as they would not be able find a tenant in the future for a demesne with its barns, byres and sheepcotes in ruins. On the estate of Canterbury Cathedral in the middle of the fifteenth century between 7 and 16 per cent of income each year was spent on building repairs, which was a greater level of investment than in the era of Henry of Eastry, the improving landlord of the thirteenth century. Many leases forbade the subletting of the land, but this often occurred, and the lords turned a blind eye, even recording in their accounts that the leasehold rent had been paid by the occupier, who was not the officially recognized tenant. Farmers who were doing well out of a lease (which they did not admit readily) might ask for the term to be extended, or ask at the end of their term for their son to be given the renewed lease.

Other manorial tenants also needed close attention. They often failed to pay their rents, and persuasion had to be used to get them to take a vacant holding. Some entire communities confronted the lord's officials, as when Thomas Huggeford and Nicholas Rody, officials of the earls of Warwick, were told by the tenants of Lighthorne in Warwickshire in 1437 that if they did not reduce the rent the tenants would leave the manor. Huggeford and Rody knew that a ring of nearby villages were in a state of near collapse, and had no desire to see Lighthorne follow the same route, so they brought down the annual rent of 15s 6d owed by each yardland holding to 10s 6d. Most of the bargaining was conducted with individuals, and concerned the terms of tenure as well as rents and dues. Sometimes tenants continued to hold their land by the former unfree or customary tenure, but with no (or very few) labour services, and the cash rent was supposed to incorporate defunct dues such as tallage. Such tenants were liable to pay an entry fine, but this was commonly negotiated down to a few shillings or even a token payment during the fifteenth century as the demand for land slackened. Heriots on death or surrender often survived in their original form of the best animal, but many lords had to accept a cash payment, or a merging of the heriot with the entry fine of the next tenant. Holdings were commonly converted into leaseholds, by which the tenant would be granted the land for a term of between five and twelve years, for a simple cash rent with no other obligations. The short term protected lord and tenant from committing themselves in unpredictable times. Some tenants held their land 'at the will of the lord' or from year to year without any formal, written agreement. Such tenures were common in Scotland, and were used in England to enable the lord to gain an income from land which otherwise would lie vacant. In the north of England 'tenant right' developed around 1500, in which holdings could be inherited, and sold, without the lord's permission. Rents were fixed, but fines were paid when a tenant died, and also on the death of the lord. Military service against the Scots was an important tenant duty.

All of this suggests that the lords had little bargaining power, but tenants did not dictate their terms. English and Welsh customary tenants were supervised by the lords' courts, and pressure could be brought to bear on them to repair buildings, and to observe the rules of the tenancy, such as not felling the trees that grew in the hedges of their tenements. The courts kept alive the memory that some families were of servile status, and the dwindling numbers of serfs were ordered to return if they left the manor without permission, or were required to pay their marriage fines. Stewards were tempted to evict tenants who broke the rules, but did so only in exceptional cases because tenants were usually in short supply. The courts still performed useful functions for the lord, for example in overseeing the transfer of holdings and recording the names of new tenants. They were still respected by tenants, who made by-laws to regulate the fields, but they made less use of the courts than in earlier centuries for recovering debts or for suing their neighbours for trespass or the return of borrowed goods.

On well-run estates, lords kept some control over tenants by making rentals (lists of tenants and rents) at regular intervals, knowing that if enquiries were not made into tenants and holdings, land might be lost and rents would lapse. Arrears of rent payment were a constant anxiety, arising from tenants who paid rents slowly, or who refused to pay selected charges at all. These could build up to very high levels, notably in the Welsh marcher lordships, where a restless peasantry asserted their independence after the Glyn Dŵr revolt. On the Brecon lordship, for example, which produced an annual revenue of about £1,000, a total of £2,453 had accumulated in arrears by 1454. In the marches arrears were an intractable dilemma, but elsewhere officials could contain the problem by cancelling rents and making concessions when necessary, while persuading and pressuring tenants to pay up when that could be achieved. Estates could make a constructive contribution to keeping tenants and cajoling them to pay their rents by helping them with the repair of buildings. They might achieve this end by letting them off their rents, or by providing materials, or in exceptional circumstances by building houses and barns themselves. Help came at modest cost to the lord on the estates of the earls of Northumberland in 1471–2, when at Great Houghton six tenants were given help with pairs of crucks, at a cost to the lord of 18d for each pair. Robert Eldere, for example, received 6s for four pairs, sufficient for rebuilding a whole house or barn. At the other extreme, the duchy of Lancaster at Brassington in Derbyshire in 1441 spent almost £7 on a complete rebuilding of a house and barn with stone walls, a timber superstructure and thatched roofs.

During the first half of the fifteenth century lords found that their lands declined in value. The manors of Canterbury Cathedral Priory produced £2,202 annually in 1419–20, after which the figure fell to £1,907 in 1454 and reached a low point in 1469 of £1,757. Reductions, in the region of 20 per cent, were normal in southern and midland England. In Cornwall, with its favourable economic conditions influenced by tin mining and other industries, the lords lost less ground: the rents for the assessionable tenants of the duchy of Cornwall (see p. 242) had stood at about £600 in the 1360s and slipped down to £500 between 1459 and 1484. The worst effects of the decline in revenues were felt in the northeast of England, which suffered severely in the bad harvests of the 1430s, and where revenues fell by a third. In Scotland lords were able to push up cash rents to compensate for the falling value of the debased currency: in the lordship of Strathearn rents rose by 40 per cent in money between 1380 and 1445, but this represents a decline in real terms. Some lords in effect went bankrupt. A number of monasteries fell into debt so seriously that administrators had to be sent in to make savings on household expenses and to install an efficient estate management. Smaller religious houses were merged with more prosperous establishments and therefore effectively closed down. The dukes of Buckingham had more acute financial difficulties than most landed magnates, and were often unable to pay their bills promptly. The third duke became reckless, and when in 1520 his debts exceeded £10,000 (two years' annual income) he was forced to sell some of his many manors.

Most lords accepted the realities of fixed or diminishing resources, and reduced their commitments. They scaled down the size of their households, introduced budgets to check on expenditure, such as the recommendation at Bury St Edmunds Abbey that each monk could be fed on 2s 6d per week. Lords audited their household accounts in person, signing their names at the end of each page. They made cuts in hospitality, and reduced the number of their houses. Earls and bishops, who before the first plague had maintained and visited twenty or more houses and castles, now focused their expenditure on three or four residences, which they could build and furnish to a higher standard. Houses like Thornbury Castle and Dartington Hall were more opulent and comfortable than the dark and draughty castles of the thirteenth century.

After a long period of retreat, the estate managers took opportunities when they reappeared after about 1470. Most lords increased their revenues in the period 1470–1520, though hesitantly, and with setbacks. Canterbury Cathedral Priory's manorial income reached its low point in 1469 and recovered to £2,056 in the early sixteenth century, which was still a little below its revenues in 1420. When officials negotiated with would-be farmers in that period they found that they could push the rent up a little, or charge a fine for entry. The customary rents paid by manorial tenants were fixed, but entry fines equivalent to two years' rent and more could be levied on manors in prospering localities, especially after 1500. Arrears dwindled as tenants paid more promptly. Direct management of agriculture experienced a revival, with more lords in the north of England and Scotland keeping livestock. Lawrence Booth, bishop of Durham, grazed 1,000 cattle and 1,000 sheep in the 1470s. James IV of Scotland (1488–1513) was pasturing large flocks of sheep, for example 6,300 in Ettrick Forest.

The reason for this modest revival in the fortunes of the great estates, which coincides with a growth in trade and industry, cannot be easily explained, as the level of population remained low and prices did not begin to rise generally until about 1517. One factor seems to have been the recovery in livestock prices. A more assertive, even more predatory style of profit-seeking entered into the mentality of the officials of the great estates at this time. We find the duke of Buckingham's men seeking out serfs who, having left the manor illicitly, had made their fortune and could be blackmailed into buying their manumission for huge sums. The royal estate (including the duchy of Lancaster) was run more efficiently, with surveyors appointed who had instructions to gain the maximum return from leases. Pastures in the Peak District of north Derbyshire were rented out in the late 1490s for sums 25 or 30 per cent higher than those which had prevailed for the previous forty years.

Lords faced with low estate incomes for much of the fifteenth century developed alternative economic strategies. Some acquired more land. This was not so easy for the great church estates, which acquired few new manors, but the monasteries steadily expanded their assets by appropriating parish churches, which allowed the monks to profit from the tithes and glebes. Each church that they took over would add an average of £10 per annum to the monastery's income, though occasionally they picked a plum worth £50. These acquisitions had to be justified, and the monasteries could spin plausible stories of plague and agricultural problems. The losers were the rectors, who when they enjoyed the income of their parishes could live like landed gentry; after appropriation they were replaced by less affluent vicars. New ecclesiastical estates were created by the fashion for founding collegiate churches, not just in Oxford or Cambridge (where Magdalen College and King's College were especially opulent examples), but also at such establishments as Eton in Berkshire and Bothwell in Lanarkshire. Much of the land for these new foundations in England came from the assets of the small monasteries and cells attached to French religious houses, which were confiscated during the Hundred Years War. These tendencies do not mean that among churchmen the units of landholding were generally increasing in size. Large numbers of chantries were being founded, sometimes attached to fraternities or small colleges. In these, one or two priests who said masses for the souls of the dead were endowed with rents often worth £10 or £20 per annum.

Lay families could plan to expand their landed resources by arranging marriage alliances, or attracting political patronage. Some successful families brought together the landed assets of a number of aristocratic estates, notably in Scotland in the late fourteenth century, when the Douglas family had accumulated three lordships and twenty-four baronies, and the Stewarts held no fewer than twelve earldoms. In England during the fifteenth century some of the great accumulators of land included the dukes of York and the earls (later dukes) of Warwick. New legal techniques were devised, above all enfeoffment to use, which enabled the aristocracy to escape from the right of overlords, including the crown, to take over an inheritance and profit from it if the heir was young or female. Aristocrats were also able to decide the descent of property and avoid the restrictions of the normal rules of succession. They could use this to keep an estate intact, for example to avoid the division of the lands among daughters when there was no son to succeed. In fifteenth-century Scotland the magnate families show a remarkable ability to continue through successive generations, which helped them to hang on to their wealth.

In England a number of tendencies prevented the aristocracy from maintaining their fortunes in the long term. Some fathers took advantage of their control of the inheritance to look after younger sons and daughters by dividing the lands. In addition, because families were so frequently dying out in the direct male line, the ranks of the aristocracy were constantly being renewed by new blood as lawyers, merchants and wealthy peasants acquired a sufficient quantity of land. So although individual families may have gained land and increased their incomes against the prevailing trend, the aristocracy as a whole did not close ranks and share the resources among fewer families.

The aristocracy believed that they could add to their incomes by participating in war and thereby gain pay, ransoms and booty. The English hoped to find especially rich pickings from campaigns in France. As well as the usual profits from plunder and prisoners, lands and offices were available to English soldiers in Normandy after Henry V took over that province in 1415. There were famous examples to prove that profit was possible, notably Sir John Fastolf who from modest beginnings rose to become a war captain in the 1420s and 1430s, and sent enough money back to England to buy lands worth £1,000 per annum. Sir Hugh Luttrell rebuilt Dunster Castle in Somerset on the basis of his service in France under Henry V. Others were not so fortunate, and incurred expenses that exceeded their profits, such as having to pay ransoms to the French. The whole enterprise ended in the 1450s, when the French expelled the English. The Scottish aristocracy suffered from similar delusions. They did gain plunder, ransoms and protection money in their raids into northern England in the late fourteenth century, but after 1400 the English were better organized. The Scots became the victim of incursions, and the obsessive but incompetent warrior, the fourth earl of Douglas, who was active between 1398 and 1424, found himself paying a ransom.

Longer-term profits could be gained by service both in peace and war through 'bastard feudalism', by which sums of money were paid by the crown, for example in Scotland in 1389–1406, to such figures as the duke of Albany, and in turn by magnates to their retainers. These financial payments among the aristocracy in both England and Scotland were not new, though they may have increased in number, for example in times of civil war.

ii. *Gentry*

The landed incomes of the higher aristocracy show adjustment to change rather than many new initiatives. The landed gentry have more of a reputation for enterprise. The lower ranks of the English aristocracy were given a new precision in this period when they were identified in legal records after the Statute of Additions in 1413 as knights, esquires and gentlemen. Contemporaries could recognize them by their houses, their numbers of servants, their style of life and their participation in govern-

ment, especially at the local level. But their defining feature was possession of a landed income, which in the case of gentlemen attained at least
£10, with a minimum of £20 for an esquire and £40 for a knight. This
meant that they often held only one or two manors, though rich knights
could have estates with a dozen.

The gentry encountered the same problems as the magnates. They
leased out their demesnes in the search for a steady income, and their
rents from lessees and peasant tenants tended to fall in the first half of
the fifteenth century. They took similar counter-measures, by compiling
rentals and if necessary putting money into peasant buildings. John
Catesby esquire, of Ashby St Ledgers in Northamptonshire, in 1385 and
1386 reviewed the 'state' of his five manors, which were valued at £123
per annum. He found much to worry him. One arable demesne was
calculated to make no profit at all, ten peasant holdings on one manor
lay 'in the lord's hands', rents were in decay or in arrears, and the cost
of reconstructing peasant buildings was calculated at £18. Manors presented the same problems, regardless of the type of lord.

The gentry served the magnates as administrators, so they were
bringing their experience as landlords on a small scale to their work as
stewards and supervisors, and no doubt returning to their own lands
with ideas gleaned from the larger estates. More of their income came
from non-landed sources. They fought in some numbers in the armies in
France, and they were the chief beneficiaries of the payment of fees and
annuities (commonly worth £5 or £10 per annum) by the magnates –
often as a reward for estate management, but also for more general
political and legal work. Above all, they manned the legal profession,
which gave a useful income to many, and allowed some stars to amass
large landed estates. Rich lawyers, like Thomas Kebell who died in 1500
with many manors in Leicestershire, became effective and innovative
estate managers.

As in the case of the higher aristocracy, individual families
united inheritances by making advantageous marriage alliances. Gentry
families in Anglesey, for example, through a combination of skilfully
negotiated marriages, office-holding and the land market, making full
use of the pridd (see p. 177), put together large accumulations of property, like the Plas Newydd estate which was built up by the Griffith family
between about 1442 and 1479. As a whole, however, the gentry did not
concentrate land into the hands of a few families; their numbers
increased in some counties by the early sixteenth century. Small institutions with similar incomes to the gentry reduced their expenditure: in the
mid-fifteenth-century depression the fellows of Exeter College, Oxford,
in view of their declining rents had to discontinue the practice of paying

themselves a bonus at Christmas, Easter and Whitsun. Economies were more difficult for lay families with a handful of servants and very restricted consumption of luxury goods. If they made any more cuts in spending they would lose their aristocratic status.

The manors of lesser lords, as in earlier periods, tended to have a high proportion of land in demesnes, and they obtained a modest income from tenant rents. Those with only a few hundred acres used much of their produce in their households, which left them with limited quantities for sale. Their great advantage over the bureaucratic estates of the magnates lay in the small scale of their operations, often adjacent to or very near to their residence, which enabled these lords to supervise agriculture and rent collection personally. Sometimes they put reeves and bailiffs in charge of manors, in which case formal accounts were submitted and audited, as on a large estate. This was especially likely for a gentry estate with a number of manors, like Catesby's. But some gentry jotted down few financial details, or compiled rough and incomplete accounts, and those with very small amounts of land did everything by word of mouth.

They clearly took a close personal interest in their lands. Gentry audited accounts, authorized payments, and attended the sheep-shearing. Sir Roger Townshend, a very rich Norfolk knight, in his account book of 1480 recorded the smallest detail, recommending that old hurdles should be sent to the household to be used as firewood, or warning shepherds to look out for dangerous dogs. When members of the gentry made their wills they revealed intimate knowledge of their livestock by bequeathing a specific animal, such as 'the black ox' or the horse with a white star. Another wealthy Norfolk family, the Pastons, kept their own sheep but lived mainly from rents. Their letters show that they observed carefully the selection of tenants, and sometimes held their own manorial courts. They received some of their rents in kind, which made them fully aware of the market for barley. John Pennington, a Lancashire knight, records in his books of accounts and memoranda written between 1486 and 1512 that he personally took the money from lessees who paid their entry fines in instalments. If gentry were active in government and service of great lords, or spent much time in the law courts or on military campaigns, their wives managed their lands. Relatives were drawn into administration, presumably because they could be trusted, and the lord's brother acted as rent collector or bailiff. The first treatise on agricultural methods to be written after the era of *Walter of Henley*, which was published in 1523, was, needless to say, not written by a manager who worked for a great estate, but by an esquire, addressing himself to a readership of gentry. John Fitzherbert, from Derbyshire, in his 'Book of Husbandry' assumed that his readers were in charge of their own manors and would profit from advice about types of plough and the best techniques for sowing corn and weeding.

Many gentry, probably a majority, depended mainly on the rents from their demesnes held by farmers and, if they were actively involved in agricultural production, concentrated on a home farm mainly for domestic consumption. They could obtain grain for the household by receiving rents in kind from their tenants, or by themselves acting as farmers for parish tithes. A significant section of them produced on a large scale for the market. They took on the demesnes of other lords as farmers, sometimes with the intention of subletting, but often they ran the demesnes as profitable enterprises. To help in this they selected their acquisitions carefully, for example leasing a piece of land next to one of their manors so as to make a larger unit of production. Usually they focused on pasture, which gave the best returns for low labour costs. The Giffard family who lived in north Gloucestershire leased out the arable demesnes of their home manors of Weston Subedge and Norton Subedge, but in the late 1440s took on lease the nearby grange of Combe from a Cistercian monastery, on which they grazed 2,156 sheep and 55 cattle. At the end of the fifteenth century John Spencer, who began his career below the gentry, accumulated in eastern Warwickshire a string of lands held on lease, most of them demesnes or the sites of villages where the fields had been converted to pasture, and in 1506 became the lord of the manor of Althorp in Northamptonshire. Land held on lease did not carry the same status as the lordship of a manor. When gentry gathered such land they did so for profit, not to gain prestige.

The gentry who were most active in agriculture specialized in livestock. The Catesbys, who after their investigation of their unprofitable arable farming leased out their demesnes, kept one in hand at Radbourn in Warwickshire, converted it entirely to pasture (including the site of the village and the peasant holdings), and added lands leased from other lords to make an even larger block of grazing land. In 1448, when lords were generally at the trough of the mid-century depression, the pasture at Radbourn was stocked with 1,643 sheep and twenty cattle, and they kept a warren which yielded 202 rabbits in a year. The whole operation in 1449 was valued at £64, three times the value of the manor when it was a mixed farming demesne with tenant rents in 1386. Later, along with a number of other midland gentry, the Catesbys bought Welsh cattle that had been driven to markets such as Bromyard in Herefordshire, and fattened them for onward sale, often to end in the hands of London butchers, or to supply the garrison in Calais. The Townshend family of Norfolk must have been the greatest sheepmasters in the whole country at the end of the fifteenth century. Between 1475 and 1490 the first Roger Townshend expanded his flocks from 7,000 to 12,000, which provided a profit of at least £200, far in excess of his income from rents. Under his successor the number of sheep rose to 18,000 in 1516. The wool was sold locally for clothmaking, and to traders in King's Lynn. There was also much money to be made by selling animals to butchers at a time of high demand for meat. Gentry with large flocks economized on cash wages by rewarding their shepherds with the right to keep their own small flock on the pasture.

The gentry also saw the advantage of investment in a wide range of commercial and industrial enterprises. We have noted their presence in towns, where they held property and joined fraternities. This was partly for prestige, as they would be the guests of honour at feasts, and they acted as political and legal advisers, but they also valued towns as outlets for their produce. They invested in a wide range of industries, such as iron-working, tin extraction, tile and glass manufacture, and the quarrying of stone for building and millstones. In Derbyshire, not just the very wealthy Vernon family but also many lesser gentry made profits from the lead industry, and near Nottingham, at Wollaton, one of the largest coal mines in England was developed by the knightly Willoughby family. Members of the gentry also owned shares in ships and invested in trading ventures.

The gentry then were actively engaged in production, but they have also gained a reputation for taking decisive actions to change the world around them in order to make larger profits. They shifted the boundaries and the size and shape of the units in which property was held. Their most notorious actions relate to the removal of peasant tenants and the seizure of village territories to create enclosed pastures, which was recorded in some detail in the reports of the enclosure commissions in 1517. In one incident, on 11 August 1495, Thomas Pigott enclosed the fields of Doddershall in Buckinghamshire with fences and ditches. Twenty-four houses in the village were allowed to fall into ruin, and 120 people left 'tearfully'. These acts of depopulation affected villages of the corn-growing open-field farming districts, and was only possible when a lord had control of a whole village or at least a substantial part of it.

More commonly, the gentry bought up land from peasants, including the customary holdings which had formerly been held by servile tenures. Thomas Tropenell, a rising lawyer and estate official, acquired a dozen holdings in Corsham in north Wiltshire between the 1430s and 1470s. The piecemeal accumulation of holdings, which could merge a number of manors, or create new ones, was a feature of the countryside surrounding London. Avery Cornborough (who died in 1487), by origin a merchant, rose in royal service to become an esquire to Edward IV. He put together holdings in Havering atte Bower to the east of London, making a total of 1,200 acres, and expanded his demesne at the expense of the tenants he inherited with his purchases. The gentry caused particular disruption by taking over areas of grazing land from peasant communities. In Norfolk they bought not the land but the the fold-courses, that is the right to pasture sheep on village fields, to the ultimate damage of the peasantry. When they enclosed common pastures in other parts of the country they were liable to cause violent hostility. A good example is Ralph Wolseley, a south Staffordshire lord, who after political service acquired rights to a large area of woodland near the small town of Rugeley and enclosed it in about 1465, some of it for grazing and a rabbit warren, and partly to provide fuel for a glasshouse. His openness to innovations is suggested by his investment in a beer brewery (in a region where ale was the main drink) and in a dyeworks. His novelties provoked the local population to riot, mainly because the enclosure deprived them of common pasture, but also because the introduction of beer threatened the local ale brewers.

After a review of the activities of the Catesby, Giffard, Spencer, Town-shend, Vernon, Willoughby and Wolseley families, we might be tempted to identify the group as a whole as entrepreneurs, exhibiting all of the hallmarks of capitalists, in their specialization in profitable lines, large scale of production, investment, technical innovations such as enclosures, and refusal to be inhibited by tradition. There would be much truth in this view, but the characteristics of this group cannot be applied to the gentry as a whole, and their acquisitive ambitions are also found among larger landlords and peasants.

Many of the smaller gentry lacked the resources for long-term invest-ment and large-scale enterprises. Humphrey Newton of Newton in Cheshire, who recorded his affairs in a rather unsystematic notebook in 1498–1505, had a finger in many pies, but all on a small scale. He culti-vated less than 100 acres of arable, and bought extra supplies of grain to feed his household. He dealt in cattle and kept about fifty sheep. He repaired his corn mill and built a new fulling mill, which brought in a rent of 26s 8d per annum. He spent money on his ponds as a source of fish for the household rather than sale. Newton, like some of his grander contemporaries, went to market, at the local towns of Macclesfield and Congleton, and the fair at Chapel-en-le-Frith, and he was interested in improving his land, devoting a lot of attention to spreading marl. He showed ingenuity, boldness, a willingness to invest and an awareness of the market, but he cannot be accused of specialization, and his efforts were devoted to keeping afloat on small assets. At Newton he increased his income from £11 to £14. Many of the gentry, of course, relied on rents, and ran their estates without much enterprise or innovation. Nicholas Franceis, with fourteen properties spead over Somerset and Devon, seems to have been content to draw £65 per annum from them in rents. The energies of many gentry were devoted to law and administration, which may well have brought them better rewards than risky investments in production.

Profit-making ventures were not confined to the gentry. Monasteries like Durham Priory kept large flocks and herds throughout this period, and the bishop of Durham invested in coal mines. Many other lords profited from tileworks and fulling mills on their estates. If the gentry were enterprising, it was often through their alliances with non-aristocratic entrepreneurs, and it is to them that we must turn next.

iii. *Farmers*

Farmers – that is the tenants of leased demesnes or granges, so called because they paid a fixed annual rent or farm – appear as a powerful new force for change in the countryside around 1400. As the lords shed their demesnes, they were handing over to the farmers the management of agricultural production of perhaps a fifth or a quarter of the agricultural land in Britain. This was not such a sudden break as first appears, because assets had been leased for centuries before. But it is the scale of the change, in a few decades, which gives it an almost revolutionary quality. Leasing of demesnes put new people in control of landed resources, established new relationships between lords and tenants, and the farmers brought new methods of production and management.

When leasing began we can sense the caution of the lords, as they often rented out their demesnes to the reeves who had already been running the manors under the system of direct management. A lord was not just choosing someone who could be trusted: the new farmer was often a customary tenant, and indeed might be a 'serf by blood', over whom the lord could hope to exercise control. To emphasize this dependency, the lease was sometimes written into the rolls of the manor court and resembled a customary tenancy; the farmer's conduct could be supervised through the court. To add to the lord's guarantee that a rash decision would not do permanent damage, the early leases were often for very short terms, even less than ten years. As the system developed, the farmers became more independent and escaped from such close supervision by the lord. However, in Kent, Warwickshire and Wiltshire, the majority of farmers continued to be recruited from the peasantry. Indeed, these figures understate the proportion of peasants actually working the leased land, as the gentry, clergy or merchants who made up the remainder of the farmers would sometimes sublet the land to peasants.

For peasants who took over the demesne in a group, becoming farmers allowed each of them to add substantially to an existing holding, perhaps to double its size. The Cistercian monastery of Coupar Angus in central Scotland leased Coupar grange in 1468 to Simon Anderson, John Olyver and eight others for five years, in return for a rent of corn, fuel and poultry. Perhaps the lessees, like the monastery, were interested in the crops they would gain for their own consumption. But many individual peasants took over a demesne of 200–400 acres for a cash rent, after their previous experience of cultivating a holding of 30–60 acres. For example, John Hickes of Durrington in Wiltshire leased a 200-acre demesne in 1401–14, having originally tenanted a single 30-acre yardland, though he later acquired three more. Many peasant farmers in the fifteenth century were recruited from outside the tenants of the manor, so they did not even bring to the task detailed knowledge of the fields and labour force. They had to adjust quickly to all of the problems of large-scale farming – raising capital, investing in equipment, buildings and livestock, hiring and managing many employees, and marketing great quantities of produce. Lords went to some trouble to identify suitable candidates to take over a farm, like William Smythe, recommended to the Pastons as 'the most able man to take a farm of land that I know in your lordship'. Most farmers stood up to the test, and stayed throughout their term.

Running a farm presented less of a challenge to the gentry, clerical or merchant lessees. We saw that the gentry might take on other lords' demesnes adjacent to their own manor in order to increase the efficiency as well as the scale of their operations. Sometimes they wished to acquire a type of land, usually extensive pasture, which was not available on their own manors. The proportion of demesnes acquired by 'gentlemen farmers' grew in the late fifteenth and sixteenth centuries, as the profits from agriculture increased. The merchants included woolmongers, clothiers, butchers and others with an obvious interest in using the produce in their businesses, but sometimes the lease was just one of their portfolio of investments.

Leases, which were contracts agreed between the parties, helped to change relationships between lords and tenants. More traditional concepts of lordship and clientage could not be banished overnight. The first farmers were sometimes serfs or customary tenants, and later farmers, like those on the Fountains Abbey estate in Yorkshire in the early sixteenth century, were expected to attend the abbot as his retainers. In essence, however, the indenture recorded a mutually advantageous

contract, and the striking feature is the lack of conditions and restrictions on tenants. They were expected to repair buildings and pay their
rent on time, but even elementary commitments were not kept. Most
farmers were not required to carry out any particular type of husbandry.
The leases after 1450 reflect the strong bargaining power of the tenants
in their length. In the south-east they often ran for fifteen to twenty years,
but in Yorkshire fifteen to forty years were commonly allowed, and in
the midlands they could stretch to sixty years and more. In Scotland,
where short leases were often granted, in the fifteenth century a growing
number were for the tenant's life. Hereditary succession was not
unknown. For example, at the bishop of Worcester's manor of Bishop's
Cleeve in Gloucestershire, Thomas Yardington held the farm from 1471
to 1525 and was succeeded by his son. It was clearly possible for the
possessors of such leases to regard the land as their own, and to do with
it virtually as they wished.

Farmers' adoption of new methods is apparent in the quantity and
layout of the land. When farmers took on leases they bargained for
acreages that they could manage. The least ambitious, like the Coupar
Angus peasants, just wanted a larger peasant holding. Those with
grander aspirations might still be daunted by very large demesnes, and
it was common for lessees of Cistercian granges which tended to run to
300–400 acres to have them divided into two. Similarly, if a demesne consisted of a number of scattered blocks as much as a mile apart, which
was not uncommon in woodland districts where the manor had developed by assarting and purchase in the twelfth and thirteenth centuries,
the lord found it easier to lease out each block separately; this led to the
building of new farmhouses out in the fields, a development normally
associated with the eighteenth century. Farmers often wished to specialize, which led to the break-up of old units, and the leasing of upland
pastures apart from the arable demesnes to which they had once been
attached. We have seen that lords began this process by keeping their
sheep pastures in hand when they first leased the arable demesnes.
The farmers could also create new combinations of land, with the
emphasis on specialization rather than the mixture of land types
favoured by the traditional estates. A good example of this new conception of an estate was John Spencer's group of leased lands on the
Warwickshire/Northamptonshire border, which consisted of extensive
pastures, often formed from the grassed-over fields of deserted villages.
The Nanfan family in Merionethshire also made a new estate out of the
leased granges of Cistercian monasteries.

Needless to say, many farmers converted arable to pasture to increase
their profits. Thomas Vicars of Strensall near York, who farmed two

demesnes, owned on his death in 1451 two ploughs, suggesting he had no more than 200 acres in cultivation, but was grazing 799 sheep, 198 cattle and 92 horses. He was evidently fattening cattle for the urban market, and breeding horses for sale. Wool merchants and clothiers could bring marketing expertise to their management of sheep pastures. Technical changes needed capital, particularly to build new structures such as sheepcotes for the increasing flocks, and enclosures in which to feed the animals. Lords commonly funded farmers' buildings in the difficult times in the mid-fifteenth century. It still happened in 1497–1507 on the bishop of Winchester's manor of Overton, where the lord spent £80 on a new house and barn for the farmer. In general the farmers were paying for their own improvements, and were able to raise loans on the basis of their profits.

The complaints of the local peasantry about the damaging changes made by farmers at this time show the degree to which they were transforming the agriculture of some demesnes by enclosure and changes in the use of land. The tenants at Quinton in Warwickshire, a manor of Magdalen College, Oxford, accused their successive farmers in 1480 and 1490 of depriving cottagers of acres of land which by informal custom they had been allowed to cultivate, of ploughing up common pasture, and generally making life difficult for tenants, who were leaving the manor and threatening the well-being of the peasant community. In this case the remote lord was persuaded to protect the peasants from the farmers. Sometimes a really radical change in the farm, involving the complete enclosure of the fields and the exclusion of the peasants, was accomplished by an alliance between lord and farmer. The Warwickshire manor of Burton Dassett was enclosed in 1497 as the result of co-operation between John Heritage, the farmer, and Edward Belknap, a young and acquisitive lord who expected to gain a higher rent as the farmer's profits increased.

iv. *Peasants*

An interpretation of the period has identified the key promoters of change as the gentry, who saw their opportunity to remove the unprofitable peasantry from their manors in order to create large and efficient units of agricultural production. We have already noted the enterprising character of gentry agriculture, their willingness to make radical changes in the landscape, and their alliance with farmers in pursuit of profits. One theory emphasizes the vulnerability of the English peasantry (in contrast with the security of tenure enjoyed by their French contemporaries), because the leaseholds or tenancies at will by which many of them held their land were easily terminated. Lords still retained arbitrary powers over the copyholders, who were the descendants of the villeins of the thirteenth and fourteenth centuries and who could display a written copy of the entry in the lord's court as evidence of their title. Lords sometimes charged such tenants very high entry fines, which could drive even those with rights of inheritance from their holdings. The gentry were not as enterprising as this view presumes: many lived on rents, and the activists were too scattered to have an overwhelming effect on the agricultural economy. Many peasants still held by hereditary tenure, such as copyhold, and while this in theory was under the control of the lords' courts, the royal court of chancery extended its protection over copyholders in the late fifteenth century. Peasants were well organized, and had recourse to many defences against a predatory farmer or lord – the peasants of Quinton, for example, mounted an effective protest by persuading their parish clergyman to petition on their behalf.

We can test the view that there was large-scale expropriation of peasant holdings by examining the 2,000 or more villages which were deserted in England between about 1370 and 1520. Together with a much larger number of villages which shrank severely, and many thousands of deserted hamlets and farms in all parts of Britain, we have apparent evidence of the lords' deliberate removal of peasants from the land.

In fact most peasants removed themselves. Far from evicting peasants, lords used their courts in often futile attempts to prevent migration and to promote repair to tenant buildings not just in the 'reaction' after the Black Death but right through the fifteenth century and even after 1500. Lords were interested in securing a healthy income of rents, and that was best secured by keeping buildings in good repair and tenants on the land. When a village was abandoned, the estate authorities were sometimes slow to take advantage, and the pasture was grazed by neighbouring villages before money was invested in enclosures and the land exploited profitably.

The villages fell victim in the long term to the fall in population, which through differences in migration affected some villages more drastically than others. Often a village survived the Black Death and later epidemics, and then its people moved away in search of better prospects. The small Oxfordshire village of Brookend which had sixteen tenants before the first plague still had fifteen in 1363, but gradually they left and were not replaced, and by 1441 only three families remained. If the villages were killed off by their lords, we would expect them to disappear rather quickly, but often they went through a long-drawn-out decline, which sometimes began in the crisis before 1348, and continued over the next century. Many villages seem to have reached the point of no return in the early fifteenth century. (Plate 19)

The inhabitants found some villages unattractive, and left them. Villages with an industrial side to their economies were rarely abandoned, and indeed a number of them expanded at the expense of purely agricultural settlements. Peasants drifted away from small villages which were not at the centre of their parishes and which lacked social variety and facilities. Chapel Ascote in Warwickshire in its decline in the early fifteenth century could muster only one brewer. When this last alehouse closed in 1451 the village's fate was sealed.

Acquisitive villagers also made life difficult for their neighbours. We find peasants taking over a number of holdings as their tenants left. At Hangleton in Sussex a peasant built his house on a site which had previously been occupied by five neighbours. These accumulators of holdings tended to behave selfishly, as the scale of their farming set them at odds with the rest of the community. Henry Chandeler of Roel in Gloucestershire, who held five tenements totalling 150 acres in 1400, was accused of overstocking the common pasture with sheep. He probably did not cultivate his large area of arable thoroughly. Such activities threatened the orderly running of the open-field system, on which the livelihood of all of the villagers depended. At Compton Verney in Warwickshire, where the village was in decay around 1400, and finally died soon after 1460, the manor court issued orders for tethering grazing horses and for the control of rooting pigs, but large sections of the arable had been converted to pasture, and tenants were holding blocks of land in the fields as if the old boundaries and rotations had been forgotten. Tenants held fragments of holdings, and the coherent yardlands that had been formed centuries before were being broken up and redistributed. Compton's fields were so ill-managed that neighbouring villages sent their flocks and herds to graze illicitly.

The lords (by no means all of them gentry) who presided over these decaying villages eventually lost patience with attempts to retain tenants or restore them to profitable health. The rents that the rump of villagers paid were very low, and the land would be worth much more if converted into enclosed pastures. Contemporaries complained that 'avaricious men' (as John Rous of Warwick called them) were destroying villages. Rous compiled in about 1486 a list of sixty villages that had been deserted, mainly in Warwickshire, and three years later public opinion had become so alarmed that legislation was passed to prevent the 'pulling down and wilful waste of houses and towns' (town meaning rural settlements, in this context). Concern continued, and in 1516 Thomas More complained that the sheep, once a meek and gentle beast, had become an eater of men.

In 1517, the government, under Cardinal Wolsey, set up a commission to investigate the 'casting down of houses' and the conversion of arable to pasture. The reports of the commissioners and the court cases that followed revealed hundreds of offences, mainly in the east midland counties, from Buckinghamshire to Nottinghamshire. They missed many deserted villages, because they had disappeared before the legislation had been passed, but they tended to catch lords who were removing the last villagers from badly shrunken settlements. For example, the depopulation of Burton Dassett in 1497 by Edward Belknap and John Heritage resulted in the loss of twelve houses, but this had been a very large manor with more than seventy tenants before the first plague. Clearly most of the inhabitants had moved out before the lord enclosed the fields.

Deserted villages attracted the attention of contemporaries like Rous and More, and have continued to fascinate modern historians because their end was so complete: a compact settlement with 100 or 200 people, cultivating complex open fields covering a territory of hundreds of acres, was transformed into a group of enclosed pastures in which the sheep and cattle were herded by a few employees. In fact, more households and land were abandoned as a result of the reduction in size of the great majority of villages from which lords gained no benefit: this was wholly the result of mortality and migration among the peasantry. Similarly, a high proportion of the half-million houses which were abandoned between 1320 and 1520 lay in hamlets and isolated farms in the regions throughout Britain where villages were rare. Often a settlement shrank down to a single farm, like the hamlet of Carneborne in Helston (Cornwall), which had once contained three holdings; by 1486 they had been taken over by a single tenant who was said to hold 'the whole vill'. In the woodlands of the west midlands half of the houses that were inhabited in about 1300 had commonly been deserted by 1520. And the traces of ruined farms scattered over the uplands of Wales and Scotland, which are rarely closely dated, include some abandoned in this period of low rural population. The loss of holdings did not lead, as in the case of the villages, to the total transformation of a section of the landscape, and it was rarely instigated by lords, but it adds to the picture of peasants choosing where to live, and leaving settlements, or avoiding moving into them, because they saw better prospects elsewhere.

Scottish tenants appear to have been more vulnerable than those in England to encroachment by landlords. Many tenants held by short, even one-year leases, but in practice these were renewed, and heirs were allowed to succeed. Similarly 'rental' tenants, whose names were included in a list of tenants, had at least some written evidence for their tenure, and the holdings could be inherited. The convention of 'kindly tenure' meant that lords were disposed to respect the rights of sons and other relatives to take a holding after a tenant's death. However ill-defined the rights of tenants may have been, they were not expelled or denied succession because in general tenants were in short supply, and the Scottish lairds, the counterparts of the gentry, did not pursue aggressive policies of direct management or the incorporation of tenants' lands into their demesnes. A new development from the mid-fifteenth century came with the adoption of *feu-ferms*, which gave tenants property rights over their holdings, if they paid an entry fine and a high annual rent. The lords gained short-term profit, but early sixteenth-century inflation made the fixed rents seem cheap, so the tenants – a third of whom were lairds, but who also included some peasants – gained in the long run.

The abandonment and shrinkage of rural settlements shows that peasants were not the victims of their lords, but decision-makers and initiators. Many peasants did not better themselves or make great changes in their economic roles in this period. In the early sixteenth century thousands of them lived in a style bearing some resemblance to that of their predecessors two centuries earlier. Between a fifth and a third of tenants worked standard holdings of 15 or 30 acres of land. They still practised mixed farming, with a strong emphasis on the cultivation of corn. Millions of acres lay in open fields, and strong village communities regulated the use of land. The techniques of cultivation and stock-rearing had not changed fundamentally. Many were either free tenants whose rents had been fixed before 1300, or in England copyholders who owed their lords rents based originally on the money value of labour which had been calculated when the services of villeins were commuted in the fourteenth century. They paid entry fines to acquire a holding, and a heriot when they died or surrendered it. Many Scottish peasants still held their land from year to year, and the Welsh pridd was used to transfer land. Hundreds of families were called serfs, and could be expected to pay marriage fines if the lord enforced them. The family was the basis of labour on the holding, and some sons worked with their fathers, and looked after them in their old age. In Wales the kin still exercised great authority over landholding. Most produce from the land was consumed within the household and farm, leaving a limited surplus for sale.

The lack of change in the peasant economy could be regarded as proof of peasants' unenterprising outlook, and their contentment with customary ways and modest profits. Rather, the persistence of a traditional peasantry reflects the fact that the economic circumstances were not especially favourable to producers – their corn in particular fetched modest prices. The cost of labour, if they were tempted to expand their holdings above the acreage that could be managed by the household,

remained high. Their rents were still a burden, and there was some truth
in their complaints that they could not afford certain rents. They asserted
themselves, however, showing that they did not accept their lot by refusing to pay selected dues, and by rebelling against new taxes in 1489, 1497
and 1525.

For all of the survival of the old ways, and the adversity of the times,
the peasants still took initiatives. The importance of migration in the
changes in the settlement pattern is clear, but the constant, even restless,
movement of people lies behind many other developments. It was not
new for peasants to uproot themselves – otherwise the clearance of
new land and growth of towns in the twelfth and thirteenth centuries
would not have been possible. But in the fifteenth century three-quarters
of the families living in some villages changed every fifty years. It was a
rare family which in 1520 had been settled in the same place continuously
since 1350. George Underhyll, a serf of Hampton Lovett in Worcestershire moved to Hartlebury, about 5 miles away, in 1479, where he made
a successful career as a landholder and seller of food and drink. His son
Richard, who was born at Hampton Lovett, migrated 20 miles to the
small town of Tewkesbury, where he worked as a tanner, and then went
to Hartlebury in 1503.

The role of the peasant family was changed not overnight by the
plagues, but in the long run. Everywhere individuals broke free from
some of the constraints of family and kinship. In East Anglia the family
had always had a limited influence on landholding, with most land transfers being made between individuals who were not related to one another
rather than passing though the family by inheritance. By the early
fifteenth century the frequent disposal of land outside the family, and
apparent reduction in inheritance as a means of transmitting property,
had spread to the midlands and the north. Children left home to find
work and land elsewhere, so that when their parent died or retired, there
was no one to inherit the land, and it passed to another family. In Wales
the group of kinsmen, the *gwely*, diminished in importance, and land
was held in larger units by individuals. This does not mean that family
sentiment came to an end, just that attitudes towards family had always
been based in some degree on the state of the market for land and
produce. In times of land scarcity it paid to be loyal to one's parents,
look after them in old age, and take over the family holding. After a
period when land was cheap and plentiful in the mid-fifteenth century,
transfers within the family tended to return with rising land values
around 1500.

Some historians might say that strong attachment to the family was a
basic peasant characteristic, and that the move away from family values

shows that the people concerned had ceased to be peasants – they had adopted capitalist notions of individualism and acquisitiveness. But peasants were not ruled entirely by emotion, and had always been motivated by some measure of self-interest. The varying attitudes in different parts of the country, and the changes in different periods, demonstrates that they were rational economic people, whose behaviour was influenced by their circumstances. The decline in family attachments may have some bearing on the greater social and economic role of the village community. After 1334 the village was made responsible for assessing and collecting its own taxes, and it seems to be in association with the collection of money for that purpose that villages developed a common box, from which poor relief was paid. In the early sixteenth century the parish was given the legal responsibility of looking after its own poor, but that function had clearly been developing for more than a century. The community was taking over some of the responsibilities to the old and sick that had previously been the duty of relatives.

At the same time, the churchwardens grew in importance, with a primary task of fundraising for the maintenance of the fabric of the parish church. Often they became ambitious to rebuild the church, or at least to add towers, porches, aisles and clerestories, or to embellish the interior with screens, images and wall paintings. In many parishes a public hall, the church house, was built by the churchwardens next to the church; here church ales could be held at which parishioners gathered to drink, and the profits of selling ale and food went to church funds. Some villages also built almshouses, advancing yet further their charitable activities. And in many parishes, especially in eastern England, religious fraternities were formed, which also raised funds, built substantial guild-halls, and made some contribution to poor relief. A growing proportion of the village's resources was devoted to public spending on these projects, and the wealthier households spent more on community projects than they paid in taxes to the crown.

Peasants knew that their lords possessed great authority and political power, but they were also aware that as the number of potential tenants declined, especially in view of the fright delivered to the aristocracy in 1381, lords could be pressurized to secure better conditions. We have already seen something of the bargaining process at work, and can appreciate that the reductions in rent, abolition of unpopular charges such as tallages, recognitions and common fines, and changes in tenancy such as the introduction of leasehold, came about through negotiations backed up by rent strikes and threats to leave the manors. Peasants still gained strength from their community organization, which meant that collective action, such as a common refusal to pay tallage, was particularly effective. One reason why we know so much about the encroachments on common pastures and other acquisitive behaviour by the gentry is that the peasants were well organized and were able to bring legal action against their lords, including making use of the royal courts. As always, the peasant suitors at the lord's courts were adept at manipulating its machinery, for example by using their influence as jurors to adjust customary laws in favour of the tenant. Peasants were becoming more closely involved in politics, as is suggested by the written programme of reform which the rebels from south-east England put forward in Cade's revolt of 1450. They were attempting to make use of the existing political machinery by agreeing with measures proposed in parliament, such as the demand that the king live on his own landed resources and not by taxing his subjects. They had apparently abandoned their attempt, as in 1381, to seek to change the social and political structure from outside.

Initiatives from the serfs put a virtual end to servile status, not by grand political actions, but by the quiet process of migration. A relatively small number of peasants paid quite large sums (£5–£10) to buy their freedom, which enabled them to live in their native village without the taint of serfdom. But for many, the desire to move from the village in search of economic benefits had the incidental effect of providing an escape from the jurisdiction of the lord: they knew that in a new home servile status would be unknown or quickly forgotten.

In pursuit of a higher standard of living, peasants rebuilt their houses in growing numbers after 1380, with a concentration of new construction in the period 1440 to 1519. Dendrochronology allows us to give a precise date for standing buildings such as the 'wealden' houses of Kent, and the cruck houses in the midland counties of Buckinghamshire, Leicestershire, Shropshire and Warwickshire. The new buildings' quality can be judged from the hundreds which survive and are still inhabited (though no longer by peasants). They were also designed to provide superior accommodation, with two storeys in the end bays of the wealden houses of the south-east, which still retained open halls; even in the midlands and Devon, in the essentially one-storey cruck houses, upper rooms were inserted at least at one end. Houses at Seacourt in Berkshire were built with external staircases against the gable. In west Yorkshire and parts of the midlands, peasant houses were being roofed with stone slates instead of the traditional thatch. A three-bay cruck house in the midlands or the north in the mid-fifteenth century measuring 15 feet by 45 feet required an outlay of about £3 on materials and the wages of craftsmen. Some houses built at this time for prospering yeomen in east and north Wales were substantial, expensive and indicate status seeking. The medieval house which is now called Leeswood Green Farm near Mold in Flint was 50 feet long by 20 feet wide, with a large hall and rooms at each end with lofts. Not only were the family provided with space and comfort, they could also impress their neighbours and visitors with a show of the large quantities of timber used in construction and the decorative carving of some of the timbers. (Plates 18a and 18b)

Peasants bought more clothing, furnishings and household equipment at this time. They also ate better. Harvest workers employed at Sedge-ford in Norfolk in 1424 were provided with a pound of meat and at least 6 pints of ale for each 2 pounds of bread. This was not just a reversal of the bread-based diet that predominated before 1300, but much higher-quality ingredients were used, with bread made from wheat flour rather than barley meal, and fresh beef instead of bacon. Many peasants would have eaten as well as the harvest workers during that season of heavy work, and would have expected to eat meat and wheat bread throughout the year. They seem to have been attempting to emulate the material conditions that they observed in towns, and in the manor houses and parsonages. Their diet, arrangement of their houses, and fur-nishings and clothing brought them closer to the models provided by better-off townspeople, gentry and clergy. In addition to individual con-sumption, they also aspired to a high level of collective spending on their churches and associated buildings.

The main means for a peasant family to raise their income was to increase the size of their holding. They achieved this by the traditional process of inheritance and marriage, but land was purchased from another tenant, or taken (more cheaply) from the lord when a tenant died or departed without heirs. There were very large variations in the size of holdings, but it was still true, as in the pre-plague era, that midland and northern peasants tended to hold standard units of yardlands or oxgangs, and the wealthier minority could commonly accumulate 45 or 60 acres. Some lords split holdings in response to demand. A typical accu-mulation was that of William White at Cowpen Bewley in County Durham, who inherited a bondland (30 acres), two cottages, and 30 acres in five holdings from his father in 1480. He brought his total holding from 60 to 80 acres by more acquisitions in 1482. In the east and south-east of England, land was held in acres rather than standard units, smallholders were more common, and the discrepancies between tenants greater. At Ickham in Kent in 1400, forty-one of fifty-one tenants held 9 acres or less, and seven held 30 acres or more, including two with 150 acres. In 1492 the smallholders with 9 acres or less had fallen to thirty, and there were individuals with 240 acres, 141 acres and 80 acres. In England as a whole by the early sixteenth century about an eighth of the rural householders held 50 acres or more, compared with the tiny percentage with so much land before the epidemics.

A new terminology to describe the English peasantry was introduced in the fifteenth century. Instead of the old distinction between free and unfree, which was becoming irrelevant, the new vocabulary was based on economic stratification, with an upper rank of yeomen, who often held 80 acres or more, a middle category of husbandmen, and at the bottom the labourers who held a few acres and had to work for wages. Yeomen of course were most likely to produce a large surplus and to employ labour. The land that defined this stratification was valuable. In Norfolk, in the depression of the market in the mid-fifteenth century as well as in the early years of the sixteenth century, customary land could command a price (that is, the money paid by the new tenant to the outgoing tenant) of 30s per acre. The busy land market meant that holdings tended to change hands in every generation, often outside the family. At Shillington in Bedfordshire, where there were about seventy tenants, 244 transfers were made in 1398–1458, so each holding changed hands about four times, mostly between unrelated parties. This land market was fed by the instability of many accumulations of land: a yeoman might build up a large holding from many parcels, but after his death it would fall apart and the parts would be used to build up new composite units.

Labour posed a serious problem for those gathering these large accumulations of land. The wages of agricultural labourers, which had risen from about 1d to 2d at the time of the Black Death, reached 3d–4d in the fifteenth and early sixteenth centuries. Real wages – assessing the value of the wage in terms of the food and other goods it would buy – increased two and a half times between 1300 and 1450. A tenant could cultivate a 30-acre holding cheaply if he had a son to help. But in the fifteenth century sons were not plentiful, and did not stay at home. One alternative was to hire young living-in servants whose labour was considerably cheaper than workers hired by the day, but again servants were in short supply because no village had a great surplus of young people. There would have been plenty of labour if the effects of the redistribution of land had worked as they did in other economic circumstances, that is to cause differentiation, with a growing number of cottagers and landless at the bottom to complement the larger holdings at the top. But all ranks of the post-plague peasantry expanded their holdings, with a general decrease in the number of cottagers. Many of the descendants of smallholders had been able to pick up a few more acres so that they no longer needed to work for wages. Presumably they were seeking the security that came from landholding rather than the cash rewards of wages. Cottagers were also highly mobile, and travelled to villages and

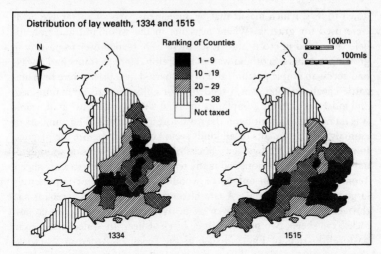

Map 11. Changes in the distribution of lay wealth, 1334 and 1515. One factor in the rise in the relative wealth of Suffolk, Essex, Kent, Gloucestershire and Somerset was the growth of the rural cloth industry.

Source: R. Schofield, 'The Geographical Distribution of Wealth in England, 1334–1649', *Economic History Review*, 2nd ser., 18 (1965).

towns where the wages were highest (Map 11). Some clothmaking settlements were as large as they had been in 1300, or even more populous. While houses everywhere were being abandoned in large numbers, in woodland villages with industrial employment, such as Sedgley in Staffordshire, new houses and cottages were being built on the waste in the late fifteenth century to accommodate the labour flowing into the community. Tenants with larger holdings attempted to solve the labour shortage by taking cottagers as subtenants, and monopolizing their labour. These tied cottages are found at Coupar Angus in the mid-fifteenth century, when ten peasant lessees of a demesne were presumed each to have two or three cottars under them. In Devon the wealthier peasants at villages such as Stokenham in the late fourteenth century gathered up the cottages as part of their larger holdings, in order to sublet them.

Peasants employers economized on labour, just like the farmers and lords, by converting their land from arable to pasture. They preferred to be self-sufficient in food, and so rarely used all of their holdings entirely as pasture. But the proportion of land under grass was increased almost everywhere in England and Wales. In open-field systems the land was put

down to leys, which meant that by agreement parts of the arable fields
were used for grazing. Where peasants in the woodland and uplands
held their land in crofts and closes these were turned over to pasture in
growing numbers. Scotland was an exception. Here peasants had always
had access to ample pasture, and in this period oats prices were high and
cattle cheap, so there was a tendency for cultivation to be maintained,
and indeed there were complaints in about 1500 that extension of arable
was damaging the hunting in the royal forest of Ettrick. The numbers of
animals kept by tenants of all kinds seem larger than before the plagues.
In midland open-field villages, flocks of 300 sheep belonging to individuals were not uncommon, and many tenants owned thirty to sixty sheep.
Yeomen, especially in upland or woodland districts, kept impressively
large numbers of animals. A late fifteenth-century Anglesey tenant had
thirteen mares and foals, eleven oxen, twenty-three cows, fourteen bul-
locks, 176 sheep, two pigs and three hives of bees. In Wales, and also in
pastoral districts of England such as the Forest of Arden in Warwickshire, peasants specialized in cattle, especially with the aim of satisfying
the market for beef. The increase in numbers of livestock caused a good
deal of friction in villages, and there were constant complaints of animals
trespassing, and of the overburdening of the commons, leading to overgrazing. Villages responded by fixing stints and repeating these limits on
the numbers of anmals that could be kept. Offenders were fined in the
manor court.

Conflict could be avoided, and land could be used more efficiently, by
changes in the management of land, and peasants in consequence reorganized their own holdings, and the common fields. In the uplands they
enclosed more open grazing land; in the woodlands, crofts which had
previously been available for common grazing were closed off and neighbours' animals denied access. The open fields could only be restructured
after a process of exchange and consolidation of strips, which t1en
formed coherent blocks of land which could be enclosed. We find individuals carrying out this process piecemeal at Stoke Fleming in Devon
around 1400, and by 1500 the village was surrounded entirely by enclosed
fields. Sometimes there was a collective agreement to enclose, like that
made by the sixteen half-yardlanders (tenants of about 15 acres) at
Sambourne in Warwickshire between 1445 and 1472, by which strips
covering 240 acres were exchanged and fenced off. Peasant enclosures
of this kind were much more numerous, and enclosed a much larger area
of land, than the enclosures carried out by the lords. They attracted less
dispute and attention because they were accepted by the peasants. Once
land had been enclosed, it could be converted to pasture, or cropped as
each peasant wished, but the common fields could be adapted, again with

collective consent. Sometimes cultivation became less intensive, with the introduction of more fallows in districts like north-east Norfolk where fallows in more pressured times had been virtually eliminated. In the same trend to cultivate the land less frequently, it might be left under grass for some years and then ploughed up, with beneficial effects on the yields of crops of the newly cultivated ground. This technique, which was once thought to have been introduced in later centuries, known as 'up-and-down' or convertible husbandry, was already in use well before 1500. Sometimes an infield–outfield system was adopted, by which part of the field system was cropped every year, and the outer furlongs were planted one year in two. This had been typical of upland regions, but now spread to villages in the midlands and East Anglia.

A quiet change in technology led to a further extension in the employment of horses rather than oxen as draught animals. John Davye of Stalbridge in Dorset, a western county where oxen predominated before the first plague, when he died in 1496 owned eight horses and six oxen. The high-quality building methods which were developed for houses were also applied to farm buildings, especially barns. At Caldecote in Hertfordshire a tenant who had absorbed the holdings of a number of neighbours built two very large barns, capable of holding the crops of 160 acres, which dwarfed his house. Peasants searched for products which gave better returns, and we find such novelties as saffron gardens, especially in north-west Essex, and the keeping of goats, which had been discouraged before 1348 because of the damage they caused to trees. In their quest for an alternative source of income when conventional crops gave poor returns, East Anglian peasants turned to sea fishing, and those inland rented fish ponds. Changes in peasant marketing are suggested by the disappearance of the small village markets. Sales were being made further afield, as peasants with vehicles and considerable knowledge of the prices in their region were willing and able to travel longer distances.

The productivity of demesne arable declined in this period. In Norfolk, famous for its high yields, lords produced about 9 to 12 bushels per acre in 1250–1350, but in the range of 8–10 bushels in 1350–1450. Yield ratios, calculated by dividing the amount of grain that was harvested by the amount sown, on the bishopric of Winchester estate reached quite a high average of 3.88 (for wheat) in 1381–1410, but slipped back to 3.66 in 1411–53, below the thirteenth-century figure. Perhaps peasant yields moved in the same direction. Both demesnes and peasant holdings had more animals, and could therefore put more manure on the land, which may have increased returns, but on the other hand both lacked labour, and it was the neglect of such activities as repeated ploughing and intensive weeding which probably lay behind the relatively low yields. The fall in the weight of sheep fleeces in this period has been blamed on the climate and the shortage of grazing, which would apply to peasant as well as demesne flocks. The low price of grain did not hurt the peasants so much, as they were often producing for their own consumption. They may even have responded to lower prices by growing greater quantities so that they could achieve the cash income that they needed. This, of course, helped to ensure that prices remained low as supply outstripped demand. The productivity of labour increased at this time, as peasants worked more land per head than in earlier centuries. Just as shepherds on demesnes were expected to tend larger flocks of sheep, and plough-men to cover more acres, so peasants, their families and employees had to work harder to deal with the tasks on large holdings.

Peasants adapted their way of life in a period of adversity. Their performance does not conform to the gloomy assumption of modern observers that low prices and scarce labour would impoverish them. Peasants in contact with the market had long been acquiring a commercial attitude towards their land and its management. John Mell of Bramfield in Suffolk, who inherited 48 acres in 1461 and through purchase and leasing increased his holding to 150 acres in 1478, managed his mixed farming so well that he could expect his executors when he made his will to raise £26 13s 4d in bequests to the younger sons and daughters of his family. He was hard-headed enough to expect that his son, who was to inherit the land, would buy the goods and chattels from the executors, presumably by borrowing money and paying back from the profits of production. This arrangement opens up a vista of peasants with a tough and realistic view of the economic world in which their offspring could make their own way. In this period the distinction begins to blur between the prosperous peasant like Mell, and many demesne farmers, themselves of peasant origin, who disposed of similar quantities of land. Townsmen who acquired and managed large acreages seem to have had a similar outlook. Andrew Bate of Lydd in Kent leased demesne land in nearby Dengemarsh, and was said in 1468 to have kept excessive numbers of cattle, which encroached on the other tenants' land and sent them away, so that he 'had driven away half [of] Dengemarsh'. This was the brave and ruthless new world at the end of the middle ages.

New ideas and new methods were making large changes in the countryside. The great lords, and to a lesser extent the gentry, were no longer the leading producers. They had to grant better conditions to their tenants, and those tenants – farmers and peasants – were running their own affairs, and changing the countryside both as individuals and as communities.

Conclusion

People in the early sixteenth century tended to depict their world according to traditional habits of thought. Edmund Dudley, writing in 1509, divided the commonwealth into the three orders of nobles, clergy and peasants, as William Langland had done in the 1370s and Aelfric soon after 1000. Little had changed in some respects over the centuries before Dudley wrote. The fundamental structure of manors and villages of his day, which provided the basis for the relationship between lords and peasants, had been formed between 850 and 1050. The urban network had also begun to take shape by about 900, though it did not reach an advanced stage until about 1300. Edmund Dudley would have encountered townspeople, such as shoemakers or bakers, and in the country peasants with middling holdings of 15 to 30 acres of land, whose way of life remained similar to that of their predecessors in the thirteenth century.

Italian visitors in the early sixteenth century saw the country differently. They noticed a thinly inhabited countryside, with expanses of pasture. They remarked on the idleness of the English, presumably in comparison with the intensive work required of Italian peasants and rural workers. Perhaps they did not visit the clothing districts, where they would have seen a busier workforce. Continental consumers showed their appreciation of English industry by their purchase of cloth from Yorkshire or Wiltshire.

The view from the continent should guide us to appreciate the transformation of the economy in the last two centuries of the middle ages. The 'new world' envisioned by the tenants of the Paston family had to some extent come about by the early sixteenth century. Lords had retreated from production, and the farmers and peasants were the main driving force behind change in the countryside. In many ways they were struggling against adversity, because of low prices and high labour costs, but that encouraged them to adopt more efficient methods which put them in a better position when conditions for producers improved in the sixteenth century. Townspeople had their problems too, but the towns maintained their importance in that their population shrank no more than the population as a whole. London strengthened its position as the centre of international trade and much else.

Contemporaries agonized over the social evils they saw about them, of depopulating enclosure and the army of vagrants. But to some extent their anxieties were being awakened unnecessarily. As the population remained low, the loss of houses and cultivation in the countryside was only to be expected. The widespread fear of beggars was provoked partly by a mobile workforce, and partly by the annoyance of employers at any signs of idleness in an economy when booming textile and metal industries were crying out for workers.

While emphasizing the many changes of the middle ages, this book has not offered a single story to explain them. This is because none of the 'grand narratives' can be made to fit the changes we can observe. The onward and upward march of commerce, money and the middle classes was not the whole story, as that movement was checked at key moments, with retreats into a degree of self-sufficiency and problems for many towns in the fifteenth century. The 'transition from feudalism to capitalism' can be applied to the emergence of the clothiers and farmers in the fifteenth century and the weakening of lords' authority at the same time. The survival of lordship, and a middling peasantry, does not accord with a complete triumph for capitalism. Also, there is little evidence for the emergence of a proletariat – a workforce entirely dependent on wages – as about 40 per cent of households lived mainly on wages in 1524–5, which is not dissimilar to calculations for the thirteenth and fourteenth centuries. The view that high levels of population and falling returns for the land precipitated a crisis in the fourteenth century and initiated a long recession fits much of the evidence, except that it is difficult to reconcile with the regions that lack high population densities and over-exploited land. The population should have bounced back once the pressure was removed by the epidemics of 1348–75, so the fact that it remained low requires some special interpretation. The idea that a powerful centralized state promoted economic growth in the tenth century, and continued to provide the framework for a more efficient system of exchange at the end of the middle ages, has something to commend it, but we must bear in mind the limitations on the power of the central government at all times, and in particular note its comparative weakness in the fifteenth century, when the 'new world' was emerging.

If none of these schemes provides a fully satisfactory explanation, some of the crucial ingredients in transforming the medieval economy must be the creation of an enduring framework for production and exchange in the two centuries after 850, and the urbanization of the period 880–1300. The dynamic tension within the feudal regime in the twelfth and thirteenth centuries, with its element of competition among the aristocracy and the lack of strict controls which enabled peasant initiatives, must be accorded great importance. The relaxation of demographic pressure in the fourteenth century and the opportunities that were given to the upper ranks of the peasantry enabled some growth in a period of apparent adversity. As lords did not take all of the peasants' surplus, they could consume enough to enable towns to grow in the thirteenth century, and the problems for producers in the next two centuries again allowed a level of consumer demand which kept industry and trade in a healthy state, especially around 1400 and again after about 1470.

These influences are presented here in an impersonal manner, but we should not forget that the medieval world developed in the way that it did because Haehstan managed his limited estate in an enterprising way (Chapter 1); Wulfhelm developed his goldsmith's craft in a new urban environment (Chapter 2); Stephen de Fretwell mismanaged his affairs and went bankrupt (Chapter 4); Robert Broun cleared new land (Chapter 5); Nicholas Symond the spurrier demanded higher wages (Chapter 8); and Thomas Vicars managed his farm in the most profitable fashion (Chapter 10). These individuals had little impact on their own, but they were part of tendencies involving many others, and their accumulated actions created the 'new world' with which the middle ages came to an end.

Further reading

This list cannot pretend to include all of the works and sources that have contributed to this book. It is a selection of books, articles and documents, but should indicate where a point can be pursued further. Most of the works listed themselves contain bibliographies which will guide readers to more specialized works. To help the reader locate the sources, they are listed in approximately the same order as the topics appear in the text. Unless otherwise stated, the place of publication is London.

Abbreviations:
AgHEW: The Agrarian History of England and Wales, vols I–IV (Cambridge, 1967–1991)
AgHR: The Agricultural History Review
CBA: Council for British Archaeology
EHR: English Historical Review
EcHR: Economic History Review
JHG: Journal of Historical Geography
Med. Arch.: Medieval Archaeology
P & P: Past and Present
TRHS: Transactions of the Royal Historical Society
VCH: Victoria County History

INTRODUCTION   APPROACHING THE ECONOMIC
HISTORY OF MEDIEVAL BRITAIN

General surveys of the economic and social history of England began with the pioneering historians of the late nineteenth and early twentieth centuries, notably J. E. Thorold Rogers, *Six Centuries of Work and Wages: The History of English Labour* (1884); W. Cunningham, *The Growth of English Industry and Commerce* (1882, enlarged in 1890); W. J. Ashley, *An Introduction to English Economic History and Theory* (1893); E. Lipson, *The Economic History of*

England (1915) and J. H. Clapham, *A Concise Economic History of Britain* (Cambridge, 1949). A distinctive American approach to the period is represented by G. C. Homans, *English Villagers of the Thirteenth Century* (Cambridge, Mass., 1941) and W. O. Ault, *Open-Field Farming in Medieval England* (1972).

Historical geography has made an important contribution to the subject, and indeed many of the authors mentioned in subsequent pages were trained as historical geographers. See H. C. Darby (ed.), *A New Historical Geography of England before 1600* (Cambridge, 1973); R. A. Dodgshon and R. A. Butlin (eds), *An Historical Geography of England and Wales* (2nd edn, 1990); G. Whittington and I. D. Whyte (eds), *An Historical Geography of Scotland* (1983). Historical atlases with economic information include P. G. B. McNeil and H. L. McQueen (eds), *Atlas of Scottish History to 1707* (Edinburgh, 1996). There are now a number of county and regional atlases, for example R. Kain and W. Ravenhill (eds), *An Historical Atlas of South-West England* (Exeter, 2000). Postan's revolutionary influence on thinking is best reflected in his essays and articles, reprinted in M. M. Postan, *Essays on Medieval Agriculture and General Problems of the Medieval Economy* (Cambridge, 1973), but see also M. M. Postan, *The Medieval Economy and Society* (1972) and his chapter in the *Cambridge Economic History of Europe*, vol. 1, *The Agrarian Life of the Middle Ages*, 2nd edn (Cambridge, 1966). General books which are broadly sympathetic to Postan's view are E. Miller and J. Hatcher, *Medieval England – Rural Society and Economic Change 1086–1348* (1978) and J. L. Bolton, *The Medieval English Economy 1150–1500* (1980).

Marxist views of the period are to be found in M. Dobb, *Studies in the Development of Capitalism* (1946) and E. A. Kosminsky, *Studies in the Agrarian History of England in the Thirteenth Century* (Oxford, 1956). Significant modifications to the orthodoxy are made by R. H. Hilton, *Class Conflict and the Crisis of Feudalism* (1985) and R. H. Hilton, *The English Peasantry in the Later Middle Ages* (1975). Another strand of Marxist thinking is expressed, and criticized, in T. H. Aston and C. H. E. Philpin (eds), *The Brenner Debate. Agrarian Class Structure and Economic Development in Pre-Industrial Europe* (Cambridge, 1985).

The wave of works critical of Postan's approach is represented by B. M. S. Campbell (ed.), *Before the Black Death. Studies in the 'Crisis' of the Early Fourteenth Century* (Manchester, 1991); R. H. Britnell and B. M. S. Campbell (eds), *A Commercialising Economy. England 1086 to c.1300* (Manchester, 1995); G. Astill and J. Langdon (eds), *Medieval Farming and Technology. The Impact of Agricultural Change in Northwest Europe* (Leiden, 1997); B. M. S. Campbell, *English Seigniorial Agriculture, 1250–1450* (Cambridge, 2000). Campbell in particular has been inspired by E. Boserup, *The Conditions of Agricultural Growth* (1965) and E. Boserup, *Population and Technology* (1981).

On commercial and urban growth the most important recent works have been S. Reynolds, *An Introduction to the History of English Medieval Towns* (Oxford, 1977); R. H. Britnell, *The Commercialisation of English Society 1000–1500* (Cambridge, 1993); E. Miller and J. Hatcher, *Medieval England.*

Towns, Commerce and Crafts (1995) and H. Swanson, *Medieval British Towns* (Basingstoke, 1999).

Medieval archaeology is summarized in D. M. Wilson (ed.), *The Archaeology of Anglo-Saxon England* (Cambridge, 1976); J. Hunter and I. Ralston (eds), *The Archaeology of Britain* (1999); G. Astill and A. Grant (eds), *The Countryside of Medieval England* (Oxford, 1988); and D. Hinton, *Archaeology, Economy and Society* (1990).

Another approach is represented by C. Dyer, *Standards of Living in the Later Middle Ages. Social Change in England, c.1200–1520* (revised edition, Cambridge, 1998); C. Dyer, *Everyday Life in Medieval England* (1994).

Scottish economic and social history of the period is covered by chapters in more general surveys: A. A. M. Duncan, *Scotland: The Making of the Kingdom* (Edinburgh, 1975); G. W. S. Barrow, *Kingship and Unity. Scotland 1000–1306* (Edinburgh, 1989); A. Grant, *Independence and Nationhood – Scotland 1306–1469* (1984).

The most useful recent book which is focused on the economy is I. Whyte *Scotland before the Industrial Revolution. An Economic and Social History, c.1050–c.1750* (1995). For archaeological evidence there is a popular survey of recent research: P. Yeoman, *Medieval Scotland. An Archaeological Perspective* (1995). For Wales, again useful surveys of the economy appear in general histories: W. Davies, *Wales in the Early Middle Ages* (Leicester, 1982); R. R. Davies, *Conquest, Coexistence and Change. Wales 1063–1415* (Oxford, 1987); G. Williams, *Recovery, Reorientation and Reformation. Wales c.1415–1642* (Oxford, 1987).

On the social history of the period, there are two surveys, M. Keen, *English Society in the Later Middle Ages* (Harmondsworth, 1990), and S. Rigby, *English Society in the Later Middle Ages. Class, Status and Gender* (Basingstoke, 1995).

On controversial terminology, 'feudal' is treated sceptically in S. Reynolds, *Fiefs and Vassals. The Medieval Evidence Reinterpreted* (Oxford, 1994). For the broad view of feudalism as a social formation, see M. Bloch, *Feudal Society* (1965).

'Aristocracy' and 'nobility' are discussed in M. Bush (ed.), *Social Orders and Social Classes in Europe since 1500* (1992).

The best definition of 'peasant' in an English context is to be found in Hilton, *English Peasantry*; the denial of a peasantry is to be found in A. Macfarlane, *The Origins of English Individualism* (Oxford, 1978).

For a clear definition of 'town' and 'urban', see R. Holt and G. Rosser (eds), *The Medieval Town. A Reader in English Urban History* (1990).

PART ONE: ORIGINS OF THE MEDIEVAL ECONOMY, *c.*850–*c.*1100

Chapter 1: Living on the land, c.850–c.1050

On the natural environment, for which most of the evidence is scientific, from animal bones and surviving traces of pollen and vegetation, see P. Dark, *The Environment of Britain in the First Millennium* AD (2000); O. Rackham, *Ancient*

Woodland (1980); O. Rackham, *The History of the Countryside* (1986); J. Rackham (ed.), *Environment and Economy in Anglo-Saxon England* (CBA Research Report, 89, 1994).

Sustainable agriculture is discussed in J. N. Pretty, 'Sustainable Agriculture in the Middle Ages: the English Manor', *AgHR*, 38 (1990); M. K. Jones, 'Agricultural Productivity in the Pre-Documentary Past', in B. M. S. Campbell and M. Overton (eds), *Land, Labour and Livestock. Historical Studies in European Agricultural Productivity* (Manchester, 1991). On the landscape, T. Williamson and L. Bellamy, *Property and Landscape. A Social History of Landownership and the English Countryside* (1987); D. Hooke, *The Landscape of Anglo-Saxon England* (1997); S. Rippon, *The Severn Estuary. Landscape Evolution and Wetland Reclamation* (Leicester, 1997); T. Williamson, *The Origins of Norfolk* (Manchester, 1993); R. Silvester, 'The Fenland Project in Retrospective', *East Anglian Archaeology*, 50 (1993); D. Hooke (ed.), *Anglo-Saxon Settlements* (Oxford, 1988); K. P. Witney, *The Jutish Forest* (1976); A. King, 'Gauber High Pasture, Ribblehead – an Interim Report', in R. A. Hall (ed.), *Viking Age York and the North* (CBA Research Report, 27, 1978); H. S. A. Fox (ed.), *Seasonal Settlements* (Leicester, 1996); J. Blair, *Anglo-Saxon Oxfordshire* (Stroud, 1994); R. Dodgshon, *Land and Society in Early Scotland* (Oxford, 1981); S. Foster and T. C. Smout (eds), *The History of Soils and Field Systems* (Aberdeen, 1994); A. Everitt, *Continuity and Colonisation: the Evolution of Kentish Settlement* (Leicester, 1986); J. Thirsk (ed.), *The English Rural Landscape* (Oxford, 2000).

On the protection of deer and their habitat, D. Hooke, 'Pre-Conquest Woodland: its Distribution and Usage', *AgHR*, 37 (1989); for Shotover, S. P. Day, 'Post-glacial Vegetational History of the Oxford Region', *New Phytologist*, 119 (1991); on venison consumption, U. Albarella and S. J. M. Davis, 'Mammals and Birds from Launceston Castle, Cornwall: Decline in Status and Rise of Agriculture', *Circaea*, 12 (1996).

The rise of the village and settlement history in general are addressed in C. C. Taylor, *Village and Farmstead. A History of Rural Settlement in England* (1983); C. Lewis, P. Mitchell-Fox and C. Dyer, *Village, Hamlet and Field. Changing Medieval Settlements in Central England* (Manchester, 1997; Macclesfield, 2001); R. Dodgshon, *The Origin of British Field Systems: An Interpretation* (1980); T. Rowley (ed.), *The Origins of Open Field Agriculture* (1981); D. Hall, 'Field Systems and Township Structure', in M. Aston, D. Austin and C. Dyer (eds), *The Rural Settlements of Medieval England* (Oxford, 1989); J. Blair, *Early Medieval Surrey: Landholding, Church and Settlement before 1300* (1991); A. Brown and G. Foard, 'The Saxon Landscape: a Regional Perspective', in P. Everson and T. Williamson (eds), *The Archaeology of Landscape* (Manchester, 1998).

On changes in technology, R. A. Hall, *Viking Age York* (1994); on woodland management, G. Milne, *Timber Building Techniques in London, c.900–1400* (London and Middlesex Archaeological Society, Special Paper 15, 1992). Norfolk turf-cutting is surveyed in T. Williamson, *The Norfolk Broads. A Landscape History* (Manchester, 1997). Drainage is discussed in Rippon, *The*

Severn Estuary. For milling, see R. Holt, *The Mills of Medieval England* (Oxford, 1988).

The 'great estate' or 'multiple estate' idea was developed by G. R. J. Jones, for example, in 'Multiple Estates and Early Settlement', in P. H. Sawyer (ed.), *Medieval Settlement* (1976); it is discussed in G. W. S. Barrow, *The Kingdom of the Scots* (1973) and in D. Hadley, 'Multiple Estates and the Origins of the Manorial Structure of the Northern Danelaw', *JHG*, 22 (1996). The Howden Charter and Hickling food rent are summarized in C. Hart (ed.), *The Early Charters of Northern England and the North Midlands* (Leicester, 1975) and Llandybie in *AgHEW*, vol. I, part 2, 43–1042.

Bampton is analysed in Blair, *Anglo-Saxon Oxfordshire*. The lease of Luddington will be found in A. J. Robertson, *Anglo-Saxon Charters* (Cambridge, 1956); and Pendock is discussed in C. Dyer, 'Dispersed Settlements in Medieval England: a Case Study of Pendock, Worcestershire', *Med. Arch.*, 34 (1990).

On the origins of the manor there is a huge literature. Its modern study began with an article by T. H. Aston, 'The Origins of the Manor', *TRHS*, 5th ser., 8 (1958); the most recent work is D. Hadley, *The Northern Danelaw. Its Social Structure, c.800–1100* (Leicester, 2000) which contains a comprehensive bibliography. The key documents for the early manor are discussed by P. D. A. Harvey in *EHR*, 108 (1993) and C. Dyer in C. Cubitt and N. P. Brooks (eds), *St. Oswald of Worcester. Life and Influence* (Leicester, 1996). Slavery and its decline have been thoroughly documented in D. Pelteret, *Slavery in Early Mediaeval England from the Reign of Alfred to the Twelfth Century* (Woodbridge, 1995). Pelteret has also edited the Hatfield list, in 'Two Old English Lists of Serfs', *Mediaeval Studies*, 48 (1986). Place names are discussed in M. Gelling, *Place-Names in the Landscape* (1984) and churches in R. Morris, *Churches in the Landscape* (1989).

The reports of bad harvests come from D. Whitelock, D. C. Douglas and S. Tucker (eds), *The Anglo-Saxon Chronicle* (1965).

Chapter 2: Crisis and new directions, c.850–c.1050

There are numerous books and articles about the Vikings; this account is influenced by P. Sawyer, *Kings and Vikings* (1982); H. R. Loyn, *The Vikings in Britain* (1977); J. Richards, *Viking Age England* (1991); B. Crawford, *Scandinavian Scotland* (Leicester, 1987); C. E. Batey and others (eds), *The Viking Age in Caithness, Orkney and the North Atlantic* (Edinburgh, 1995); J. Graham-Campbell and C. E. Batey, *The Vikings in Scotland* (Edinburgh, 1998); D. Hadley, ' "Cockle Among the Wheat": The Scandinavian Settlement of England', in W. O. Frazer and A. Tyrrell (eds), *Social Identity in Early Medieval Britain* (Leicester, 2000); A. Richie, 'Excavations of Pictish and Viking-Age Farmsteads at Buckquoy, Orkney', *Proceedings of the Society of Antiquaries of Scotland*, 108 (1976–7); J. R. Hunter, 'Rescue Excavations on the Brough of Birsay, 1974–82', *Society of Antiquaries of Scotland, Monograph* 4 (1986). On the English reaction, N. P. Brooks, 'England in the Ninth Century: The Crucible of Defeat', *TRHS*, 5th ser., 29 (1979).

For the Anglo-Saxon state, H. R. Loyn, *The Governance of Anglo-Saxon England 500–1087* (1984); J. Campbell, 'The Late Anglo-Saxon State: A Maximum View', *Proceedings of the British Academy*, 87 (1995).

On the burh system, J. Haslam, *Anglo-Saxon Towns in Southern England* (Chichester, 1984); D. Hill and A. Rumble (eds), *The Defence of Wessex* (Manchester, 1996). On the relationship between burh and town, see R. Hodges, *The Anglo-Saxon Achievement: Archaeology and the Beginning of English Society* (1989); and S. R. H. Jones, 'Transaction Costs, Institutional Change, and the Emergence of a Market Economy in Late Anglo-Saxon England', *EcHR*, 46 (1993).

On the 'feudal revolution' see T. N. Bisson, 'The "Feudal Revolution"', *P & P*, 142 (1994), and the 'Debate' in *P & P*, 152 (1996), and 155 (1997); The system of coinage is discussed in R. H. M. Dolley (ed.), *Anglo-Saxon Coins* (1961); M. A. S. Blackburn (ed.), *Anglo-Saxon Monetary History* (Leicester, 1986); P. Spufford, *Money and its Use in Medieval Europe* (Oxford, 1988).

On town origins, J. H. Williams, 'A Review of late Saxon Urban Origins and Developments', in M. L. Faull (ed.), *Studies in Late Anglo-Saxon Settlement* (Oxford, 1984); R. Hodges and B. Hobley (eds), *The Rebirth of Towns in the West AD 700–1050* (CBA Research Report, 68, 1988); G. G. Astill, 'Towns and Town Hierarchies in Saxon England', *Oxford Journal of Archaeology*, 10 (1991); R. Fleming, 'Rural Elites and Urban Communities in Late Saxon England', *P & P*, 141 (1993); N. J. Baker and R. A. Holt, 'The City of Worcester in the Tenth Century', in N. P. Brooks and C. Cubitt (eds), *St. Oswald of Worcester: Life and Influence* (1996); A. Vince, *Saxon London: An Archaeological Investigation* (1990); Blair, *Anglo-Saxon Oxfordshire*.

Domesday's towns are conveniently listed in H. C. Darby, *Domesday England* (Cambridge, 1977). They are discussed in G. H. Martin, 'Domesday Book and the Boroughs', in P. Sawyer (ed.), *Domesday Book: a Reassessment* (1985) and S. Reynolds, 'Towns in Domesday Book', in J. C. Holt (ed.), *Domesday Studies* (Woodbridge, 1987). See also C. Dyer, 'Towns and Cottages in Eleventh Century England', in H. Mayr-Harting and R. I. Moore (eds), *Studies in Medieval History Presented to R. H. C. Davis* (1985).

The archaeological evidence for early York is summed up in R. A. Hall, *Viking Age York* (1994). For excavations in other towns see M. O. H. Carver, 'Three Saxon-Norman Tenements in Durham City', *Med. Arch.*, 23 (1979) and P. Ottaway, *Archaeology in British Towns* (1992).

On the towns in general, D. Palliser (ed.), *The Cambridge Urban History of Britain*, vol. 1, *600–1540* (Cambridge, 2000). For proto-urban settlements, P. Hill, *Whithorn and St. Ninian* (Stroud, 1997); P. Courtney, *Medieval and Later Usk* (Cardiff, 1994).

For the debate on the supposed wealth of England, see P. H. Sawyer, 'The Wealth of England in the Eleventh Century', *TRHS*, 5th ser., 15 (1965); M. K. Lawson, 'The Collection of Danegeld and Heregeld in the Reigns of Aethelred II and Cnut', *EHR*, 99 (1984), and the subsequent exchange of views between J. Gillingham and M. Lawson in *EHR*, 104 (1989) and 105 (1990). On trade

M. Gardiner, 'Shipping and Trade between England and the Continent during the Eleventh Century', *Anglo-Norman Studies*, 22 (1999).

Chapter 3: Conquest c.1050–c.1100

On the pre-Conquest aristocracy the best study is P. A. Clarke, *The English Nobility under Edward the Confessor* (Oxford, 1994); on military institutions see R. Abel, *Lordship and Military Obligation in Anglo-Saxon England* (Berkeley, 1988); N. P. Brooks, *Communities and Warfare, 700–1400* (2000). Local studies include A. Wareham, 'Saint Oswald's Family and Kin', and V. King, 'St. Oswald's Tenants', in Brooks and Cubitt (eds), *St. Oswald of Worcester*. On the three orders see T. E. Powell, 'The "Three Orders" of Society in Anglo-Saxon England', *Anglo-Saxon England*, 23 (1994). Studies of aristocratic residences include G. Beresford, *Goltho. The Development of an Early Medieval Manor, c.850–1150* (English Heritage, Archaeological Report, 4, 1987); J. Fairbrother, *Faccombe Netherton: Excavations of a Saxon and Medieval Manorial Complex* (1990).

On changes in the church, F. Barlow, *The English Church 1066–1154* (1979); J. Burton, *Monastic and Religious Orders in Britain 1000–1300* (Cambridge, 1994). The huge literature on the Norman Conquest includes A. Williams, *The English and the Norman Conquest* (Woodbridge, 1995) and B. Golding, *Conquest and Colonisation: the Normans in Britain 1066–1100* (1994). R. Fleming, *Kings and Lords in Conquest England* (Cambridge, 1991) disagrees on the land settlement with P. Sawyer, '1066–1086: a Tenural Revolution?', in P. Sawyer (ed.), *Domesday Book. A Reassessment* (1985). On the aristocracy see C. P. Lewis, 'The Early Earls of Norman England', *Anglo-Norman Studies*, 13 (1970); S. Harvey, 'The Knight and the Knight's Fee in England', *P & P*, 49 (1970).

On Domesday see Sawyer (ed.), *Domesday Book. A Reassessment*; J. C. Holt (ed.), *Domesday Studies* (Woodbridge, 1987); D. Roffe, *Domesday. The Inquest and the Book* (Oxford, 2000); J. J. N. Palmer, 'The Wealth of the Secular Aristocracy in 1086', *Anglo-Norman Studies*, 22 (1999). The text of Domesday is available in translation in the Phillimore series, edited by J. Morris; for many counties there is an authoritative translation and commentary in the *VCH*.

The economic consequences in terms of destruction are discussed in R. Welldon Finn, *The Norman Conquest and its Effects on the Economy* (1971). A more rounded picture comes from W. E. Kapelle, *The Norman Conquest of the North: The Region and its Transformation, 1000–1135* (1979); D. Palliser, 'Domesday Book and the "Harrying of the North"', *Northern History*, 29 (1993); M. Chibnall, *Anglo-Norman England 1066–1166* (Oxford, 1986). On the rural scene, see S. Harvey, 'Domesday England', in *AgHEW*, vol. II; for the towns in Domesday, see the titles given above for Chapter 2.

The Pinbury survey is in M. Chibnall (ed.), *Charters and Custumals of the Abbey of Holy Trinity Caen* (British Academy, Records of Economic and Social History, new ser., 5, 1982).

For Domesday population, see J. Moore, ' "Quot homines?" The Population of Domesday England', *Anglo-Norman Studies*, 19 (1996). The monumental series of volumes on the Domesday geography of each region is summed up in H. C. Darby, *Domesday England* (Cambridge, 1977).

PART TWO: EXPANSION AND CRISIS, *c.*1100–*c.*1350

The estimates of population vary: R. Smith, 'Human Resources', in Astill and Grant (eds), *Countryside*; Campbell, *English Seigniorial Agriculture*. The Scottish and Welsh estimates come from Whyte, *Scotland before the Industrial Revolution* and Davies, *Conquest, Coexistence and Change*.

On money see N. J. Mayhew, 'Modelling Medieval Monetisation', in R. H. Britnell and B. M. S. Campbell (eds), *A Commercialising Economy. England 1086 to c.1300* (Manchester, 1995); D. M. Metcalfe (ed.), *Coinage in Medieval Scotland* (British Archaeological Reports, 45, 1977).

The economic effects of Stephen's reign are discussed in E. King (ed.), *The Anarchy of King Stephen's Reign* (Oxford, 1994); E. Amt, *The Accession of Henry II in England. Royal Government Restored, 1149–59* (Woodbridge, 1993); G. White, *Restoration and Reform, 1153–1165. Recovery from Civil War in England* (Cambridge, 2000).

On the growth in documents, M. T. Clanchy, *From Memory to Written Record* (1979).

Chapter 4: Lords, c.1100–c.1315

The importance of the honour was argued in F. M. Stenton, *The First Century of English Feudalism, 1066–1166* (2nd edn, Oxford, 1961). This has since been modified by J. Green, *The Aristocracy of Norman England* (Cambridge, 1997); S. F. C. Milsom, *The Legal Framework of English Feudalism* (Cambridge, 1976); J. Hudson, *The Formation of the English Common Law* (1996); J. C. Holt, 'Feudal Society and the Family in Early Medieval England', *TRHS*, 5th ser., 32–5 (1982–5). J. M. W. Bean, *The Decline of English Feudalism* (Manchester, 1968); H. M. Thomas, *Vassals, Heiresses, Crusaders and Thugs: The Gentry of Angevin Yorkshire, 1154–1216* (Philadelphia, 1993); D. A. Carpenter, 'The Second Century of English Feudalism', *P & P*, 168 (2000).

On the Scottish and Welsh aristocracy, see K. J. Stringer (ed.), *Essays on the Nobility of Medieval Scotland* (Edinburgh, 1985); R. A. McDonald, *The Kingdom of the Isles, Scotland's Western Seaboard, c.1100–c.1336* (East Linton, 1997); T. Brotherstone and D. Ditchburn (eds), *Freedom and Authority. Scotland c.1050–c.1650* (East Linton, 2000); R. R. Davies, *The First English Empire. Power and Identities in the British Isles 1093–1343* (Oxford, 2000). Much of the generalization in this chapter derives from studies of individuals, families and institutions. On the lay aristocracy these include M. Altschul, *A Baronial Family in Medieval England. The Clares, 1217–1314* (Baltimore, 1965); W. E.

Wightman, *The Lacy Family in England and Normandy 1066–1194* (Oxford, 1966); D. Crouch, *The Beaumont Twins. The Roots and Branches of Power in the Twelfth Century* (Cambridge, 1986); D. Crouch, *William the Marshal. Court, Career and Chivalry in the Angevin Empire, 1147–1219* (1990); B. English *The Lords of Holderness 1086–1260* (Oxford, 1979); K. Stringer, *Earl David of Huntingdon 1152–1219* (Edinburgh, 1986); P. Dalton, *Conquest, Anarchy and Lordship. Yorkshire 1066–1154* (Cambridge, 1994); R. R. Davies, *Lordship and Society in the March of Wales* (Oxford, 1978).

For church estates, historians have been able to say more about estate management and agricultural production. Some of the most substantial works which emphasize the period up to 1315 are R. A. L. Smith, *Canterbury Cathedral Priory* (Cambridge, 1943); E. Miller, *The Abbey and Bishopric of Ely* (Cambridge, 1951); J. A. Raftis, *The Estates of Ramsey Abbey* (Toronto, 1957); F. R. H. Du Boulay, *The Lordship of Canterbury* (1966); E. King, *Peterborough Abbey 1086–1310* (Cambridge, 1973); C. Dyer, *Lords and Peasants in a Changing Society. The Estates of the Bishopric of Worcester, 680–1540* (Cambridge, 1980); J. I. Catto (ed.), *The History of the University of Oxford* (Oxford, 1984). Studies specifically of the administration of estates and of the methods of agriculture include N. Denholm-Young, *Seigniorial Administration in England* (Oxford, 1937); P. D. A. Harvey, *Manorial Records* (British Records Association, 2nd edn, 2000), D. Oschinsky (ed.), *Walter of Henley and Other Treatises on Estate Management and Accounting* (Oxford, 1971); B. M. S. Campbell, *English Seigniorial Agriculture 1250–1450* (Cambridge, 2000); B. M. S. Campbell and M. Overton (eds), *Land, Labour and Livestock: Historical Studies in European Agricultural Productivity* (Manchester, 1991); J. Langdon, *Horses, Oxen and Technological Innovation: The Use of Draught Animals in English Farming from 1066–1500* (Cambridge, 1986); G. Astill and J. Langdon (eds), *Medieval Farming and Technology: The Impact of Agricultural Change in North-West Europe in the Middle Ages* (Leiden, 1997); R. Holt, 'Whose Were the Profits of Corn Milling?', *P & P*, 116 (1987); J. Langdon, 'Lordship and Peasant Consumerism in the Milling Industry of Early Fourteenth-Century England', *P & P*, 145 (1994); M. A. Atkin, 'Land Use and Management in the Upland Demesne of the De Lacy Estate of Blackburnshire', *AgHR*, 42 (1994).

On the leasing of demesnes, P. D. A. Harvey, 'The English Inflation of 1180–1220', in R. H. Hilton (ed.), *Peasants, Knights and Heretics* (Cambridge, 1976). The lease of Kensworth is in W. H. Hale (ed.), *The Domesday of St. Paul's* (Camden Society, 1858).

For the new monastic lords, see R. A. Donkin, *The Cistercians. Studies in the Geography of Medieval England and Wales* (Toronto, 1978); C. Platt, *The Monastic Grange in Medieval England* (1969); D. H. Williams, *The Welsh Cistercians* (Pontypool, 1969); B. Golding, *Gilbert of Sempringham and the Gilbertine Order c.1130 to c.1300* (Oxford, 1995); J. Burton, *The Monastic Order in Yorkshire, 1069–1215* (Cambridge, 1999); the special character of Cistercian lordship is doubted in I. Alfonso, 'Cistercians and Feudalism', *P & P*, 133 (1991).

For lords' relations with peasants some important works include R. H. Hilton, 'Freedom and Villeinage in England', in Hilton (ed.), *Peasants, Knights and Heretics*; P. R. Hyams, *Kings, Lords, and Peasants in Medieval England: The Common Law of Villeinage in the Twelfth and Thirteenth Centuries* (Oxford, 1980); J. Hatcher, 'English Serfdom and Villeinage: Towards a Reassessment', in T. H. Aston (ed.), *Landlords, Peasants and Politics in Medieval England* (Cambridge, 1987); C. Dyer, 'Memories of Freedom: Attitudes towards Serfdom in England, 1200–1350', in M. L. Bush (ed.), *Serfdom and Slavery. Studies in Legal Bondage* (1996).

On knights and small landowners see P. R. Coss, *The Knight in Medieval England 1000–1400* (Stroud, 1993); P. R. Coss, *Lordship, Knighthood and Locality. A Study in English Society c.1180–c.1280* (Cambridge, 1991); P. R. Coss, 'Sir Geoffrey de Langley and the Crisis of the Knightly Class in Thirteenth Century England', *P & P*, 68 (1975); D. A. Carpenter, 'Was There a Crisis of the Knightly Class in the Thirteenth Century? The Oxfordshire Evidence', *EHR*, 95 (1980); P. R. Coss, 'Bastard Feudalism Revised', *P & P*, 125 (1989), and the 'Debate' that followed in *P & P*, 131 (1991); P. R. Coss, 'The Formation of the English Gentry', *P & P*, 147 (1995); K. Faulkner, 'The Transformation of Knighthood in Early Thirteenth Century England', *EHR*, 111 (1996); P. Brand, *The Origins of the English Legal Profession* (Oxford, 1992); on military roles, M. Prestwich, *Armies and Warfare in the Middle Ages* (New Haven and London, 1996); The documents used are from H. E. Salter (ed.), *Eynsham Cartulary* (Oxford Historical Society, 1907), and John Rylands Library (Manchester), Phillipps Ch. 17.

Other sources of information about peasants' relationship with lords (apart from the estate histories listed above) are P. D. A. Harvey (ed.), *The Peasant Land Market in Medieval England* (Oxford, 1984); P. D. A. Harvey, *A Medieval Oxfordshire Village. Cuxham 1240–1400* (Oxford, 1965); J. Hatcher, *Rural Economy and Society in the Duchy of Cornwall 1300–1500* (Cambridge, 1970); Z. Razi and R. Smith (eds), *Medieval Society and the Manor Court* (Oxford, 1996); R. H. Hilton, 'Gloucester Abbey Leases of the Late Thirteenth Century', in Hilton, *English Peasantry in the Later Middle Ages*; T. Jones Pierce, *Medieval Welsh Society* (Cardiff, 1972).

The documents quoted are (for Navestock), Hale (ed.), *The Domesday of St. Paul's*; (for Street) C. J. Elton (ed.), *Rentalia et Custumaria* (Somerset Record Society, 5, 1891); (for Weedon), F. W. Maitland (ed.), *Select Pleas in Manorial and other Seignorial Courts* (Selden Society, 2, 1888).

For lords' relations with towns, see the reading for Chapter 6.

Chapter 5: Peasants, c.1100–c.1315

This is informed by a number of the histories of estates listed for Chapter 4. A great deal of information is embedded in *AgHEW*, vol. II. On population, there are R. M. Smith's essays in Astill and Grant (eds), *Countryside*, and B. M. S. Campbell (ed.), *Before the Black Death* (Manchester, 1991). On marriage and families, see J. Hajnal, 'European Marriage Patterns in Perspective', in

D. V. Glass and D. E. C. Eversley (eds), *Population in History* (1965); R. Helmholz, *Marriage Litigation in Medieval England* (Cambridge, 1974); M. Sheehan, 'Marriage Theory and Practice. The Diocesan Legislation of Medieval England', *Mediaeval Studies*, 40 (1978); E. Clark, 'The Decision to Marry in Thirteenth and Early Fourteenth Century Norfolk', *Mediaeval Studies*, 49 (1987); P. Biller, 'Birth Control in the West in the Thirteenth and Early Fourteenth Centuries', *P & P*, 94 (1982); Z. Razi, 'The Myth of the Immutable English Family', *P & P*, 140 (1993).

On the relationship between population and landholding, see Z. Razi, *Life, Marriage and Death in a Medieval Parish. Economy, Society and Demography in Halesowen, 1270–1400* (Cambridge, 1980); R. M. Smith (ed.), *Land, Kinship and Lifecycle* (Cambridge, 1984); C. Clarke, 'Peasant Society and Land Transactions in Chesterton, Cambridgeshire, 1277–1325' (University of Oxford DPhil. thesis, 1985).

The idea of 'cottage economy' is used in D. Levine, *Reproducing Families* (Cambridge, 1987). The record of Elyas de Bretendon is from J. A. Raftis, *Tenure and Mobility. Studies in the Social History of the Mediaeval English Village* (Toronto, 1964).

On expansion there are many studies, such as H. E. Hallam, *Settlement and Society: A Study of the Early Agrarian History of South Lincolnshire* (Cambridge, 1965); J. McDonnell, 'Medieval Assarting Hamlets in Bilsdale, North-East Yorkshire', *Northern History*, 22 (1986); J. Kissock, ' "God Made Nature and Men Made Towns": Post-Conquest and Pre-Conquest Villages in Pembrokeshire', in N. Edwards (ed.), *Landscape and Settlement in Medieval Wales* (Oxford, 1997); Rippon, *Severn Estuary*; M. Parry, *Climatic Change, Agriculture and Settlement* (Folkestone, 1978).

For contrasts between woodland settlement and a 'champion' village C. Dyer, *Hanbury, Settlement and Society in a Woodland Landscape* (Leicester University Department of English Local History, 1991) and C. Dyer, 'Compton Verney: Landscape and People in the Middle Ages', in R. Bearman (ed.), *Compton Verney. A History of the House and its Owners* (Stratford-upon-Avon, 2000). The record of assarting comes from J. Birrell (ed.), *The Forests of Cannock and Kinver: Select Documents 1235–1372* (Staffordshire Record Society, 4th ser., 18, 1999). The Halesowen preservation of the common pasture comes from R. A. Wilson (ed.), *Court Rolls of the Manor of Hales*, part 3 (Worcestershire Historical Society, 1933). For size of holdings E. A. Kosminsky, *Studies in the Agrarian History of England in the Thirteenth Century* (Oxford, 1956), and *AgHEW*, vol. II. For the peasant budget, C. Dyer, *Standards of Living in the Later Middle Ages* (revised edn, Cambridge, 1998).

On the pastoral dimension, K. Williams-Jones (ed.), *The Merioneth Lay Subsidy Roll, 1292–3* (Cardiff, 1976); M. Page (ed.), *The Pipe Roll of the Bishopric of Winchester 1301–2* (Hampshire Record Series, 14, 1996); on the general commitment of peasants to the sale of produce, Britnell, *Commercialisation of English Society*.

Land management and technical changes are discussed in A. R. H. Baker and R. A. Butlin (eds), *Studies of Field Systems in the British Isles* (Cambridge, 1973); H. S. A. Fox, 'The Alleged Transformation from Two-Field to Three-Field Systems in Medieval England', *EcHR*, 2nd ser., 39 (1986); Langdon, *Horses, Oxen and Technological Innovation*; B. M. S. Campbell and M. Overton, 'A New Perspective on Medieval and Early Modern Agriculture: Six Centuries of Norfolk Farming, *c.*1250–*c.*1850', *P & P*, 141 (1993); Astill and Langdon, *Medieval Farming and Technology*.

For rural industries see J. R. Birrell, 'Peasant Craftsmen in the Medieval Forest', *AgHR*, 17 (1969); H. E. J. Le Patourel, 'Documentary Evidence and the Medieval Pottery Industry', *Med. Arch.*, 12 (1968), and for women's brewing J. M. Bennett, *Women in the Medieval English Countryside. Gender and Household in Brigstock before the Plague* (New York, 1987); J. M. Bennett, *Ale, Beer and Brewsters in England: Women's Work in a Changing World, 1300–1600* (New York and Oxford, 1996).

For revised views on peasant houses, C. Dyer, 'English Peasant Buildings in the Later Middle Ages', *Med. Arch.*, 30 (1986); J. Grenville, *Medieval Housing* (Leicester, 1997); M. Gardiner, 'Vernacular Buildings and the Development of the Late Medieval Domestic Plan in England', *Med. Arch.*, 44 (2000). For dates of buildings, and much else, the journal *Vernacular Architecture*.

William Lene's inventory is published in R. Lock (ed.), *The Court Rolls of Walsham le Willows 1303–1350* (Suffolk Records Society, 41, 1998); for Sturminster Newton, Elton (ed.), *Rentalia et Custumaria*. For other peasant purchases, R. S. Kelly, 'The Excavation of a Medieval Farmstead at Cefn Graeanog, Clynnog, Gwynedd', *Bulletin of the Board of Celtic Studies*, 29 (1982); P. A. Rahtz, 'Upton, Gloucestershire, 1964–8', *Transactions of the Bristol and Gloucestershire Archaeological Society*, 88 (1969).

The examples of land transfers are from G. J. Turner and H. E. Salter (eds), *The Register of St. Augustine's Abbey, Canterbury* (1924); Maitland (ed.), *Select Pleas in Manorial Courts*. On various aspects of the peasant land market, see Harvey (ed.), *Peasant Land Market* and Smith (ed.), *Land, Kinship and Lifecycle*. Specific examples given here come from M. K. McIntosh, *Autonomy and Community. The Royal Manor of Havering, 1200–1500* (Cambridge, 1986); King, *Peterborough Abbey*; D. W. Ko, 'Society and Conflict in Barnet, Hertfordshire, 1337–1450', (University of Birmingham PhD thesis, 1994); Razi, *Life, Marriage and Death*; A. Jones, 'Caddington, Kensworth and Dunstable in 1297', *EcHR*, 2nd ser., 32 (1979); P. Schofield, 'Dearth, Debt and the Local Land Market in Late Thirteenth-Century Village Community', *AgHR*, 45 (1997); L. B. Smith, 'The Gage and the Land Market in Late Medieval Wales', *EcHR*, 2nd ser., 29 (1976); L. B. Smith, 'Deeds of Gage of Land in Late Medieval Wales', *Bulletin of the Board of Celtic Studies*, 27 (1977).

The various cases of unrest and rebellion come from B. F. Harvey, *Westminster Abbey and its Estates in the Middle Ages* (Oxford, 1977); A. D. Carr, 'The Bondsmen of Penrhosllugwy: A Community's Complaint', *Transactions of the Anglesey Antiquarian Society and Field Club* (1988); E. Searle, *Lordship and Community. Battle Abbey and its Banlieu 1066–1538* (Toronto, 1974);

J. R. Birrell, 'Common Rights in the Medieval Forest: Disputes and Conflicts in the Thirteenth Century', *P & P*, 117 (1987); J. H. Bettey, *Wessex from AD 1000* (1986).

On strains within communities, H. S. A. Fox, 'Exploitation of the Landless by Lords and Tenants in Early Medieval England', in Razi and Smith (eds), *Medieval Society and the Manor Court*; W. O. Ault, *Open-Field Farming in Medieval England* (1972); L. Poos, 'Population Turnover in Medieval Essex: The Evidence of Some Early Fourteenth Century Tithing Lists', in L. Bonfield, R. M. Smith and K. Wrightson (eds), *The World We Have Gained* (Oxford, 1986); C. Dyer, 'The English Village Community and its Decline', *Journal of British Studies*, 33 (1994); R. M. Smith, 'Kin and Neighbours in a Thirteenth-Century Suffolk Community', *Journal of Family History*, 4 (1979).

Chapter 6: Towns and commerce, c.1100–c.1315

On towns in general in this period, D. Palliser (ed.), *The Cambridge Urban History of Britain*, vol. 1, 600–1540 (Cambridge, 2000) surveys every aspect of the subject. Other overviews include S. Reynolds, *An Introduction to the History of English Medieval Towns* (Oxford, 1977); E. Miller and J. Hatcher, *Medieval England. Town, Commerce and Crafts* (1995) and H. Swanson, *Medieval British Towns* (Basingstoke, 1999). A remarkable work which locates towns in society as a whole is R. H. Hilton, *English and French Towns in Feudal Society. A Comparative Study* (Cambridge, 1992). Another book which views towns in their rural surroundings is J. Masschaele, *Peasants, Merchants and Markets. Inland Trade in Medieval England, 1150–1350* (New York, 1997). On Scotland and Wales, I. Adams, *The Making of Urban Scotland* (1978); M. Lynch (ed.), *The Scottish Medieval Town* (Edinburgh, 1988); E. Ewen, *Townlife in Fourteenth-Century Scotland* (Edinburgh, 1990); R. A. Griffiths (ed.), *Boroughs of Mediaeval Wales* (Cardiff, 1978), and I. Soulsby, *The Towns of Medieval Wales* (Chichester, 1983). On the new towns M. W. Beresford, *New Towns of the Middle Ages. Town Plantations of England, Wales and Gascony* (London, 1967).

The section on the urban hierarchy is based on numerous detailed studies. For example, on markets see R. H. Britnell, 'The Proliferation of Markets in England, 1200–1349', *EcHR*, 2nd ser., 34 (1981); T. Unwin, 'Rural Marketing in Medieval Nottinghamshire', *JHG*, 7 (1981), D. Postles, 'Markets for Rural Produce in Oxfordshire, 1086–1350', *Midland History*, 12 (1987).

For fairs, E. W. Moore, *The Fairs of Medieval England* (Toronto, 1985). On small and large towns R. H. Hilton, 'Small Town Society in England before the Black Death', *P & P*, 97 (1982); R. H. Hilton, 'Medieval Market Towns and Simple Commodity Production', *P & P*, 109 (1985); J. Laughton and C. Dyer, 'Small Towns in the East and West Midlands in the Later Middle Ages: A Comparison', *Midland History*, 24 (1999); M. Kowaleski, *Local Markets and Regional Trade in Medieval Exeter* (Cambridge, 1995); H. Summerson, *Medieval Carlisle: The City and the Borders from the Late Eleventh to the mid-Sixteenth Century* (Cumberland and Westmorland Antiquarian and

Archaeological Society, extra ser., 25, 1993). For the country people attached to towns, J. Masschaele, 'Urban Trade in Medieval England: The Evidence of Foreign Gild Membership Lists', *Thirteenth Century England*, 5 (1994); I. J. Sanders, 'Trade and Industry in Some Cardiganshire Towns in the Middle Ages', *Ceredigion*, 3 (1959).

On London's influence, B. M. S. Campbell, J. A. Galloway, D. Keene and M. Murphy, *A Medieval Capital and its Grain Supply* (Historical Geography Research 30, 1993); C. Barron, 'Centres of Conspicuous Consumption: The Aristocratic Town House in London, 1200–1550', *London Journal*, 20 (1995); D. Keene, 'Wardrobes in the City: Houses of Consumption, Finance and Power', *Thirteenth-Century England*, 7 (1999); D. Keene, 'Small Towns and the Metropolis: The Experience of Medieval England', in J. M. Duvosquel and E. Thoen (eds), *Peasants and Townsmen in Medieval Europe. Studies in Honorem Adriaan Verhulst* (Ghent, 1995). Bishop Swinfield's purchases are recorded in J. Webb (ed.), *A Roll of the Household Expenses of Richard de Swinfield* (Camden Society, 56, 62, 1854–5).

On migration, the sudden death of an immigrant was recorded in R. R. Sharpe (ed.), *Calendar of Coroners' Rolls of the City of London AD 1300–1378* (1913). Historical comments include P. McClure, 'Patterns of Migration in the Late Middle Ages: The Evidence of English Place-Name Surnames', *EcHR*, 2nd ser., 32 (1979); E. D. Jones, 'Some Spalding Priory Vagabonds of the Twelve-Sixties', *Historical Research*, 73 (2000); C. Dyer, 'Stratford-upon-Avon: A Successful Small Town', in R. Bearman (ed.), *The History of an English Borough. Stratford-upon-Avon 1196–1996* (Stroud and Stratford, 1997); E. Miller, 'Medieval York', *VCH Yorkshire, City of York* (1961); T. James, 'Medieval Carmarthen and its Burgesses. A Study of Town Growth and Burgess Families in the Later Thirteenth Century', *Carmarthenshire Antiquary*, 25 (1989); A. J. L. Winchester, *Landscape and Society in Medieval Cumbria* (Edinburgh, 1987).

On urban topography, T. R. Slater, 'Ideal and Reality in English Episcopal Medieval Town Planning', *Transactions of the Institute of British Geographers*, new ser., 12 (1987); T. R. Slater, 'Understanding the Landscape of Towns', in D. Hooke (ed.), *Landscape. The Richest Historical Record* (Society for Landscape Studies supplementary ser., 1, 2001). On urban property and the environment, S. Penn, 'Social and Economic Aspects of Fourteenth Century Bristol' (University of Birmingham PhD thesis, 1989); W. Urry, *Canterbury under the Angevin Kings* (1967); R. Goddard, 'Bullish Markets: the Property Market in Thirteenth-Century Coventry', *Midland History*, 23 (1998); D. Keene, 'Shops and Shopping in Medieval London', in L. Grant (ed.), *Medieval Art, Architecture and Archaeology in London* (British Archaeological Association, 1990); Grenville, *Medieval Housing*; P. Holdsworth (ed.), *Excavations in the Medieval Burgh of Perth, 1979–81* (Society of Antiquaries of Scotland, Monograph ser. 5, 1987); C. Moloney and R. Coleman, 'The Development of a Medieval Street Frontage: The Evidence from Excavations at 80–86, High Street, Perth', *Proceedings of the Society of Antiquaries of Scotland*, 127 (1997). The leaking cesspit is recorded in H. M. Chew and W. Kellaway (eds), *London Assize of Nuisance 1301–1431* (London Record Society, 10, 1973). For London's fuel crisis, J. A. Galloway,

D. Keene and M. Murphy, 'Fuelling the City: Production and Distribution of Firewood and Fuel in London's Region, 1290–1400', *EcHR*, 49 (1996).

On the variety of urban occupations, R. Karras, *Common Women: Prostitution and Sexuality in Medieval England* (New York and Oxford, 1996); R. H. Hilton, 'Towns in English Feudal Society', in his *Class Conflict and the Crisis of Feudalism* (1985); D. and R. Cromarty (eds), *The Wealth of Shrewsbury in the Early Fourteenth Century* (Shrewsbury Archaeological and Historical Society, 1997), D. Keene, *Survey of Medieval Winchester* (Oxford, 1985), P. J. P. Goldberg, 'Urban Identity and the Poll Taxes of 1377, 1379 and 1381', *EcHR*, 2nd ser., 43 (1990), J. H. Munro, *Textiles, Towns and Trade* (Aldershot, 1994); G. Egan and F. Pritchard (eds), *Dress Accessories, c.1150–c.1450* (1991); G. Egan (ed.), *The Medieval Household. Daily Living c.1150–c.1450* (1988) (these are two in a series of publications entitled *Medieval Finds from Excavations in London*). The thirteenth-century lists of towns' specialisms is printed in H. Rothwell (ed.), *English Historical Documents, 1189–1327* (1975). The herring fishery is described in A. R. Saul, 'Great Yarmouth in the Fourteenth Century. A Study in Trade, Politics and Society' (University of Oxford DPhil. thesis, 1975).

My main sources for trade have been E. Ashtor, *Levant Trade in the Later Middle Ages* (Princeton, NJ, 1983); T. H. Lloyd, *The English Wool Trade in the Middle Ages* (1977); W. R. Childs, *Anglo-Castilian Trade in the Later Middle Ages* (Manchester, 1978); P. Nightingale, *A Medieval Mercantile Community. The Grocers' Company and the Politics and Trade of London, 1000–1485* (New Haven and London, 1995); C. Platt, *Medieval Southampton. The Port and Trading Community, 1000–1600* (1973); J. Donnelly, 'Thomas of Coldingham, Merchant and Burgess of Berwick upon Tweed', *Scottish Historical Review*, 59 (1980); J. Donnelly, 'An Open Port: The Berwick Export Trade, 1311–1373', *Scottish Historical Review*, 78 (1999); M. K. James, *Studies in the Medieval Wine Trade* (Oxford, 1971); E. M. Carus-Wilson, *Medieval Merchant Venturers* (1954); T. H. Lloyd, *Alien Merchants in England in the High Middle Ages* (Brighton, 1982); J. W. F. Hill, *Medieval Lincoln* (1948).

On credit, important articles by M. M. Postan are reprinted in his *Medieval Trade and Finance* (Cambridge, 1973). See also H. Jenkinson, 'William Cade, a Financier of the Twelfth Century', *EHR*, 28 (1913); H. G. Richardson, *The English Jewry under Angevin Kings* (1960); R. Stacey, 'Jewish Lending and the Medieval English Economy', in Britnell and Campbell (eds), *A Commercialising Economy*; R. R. Mundill, *English Jewish Solution. Experiment and Expulsion, 1262–1290* (Cambridge, 1998); R. Kaeuper, *Bankers to the Crown: The Riccardi of Lucca and Edward I* (Princeton, 1973). For industry see J. Blair and N. Ramsay (eds), *English Medieval Industries* (1991); D. Crossley (ed.), *Medieval Industry* (CBA Research Report, 40, 1981); R. Holt, *The Mills of Medieval England* (Oxford, 1988). The controversy over fulling mills is raised in A. R. Bridbury, *Medieval English Clothmaking* (1982). On other aspects of technology, G. G. Astill, *A Medieval Industrial Complex and its Landscape* (CBA Research Report 92, 1993); M. K. McCarthy and C. M. Brooks, *Medieval Pottery in Britain AD 900–1600* (Leicester, 1988).

For transport F. M. Stenton, 'The Road System of Medieval England', *EcHR*, 7 (1936–8); C. C. Taylor, *Roads and Tracks of Britain* (1979); B. P. Hindle, *Medieval Roads* (Princes Risborough, 1982); J. Langdon, 'Horse Hauling: A Revolution in Vehicle Transport in Twelfth and Thirteenth Century England', in T. H. Aston (ed.), *Landlords, Peasants and Politics in Medieval England* (Cambridge, 1987); D. Harrison, 'Bridges and Economic Development, 1300–1800', *EcHR*, 45 (1992); J. Masschaele, 'Transport Costs in Medieval England', *EcHR*, 46 (1993). A debate on inland water transport between B. P. Hindle, J. Edwards, E. Jones and J. Langdon will be found in *JHG*, 17 (1991); 19 (1993), and 25 (1999). For shipping see G. Hutchinson, *Medieval Ships and Shipping* (Leicester, 1994) and I. Friel, *The Good Ship* (1995).

On trading techniques an essay on partnerships by J. Masschaele and on the Exeter grain trade by M. Kowaleski will be found in E. B. Dewindt (ed.), *The Salt of Common Life. Individuality and Choice in the Medieval Town, Countryside and Church* (Kalamazoo, Mich., 1995). For the shopping technology of Chester, A. Brown (ed.), *The Rows of Chester* (English Heritage Archaeological Report, 16, 1999). Coinage and currency are discussed in N. J. Mayhew, 'Modelling Medieval Monetization', in Britnell and Campbell (eds), *Commercialising Economy*; N. Mayhew, 'Alexander III – a Silver Age? An Essay in Scottish Medieval Economic History', in N. H. Reid (ed.), *Scotland in the Reign of Alexander III, 1249–1286* (Edinburgh, 1988); D. Metcalf (ed.), *Coinage in Medieval Scotland (1100–1600)* (British Archaeological Report, 45, 1977).

On boroughs the classic work is J. Tait, *The Medieval English Borough* (Manchester, 1936), together with C. Gross, *The Gild Merchant* (Oxford, 1890). Additional works include M. McKisack, *The Parliamentary Representation of the English Borough during the Middle Ages* (Oxford, 1932). The most thorough study of a struggle between a monastery and its town is M. D. Lobel, *The Borough of Bury St. Edmunds* (Oxford, 1935).

A self-governing town has been revealed in R. B. Peberdy, 'The Economy, Society and Government of a Small Town in Late Medieval England: A Study of Henley-on-Thames from *c.*1300–*c.*1540' (University of Leicester PhD thesis, 1994). For the monopolies of Welsh and Scottish towns see Griffiths (ed.), *Boroughs of Mediaeval Wales*; J. M. Houston, 'The Scottish Burgh', *Town Planning Review*, 25 (1954–5); A. Gibb and R. Paddison, 'The Rise and Fall of Burghal Monopolies in Scotland: The Case of the North-East', *Scottish Geographical Magazine*, 99 (1983).

Trade restrictions are recorded in R. W. Greaves (ed.), *The First Ledger Book of High Wycombe* (Buckinghamshire Record Society, 2, 1947); M. Bateson (ed.), *Records of the Borough of Leicester* (Cambridge, 1899).

Chapter 7: Crisis, *c.1290–c.1350*

W. C. Jordan, *The Great Famine. Northern Europe in the Early Fourteenth Century* (Princeton, 1996) deals with northern Europe as a whole, and plays down the events. Many aspects of the crisis of the first half of the fourteenth century appear in Campbell (ed.), *Before the Black Death*.

For the famine in England, I. Kershaw, 'The Great Famine and Agrarian Crisis in England 1315–1322', *P & P*, 59 (1973); I. Kershaw, *Bolton Priory: The Economy of a Northern Monastery 1286–1325* (Oxford, 1973); Smith (ed.), *Land, Kinship and Lifecycle*; M. Stinson, 'Assarting and Poverty in Early Fourteenth Century West Yorkshire', *Landscape History*, 5 (1983); B. Hanawalt, 'Economic Influence on the Pattern of Crime in England, 1300–1348', *American Journal of Legal History*, 18 (1974); J. Lister (ed.), *Court Rolls of the Manor of Wakefield*, vol. 4 (Yorkshire Archaeological Society Record Ser., 78, 1930); Dyer, 'English Village Community'; Catto (ed.), *University of Oxford*.

The mortality estimates are reviewed in Smith's essay in Campbell, *Before the Black Death*; but see also M. Eccleston, 'Mortality of Rural Landless Men before the Black Death: The Glastonbury Head-Tax Lists', *Local Population Studies*, 63 (1999). For mortality after the famine, M. C. Coleman, *Downham-in-the Isle. A Study of an Ecclesiastical Manor in the Thirteenth and Fourteenth Centuries* (Woodbridge, 1984).

On the decline in cultivation, J. Birrell, 'Agrarian History', *VCH Staffordshire*, 6 (1979); A. R. H. Baker, 'Evidence in the *Nonarum Inquisitiones* of Contracting Arable Lands in England during the Early Fourteenth Century', *EcHR*, 2nd ser., 19 (1966); C. Dyer, 'The Rise and Fall of a Medieval Village: Little Aston (in Aston Blank), Gloucestershire', *Transactions of the Bristol and Gloucestershire Archaeological Society*, 105 (1987); D. Austin and M. J. C. Walker, 'A New Landscape Context for Houndtor, Devon', *Med. Arch.*, 29 (1985); Kelly, 'Excavation of a Medieval Farmstead'; L. A. Toft, 'A Study of Coastal Village Abandonment in the Swansea Bay Region, 1270–1540', *Morgannwg*, 32 (1988).

On yields, D. L. Farmer, 'Grain Yields on the Winchester Manors in the Later Middle Ages', *EcHR*, 2nd ser., 30 (1977); E. I. Newman and P. D. A. Harvey, 'Did Soil Fertility Decline in Medieval English Farms? Evidence from Cuxham, Oxfordshire, 1320–1340', *AgHR*, 45 (1997).

The information on prices and wages, calculated by D. L. Farmer, is from *AgHEW*, vol. II; on the meals of harvest workers, C. Dyer, 'Changes in Diet in the Late Middle Ages: The Case of Harvest Workers', *AgHR*, 36 (1988).

On land purchases, S. F. Hockey, *Quarr Abbey and its Lands, 1132–1632* (Leicester, 1970); S. Raban, *The Estates of Thorney and Crowland: A Study in Medieval Monastic Land Tenure* (Cambridge, 1977); G. A. Holmes, *The Estates of the Higher Nobility in Fourteenth Century England* (Cambridge, 1957).

Information on entry fines and variable rents comes from Raftis, *Ramsey Abbey*; J. Z. Titow, *English Rural Society, 1200–1349* (1969); J. Hatcher, *Rural Economy and Society in the Duchy of Cornwall 1300–1500* (Cambridge, 1970); M. Mate, 'The Estates of Canterbury Cathedral Priory before the Black Death', *Studies in Medieval and Renaissance History*, 8 (1987).

The problems of aristocratic expenditure are highlighted in Dyer, *Standards of Living*. On repercussions in towns, Beresford, *New Towns*; G. Rosser,

Medieval Westminster 1200–1540 (Oxford, 1989); M. Carlin, *Medieval Southwark* (1996); R. H. Britnell, *Growth and Decline in Colchester, 1300–1525* (Cambridge, 1986); P. Short, 'The Medieval Rows of York', *Archaeological Journal*, 137 (1980).

The statistics of overseas trade given here, and in subsequent chapters, come from E. M. Carus-Wilson and O. Coleman, *England's Export Trade, 1275–1547* (Oxford, 1963); J. Hatcher, *English Tin Production and Trade before 1550* (Oxford, 1973); James, *Wine Trade*. For major churches see R. Morris, *Cathedrals and Abbeys of England and Wales* (1979). The comments on cloth are based on J. H. Munro, 'The "Industrial Crisis" of the English TextileTown, *c.*1290–*c.*1330', *Thirteenth-Century England*, 7 (1997).

On the debate, the key works have been indicated in the books listed for the Introduction, above. Continental approaches can be seen in W. Abel, *Agricultural Fluctuations in Europe* (1980). The most thorough investigation of 'marginal' land is in M. Bailey, *A Marginal Economy? East Anglian Breckland in the Later Middle Ages* (Cambridge, 1989).

For Scotland in this period, Whyte, *Scotland before the Industrial Revolution*; E. Gemmill and N. Mayhew, *Changing Values in Medieval Scotland. A Study of Prices, Money and Weights and Measures* (Cambridge, 1995); Duncan, *Scotland: The Making of a Kingdom*; Grant, *Independence and Nationhood*; P. Dixon, 'A Rural Medieval Settlement in Roxburghshire: Excavations at Springwood Park, Kelso, 1985–6', *Proceedings of the Society of Antiquaries of Scotland*, 128 (1998); Moloney and Coleman, 'Development of a Medieval Street Frontage'.

For climate, the best survey is M. L. Parry, *Climatic Change, Agriculture and Settlement* (Folkestone, 1978); on money N. J. Mayhew (ed.), *Edwardian Monetary Affairs (1279–1344)* (British Archaeological Reports, 36, 1977); N. J. Mayhew, 'Money and Prices in England from Henry II to Edward III', *AgHR*, 35 (1987). For arbitrary lordship in the Welsh marches, Davies, *Lordship and Society*; W. Rees, *South Wales and the March, 1284–1415* (Oxford, 1924); L. B. Smith, 'The Arundel Charters to the Lordship of Chirk in the Fourteenth Century', *Bulletin of the Board of Celtic Studies*, 23 (1968).

On war in general, M. Prestwich, *War, Politics and Finance under Edward I* (1972); H. J. Hewitt, *The Organisation of War under Edward III 1338–62* (Manchester, 1966); Prestwich, *Armies and Warfare*; C. McNamee, *The Wars of the Bruces. Scotland, England and Ireland, 1306–1328* (East Linton, 1997); R. Lomas, 'The Impact of Border Warfare: The Scots and South Tweedside, *c.*1290–*c.*1520', *Scottish Historical Review*, 75 (1996); A. J. Taylor, 'Scorched Earth and Flint in 1294', *Flintshire Historical Society Journal*, 30 (1981–2).

On the total tax burden, M. Ormrod, 'England in the Middle Ages', in R. Bonney (ed.), *The Rise of the Fiscal State in Europe c.1200–1815* (Oxford, 1999); for the experience of the taxpayers, J. R. Maddicott, *The English Peasantry and the Demands of the Crown, 1294–1341) (P & P* supplement, 1, 1975). E. B. Fryde, *William de la Pole* (1988), deals with the wool monopoly, as does Lloyd, *Wool Trade*.

PART THREE: MAKING A NEW WORLD c.1350–c.1520

The primary sources in this introductory section include W. Nelson (ed.), *A Fifteenth Century School Book* (Oxford, 1956); J. Gower, *Confessio Amantis* (Harmondsworth, 1966); N. Davis (ed.), *Paston Letters and Papers of the Fifteenth Century* (2 vols, Oxford, 1971, 1976).

On money, J. Day, 'The Great Bullion Famine of the Fifteenth Century', *P & P*, 79 (1978); N. J. Mayhew, 'Population, Money Supply, and the Velocity of Circulation in England, 1300–1700', *EcHR*, 48 (1995); Spufford, *Money and its Use*; Gemmill and Mayhew, *Changing Values in Medieval Scotland*; W. W. Scott, 'Sterling and the Usual Money of Scotland, 1370–1495', *Scottish Economic and Social History*, 5 (1985).

The best sources of information on prices and wages in England and Wales are the chapters by D. Farmer in *AgHEW*, vols II and III, and Bowden's chapter in *AgHEW*, vol. IV.

Chapter 8: The Black Death and its aftermath, c.1348–c.1520

On plague and its effects see J. Hatcher, *Plague, Population and the English Economy 1348–1530* (1977); C. Platt, *King Death. The Black Death and its Aftermath in Late Medieval England* (1996); M. Ormrod and P. Lindley (eds), *The Black Death in England* (Stamford, 1996). The primary sources used are R. H. Hilton (ed.), *The Stoneleigh Leger Book* (Dugdale Society, 24, 1960); Westminster Abbey Muniments, 21037–9; J. Toomey (ed.), *Records of Hanley Castle Worcestershire*, c.1147–1547 (Worcestershire Historical Society, 18, 2001). R. Horrox (ed.), *The Black Death* (Manchester, 1994) conveniently gathers together chroniclers' descriptions. For the archaeological evidence, D. Hawkins, 'The Black Death and the New London Cemeteries of 1348', *Antiquity*, 64 (1990). On ruined houses in the countryside, P. Hargreaves, 'Seigniorial Reaction and Peasant Responses: Worcester Priory and its Peasants after the Black Death', *Midland History*, 24 (1999).

For mortality after 1350 see A.-B. Fitch, 'Assumptions about Plague in Late Medieval Scotland', *Scotia*, 11 (1987); R. Gottfried, *Epidemic Disease in Fifteenth-Century England* (Leicester, 1978); J. Hatcher, 'Mortality in the Fifteenth Century: Some New Evidence', *EcHR*, 2nd ser., 39 (1986); B. Harvey, *Living and Dying in England 1100–1540. The Monastic Experience* (Oxford, 1993); L. R. Poos, *A Rural Society after the Black Death. Essex 1350–1520* (Cambridge, 1991); Razi, *Life, Marriage and Death*; A. J. F. Dulley, 'Four Kent Towns at the End of the Middle Ages', in M. Roake and J. Whyman (eds), *Essays in Kentish History* (1973).

Delayed marriage and the shortage of children are highlighted in P. J. P. Goldberg, *Women, Work and Life Cycle in a Medieval Economy: York and Yorkshire, c.1300–1520* (Oxford, 1992); on families, Z. Razi, 'The Myth of the Immutable English Family', *P & P*, 140 (1993).

On the liberation of the lower orders, R. H. Hilton, *The Decline of Serfdom in England* (1968); S. A. C. Penn and C. Dyer, 'Wages and Earnings in Late Medieval England: Evidence from the Enforcement of the Labour Laws', *EcHR*, 2nd ser., 43 (1990); M. Rubin, *Charity and Community in Medieval Cambridge* (Cambridge, 1987); C. Dyer, 'The English Medieval Village Community and its Decline', *Journal of British Studies*, 33 (1994); Z. Razi, 'Family, Land and the Village Community in Later Medieval England', *P & P*, 93 (1982); Hilton, *English Peasantry*; C. Barron, 'The Golden Age of Women in Medieval London', *Reading Medieval Studies*, 15 (1989); C. Barron and A. Sutton (eds), *Medieval London Widows 1300–1500* (1994); M. E. Mate, *Women in Medieval English Society* (Cambridge, 1999); R. M. Smith, 'Coping with Uncertainty: Women's Tenure of Customary Land in England 1370–1430', in J. Kermode (ed.), *Enterprise and Individuals*.

The primary sources quoted in this section are from Raftis, *Tenure and Mobility*; R. Sillem (ed.), *Records of Some Sessions of the Peace in Lincolnshire 1360–1375* (Lincoln Record Society, 30, 1937); C. Gross (ed.), *Select Cases from the Coroners' Rolls 1265–1413* (Selden Society, 9, 1895); A. V. C. Schmidt (ed.), *William Langland. Piers Plowman* (Oxford, 1992); E. C. Furber (ed.), *Essex Sessions of the Peace 1351, 1377–1379* (Essex Archaeological Society, 1953).

For the origins and course of the 1381 rising, R. H. Hilton, *Bondmen Made Free: Medieval Peasant Movements and the English Rising of 1381* (1973); W. M. Ormrod, 'The Peasants' Revolt and the Government of England', *Journal of British Studies*, 29 (1990); R. H. Hilton and T. H. Aston (eds), *The English Rising of 1381* (Cambridge, 1984); C. Dyer, 'The Rising of 1381 in Suffolk: Its Origins and Participants', in Dyer, *Everyday Life*; R. B. Dobson (ed.), *The Peasants' Revolt of 1381* (2nd edn, 1983); S. Justice, *Writing and Rebellion: England in 1381* (Berkeley, Cal., 1994); H. Eiden, 'Joint Action against "Bad" Lordship: The Peasants' Revolt in Essex and Norfolk', *History*, 83 (1998).

William Smith's story is in Wadham College, Oxford, 44 B/1. On the Welsh revolt, R. R. Davies, *The Revolt of Owain Glyn Dŵr* (Oxford, 1997); L. B. Smith, 'Seignorial Income in the Fourteenth Century: The Arundels in Chirk', *Bulletin of the Board of Celtic Studies*, 28 (1979).

On the economy in the late fourteenth century, see A. R. Bridbury, 'The Black Death', *EcHR*, 2nd ser., 26 (1973); J. Hatcher, 'England in the Aftermath of the Black Death', *P & P*, 144 (1994); L. R. Poos, *A Rural Society after the Black Death: Essex 1350–1525* (Cambridge, 1990); Grant, *Independence and Nationhood*; Bailey, *A Marginal Economy?*; Hatcher, *Rural Economy and Society*; H. Grieve, *The Sleepers and the Shadows. Chelmsford: A Town, its People, and its Past* (Chelmsford, 1988).

Chapter 9: Towns, trade and industry, c.1350–c.1520

See Chapter 6 for a list of books on towns, many of which cover this period. On urban decline, A. D. Dyer, *Decline and Growth in English Towns 1400–1640* (Cambridge, 1995); S. Rigby, *Medieval Grimsby. Growth and Decline* (Hull,

1993); R. Holt, 'Gloucester in the Century after the Black Death', in Holt and Rosser (eds), *Medieval Town*; J. M. Bartlett, 'The Expansion and Decline of York in the Later Middle Ages', *EcHR*, 2nd ser., 12 (1959–60); A. F. Butcher, 'Rents and the Urban Economy: Oxford and Canterbury in the Later Middle Ages', *Southern History*, 1 (1979); A. F. Butcher, 'Rent, Population and Economic Change in Late-Medieval Newcastle', *Northern History*, 14 (1978). On buildings, Griffiths (ed.), *Boroughs of Mediaeval Wales*; Keene, *Medieval Winchester*. On civic duties, J. I. Kermode, 'Urban Decline? The Flight from Office in Late Medieval York', *EcHR*, 2nd ser., 35 (1982).

On town populations and failed towns, A. Dyer, '"Urban Decline" in England, 1377–1525', in T. R. Slater (ed.), *Towns in Decline AD 100–1600* (Aldershot, 2000); I. Adams, *The Making of Urban Scotland* (1978). On the ups and downs of trade, T. H. Lloyd, *England and the German Hansa, 1157–1611* (Cambridge, 1991); J. Kermode, *Medieval Merchants. York, Beverley and Hull in the Later Middle Ages* (Cambridge, 1998).

On London, C. Barron, 'Richard Whittington: The Man Behind the Myth', in A. E. J. Hollaender and W. Kellaway (eds), *Studies in London History* (1969); P. Nightingale, *A Medieval Mercantile Community. The Grocers' Company and the Politics and Trade of London, 1000–1485* (New Haven and London, 1995); Blair and Ramsay (eds), *English Medieval Industries*; M. Norris, *Monumental Brasses, the Memorials* (1977); J. Galloway (ed.), *Trade, Urban Hinterlands and Market Integration c.1300–1600* (2000).

On individual towns, Courtney, *Medieval Usk*; C. Phythian-Adams, *Desolation of a City. Coventry and the Urban Crisis of the Later Middle Ages* (Cambridge, 1979); R. H. Britnell, *Growth and Decline in Colchester, 1300–1525* (Cambridge, 1986); E. M. Carus-Wilson, *The Expansion of Exeter at the Close of the Middle Ages* (Exeter, 1963). There are also regional studies: H. S. A. Fox, 'Medieval Urban Development', in Kain and Ravenhill (eds), *Historical Atlas of South-West England*; G. Sheeran, *Medieval Yorkshire Towns. People, Buildings and Space* (Edinburgh, 1998); Laughton and Dyer, 'Small Towns in the East and West Midlands'; A. J. L. Winchester, *Landscape and Society in Medieval Cumbria* (Edinburgh, 1987).

On merchants S. Thrupp, *The Merchant Class of Medieval London* (Chicago, 1948); A. Hanham, *The Celys and Their World. An English Merchant Family of the Fifteenth Century* (Cambridge, 1985); H. W. Booton, 'Sir John Rutherford: A Fifteenth-Century Aberdeen Burgess', *Scottish Economic and Social History*, 10 (1990).

For artisans, Swanson, *Medieval Artisans*; H. Booton, 'The Craftsmen of Aberdeen between 1400 and 1550', *Northern Scotland*, 13 (1993); Grenville, *Medieval Housing*; J. Schofield, *Medieval London Houses* (New Haven, 1994); J. Schofield, 'Urban Housing in England, 1400–1600', in D. Gaimster and P. Stamper (eds), *The Age of Transition. The Archaeology of English Culture, 1400–1600* (Oxford, 1997).

John Symond's will is in Suffolk Record Office, Ipswich branch, J 421/3. fo. 5.

For hospitals and almshouses, N. Orme and M. Webster, *The English Hospital, 1070–1570* (New Haven and London, 1995).

On civic pride and urban regulation, L. Toulmin Smith (ed.), *The Maire of Bristowe is Kalendar by Robert Ricart* (Camden Society, new ser., 5, 1872); J. R. Green, *Town Life in the Fifteenth Century* (1894); Gemmill and Mayhew, *Changing Values*; W. B. Bickley (ed.), *The Little Red Book of Bristol* (Bristol, 1900); H. Swanson, 'The Illusion of Economic Structure: Craft Guilds in Late Medieval Towns', *P & P*, 121 (1988); G. Rosser, 'Crafts, Guilds and the Negotiation of Work in the Medieval Town', *P & P*, 154 (1997); R. H. Hilton, *English and French Towns in Feudal Society. A Comparative Study* (Cambridge, 1992); A. H. Thomas and P. E. Jones, *Calendar of Plea and Memoranda Rolls of the City of London* (6 vols, Cambridge, 1926–61); *VCH Cambridgeshire*, vol. 4; G. Rosser, 'Communities of Parish and Guild in the Late Middle Ages', in S. J. Wright (ed.), *Parish, Church and People* (1988); D. G. Shaw, *The Creation of a Community. The City of Wells in the Middle Ages* (Oxford, 1993); J. A. F. Thomson (ed.), *Towns and Townspeople in the Fifteenth Century* (Gloucester, 1988) contains essays by Rigby, Kermode and Horrox on elites.

On the informalities of small towns and trading places, M. Bailey, 'A Tale of Two Towns: Buntingford and Standon in the Later Middle Ages', *Journal of Medieval History*, 19 (1993); C. Dyer, 'The Hidden Trade of the Middle Ages: Evidence from the West Midlands of England', *JHG*, 18 (1992); P. J. P. Goldberg, 'Urban Identity and the Poll Taxes of 1377, 1379, and 1381', *EcHR*, 2nd ser., 43 (1990).

For consumption, H. S. Cobb, 'Textile Imports in the Fifteenth Century: The Evidence of Customs Accounts', *Costume*, 29 (1995); Bennett, *Ale, Beer and Brewsters*; A. Sutton, 'Mercery through Four Centuries, 1130–1500', *Nottingham Medieval Studies*, 41 (1997). M. Mellor, 'A Synthesis of Middle and Late Saxon, Medieval and Early Post-Medieval Pottery in the Oxford Region', *Oxoniensia*, 59 (1994); M. Threlfall-Holmes, 'Late Medieval Iron Production and Trade in the North-East', *Archaeologia Aeliana*, 27 (1999); R. I. Jack, 'The Cloth Industry in Medieval Wales', *Welsh History Review*, 10 (1981); E. Power, *The Paycockes of Coggeshall* (1920); J. Hatcher, *History of the British Coal Industry vol. 1: Before 1700* (Oxford, 1993).

Capitalism and credit are discussed in a number of essays in Kermode (ed.), *Enterprise and Individuals*; J. Kermode, 'Money and Credit in the Fifteenth Century: Some Lessons from Yorkshire', *Business History Review*, 65 (1991). On a new outlook, M. K. McIntosh, *Controlling Misbehavior in England, 1370–1600* (Cambridge, 1998); C. Dyer, 'Work Ethics in the Fourteenth Century', in J. Bothwell, P. J. P. Goldberg and W. M. Ormrod (eds), *The Problem of Labour in Fourteenth Century England* (Woodbridge, 2000).

Chapter 10: The countryside, c.1350–c.1520

AgHEW, vol. III is a very important source for this period. On the policies of lords while they kept their demesnes in cultivation Campbell, *English Seigniorial*

Agriculture; H. P. R. Finberg, *Tavistock Abbey. A Study in the Social and Economic History of Devon* (Newton Abbot, 1969); R. H. Hilton, *The Economic Development of Some Leicestershire Estates in the Fourteenth and Fifteenth Centuries* (Oxford, 1947); Harvey, *Westminster Abbey*; Hilton, *English Peasantry*; M. Carlin, 'Christ Church, Canterbury and its Lands . . . 1391–1540' (Oxford University B.Litt. thesis, 1970); Du Boulay, *Lordship of Canterbury*; Dyer, *Lords and Peasants*; T. H. Lloyd, *The Movement of Wool Prices in Medieval England* (*EcHR* Supplement 6, 1973).

For the administration of the leased estate, K. B. McFarlane, *England in the Fifteenth Century* (1981); K. B. McFarlane, *The Nobility of Later Medieval England* (Oxford, 1973); R. Britnell, 'The Pastons and Their Norfolk', *AgHR*, 36 (1988); T. B. Pugh (ed.), *The Marcher Lordships of South Wales, 1415–1536* (Cardiff, 1963); J. C. Hodgson (ed.), *Percy Bailiff's Rolls of the Fifteenth Century* (Surtees Society, 134, 1921).

On revenues, Carlin, 'Canterbury and its Lands'; Hatcher, *Earldom of Cornwall*; A. J. Pollard, *North Eastern England during the Wars of the Roses. Lay Society, War and Politics 1450–1500* (Oxford, 1990); C. Rawcliffe, *The Staffords, Earls of Stafford and Dukes of Buckingham 1394–1521* (Cambridge, 1978); J. M. Gilbert, *Hunting and Hunting Reserves in Medieval Scotland* (Edinburgh, 1979); I. S. W. Blanchard, *The Duchy of Lancaster's Estates in Derbyshire 1485–1540* (Derbyshire Archaeological Society Record Series, 3, 1971).

For the gentry C. Dyer, *Warwickshire Farming, 1349–c.1520* (Dugdale Society Occasional Paper, 27, 1981); C. Carpenter, *Locality and Polity. A Study of Warwickshire Landed Society, 1401–1499* (Cambridge, 1992); E. W. Ives, *The Common Lawyers of Pre-Reformation England* (Cambridge, 1983); A. D. Carr, *Medieval Anglesey* (Llangefni, 1982); C. E. Moreton, *The Townshends and their World: Gentry, Law and Land in Norfolk, c.1450–1551* (Oxford, 1992); H. Thorpe, 'The Lord and the Landscape', *Transactions of the Birmingham and Warwickshire Archaeological Society* 80 (1962); S. M. Wright, *The Derbyshire Gentry in the Fifteenth Century* (Derbyshire Record Society, 8, 1983); the documents cited include Public Record Office, E101/691/41; Cumbria Record Office D/Penn/200 (Pennington); Dorset County Record Office, D10/M231 (Giffard); W. W. Skeat (ed.), *The Boke of Husbandry by Master Fitzherbert* (English Dialect Society, 1882); I. S. Leadam (ed.), *The Domesday of Inclosures, 1517–1518* (Royal Historical Society, 1897).

For gentry creating new manors and units of production F. C. Taylor, 'Thomas Tropenell, Esquire: A Local Lawyer, the Gentry and Estate Creation' (University of Birmingham MPhil thesis, 1997); McIntosh, *Autonomy and Community*; C. Welch, 'Glassmaking in Wolseley, Staffordshire', *Post-Medieval Archaeology*, 31 (1997); D. Youngs, 'Estate Management, Investment and the Gentleman Landlord in Later Medieval England', *Historical Research*, 73 (2000).

There are many local studies of farmers, for example J. N. Hare, 'The Demesne Lessees of Fifteenth-Century Wiltshire', *AgHR*, 29 (1981), which cites earlier writings on the subject; see also J. N. Hare, 'Durrington, a Chalkland

Village in the Later Middle Ages', *Wiltshire Archaeological Magazine*, 74/5 (1979–80); E. Roberts, 'Overton Court Farm and the Late-Medieval Farmhouses of Demesne Lessees in Hampshire', *Proceedings of the Hampshire Field Club*, 51 (1995), C. Dyer, 'Were There Any Capitalists in Fifteenth-Century England?', in Kermode (ed.), *Enterprise and Individuals*. Documents cited include D. J. H. Michelmore (ed.), *The Fountains Abbey Lease Book* (Yorkshire Archaeological Society Record Series, 140, 1981); C. Rogers (ed.), *Rental Book of the Cistercian Abbey of Coupar-Angus* (Grampian Club, 1879); J. Raine (ed.), *Testamenta Eboracensia*, vol. 3 (Surtees Society, 45, 1864).

The most recent view of the importance of expropriation is R. Brenner, whose views provoked a debate: T. H. Aston and C. H. E. Philpin (eds), *The Brenner Debate* (Cambridge, 1985). The view here is expounded in C. Dyer, 'Deserted Medieval Villages in the West Midlands', *EcHR*, 2nd ser., 35 (1982); C. Dyer, 'Peasants and Farmers: Rural Settlements in an Age of Transition', in D. Gaimster and P. Stamper (eds), *The Age of Transition. The Archaeology of English Culture, 1400–1600* (Oxford, 1997).

For peasants, in addition to the reading recommended for Chapters 5, 7 and 8, J. Whittle, *The Development of Agrarian Capitalism. Land and Labour in Norfolk 1440–1580* (Oxford, 2000); R. K. Field, 'Migration in the Later Middle Ages: The Case of the Hampton Lovett Villeins', *Midland History*, 8 (1983); P. D. A. Harvey (ed.), *The Peasant Land Market in Medieval England* (Oxford, 1984); A. Watkins, 'Cattle Grazing in the Forest of Arden in the Later Middle Ages', *AgHR*, 37 (1989); M. Yates, 'Change and Continuities in Rural Society from the Later Middle Ages to the Sixteenth Century: The Contribution of West Berkshire', *EcHR*, 52 (1999); I. Harvey, *Jack Cade's Rebellion of 1450* (Oxford, 1991).

John Mell of Bramfield: Suffolk Record Office (Ipswich branch), J421/3, fo. 117r; HB26, 371: 41, 71, 110; for enclosure of Lydd, S. Dimmock, 'English Small Towns and the Emergence of Capitalist Relations, *c.*1450–1550', *Urban History*, 28 (2001).

Index